Unraveling the Right

Unraveling the Right

The New Conservatism in American Thought and Politics

edited by
Amy E. Ansell

A Member of the Perseus Books Group

All rights reserved. Printed in the United States of America. No part of this publication may be reproduced or transmitted in any form or by any means, electronic or mechanical, including photocopy, recording, or any information storage and retrieval system, without permission in writing from the publisher.

Copyright © 2001 **Published by Westview Press, A Member of the Perseus Books Group**

First published in 1998 in the United States of America by Westview Press, 5500 Central Avenue, Boulder, Colorado 80301-2877, and in the United Kingdom by Westview Press, 12 Hid's Copse Road, Cumnor Hill, Oxford OX2 9JJ

First paperback printing 2001.

Library of Congress Cataloging-in-Publication Data
Unraveling the right : the new conservatism in American thought and
   politics / edited by Amy Ansell.
      p.   cm.
   Includes biblographical references and index.
   ISBN 0-8133-3146-3 (hardcover); ISBN 0-8133-3147-1 (paperback)
   1. Conservatism—United States.   2. United States—Politics and
government—1993–   .   I. Ansell, Amy Elizabeth, 1964–   .
JC573.2.U6U57   1998
320.52'0973—dc21   98-9569
                                                                                    CIP

The paper used in this publication meets the requirements of the American National Standard for Permanence of Paper for Printed Library Materials Z39.48-1984.

10   9   8   7   6   5   4   3   2   1

Contents

Foreword	vii
Introduction, *Amy E. Ansell*	1

Part One   Organizational Currents

1 Following the Threads, *Chip Berlet*	17
2 The Personal Is Political: The Role of Cultural Projects in the Mobilization of the Christian Right, *Sara Diamond*	41
3 Inventing an American Conservatism: The Neoconservative Episode, *Gary Dorrien*	56
4 Business Conflict and Right-Wing Movements, *Matthew N. Lyons*	80

Part Two   Ideological and Policy Currents

5 Kitchen Table Backlash: The Antifeminist Women's Movement, *Jean Hardisty*	105
6 Fulfilling Fears and Fantasies: The Role of Welfare in Right-Wing Social Thought and Strategy, *Ann Withorn*	126
7 Why Did Armey Apologize? Hegemony, Homophobia, and the Religious Right, *Anna Marie Smith*	148
8 The Color of America's Culture Wars, *Amy E. Ansell*	173
9 The Military-Industrial Complex and U.S. Foreign Policy: Institutionalizing the New Right Agenda in the Post–Cold War Period, *Ronald W. Cox*	192
10 The New Right's Economics: A Diagnosis and Counterattack, *Richard D. Wolff*	211

v

11 Mastering the New Political Arithmetic:
   Volatile Voters, Declining Living Standards, and
   Non-College-Educated Whites,
   Ruy A. Teixeira and Joel Rogers   228

Notes on the Editor and Contributors   249
Index   253

Foreword

This volume analyzes the most central and most significant public issues confronting our society at the end of the twentieth century, and it does so in a remarkably helpful way. The new conservatism not only shapes the quality of our lives but presents a number of haunting issues that are not easily resolved.

The implications of the new conservatism for values and for ideology are basic. This ideology elevates a religious minority, the Christian Right, and an affluent minority over the great majority and defines these as more worthwhile, arbitrarily defining them as making the chief contribution to society.

Because these groups enjoy more ready access to the media than most of the population, they can inculcate this warped view widely, especially among those who are chiefly influenced by the electronic media. The reason for such a bias lies in the tendency of news and commentary on radio and television to focus on their entertainment value and on propaganda that is advantageous to the ambitions of the powerful. This tendency discourages a critical stance from listeners and viewers.

Students of organization are aware, moreover, that it is often subordinate employees, such as schoolteachers and store clerks, who most decisively influence the decisions that determine the quality of life, while their hierarchical superiors get the credit for doing so, although their "decisions" are typically ambiguous and inconclusive. The claims of the conservative Right to monitor and improve societal values are therefore largely misleading and hypocritical.

The worse living conditions and standards become for a significant part of the public, the more cynical these people are likely to be and the more enticing the appeal of conservative ideology will be for them. This relatively recent phenomenon is a stark departure from the long-held assumption that poverty, unemployment, and other burdensome developments encourage adherence to leftist or liberal causes.

In the course of argument about desirable public policy, adherents to a particular view are likely to define it as moderate, whereas its opponents see it as extreme. But "extreme" and "moderate" are highly volatile terms, shaped by the ideologies of those who use them. Right-wing positions regarded as extreme through most of the twentieth century are now defined by newspaper editorials and political spokespersons as moderate.

This volume is a major and admirable contribution to our knowledge of symbolic politics and of contemporary issues. It will continue for a long time to deepen and clarify our understanding of political and social trends.

Murray Edelman
Madison, WI

Introduction

Amy E. Ansell

Beginning in the mid-1970s, an increasing amount of media and scholarly attention has been showered on what has been alternatively defined as the "New/Christian Right," the "new conservatism," the "respectable Right," and the "counter-counterestablishment." Such attention makes a great deal of sense since evidence of a new conservative mobilization has been palpable in a myriad of cultural and political arenas: the bombing of abortion clinics by Christian Right fundamentalists; the passage of anti-gay and lesbian rights initiatives in Oregon and Colorado by right-wing homophobic forces; the success of anti-immigrant legislation pioneered by the racist Right at the polls in California; passage of the California Civil Rights Initiative (CCRI) that legislated abandonment of affirmative action programs in effect for the past two decades; the rise of the antigovernment militia movement and its link with the bombing of the Oklahoma federal building; and, perhaps most poignantly, the so-called Republican revolution in the 1994 midterm elections, which brought right-wing Republicans to a dominant position in Congress for the first time in over forty years.

These are only some of the most salient examples of the apparent power and influence of a new strain of conservatism in American thought and policy. Conventional wisdom would have us believe that such right-wing activity represents the marginal influence of right-wing radicals who have only a peripheral influence on the political mainstream, which has shown itself to be highly resilient to attacks upon it. Despite the fact that a rightist agenda was front and center throughout the Reagan administration as it undermined key Great Society commitments in economic and social policy and that this agenda was clearly evident in the Clinton administration's signing of welfare legislation that abandons central tenets of the welfare state in place since the New Deal, conventional reasoning continues to interpret American conservatism as an aberrational phenomenon that swims against the dominant currents of liberal democratic thought and policy. The fall of the Berlin Wall and the end of the cold war have further reinforced such reasoning as pundits pronounce that liberal democracy has become the only game in the now global town. Sounding suspiciously similar to the "end of ideology" thesis touted some three decades earlier, the rhetoric of the triumph of liberal democracy legitimates the conventional view of the right wing as essentially extraneous to the mainstream of the economy and society of liberal democracies such as the United States; the Right is the extreme that merely serves to give definition to the hegemonic center.

The preponderance of this conventional view, itself based upon a pluralist model of politics, contends that the right wing gains influence because of its successful mobilization of resources at hand (media technology, formerly apolitical Christian voters, manipulation of the reactionary sentiments of "angry white males," and so on) or because it decides to infiltrate the mainstream when other avenues of achieving change are closed. Whether the Right wins or loses is explained by assessing its ability to attract voters to its value system, to favorably translate its policy agenda into a legislative platform in competition with other contending platforms, and to successfully hide its extremism and appear respectable. The current consensus deems that although the right wing exercised some degree of influence during periods of the Reagan, Bush, and even Clinton administrations, its influence has waned as part of the natural swing of the political pendulum. In other words, although the Right may have won specific political battles, the liberal democratic center continues to be the victor in the war over the meaning of the American political tradition. Such a perspective has unwittingly added credence to the views of those who declare that American politics has moved beyond Left and Right. The practical political implications of the pluralist perspective for those interested in combating the right wing is to unmask the loony Right agenda for "what it really is" and thus expose right-wing radicals as extremists beyond the pale, that is, outside the legitimate political spectrum.

Each author in this volume contributes to an alternative perspective on the relevance of today's conservatism in American thought and politics. The authors all recognize that the 1994 victory represented much more than the temporary infiltration of right-wing extremists or the spontaneous combustion of reactionary sentiments by part of the public but rather that it resulted from twenty-plus years of diligent, conscientious organizing by new actors on the right-wing of the political spectrum. Further, the contributors to this volume agree that the American right wing continues to be an important force to be reckoned with. Despite the apparent failure of the "Republican revolution" and the subsequent re-election of President Clinton in 1996, the political and sociocultural forces that contributed to the 1994 victory are still very much at play, demand-

Introduction 3

ing that those interested in reversing the rightward drift of political opinion and government policy formation thoroughly understand the processes at work if another swing to the right (one that is almost certainly to occur) is to be successfully combated.

This volume has been organized to challenge the conventional view of the right wing as essentially extraneous to the mainstream U.S. political tradition and social imagination; as Chip Berlet argues in Chapter 1, the right wing is an integral part of the U.S. political tapestry. The contemporary conservative movement represents something much more than a rearguard, irrational movement of status-anxious individuals. Rather, today's conservatives are engaged in an important effort to contest and rearticulate the very "truths" that are taken for granted in the U.S. liberal democratic tradition. Rather than regarding the right wing as kooks seeking entry to the halls of Congress, an overly conciliatory view that trivializes the sociocultural force of today's conservative movement and its popular appeal, the contributing authors argue that the right wing is the most potent of the political and sociocultural forces taking aim at the already disintegrating postwar consensus. And it is the same conservative movement that is attempting to rebuild a new hegemonic consensus around conservative values and principles: individualism and individual rights, personal responsibility, free market economics, traditional gender/sexual roles, family values, and white racial nationalism. Thus, rather than viewing the right wing as aberrational, as somehow outside the mainstream U.S. political tradition, like a coat of paint that can be peeled away to reveal the healthy underside, we argue that today's right wing sits at the center of the most salient social debates and political processes of the day.

From this perspective, there is no need to search for reactionary or antiliberal sentiment cloaked in democratic platitudes in order to expose the right wing as cranks, although such opportunistic circumvention of the liberal democratic tradition does indeed occur; rather, progressive opponents of today's conservatism need to recognize the degree to which the right wing is contributing to a shift toward a more authoritarian form of democracy by reinterpreting the core values and assumptions of the liberal democratic tradition itself. From the mid-1970s until today, the right wing has waged a formidable struggle in the realm of culture and ideas to map out new ideological territories and symbolic repertoires that both shape and reinforce Republican (and now New Democrat) mantras: that the government is now part of the problem rather than the solution, that individuals are responsible for their own social location, that current social and economic problems result from overly indulgent liberal social engineering, and so on. Such symbolic conflict over the meaning of past events and recipes for future well-being carry significant consequences at both the macrosocial level (for example, which government policies are deemed legitimate and which unsound) and in the most intimate details of people's everyday lives.

In addition to propounding the symbolic conflict perspective on the new conservatism in American thought and politics just outlined, this book also considers three broad questions, although the contributing authors do not always agree on their answers. These questions are: (1) Is there a New Right, and if so, what is it and why is it characterized as "new"? (2) What is the role of conservative ideas in contributing to the right turn in government policy formation? and (3) What are the implications of the new conservatism for the future character of American democracy? In the following sections, I review each of these questions in turn.

Is There a New Right?

All the contributors to this volume agree that the recent rise in right-wing ideas and policies represents something important and new in U.S. politics; however, differences of opinion emerge over the application of the term "New Right." Rather than being merely semantic, such differences of opinion indicate the need to clarify our understanding of the relationship of today's conservative forces with right-wing movements of the past, as well as with other factions of the contemporary Right. There is a continuum of opinion on these questions that the chapters reveal.

At one end of the spectrum is the perception that the strategies and beliefs of the contemporary right wing are fundamentally consistent with the right wing of the past. These authors point out that right-wingers themselves have not used the term since the 1970s and object that the term obscures the continuity between current right-wing movements and their predecessors of the 1940s and 1950s. In this view, the term "right-wing movements" is preferred, in order to avoid making an analytic distinction between postwar generations of the right wing.

Others believe that although there was something "new" about the New Right in the mid-1970s and early 1980s, it is not germane to continue to label these forces on the right of the political spectrum as "new" in the 1990s. Moreover, these authors note that many of the organizations of the so-called New Right of the Reagan era are now defunct. In this perspective, the term "conservative movement" is preferred because the right wing of the 1990s is much more than a limited set of organizations or a network of personalities and, as such, is more deeply institutionally embedded than the right wing of only a decade ago.

At the other end of the spectrum are those who believe that the right wing of the past two decades is qualitatively distinct from the so-called Old Right, and they therefore continue to apply the label "New Right." These authors emphasize that which is distinct about the constellation of

Introduction

political forces on the right of the political spectrum that emerged in the mid-1970s. Among the features that mark the New Right as distinct from right-wing movements of the past are its populist and sometimes even revolutionary rhetoric; a hybrid ideological fusion of neoliberalism and social conservatism; avoidance of extremism and the centering of its discourse as part of an aggressive bid for political power; mobilization of new blocs of voters around a broad range of social issues; and success at coalition building and attention to organizational detail.

Each of these perspectives overlaps considerably in practice, and they are often consistent with one another in application. Each has merit and points to important questions for any student of right-wing movements: How long can a movement or ideology be defined as new? Can we speak of a coherent, singular movement when important differences exist between the religious, secular-political, and intellectual factions of the Right? Should a movement be defined by reference to a specific set of organizations and the individuals associated with them or by reference to the content and style of its discourse and ideology?

With such questions in mind, this book attempts to clarify how the contemporary Right is similar to and distinct from more extreme, Far Right groupings and from previous breeds of conservatism in U.S. history. Moreover, it examines the degree to which there are meaningful differences between the New Right movement that emerged in the mid-1970s and the myriad of conservative voices that characterize the politics of the Right in the 1990s. As the chapters attest, any understanding of the distinctive qualities of the present incarnation of the conservative movement turns on an estimation of new players (for example, the Christian Coalition, the so-called minicons [the newer, younger neoconservative generation, in many cases, actually children of the 1970–1980 generation], Newt Republicans, and so on), changes in historical context (especially the end of the cold war), the rhetorical circumvention of New Left themes (for example, color blindness, equality, special rights, and so on), and the significance of current divisions and fissures within today's conservative movement.

Populism or Ventriloquism: The Role of Ideology

Although an analysis of conservative ideology is not sufficient to combat the rise of right-wing policies in recent years, it is certainly vital to understand its popular appeal and social functions. Contributors differ in opinion, however, about the extent to which the conservative movement should be understood in terms of its ideology, and they also disagree on the question of the relationship of ideology to political practice. In this respect, the book raises important and long-standing questions about the role of ideology in social processes.

6   *Amy E. Ansell*

In general, however, the chapter authors agree that the conservative-led culture wars represent something more than a battle of ideas. The policy debates in which conservatives are engaged are also about class strategies, economic restructuring, business mobilization, the defeat of the Left, and so on. There is no doubt that ideas have consequences, as conservatives are fond of saying, but these ideas also have interests, advocates, opponents, and, most important of all, relations of power and inequality at stake. Thus, although the contributors agree on the danger of reducing the study of the new conservatism to a struggle over values, or a struggle between right-wing ideas and left-wing ideas, there is broad agreement on the usefulness of examining the critical role right-wing ideology has played in the reorganization of key features long taken for granted on the U.S. political landscape.

Each of the chapters speaks to the relationships among the historical context out of which the New Right emerged, the political realities that inform and shape the sociopolitical and cultural engagements of today's conservatives, and the culturally specific modes of signification that render current right-wing discourse and symbolism so evocative in the wider social imagination. It is this complex and materially grounded relationship that we mean to invoke when we speak of ideology. Too often, studies of the so-called culture wars or other right-wing symbolic campaigns are detached from the very relations of power and inequality that give them purchase. This is not to say that right-wing ideology is purely ventriloquist in nature; in order for ideology to work, it must respond in a compelling way to the everyday realities of people's lives. But neither is right-wing ideology a simple function of unmediated populist sentiment, for populist rhetoric can just as easily function as a legitimating tool for elites as it can represent a true expression of popular support.

The authors are concerned with the ideological functioning of conservative policy proposals—to organize perception, interpret events, and justify certain courses of action over others. More specifically, the chapters examine the endeavor by conservatives to appropriate evocative symbols—such as those related to race, gender, sexuality, morality, and nation—to serve as ideological articulators of the recent exit from consensus politics in the post–cold war era United States. In its bid to explain contemporary realities in a popular idiom, the conservative movement has helped bring to the fore of the political landscape such contested symbols and, in so doing, has helped to justify and shape the right turn in policy formation that is becoming increasingly normalized and bipartisan.

The New Conservatism: Implications for Democracy

The essays in this book implicitly raise important questions about the implications for democracy posed by the new conservatism in American

Introduction 7

thought and politics. The complex assemblage of symbolic themes within the right-wing worldview is helping to forge a new political imagination and right-wing consensus that links recipes for national revival to often exclusionary images of the national community. Without minimizing the potential that such exclusionary images signal a dangerous turn toward a more mean-spirited form of politics, the authors avoid unnecessary hyperbole and instead emphasize the new and more indirect forms of exclusion established and maintained by relatively mainstream cultural codes and institutional practices.

To the extent that the new conservatism does pose a threat to liberal forms of democracy, the danger owes less to a set of illicit or surreptitious intentions on the part of right-wingers than to the real potential for the New Right's hegemonic project to succeed in furthering the disintegration of the postwar liberal democratic consensus and its positive vision of the role of government in pursuing liberal equality policies. The symbolic dimensions of policy formation are being orchestrated at the expense of substantive benefits and are serving to foreclose discussion of policies oriented toward other, more structural interpretations of the nation's present difficulties. Not only have the symbolic dimensions of policy formation shaped and reinforced public animosity to new folk devils such as illegal immigrants and "welfare queens" (folk devils who themselves implicate and stigmatize the liberal/Left opposition) but they have also offered a convenient way to deny the need for policymakers to confront the difficult social and economic realities that are emerging and to justify the retreat from the idea that the government has an obligation to ensure a decent social wage.

In their own respective ways, these authors articulate a need for a concerted effort by progressive opponents of the new conservatism to reframe the political debate at the sociocultural—and not only the policy—level. This means recognizing, as the new conservatives do, the importance of the act of framing public discourse for political advantage. Policy formation processes always involve competing narratives, metaphors, and discursive practices that seek to bolster one view of what the issue is, why it is there, and what to do about it. In many ways, the problems in need of policy resolution are created in and through the policymaking process, a counterintuitive insight that is missed by those who approach the policy arena from a narrowly empiricist perspective. Only with an appreciation of the symbolic dimensions of the policymaking process is it possible to appreciate that the narratives mobilized and the metaphors employed often reveal more about the perspectives and interests of those in the dominant society who are attempting to resolve a "problem" than about the so-called deviants who are the ostensible focus of the policymaking effort. In this sense, the ideology of the new conservatism is as much about an effort to construct a nonproblematic American identity and to justify the operation of the meritocratic ideal in a context of structural inequality as it is about combating the "special rights" of homosexual people or the irresponsible behaviors associated with the "dependency culture."

Of course, to understand and combat the cultural codes and symbolic themes that justify and maintain patterns of indirect exclusion is not sufficient in and of itself to reverse the whole myriad of economic, political, and sociocultural shifts that we now associate with the right turn; it is but one limited yet vital contribution to that reversal. The authors disagree on the degree to which progressives should focus on strategies of ideological as opposed to material bases of counterhegemony. This volume aims to air such strategic debates to aid those who wish to contribute to a reversal of the gains made by the new conservatives in recent years.

Organization of the Book

The volume is organized in two parts: Part One surveys various organizational currents that characterize the contemporary right, and Part Two surveys a variety of thematic arenas that involve the new conservatism.

The new conservatism includes within it a variety of organizational currents, most important among them the secular-political Right, the Christian Right, the intellectual Right (otherwise known as neoconservatism), and the business Right. In Chapter 1, Chip Berlet provides an overview of the terrain occupied by the new conservatism in the United States. Defining the political Right as an integral part of the U.S. political tapestry, Berlet documents the historical phases through which the prewar and postwar Right has passed: from the Old Right's explicit defense of unequal access to privilege and power to the postwar fusionist themes of economic liberalism, social conservatism, and militant anticommunism to the New Right's aggressive attempt to dominate the Republican Party by eschewing the nativist baggage and extremist rhetoric of the Old Right, thereby mainstreaming its image. After synthesizing such an enormous amount of historical material, Berlet proceeds to document the current points of overlap and fissure within the now fraying threads of the contemporary Right in the post–cold war era.

In Chapter 2, Sara Diamond examines the process whereby the Christian Right has become "the largest, most influential social movement active in U.S. politics." Of central importance to Diamond are what she labels the Christian Right's "cultural politics," which inform the practices of everyday life; Diamond finds cultural politics to be as, if not more, important to the Christian Right's success as the conventionally studied politics of the ballot box. Although it has become common in recent years for commentators to pronounce the movement's "fall from grace," Dia-

Introduction 9

mond argues that it is through the Christian Right's seemingly nonpolitical cultural projects and subcultural institutions such as the religious broadcasting industry, the evangelical publishing and print media, the Promise Keepers' men's rallies, and the racial reconciliation projects within evangelical churches that the real and continuing source of the strength, popular appeal, and longevity of the Christian Right can be ascertained.

In Chapter 3, Gary Dorrien examines an important moment in the history of U.S. intellectual conservatism, a period he labels the "neoconservative episode." The neoconservatives—a group of mainly male, Jewish, New York intellectual refugees of the radical Left—emerged in the 1960s as a new, more modern face of the intellectual Right. They referred to themselves as "realist meliorists," or in neoconservative Irving Kristol's famous phrase, "liberals who have been mugged by reality." By the beginning of the first Reagan administration, the neoconservatives had assumed an influential movement posture and were decrying the excesses of the counterculture and the indulgences of liberal social engineering while advocating core concerns such as militant anticommunism, capitalist economics, a minimal welfare state, the rule of established elites, and the return to traditional cultural values. Dorrien documents how the movement has since disintegrated as a unified intellectual force in the post–cold war era, as anticommunism had previously provided a sort of glue for otherwise very disparate concerns and personalities. The chapter concludes with an examination of "the lasting commitments that a dissolving neoconservative movement has contributed to a reconstituted American Right," the most important of these being the mainstreaming of a breed of intellectual conservatism that accepts no guilt for the reactionary movements of the past, such that the more recent generation of neoconservative thinkers (the so-called minicons) simply refer to themselves as conservatives.

Matthew Lyons begins Chapter 4 by stating: "The right-wing offensive of the last twenty years has been a gold mine for big business." Having posited such a positive relationship between the Right and business from the outset, Lyons proceeds to demonstrate that the alliance between the two sets of actors has been far from simple. Employing a business conflict analysis (also advanced by Ronald Cox in Chapter 9), Lyons highlights the degree to which right-wing splits and clashes over policy in recent years have often paralleled capitalist factional divisions. He alerts us to the ways in which right-wing appeals and the changing and often inconsistent interests of business actors interacted to deliver Reagan the White House in 1980 and again in 1984 and then concludes that this same interaction helps explain the breakup of this right-wing coalition in the late 1980s and early 1990s.

Part Two surveys a variety of thematic concerns in which the contemporary Right has been involved. In Chapter 5, Jean Hardisty examines the antifeminist women's movement. Rather than propounding theories of false consciousness, Hardisty analyzes the process the contemporary Right has used to address complex areas of concern and distress for conservative women who hold traditional values, thereby recruiting these women to aid in its efforts to roll back the gains of the women's movement and politically neutralize feminism. Focusing chiefly on the core themes and activities of two organizations—Phyllis Schlafly's Eagle Forum and Beverly LaHaye's Concerned Women for America (CWA)—Hardisty argues that the antifeminist women's movement has been quite successful in drawing women into an activist position supportive of the wider agenda and ideology of the conservative movement.

In Chapter 6, Ann Withorn documents the process whereby conservative opposition to welfare has shifted from a political issue on the back burner in the 1970s to a central organizing theme for right-wing fantasies in the 1980s and 1990s. Especially in the post–cold war era, Withorn argues, conservative opposition to welfare has emerged as both a unifying enemy for an otherwise splintering right wing and also as a wedge issue par excellence in the struggle to discredit the legacies of the New Deal and the Great Society. Withorn concludes by acknowledging the degree to which the insurgent conservative consensus on welfare reform has become institutionalized in the welfare legislation signed by the Clinton administration in 1996, quite possibly signaling "the point of no return on the democratic promises" of the U.S. liberal democratic tradition.

Anna Marie Smith begins Chapter 7 on homophobia and the Religious Right with a recounting of the controversy surrounding Representative Dick Armey's "slip of the tongue" in referring to Representative Barney Frank as "Barney Fag" and Armey's subsequent apology. Challenging the conventional pluralist assumption that Armey's apology had to do with the Republican concern not to alienate the gay and lesbian vote, Smith shifts attention to the symbolic dimensions of right-wing homophobic discourse by highlighting the ways in which that discourse has become increasingly sophisticated in avoiding blatantly homophobic and exclusionary language in favor of pseudo-democratic denunciations of the "special rights" of lesbians and gay men. Rather than simply viewing conservative opposition to gay rights as evidence of hidden or covert antidemocratic sentiment or mean-spirited affect on the part of the Religious Right, neoconservatives, or the new racists, Smith argues that Armey's slip and subsequent apology must be understood in terms of the contemporary Right's attempt to mainstream Republican extremism and redefine the very meaning of the democratic tradition.

In Chapter 8, I document the way in which race has become a key symbol in the New Right's attempt to forge a new authoritarian democratic

Introduction 11

consensus. In order to reconcile America's democratic ideals with the politics of indirect exclusion in policy arenas as diverse as immigration, affirmative action, welfare, and traditional values, the new conservatives have contested previously dominant cultural codes and policy assumptions related to the liberal pursuit of racial equality. In the process, a new breed of racism characterized largely by an absence of antiblack sentiment or extremist intolerance has been brought to bear in the New Right's project to center its discourse on race and normalize it in relation to other more mainstream democratic discourses and cultural codes. The chapter concludes with an argument that an understanding of the new racism of the New Right is crucial if progressives are to effectively intervene in and combat recent debates that assume a nonracialist form but nevertheless serve to establish and maintain relations of racial inequality.

In Chapter 9 on the institutionalization of the New Right agenda in the U.S. foreign policy arena, Ronald Cox attempts to answer the question of why the military budget remains, in the post–cold war era, at levels above the cold war average, especially in an era when Newt Republicans and New Democrats are on a budget-cutting spree. His answer turns on the importance he attributes to the role of the military industrial complex and its strong connections with the New Right and congressional Republicans. Arguing that the New Right never had power on its own but was highly dependent on political officials and business elites whose commitments to increases in military spending provided legitimacy for conservative foreign policy ideology and practice, Cox argues that the continued salience of right-wing thought in foreign policy has to do with the creation of a war-fighting strategy doctrine championed by a coalition of congressional conservatives, executive branch officials, the military-industrial complex, and sectors of a now splintering New Right. Analyzing events such as the Gulf War and the 1994 midterm election Republican revolution, Cox concludes by arguing that New Right proposals for increasing the military budget have been effectively institutionalized during the post–cold war era.

In Chapter 10, Richard Wolff takes on the essential task of diagnosing and providing a critique of the New Right's economics. In an examination of how the consensus around economic theories has been challenged and reformulated in the rightward thrust of the past two decades, Wolff argues that the conservative movement and agenda in economics has provided the Liberal Right with a new opportunity to blame current economic problems on state economic intervention, thereby legitimating its far-from-novel policy recommendation to dismantle such intervention and allow the free market to reign unhampered. Wolff explains that although institutional checks were placed on the system of free market capitalism beginning in the 1930s because of the intolerability of that system, the recent historical context—characterized by mounting social dissatisfactions and a weak Left at home and the demise of the USSR and its Eastern European allies abroad—has created an opportunity for the new conservatism in economic thought to wage a comeback by linking mass dissatisfaction with social conditions to the purported destructive policies of government intervention in the economy and by assaulting Keynesian dominance at all governmental levels.

In Chapter 11, Ruy Teixeira and Joel Rogers provide an analysis of electoral data from the 1992, 1994, and 1996 elections to support their contention that the volatility in voter behavior over the course of the last half decade has less to do with big ideological swings in the electorate, fickle value metamorphoses, or the increased role of religion in politics than with the electoral upshot of declining living standards "and the persistent failure of either political party to successfully address this problem." Rather than viewing the increased salience of the new conservatism as evidence of the inherent ideological conservatism of the electorate, Teixeira and Rogers argue that the Democratic opposition has been hampered by the dominance of the conservative antigovernment story that explains the long-term decline in living standards as caused by useless and often counterproductive government spending. To the extent that the Democrats have surrendered so much symbolic terrain to the new conservatives, they have been vulnerable to the Right's portrayal of their programs as yet another big government intrusion that will do little to benefit the middle class. Teixeira and Rogers conclude by suggesting that the central challenge of U.S. politics today is to capture especially the loyalty of the most volatile voters (that is, non-college-educated whites) by providing effective counterstories to the dominant antigovernment version of events and to address the declining living standards of the middle classes as a values issue. If there is to be any lasting shift away from the new conservatism in American thought and politics, the authors argue, there is a need for a broad national program to raise living standards.

The Political Implications of Unraveling the Right

The project of unraveling the Right carries important implications for both understanding and combating the rise of right-wing ideas and policies in recent years. The works collected here suggest a way to understand the Right that transcends a focus on single-issue politics and instead shifts attention to how a variety of right-wing forces have worked together as a hegemonic coalition to recontextualize and rearticulate the "truths" taken for granted in the U.S. political tradition. Rather than viewing the contemporary right wing as essentially extraneous to the mainstream economy and society of the United States, each of the contributing authors demonstrates the myriad ways in which the new con-

Introduction

servatism is profoundly implicated in the ideological debates, political processes, and policy challenges of the day.

The writings collected here also exhibit novel implications for the project of combating the new conservatism. Rather than directing their energy solely toward exposing the covert antidemocratic sentiments of the right-wing fringe, a strategy that neglects the Right's successful mainstreaming of its extremism and trivializes the degree to which it offers a compelling explanation for the present difficulties of people looking for easy answers, the contributing authors suggest the need to inaugurate a national conversation on the meaning of the American liberal democratic tradition that recognizes that far from declining in power, the new conservatism has successfully moved the entire mainstream political terrain considerably to the right.

PART ONE

Organizational Currents

1

Following the Threads

Chip Berlet

If the Right is right, the poor will always be with us, but pity poor us, the Right will always be with us as well. There will always be a political Right because there will always be people seeking to defend or extend unequal access to privilege and power. The demise of the Right is prematurely reported on a periodic basis by pundits with paltry skills of perception. If the Right is so weak, how did it elect so many members of Congress in 1994? If it collapsed after failing to completely dominate the 1996 elections, why did President Clinton sign legislation slashing the social safety net, demonizing immigrants, and eroding civil liberties? If the Right is marginal, why is there a long list of issues—from attacks on gay rights to continued terrorism aimed at reproductive rights clinics to the rollback of affirmative action—in which the Right has played a significant role?

In challenging the conventional view that the Right is weak and marginal in the United States, this chapter argues that U.S. society has been yanked to the right since the late 1970s in the most sustained political backlash since the redemptionist attacks on Reconstruction after the Civil War.[1] Efforts to reshuffle the New Deal and encage the social liberation movements of the 1960s and 1970s have scored many successes. Even when specific legislative or electoral campaigns have been lost by the Right, its strategists have been skillful in using these losses to further educate, recruit, and mobilize supporters. A phalanx of right-wing think tanks now dominates public discourse on many issues including welfare, taxes, affirmative action, and immigration.

Any serious response that might challenge the right-wing backlash requires an accurate and effective analytical model incorporating the complexity and fluidity of the Right. It is a stereotype to perceive every leader and follower in the Right as cut from the same cloth. The Right is an integral part of the U.S. political tapestry, with many individual patterns and threads woven throughout. To unravel the Right we must follow its many threads and begin to tease apart the loose ends.[2]

What Is Right About the Right?

When terms like "conservative" and "reactionary" are used to describe those in the former Soviet Union who wistfully yearn for a return to communism (or even Stalinism), the terms "Left" and "Right" can certainly seem muddled. Sometimes the waters are muddled by those who insist we have reached an end to ideology because for them the hegemony of the status quo is invisible. Others argue that Left and Right are meaningless terms because they have themselves adopted one or more right-wing doctrines and now want to redefine these regressive ideas as mainstream or even progressive. Some seek idealized community and want dissidents of the Left and Right to shut up and sit down. Arguments about the meaninglessness of "Left" and "Right" are made more persuasive when definitions of the political Right by the Left are overly simplistic, stereotypical, demonizing, or didactic.

Despite all the hullabaloo, this volume argues that there is a political Right. It is composed of a complex and organic network of overlapping political, electoral, cultural, and social structures. There are distinct sectors of the Right in terms of ideology, zealousness, and methodology. Each sector is composed of elite institutions, core leaders, information networks, and grassroots social movements that form, dissolve, and reform coalitions over time based on multiple factors. These diverse sectors have various wings that sometimes agree and sometimes challenge each other over issues such as commercial materialism, federal intrusion into private matters, and whether Hollywood is the new Babylon.

This conceptualization of the Right assumes a range of beliefs that stretch along many continuums and thus challenges the concept that there is an "extremist" or "radical" Right that is outside of and detached from the mainstream political system. Racism, sexism, homophobia, and anti-Semitism—along with other forms of supremacist ideology—are not the exclusive domain of militant organized hate groups but are also domiciled in mainstream culture and politics. Authoritarianism can take an individualized form such as a Ku Klux Klan lynching or a gay bashing, or it can appear in an institutional setting such as in the passage of draconian drug laws or anti-immigrant legislation (promoted in the mid-1990s by both Republican and Democratic politicians). In all these examples, the themes of prejudice, supremacy, and ethnocentrism are also present. Additional themes that emerge from a study of the U.S. political Right include nativism, orthodox religious beliefs (primarily Christian), hierarchical male-dominated family structures, support for unregulated

Following the Threads   *19*

free market capitalism, rugged individualism, and belief in conspiratorial subversion myths and scapegoating.

The diversity within the Right can be confusing, yet there is a back beat to these many melodies of the Right—the issue of equality. Sara Diamond has proposed a deceptively simple yet comprehensive definition of the political Right: "To be right-wing means to support the state in its capacity as *enforcer* of order and to oppose the state as *distributor* of wealth and power downward and more equitably in society."[3] Using this definition and viewing the Right in terms of its political and social mobilization around certain core themes, Diamond in *Roads to Dominion* divided the American Right between World War II and the end of the cold war into four broad movements: the anticommunist Right, the racist Right, the Christian Right, and the neoconservatives. Each of these sectors had adherents that ranged from moderate to militant, pursued various methodological strategies and tactics, and stressed different themes in an infinite matrix of individualized combinations. What a particular right-wing social or political movement views as the legitimate enforcement functions of the state depends on its key topical demands.

As Diamond and others have documented, there is a dynamic relationship among the various sectors of the Right. The activist Right pulls conservatism over in terms of both militancy and ideology, simultaneously pressuring liberals to concede the center and retrench. A vigorous activist Right opens recruitment opportunities for the Far Right. At the same time the dramatic excesses of the Far Right provide a cover for ideological victories of the activist Right and conservative Right and makes them seem more reasonable.

Diamond has pointed out that the distinct sectors of the Right are sometimes system supportive and sometimes system oppositional. They form shifting alliances based on shared goals that vary across time and topic.[4] This is an especially useful concept since the same type of paramilitary Far Right groups that assisted government agencies in spying on civil-rights and antiwar dissidents in the 1960s were busy forming antigovernment armed militias and blowing up federal buildings in the 1990s.

It is erroneous to conclude that since there are often shared themes on the right, all right-wing groups work together. For instance, the conservative Heritage Foundation is a long-standing critic of the Far Right LaRouche network, whereas some traditional conservatives are offended by the sweeping changes proposed by the more reactionary and ultraconservative activists in the New Right. The Far Right views both the activist Right and the conservative Right as weak-willed wimps or active agents of the global conspiracy to enslave patriotic white Americans. Far Right groups such as the LaRouche network, Liberty Lobby, and the Christian Identity movement attempt to join more moderate activist

Right and conservative coalitions, but guilt by association is unethical and inaccurate, despite its popularity as a direct-mail fund-raising pitch by liberal watchdog groups. It is not fair to presume that all conservatives are on a slippery slope toward reaction or that all reactionaries are inevitably borne on a transmission belt toward fascism. Migrations do occur, but they occur in both directions, just as on the left.

Building Blocks of the Contemporary Right:
From Roosevelt to Reagan

In the rest of this chapter, an effort is made to unravel the different threads (organizational, ideological and policy/political) that have defined the right wing in the United States during this century.

The Old Right Stuff

The roots of various contemporary right-wing movements and intellectual currents in the United States derive from a variety of historic ideological sources that are generally rooted in the early hegemony of white Anglo-Saxon Protestantism and consist of Eurocentrism, white supremacy, male privilege, heterosexual norms, and Christian superiority. As a settler society, the United States has also produced a political Right that is intrinsically linked to the assumptions of the early dominant settlers. The resulting ethnocentric and nativist movements have reinforced the current of white supremacy that infuses U.S. culture. It influences institutions and individuals in ways that are frequently invisible to those with disproportionate access to power and privilege based on racial, ethnic, religious, or gender identity.

Between World War I and the Great Depression, the map of the political Right was drawn in broad strokes with the palette knife of racialized nativism. The Ku Klux Klan, born out of the social and economic chaos of Reconstruction to defend white privilege against federal intervention in the South on behalf of freed slaves, saw a resurgence as the violent wing of the nativist sector in the 1920s in a period of economic growth prior to the depression. In this case, social stress was a more causatory factor than economic stress. White supremacy, however, was not merely a marginal activity of the "extreme" Klan but could be found in respectable academic and political circles in the form of the eugenics movement and anti-immigrant organizing. Prejudice against Negroes was so widespread it would be difficult to argue that it represented a uniquely right-wing viewpoint. Antipathy toward Asians and Mexicans was the norm. Anti-Semitism was considered unremarkable. Henry Ford had no qualms about identifying the alien "Other" as "The International Jew" in

Following the Threads 21

the *Dearborn Independent*. Buy a Ford motorcar and you might find an anti-Semitic tract slipped into the glove box.

Catholicism was still suspect well after the turn of the century, but for many the identity of the main alien threat was ideological bolshevism and anarchism—often linked to Jews—though these ideas were also racialized as they were popularly associated with non-Anglo-Saxon southern Europeans such as Italians, and eastern Europeans such as Slavs. The Palmer Raids starting in late 1919 are an example of state authoritarian repression that enjoyed widespread public support as a bulwark against alien ideas and individuals. Deportation ships set off to deliver the foreign threat back to Italy and Russia. Additionally, the Scopes (or "Monkey") trial over the teaching of evolution instead of creationism and the reinvigorated temperance movement leading to Prohibition represent efforts by evangelicals to restore America to the proper path. Godless permissiveness leading to immorality, coupled with godless collectivism leading to communism, were the twin evils being perpetrated on the idealized nation by modernist liberals with their secular and foreign ideas.

Diamond observed that the "American Right of the Depression was characterized by (1) the strident racism and anti-Semitism of its large, mass-based organizations (associated with William Dudley Pelley, Gerald Winrod, Gerald L. K. Smith, and Father Charles E. Coughlin); and (2) the anti–New Deal economic agenda of its corporate lobbies." Both camps were strongly nationalistic, and both shared an aversion to U.S. government intervention abroad. Some economic conservatives opposed Franklin D. Roosevelt as a tool of collectivist organized labor, some thought him an outright socialist, some preferred their antibolshevism in the earth tones of fascism. Elizabeth Dilling's *Roosevelt's Red Record* is a vivid example of the conspiratorial scapegoating that accompanied many attacks on Roosevelt from the Far Right.

The ideas of the Old Right were complex and often contradictory, but if we were flies on the wall at a Newport Beach mansion during a cocktail party celebrating the end of World War II, we would probably have heard the following sentiments:

- Natural oligarchies of governance were composed of those persons with the "proper breeding," a popular phrase that valued the bloodlines and racial hierarchies that motivated the interwar eugenics movement. Dark-skinned immigrants and Negroes could be trained to *act* like Americans but could never really *be* Americans.
- Roosevelt's New Deal was a socialist experiment slowly emasculating democracy, which relied on the vigor of an unrestricted capitalist marketplace.

22   *Chip Berlet*

- We had been pulled into World War II, but now that it was over, it was time to heed George Washington's admonition to beware foreign entanglements and pay attention to rebuilding our nation's business and industry and disciplining the unruly labor unions.
- "Parlor pink" liberals were greasing the skids toward communism with subversive moles burrowing into federal agencies to gnaw from within.
- Freud and Dewey (and perhaps Darwin) were crackpots whose disciples ran through the streets overturning the applecarts of order and discipline. Dewey especially had destroyed public education by taking biblical morality out and putting in a utopian quest for values and meaning that called into question God-given parental authority and natural hierarchies.

Over by the wet bar, there would be whispers that it was the Jews to blame for poisoning the wellspring of American liberty—although such ideas would not be proper to mention in public.

Postwar Fusionism

European fascism and Nazism gave the militant domestic nativists and their right-wing populist mass movements a bad name. After World War II the so-called respectable Right sought to distance itself from the fascist movements and to craft an electoral coalition to roll back communism overseas, restore traditional morality, return gender (and, for some, racial) roles to prewar status, and challenge the statist and collectivist assumptions of Roosevelt's New Deal at home. What emerged was modern conservatism, built around economic libertarianism, social traditionalism, and militant anticommunism.[5] Jerome L. Himmelstein wrote, "The core assumption that binds these three elements is the belief that American society on all levels has an organic order—harmonious, beneficent, and self-regulating—disturbed only by misguided ideas and policies, especially those propagated by a liberal elite in the government, the media, and the universities."[6] The attempt to build a working coalition was called fusionism, and the chief architects were Frank Meyer, M. Stanton Evans, and William F. Buckley Jr. Buckley, who had written for the Libertarian journal *Freeman*, went on to found the influential *National Review* in 1955.[7]

Key Libertarian influences, according to Himmelstein, came from "leaders of the Old Republican Right like Herbert Hoover and Robert Taft; neoclassical economists like Friedrich Hayek, Ludwig von Mises, and Milton Friedman; and a variety of iconoclastic individualists and objectivists like Albert Jay Nock and Ayn Rand."[8] Himmelstein found that social traditionalist influences were equally diverse, with "arguments rooted in natural law, Christian theology, and nineteenth-century European conservatism and its notions of tradition."[9] Post–World War II influential thinkers included Leo Strauss, Eric Vogelin, Robert Nisbet, Russell Kirk, and Richard Weaver.

Militant anticommunism was spread through a series of interlocking organizations such as the National Association of Manufacturers, the Hoover Institution, *Reader's Digest*, the Foreign Policy Research Institute, Crusade for Freedom, the American Legion, and the Reserve Officers Association.[10] Specific constituencies were networked by groups that carried on the themes of the McCarthy period after the congressional witch hunt was discredited in elite circles. These groups included the reactionary John Birch Society (JBS) and the Far Right's Liberty Lobby.[11]

Simultaneous with the rise of the cold war, there was a resurgence of Christian evangelical fervor. This new awakening is best known through the crusades of the Reverend Billy Graham, who facilitated the reemergence of evangelicals into the public social sphere following a long period of inward direction that occupied most evangelicals following the public humiliation they had suffered after the Scopes trial.[12] More politicized parachurch ministries such as Moral Rearmament emerged to combat godless communism, and more secularized groups, albeit still implicitly rooted in Christian social traditionalism and moral orthodoxy, were also formed. The Freedom Foundation at Valley Forge and the Christian Anti-Communist Crusade are typical examples.[13] At the same time, fundamentalists, Pentecostals, and charismatics moved toward more acceptance and respectability, first within the evangelical movement, then within denominational Protestantism, and then into the larger secular sphere.

Throughout this period, the Far Right (race haters, anti-Semites, white supremacists, the Ku Klux Klan, and neo-Nazi groups) mobilized primarily to oppose the civil rights movement.

The New Right Coalition: Rebuilding After Goldwater

The 1964 Barry Goldwater presidential campaign was the high point of Old Right fusionism. Most influential Goldwater supporters were not marginal Far Right activists, as many liberal academics postulated at the time, but had been Republican Party regulars for years, representing a vocal reactionary wing far to the right of many who usually voted Republican. This reactionary wing had an image problem, which was amply demonstrated by the devastating defeat of Goldwater in the general election.

If reactionaries wanted to dominate the Republican Party, they had to face their image problem. This meant creating a "New Right" that dis-

24   *Chip Berlet*

tanced itself (at least publicly) from several problematic sectors of the Old Right. Overt white supremacists and segregationists had to go, as did obvious anti-Jewish bigots. The conspiratorial rhetoric of the isolationist John Birch Society was pronounced unacceptable by interventionist William F. Buckley Jr., whose *National Review* was the authoritative journal of fusionist conservatism. While the Old Right's image was being modernized, emerging technologies and techniques using computers, direct mail, and television were brought into play to build the New Right. Richard Viguerie built the first right-wing direct mail empire by computerizing the list of Barry Goldwater and George Wallace contributors.

When Richard Nixon was elected president in 1968, his campaign payoff to the emerging New Right included appointing conservative activists such as Howard Phillips to government posts. Phillips was sent to the Office of Economic Opportunity with a mandate to dismantle social programs allegedly dominated by liberals and radicals. Conservatives and reactionaries joined in a "Defund the Left" campaign. As conservatives in Congress sought to gut social welfare programs, corporate funders were urged to switch their charitable donations to build a network of conservative think tanks and other institutions to challenge what was seen as the intellectual dominance of Congress and society held by such liberal think tanks as the Brookings Institution.[14] Starting in the mid-1970s, a large and vigorous network of national and statewide think tanks, periodicals, and electronic media emerged to eclipse liberal intellectual dominance in domestic and foreign policy debates.

A New Evangelical Awakening

But corporate millionaires and zealous right-wing activists cannot deliver votes without a grassroots constituency that responds to the rhetoric. Conveniently, the New Right's need for foot soldiers arrived just as the growing number of Protestant evangelicals marched onward toward a renewed interest in the political process.

A more aggressive form of evangelicalism emerged in the 1970s, typified by right-wing evangelical activist Francis A. Schaeffer, founder of the L'Abri Fellowship in Switzerland and author of *How Should We Then Live?*, which challenged Christians to take control of a sinful secular society.[15] Schaeffer (and his son Franky) influenced many of today's Religious Right activists, including Jerry Falwell, Timothy LaHaye, and John W. Whitehead, who have gone off in several theological and political directions, though they all adhere to the notion that the Old Testament scriptures reveal that man has been given dominion over the earth and that if the New Testament transfers God's covenant to Christians, then Christians owe it to God to seize the reins of secular society to exercise this dominion.[16]

Following the Threads

The most extreme interpretation of this "dominionism" is a movement called reconstructionism, led by right-wing Presbyterians who argue that secular law is always secondary to biblical law. Although the reconstructionists represent only a small minority within Protestant theological circles, they have had significant influence on the Christian Right.[17] Dominionism is a factor behind the increased violence in the antiabortion movement, the nastiest of attacks on gays and lesbians, and the new wave of battles over alleged secular humanist influence in the public schools. Some militant reconstructionists even support the death penalty for adulterers, homosexuals, and recalcitrant children.

While dominionism spread, the numbers of people identifying themselves as born-again Christians was growing. By the mid-1970s, rightists were making a concerted effort to link Christian evangelicals to conservative ideology. The coalition really jelled in 1979, when Robert Billings of the National Christian Action Council invited rising televangelist Jerry Falwell to a meeting with right-wing strategists Paul Weyrich, Howard Phillips, Richard Viguerie, and Ed McAteer. The idea was to push the issue of abortion as a way to split social conservatives away from the Democratic Party. This meeting came up with the idea of the Moral Majority, which Falwell turned into an organization.

While the Moral Majority began hammering on the issue of abortion, the core founding partners of the New Right were joined in a coalition by the growing neoconservative movement of former liberal intellectuals concerned over what they perceived as a growing communist military threat and the appalling immorality and irrationality of the 1960s counterculture. Reluctantly, the remnants of the Old Right hitched a ride on the only electoral wagon moving to the right. To reach the grassroots activists and voters, New Right strategists openly adopted the successful organizing, research, and training methods that had been pioneered by the labor and civil rights movements. Viguerie especially championed the idea of using populist rhetoric to build a mass base for conservatism.[18]

The New Right coalition of the late 1970s "represented a reassertion of the 'fusionist' triad of moral traditionalism, economic libertarianism, and militarist anticommunism," Sara Diamond has explained.[19] On the economic front, the idea was to roll back federal policy to eradicate the influence of New Deal social welfarism and state regulation of corporate prerogatives. Socially, there was a backlash mobilization of people horrified—or at least discomforted—by the social liberation movements of the 1960s and 1970s, which had sent a shock through traditionalist communities. It was bad enough that women wanted to be on top—they wanted to be on top of each other! If America was to reject the harlot of Babylon, decent people had to fight back. In 1980, Republican presidential candidate Ronald Reagan sauntered all the way to the White House by strumming these economic and social themes.

Reagan did try to push some of the social issues favored by the Christian Right in Congress, but many mainstream Republicans refused to go along. Congress continued to pass bits and pieces of the lengthy (and sometimes competing) agendas put forward by the Christian Right, economic Libertarians, militarists, and xenophobic authoritarians, but some sectors of the Christian Right felt betrayed by the failure to deliver on promises to outlaw abortions, sanctify prayer in the public schools, and exorcise the Department of Education. Key hard-right activists such as Phillips and Viguerie denounced Reagan for negotiating with the Soviets over arms reductions, joining with militarists to drive another wedge into the New Right.[20]

The election of George Bush—eastern, elite, educated at Yale, for God's sake—further alienated the Christian Right, despite Bush's selection of Dan Quayle as a running mate to pacify social traditionalists. The Christian Right did briefly keep its ties to the Bush White House through chief of staff John H. Sununu, who worked closely with the Free Congress Foundation (FCF). The Bush White House also staffed an outreach office to maintain a liaison with evangelicals. This cozy relationship, however, soon changed as pragmatic secular operatives elbowed social conservatives out of the Oval Office. Meanwhile, the militant tactics of Operation Rescue and other aggressive antiabortion groups highlighted a woman's right to choose as a wedge issue that further split Republicans. Out of this frisson came a revanchist movement whose members dubbed themselves paleoconservatives to show their allegiance to key themes of the Old Right, especially Eurocentric monoculturalism, white cultural or racial superiority, heterosexual patriarchy, and isolationist nationalism.

Frays on the Right in the Post-Reagan Era

Toppling Blocks and Shifting Sands

The edifice of the U.S. political Right seemed doomed to topple along with the Berlin Wall in late 1989. With the end of the cold war, who needed cold warriors? The Christian Right was itself tipsy from news of important leaders caught with their hands in the till or handling prostitutes. The trickle-down theory had mostly dried up. The New Right alliance that had been cobbled together to support Reagan eventually collapsed. After the scandals of Jimmy Swaggart and Jim Bakker which rocked televangelism, and Pat Robertson's failed 1988 presidential bid, some pundits predicted the demise of the Christian Right. But they overlooked the huge grassroots constituency that remained connected

Following the Threads   27

through an infrastructure of conferences, publications, radio and television programs, audiotapes, and so forth. The new conservatism reformed and continued on in diverse ways.

How did various right-wing groups take the end of the cold war so easily in stride and come to construct the government as the new subversive enemy? The "red menace" was the central scapegoat for the political Right during the twentieth century, and state collaboration with right-wing countersubversion movements was common. Many periods of economic or social conflict that generated right-wing populism preceded the rise of communism and anticommunism. After the collapse of communism in Europe, sectors of the conspiracist Right simply reached into their historic baggage and pulled out old clothes to put on the new scapegoat. They claimed the goal of the age-old collectivist enemy was still a "New World Order," just as they had been predicting for centuries. Furthermore, this sector of the Americanist Right had long asserted that a primary danger of communism was internal subversion, not just external invasion. And the John Birch Society and the Liberty Lobby had argued that behind communism hid the shadowy elites who also manipulated Wall Street.[21]

This transition was particularly painless for the new Christian Right because prior to the collapse of communism, many of its leaders had embraced a new variation on the theme: the secular humanist conspiracist theory.[22] According to George Marsden, this new analysis "revitalized fundamentalist conspiracy theory."

> Fundamentalists always had been alarmed at moral decline within America but often had been vague as to whom, other than the Devil, to blame. The "secular humanist" thesis gave this concern a clearer focus that was more plausible and of wider appeal than the old mono-causal communist-conspiracy accounts. Communism and socialism could, of course, be fit right into the humanist picture; but so could all the moral and legal changes at home without implausible scenarios of Russian agents infiltrating American schools, government, reform movements, and mainline churches.[23]

A number of Christian Right ideologues adopted the secular humanist conspiracist theory, including Timothy and Beverly LaHaye and Dr. James Dobson. Goldwater supporter John Stormer updated his 1960s book for the 1990s and shifted his focus from anticommunism to claim secular humanism now played a key subversive role in undermining America.[24] In a similar way, militant Protestant fundamentalist elements in the antiabortion movement claimed a conspiracy of secular humanists as the source of godless disregard for what they argued was sinful murder of the unborn.[25]

One of the core ideas of the Right in the United States during this century has been that modern secular liberalism was a handmaiden for collectivist godless communism. The secular humanist conspiracist theory decouples scapegoating allegations from godless anticommunism and returns them to the earlier underlying tracks leading from the original antimodernist and anti-Enlightenment fundamentalist impulses and allegations about demonic conspiracies.[26] As a result, sectors of the new Christian Right now compete with the John Birch Society and the Liberty Lobby as major sources of conspiracist narrative in the United States.

Secular humanists, pictured as the torchbearers of liberal godlessness and New Deal statism, could be scapegoated from a variety of perspectives—economic, antielitist, and moral, as well as religious. The idea of the secular humanist conspiracy also paralleled and buttressed the resurgent Libertarian theme that collectivism drains the precious bodily fluids from individual initiative and also saps the vigor of the free market system. Further, it echoed the concern of conservatives, neoconservatives, and paleoconservatives over creeping moral decay and the failure of New Deal liberalism. This resulted in some remarkable tactical coalitions following the rise of the New Right, especially around issues of public school curricula and government funding for education.

The strongest glue that bound the New Right pro-Reagan coalition together was anticommunist militarism. Neoconservatives, some of them Jewish, were often willing to overlook the long-standing tolerance of racist and anti-Jewish sentiments among some in the Old Right. When Bush enthused about a New World Order as he sent troops off to storm the desert sands of Kuwait, it signaled the end of the original New Right coalition. Isolationists, right-wing economic populists, and business nationalists formed a new coalition to oppose the Gulf War. Neoconservatives, who were overwhelmingly interventionist, attempted to vilify the emerging isolationist paleoconservatives by decrying their racialist and anti-Semitic credentials. Paleoconservative Pat Buchanan's long-standing bigotry was suddenly "discovered" and denounced by his former allies.

Strange Bedfellows: Electoral Conservatives Regroup at the Grass Roots

Culling a cadre from campaign contributors to his failed 1988 presidential bid, Pat Robertson went back to the future with a scheme to take over the Republican Party from the ground up. Robertson and organizer Ralph Reed created the Christian Coalition, which moved quickly into the local and state electoral arena. The Christian Coalition joined with other Christian Right groups, such as the Traditional Values Coalition (TVC) of Lou Sheldon, and Concerned Women for America led by Beverly LaHaye, to

Following the Threads

target school boards, public libraries, and state legislatures. Meanwhile, the Washington, D.C. chain of right-wing institutions such as the Free Congress Foundation, Madison Center, and the Heritage Foundation continued to train conservative activists from college newspaper reporters to elected state officials. The Christian Right reassembled its key components, then launched an outreach campaign to conservative Catholics and moral traditionalists, even reaching out to include a handful of high-profile Jews. Antihomosexual campaigns overtook antiabortion organizing as the hot-button issue and fund-raising focus for social issue conservatives.[27]

The 1992 Republican convention represented the ascendancy of the activist Right, with politically mobilized conservative Christians emerging as the largest voting block within the GOP. Meanwhile, neoconservatives, who championed the anti-Sandinista Nicaraguan contras, were given posts in the Clinton administration as it scuttled to the right. Even Barry Goldwater, toast of the reactionaries in 1964, lambasted the narrow-minded bigotry of the Christian Right, which traced its paternity to his failed presidential bid. The militant apocalyptic rhetoric of Buchanan and others at the 1992 Republican convention was condemned by liberal and conservative pundits, but despite many claims otherwise, there is no evidence that this had a significant effect on voting outcomes.

The base-broadening effort of social conservatives continued, with Ralph Reed of the Christian Coalition writing in the Heritage Foundation's *Policy Review* about the need for the Right to move from such controversial topics as abortion and homosexuality toward bread-and-butter issues such as taxes—a tactical move that did not reflect any change in the basic belief structure. Sex education, abortion, objections to lesbian and gay rights, resistance to pluralism and diversity, demonization of feminism and working mothers—these are core values of the coalition being built by the Christian Right and its allies. By November 1994, the electoral activist Right had gained control of significant sectors of the Republican Party and helped sweep into the House of Representatives a large number of conservative and reactionary politicians.

One of the key organizing tactics of the Christian Right has been the use of populist rhetoric. As globalization has disrupted social, political, and economic systems across the planet, many different types of right-wing populist movements have appeared in response. For a growing portion of the population in the 1990s, neither the Democrats nor the Republicans offered hope for redress of grievances. Conservative analyst Kevin Phillips wrote: "The sad truth is that frustration politics has built to a possibly scary level precisely because of the unnerving weakness of the major parties and their prevailing philosophies." Phillips cited both Republicans and Democrats for "ineptness and miscalculation." After decrying liberal elitism and arrogance, Phillips condemned Republican politicians who have "periodically unleashed the anti-black and anti-Israel messages they now complain about in more blunt politicians as 'bigotry.'" According to Phillips, "If Patrick Buchanan is to be put in a 1930-something context, so should the second-rate conservatives and liberals responsible for the economic and social failures from which he and other outsiders have drawn so many angry votes."[28]

Serious statistical research on this subject is scarce in the United States, but in his study *Radical Right-Wing Populism in Western Europe*, Hans-Georg Betz noted one common theme in Western Europe was xenophobia and racist scapegoating of immigrants and asylum seekers in an electoral context.[29] Betz's review of voting demographics in Europe reveals that right-wing populist parties attract a disproportionate number of men, individuals employed in the private sector, and younger voters. In terms of social base, two versions of right-wing populism have emerged: one centered around "get the government off my back" economic libertarianism coupled with a rejection of mainstream political parties (more attractive to the upper middle class and small entrepreneurs), the other based on xenophobia and ethnocentric nationalism (more attractive to the lower middle class and wageworkers).[30] These different constituencies unite behind candidates who attack the current regime since both constituencies identify an intrusive and incompetent government as the cause of their grievances. Anecdotal evidence suggests a similar constituency for right-wing populists in the United States.[31]

Further to the right in this country, a series of overlapping right-wing social movements with militant factions coalesced into the Patriot movement, which has an armed wing—the citizen militias—that spawns violent confrontations. Remnants of the Christian Patriot movement and members of the neo-Nazi underground interacted with the militia movement. Anger over gross government abuse of power against the Weaver family at Ruby Ridge, Idaho, and the Branch Davidian sect at Waco, Texas, swirled into a frenzy that exploded in the bombing of the federal building in Oklahoma City. During the mid-1990s, armed militias were sporadically active in all fifty states, with numbers estimated at between 20,000 and 60,000. The larger and broader Patriot movement involved as many as 5 million people who suspected the government was manipulated by secret elites and planned some form of tyranny.[32] This sector overlapped with a resurgent states' rights and county supremacy movement, with its novel manifestation, common law courts, set up by "sovereign" citizens claiming jurisdiction and dismissing the U.S. judicial system as corrupt.[33]

The use of scapegoating as a political tool has accompanied the backlash against social liberation and global corporatism. In studying the debate over welfare, Lucy A. Williams has argued the importance of the fact that "the development of a right-wing populist movement, based on fear and nostalgia . . . led to the scapegoating of welfare recipients as the cause of all economic and social woes. Race and gender played central roles in the promotion of the stereotype of the unworthy welfare recipient. The Right utilized welfare as a wedge issue, an issue which could pry voters away from their traditional allegiances."[34] As Jean Hardisty has observed, "Several different forms of prejudice can now be advocated under the guise of populism."[35] Scapegoating has already become mainstream in political and electoral circles, and it has both economic and social roots.

Whether religious or secular in style, various right-wing populist movements can cause serious damage to a society because they often popularize xenophobia, authoritarianism, scapegoating, and conspiracism. This can lure mainstream politicians to adopt these themes to attract voters, and it can even legitimize acts of discrimination (or even violence).

Cracks and Fissures in the Electoral Right

Although the Far Right flirtation with fascism makes for colorful headlines, the largest and most influential sector of the Right in the United States are the electoral conservative coalitions. Jean Hardisty has argued that it is the confluence of several factors that has assisted this success of the resurgent Right since the 1970s: a conservative religious revitalization, economic contraction and restructuring, race resentment and bigotry, backlash and social stress, and a well-funded network of right-wing organizations. The synergy is key, according to Hardisty:

> Each of these conditions has existed at previous times in U.S. history. While they usually overlap to some extent, they also can be seen as distinct, identifiable phenomena. The lightning speed of the right's rise can be explained by the simultaneous existence of all five factors. Further, in this period they not only overlap, but reinforce each other. This mutual reinforcement accounts for the exceptional force of the current rightward swing.[36]

While the electoral Right has been resurgent, it has been continuously bickering. By the late 1980s the New Right coalition was fraying at the seams, and the collapse of communism in Eastern Europe further tore the fabric.[37] As John Judis explained:

> During the Bush years, strife among these groups was rampant. Tory "neocons" and Old Right "paleocons" warred over Israel and immigration, while libertarians and the Christian right quarreled over family matters. In the 1992 Republican presidential primary [neoconservative] Bill Bennett accused Bush challenger Buchanan of "flirting with fascism." Ross Perot's third-party candidacy divided the movement further, drawing off Old Right and laissez-faire conservatives."[38]

The outcomes of these ongoing internal struggles are difficult to predict, but the cleavages are useful to examine for both tactical and strategic reasons because the shape of the Right will reflect how the dominant sectors either win these debates or demote them below the primary principles of unity for new tactical and strategic coalitions. It would be a serious mistake, however, to equate internal contradictions and realignment of coalitions with the collapse of the Right.

With the ascendancy of the Christian Right in the 1980s, the social conservative theme of the culture war bested economic libertarianism as the new central metaphor for the struggle between conservatives and liberals.[39] For many years, Paul Weyrich had proposed cultural conservatism as the new glue for conservative mobilization. The idea of a culture war has its primary effect on public policy through demands that the state play a role in policing monocultural concepts of morality rooted in shared mandates of Protestant and Catholic orthodoxy. This provokes an intrinsic conflict with Libertarians, who rage against most statist intervention other than narrow government activity to protect property and wealth such as national defense and law enforcement.

One domestic example of this monoculturalism is the Christian Right's core focus on sexuality, especially any attempt by women—or men—to step outside the limits of conservative Christian patriarchal assumptions of family.[40] Antigay sentiments attracted support from many neoconservatives who called for an idealized level playing field for women and people of color but did not want homosexuals to leave the locker-room closet. Meanwhile, some economic Libertarians, including a small but vocal group of gay conservatives, pestered the Christian Right for its obsession with passing laws curtailing rights based on sexual identity.[41] Antiabortion strategy sparked a fierce debate over the text of the Republican Party platform in 1996, with candidate Bob Dole failing in an effort to offer pro-choice Republicans at least a rhetorical refuge against the dogmatism of the Christian Right ideologues who dominated the party at the grass roots.[42] Moreover, most Libertarians and even some traditional Republican Party conservatives were uncomfortable with the Christian Right's attack on comprehensive sexuality education (in the latter's promotion of abstinence-only curricula) in the era of AIDS.

In terms of foreign policy, culture war themes extend well into the mainstream. Samuel Huntington in *The Clash of Civilizations and the Remaking of World Order* argued that the crucial global division in the post–cold war period was between cultures. Huntington now saw ethnoreligious worldviews pitted against each other, with global blocs of Islamic, Orthodox, Japanese, and other cultures battling the beleaguered (heroic, idealized, preferred) Western culture. Noting this paradigm omits consideration of other cleavages, such as those between mod-

Following the Threads 33

ernists and traditionalists and between the haves and have-nots, as Ronald Steel has observed: "Indeed, the whole 'civilization' thesis sometimes seems motivated by a profound distaste for multiculturalism at home, and can be viewed as an elaborate 'decadence of the West' alarm that requires battening down the hatches against cultural assaults from within as well as without."[43]

Some economic Libertarians found themselves at odds with monoculturalists who opposed immigration. Some Libertarian think tanks, with an eye toward cheap labor and an arm against state regulation, were quick to point out that most immigrants, over time, pay more in taxes than they use in social services. Some xenophobic Libertarians, however, sided with the anti-immigrant campaign, arguing that capitalism and democracy work best in monocultural societies where (they allege) less government regulation is needed, given widely shared values.

Even those who supported the culture war argued over whether it was based on behavior or bloodline. The 1990s saw a renewal of the biological determinist claim that genetic racial differences accounted for class inequalities. This focus on race played out in policy debates over street crime, welfare, and immigration. The loudest salvo from the biological determinists came with the publication of *The Bell Curve*, by Richard J. Herrnstein and Charles Murray.[44] *The Bell Curve* argued that blacks and Latinos were genetically inferior and then concluded that most affirmative action and social welfare programs were doomed to failure.[45] Much of the underlying research was funded by the white supremacist Pioneer Fund, including a number of studies published by the Institute for the Study of Man, a racialist group that promotes the same debunked pseudoanthropological claims of a racial Aryanist diaspora favored by the Nazis.[46] It is interesting to note that not all critics of *The Bell Curve* were on the left. A stinging rebuke of the thesis was published in an antiabortion publication by a conservative author who warned that eugenicist thinking in the past had led to calls for terminating individuals and bloodlines thought to be dysgenic.

Another important division among contemporary conservatives that has inflicted continuing repercussions is the well-publicized fracture between the neoconservatives and the paleoconservatives.[47] The split began in the mid-1980s as an elite intellectual debate appearing in the pages of the neoconservative *Commentary* and in two periodicals with paleoconservative leanings, *National Review* and *Intercollegiate Review*.[48] It reached a boiling point in 1989 during a feud involving theologian Reverend Richard John Neuhaus at the Center for Religion and Society, a think tank in New York City that networked closely with leading neoconservatives. Neuhaus and his staff were fired and locked out of their offices by the parent organization, the paleoconservative Rockford Institute in Illinois.[49] According to the *New York Times*:

The raid on the center's office was provoked by Pastor Neuhaus's complaint, supported by a number of leading conservative figures, that the Rockford Institute's monthly publication, *Chronicles*, was tilting toward views favoring native-born citizens and values and that it was "insensitive to the classic language of anti-Semitism."[50]

Rockford is hardly a marginal institution on the Right. Pat Buchanan endorsed the work of the Rockford Institute after the Neuhaus incident. Ross Perot's running mate, James B. Stockdale, was on the Board of Directors of Rockford in 1989. After Buchanan's anti-Semitism was outed during the Gulf War, other paleocons made bigoted references about the people who "control" the neocon movement, leading neocon critics to charge with much justification that the paleocons were tainted by "anti-Semitism" and "nativism."[51] Since then the split has widened.

The revolutionary Right frame of some reactionary paleocons such as Sam Francis is easy to demonstrate from their own arguments. Francis allies himself with other paleocons such as Thomas Fleming, editor of Rockford's *Chronicles* magazine; Paul Gottfried, author of *The Conservative Movement*; and E. Christian Kopff, a contributing editor to *Chronicles*. Citing speeches delivered by himself and these colleagues at a conference of the rightist American Cause group, Francis described the theme of their presentations as involving "a mission of challenging and overthrowing the incumbent elites of education and culture, not conserving them or fighting them" with reasonable arguments drawn from Republican Party rhetoric.[52] Francis explained that his speech "dealt with the theory and practice of Antonio Gramsci's concept of 'cultural hegemony' and how it might be applied to the causes of the right."

Along with the Rockford Institute, the Ludwig von Mises Institute and the Independent Institute have been singled out as paleoconservative havens.[53] Influential conservative foundations that paleocons decry as seized by neocons include the Bradley, Olin, Scaife, and Smith Richardson Foundations.[54]

Another current division within the contemporary Right is between the neocons and the "theocons," the Christian Right fundamentalists. Despite many differences, modernist neocons and theocons could agree on many socially conservative legislative and policy matters. But neoconservatives could not overlook increasingly open suggestions by some sectors of the Christian Right that the real solution to the moral crisis was the reassertion that America was a Christian nation. Conservative Christian evangelicals were one thing, but theocratic dominionists were quite another. Another tension that contributed to the move of some neoconservatives back to the Democratic Party to support Clinton was the growth of economic nationalist and isolationist tendencies, not only in the Republican Party but also in the activist and Far Right.[55]

Following the Threads   35

The neocon retreat from the antidemocratic trajectory of their own political engagement has also been fueled by broader trends and bickering between purists and pragmatists within the Christian Right. In 1996, militant Protestants and Catholics unhappy with the pragmatism of the Christian Coalition began to question the legitimacy of electoral politics, the judiciary, and the regime itself. These groups began to push openly theocratic arguments.[56] A predominantly Catholic movement emerged from this sector to suggest civil disobedience against abortion was mandated by the primacy of natural law over the constitutional separation of powers that allowed the judiciary to protect abortion rights.[57]

Decrying pragmatism, Howard Phillips used his U.S. Taxpayers Party in an unsuccessful attempt to lure Pat Buchanan to run for president under the purist banner. Although Buchanan was a paleocon, a racial nationalist, and a theocratic Christian nationalist, he was nonetheless a team player and a pragmatist. Phillips went on in another failed attempt to prod Christian Right leader James Dobson of Focus on the Family to denounce the pragmatists. Although these electoral efforts were unsuccessful, the purist sector in the Christian Right has continued to grow.[58]

Toward an Effective Response

The new conservatism has been successful because it has built a movement that serves as an umbrella under which political, religious, cultural, electoral, and economic sectors of conservatism and reaction can gather around shared concerns while still disagreeing about specific topical issues and long-term methodology. The great irony is that several rightist leaders admit they learned this coalition-building strategy from the labor, civil rights, and antiwar movements of the Left.

It is important to understand that the various sectors of the political Right have tapped into genuine anger and disillusionment within the middle and working classes. In some cases, for those with bleak economic futures and declining pay scales, the complaints are legitimate. In some other cases, like majority backlash responses to the demands for social justice from marginalized groups, the complaints are illegitimate. But either way the sense of grievance is real. The sleight of hand employed by demagogues of the Right is to focus this sense of grievance on scapegoats and conspiracist theories of secret liberal elites.

Progressives need to engage in three activities simultaneously: challenging the scapegoating, prejudice, and myths; providing clear strategic analysis and real alternatives that respond to people's specific legitimate concerns and needs; and joining in broad and diverse community-based coalitions engaged in joint work to solve specific problems.

Recognizing who has gained and who has lost in the current economic climate must be part of the discussion. As Frederick Douglass noted, those with power and privilege concede nothing without a struggle. The rightist backlash would have been less destabilizing had there been progressive leadership able to help pilot the society through the roaring ocean waves tossed up in reaction to demands for rectifying centuries of economic and social injustice. For instance, blaming massive job loss and underemployment on affirmative action is scapegoating, but it would be a difficult scapegoat for the Right to peddle in a full employment economy.

The cleverest trick is how the Right has empowered and elevated spokespersons who claim to represent vast constituencies: African Americans who oppose affirmative action, women who oppose feminism, Mexican Americans who call for immigration control. Their discourse is counterintuitive in its opposition to apparent self-interest and is thus the hardest to decode and confront as scapegoating. Our most effective response as progressives is to empower and elevate as leaders people whose core identities and beliefs transcend boundaries: Latino/a artists who support free expression and immigration rights, Christians who support separation of church and state, African-American lesbians who speak out against racism and homophobia, veterans who oppose militarism, comedians who gleefully dissect the absurd claims of our emperor politicians who flap about wearing no intellectual clothes.

In confronting scapegoating, it is important to isolate the handful of ideologues cynically promoting racism, sexism, homophobia, anti-Semitism and other forms of supremacy from their audience, which may embrace these ideas consciously or unconsciously but whose prejudice and discrimination has not hardened into a zealous worldview. The Right has gained many of these converts because it is the only organized oppositional movement challenging the status quo in a coherent manner that provides seemingly plausible explanations and solutions. Labeling and demonizing members of the Right as radicals and extremists who should be shunned is like helping miners pan for fool's gold on Saturday when we should be spending our workweek organizing them to take control of the mines.

The media have been easily manipulated by those adept at scapegoating and demagoguery. In part, this is due to the degrading of news as corporate empires gobble up media outlets and to the reduction of resources made available for serious research while advertising pressures increasingly drive style and content. There are structural and stylistic reasons as well, including the emphasis on short takes and sound bites over more thoughtful longer discussions, the need for exciting images, the rise of "infotainment" and shock talk shows. Perhaps most influential has been the massive funding for right-wing think tanks that churn out talking heads like chicken nuggets and send them off to interviews surrounded by skillful publicity agents and media-packaging professionals.

Following the Threads

Democratic public discourse is disrupted by scapegoating. Opposing scapegoating is both a moral issue and strategically vital because of the role scapegoating plays in building right-wing populism that can be harvested by fascism. Fascism begins by organizing a mass movement with bitter antiregime rhetoric. Human rights organizers working for social and economic justice need to encourage forms of mass political participation, including democratic forms of populism, while simultaneously opposing the scapegoating and conspiracism that often accompanies right-wing populism.

The removal of the obvious anticommunist underpinnings assisted left-wing conspiracists in creating a parody of the fundamentalist and Libertarian conspiracist critiques. Left-wing conspiracists strip away the underlying religious fundamentalism, anti-Semitism, and economic social Darwinism and peddle the repackaged product like carnival snake-oil salesmen to unsuspecting sectors of the Left. Those on the Left who only see the antielitist aspects of right-wing populism and claim they are praiseworthy are playing with fire. Radical-sounding conspiracist critiques of the status quo are the wedge that fascism uses to penetrate and recruit from the Left.

Given the trends we are facing, people who want to defend democracy have to fight on four fronts. We must organize against:

- The rise of reactionary populism, nativism, and fascism with roots in white supremacy, anti-Semitism, subversion myths, and the many mutating offspring of the Freemason/Jewish banker conspiracy theories
- Theocracy and other antidemocratic forms of religious fundamentalism around the world, which in the United States are based in white Anglo-Saxon Protestantism with its subtexts of patriarchy and homophobia
- Authoritarian state actions in the form of militarism and interventionism abroad and government repression and erosion of civil liberties at home
- The antidemocratic neocorporatism of multinational capital with its attack on the standard of living of working people around the globe

As we promote progressive solutions, we must also join with all people across the political spectrum to defend the basic ideas of mass democracy, even as we argue that it is an idea that has never been real for many here in our country. The principles of the Enlightenment are not our goal, but resisting attempts to push political discourse back to pre-Enlightenment principles is nonetheless a worthy effort.

Notes

1. For haunting parallels, see Eric Foner, *Reconstruction: America's Unfinished Revolution, 1863–1877* (New York: Harper and Row, 1988), especially pp. 585–612.

2. For general background on various sectors of the U.S. Right, the best overview is Sara Diamond, *Roads to Dominion: Right-Wing Movements and Political Power in the United States* (New York: Guilford, 1995); in addition, see George Marsden, *Understanding Fundamentalism and Evangelicalism* (Grand Rapids, MI: William B. Eerdmans Publishing, 1991); Jerome L. Himmelstein, *To the Right: The Transformation of American Conservatism* (Berkeley: University of California Press, 1990); James Corcoran, *Bitter Harvest: The Birth of Paramilitary Terrorism in the Heartland* (New York: Viking Penguin, 1995 [1990]); Frank P. Mintz, *The Liberty Lobby and the American Right: Race, Conspiracy, and Culture* (Westport, CT: Greenwood Press, 1985); Leo P. Ribuffo, *The Old Christian Right: The Protestant Hard Right from the Great Depression to the Cold War* (Philadelphia: Temple University Press, 1983).

3. Diamond, *Roads*, p. 9.

4. Ibid., pp. 10–11.

5. Jerome L. Himmelstein, *To the Right*, p. 14.

6. Ibid. Himmelstein's discussion of the practical problems of uniting the three strands into a conservative movement is especially useful and perceptive; see pp. 43–60.

7. Ibid., pp. 43–44.

8. Ibid., p. 46.

9. Ibid., p. 49.

10. Russ Bellant, *Old Nazis, the New Right, and the Reagan Administration: The Role of Domestic Fascist Networks in the Republican Party and Their Effect on U.S. Cold War Policies* (Boston: South End Press/PRA, 1991), pp. 33–38; Christopher Simpson, *Blowback: America's Recruitment of Nazis and Its Effects on the Cold War* (New York: Macmillan Publishing Company, Collier Books, 1988), p. 219.

11. Bellant, *Old Nazis*, pp. 38–39.

12. William Martin, *With God on Our Side: The Rise of the Religious Right in America* (New York: Broadway Books, 1996), pp. 25–46. Although creationists won the case, they lost public favor.

13. Diamond, *Roads*, pp. 92–106; Russ Bellant, *The Coors Connection: How Coors Family Philanthropy Undermines Democratic Pluralism* (Boston: South End Press/PRA, 1991), p.125.

14. Himmelstein, *To the Right*, pp. 9, 129–164. Portions of this section first appeared as Chip Berlet, "The Right Rides High," The Progressive, October 1994, and were later adapted in Chip Berlet and Margaret Quigley, "Theocracy and White Supremacy," in *Eyes Right: Challenging the Right Wing Backlash* (Boston: South End Press, 1995).

15. Martin, *With God*, pp. 194–198.

16. An excellent survey of dominionism and reconstructionism is Bruce Barron, *Heaven on Earth? The Social and Political Agendas of Dominion Theology* (Grand Rapids, MI: Zondervon, 1992).

17. Fred Clarkson, "Christian Reconstructionism: Theocratic Dominionism Gains Influence," in *Eyes Right! Challenging the Right-Wing Backlash*, ed. Chip Berlet (Boston: South End Press, 1995), pp. 60–61.

Following the Threads

39

18. Himmelstein, *To the Right*, pp. 80–94; Diamond, *Roads*, pp. 127–138; Michael Kazin, *The Populist Persuasion: An American History* (New York: Basic Books, 1995), pp. 255–260.

19. Diamond, *Roads*, pp. 127–131, 179–180.

20. Ibid., pp. 261–262.

21. This section is adapted from a draft of Chip Berlet and Matthew N. Lyons's *Too Close for Comfort: Right-Wing Populism, Scapegoating, and Fascist Potentials in U.S. Political Traditions* (Boston: South End Press, Forthcoming).

22. George Johnson, *Architects of Fear: Conspiracy Theories and Paranoia in American Politics* (Los Angeles: Tarcher/Houghton Mifflin, 1983), pp. 169–173; Sara Diamond, *Spiritual Warfare: The Politics of the Christian Right* (Boston: South End Press, 1989), pp. 84–87, 233.

23. Marsden, *Understanding Fundamentalism and Evangelicalism*, pp. 109; see also Diamond, *Roads*, pp. 246–248; William Martin, *With God on Our Side: The Rise of the Religious Right in America* (New York: Broadway Books, 1996), pp. 194–198, 331–333, 344–347.

24. John Stormer, *None Dare Call It Treason . . . 25 Years Later*, (Flourissant, MO: Liberty Bell Press, 1992).

25. Martin, *With God on Our Side*, pp. 194–197; Dallas A. Blanchard, *The Anti-Abortion Movement and the Rise of the Religious Right* (New York: Twayne Publishers, 1994), p. 97. Francis A. Schaeffer, *A Christian Manifesto*, rev. ed. (Westchester, IL: Crossway Books, 1982 [1981]), pp. 117–130; Franky Schaeffer, *A Time for Anger: The Myth of Neutrality* (Westchester, IL: Crossway Books, 1982), pp. 15–25, 76–78; John W. Whitehead, *The Stealing of America* (Westchester, IL: Crossway Books, 1987), pp. 31–59; Tim LaHaye, *The Battle for the Mind* (Old Tappan, NJ: Fleming H. Revell, 1980), pp. 141–179.

26. Fred Clarkson, *Eternal Hostility: The Struggle Between Theocracy and Democracy* (Monroe, ME: Common Courage, 1997), pp. 125–138.

27. Jean Hardisty, "Constructing Homophobia," in *Eyes Right!* pp. 86–104.

28. Kevin Phillips, "The Politics of Frustration," *New York Times Magazine,* April 12, 1992, p. 42.

29. Hans-Georg Betz, *Radical Right-Wing Populism in Western Europe* (New York: St. Martin's Press, 1994), pp. 106–108.

30. Ibid., pp. 106–108, 174; "America's New Populism," *Business Week*, cover story, March 13, 1995.

31. "Portrait of an Anxious Public," in special report on "The New Populism," *Business Week*, March 13, 1995, p. 80.

32. Kenneth S. Stern, *A Force Upon the Plain: The American Militia Movement and the Politics of Hate* (New York: Simon and Schuster, 1996); Philip Lamy, *Millennium Rage: Survivalists, White Supremacists, and the Doomsday Prophecy* (New York: Plenum, 1996).

33. Devin Burghart and Robert Crawford, *Guns and Gavels: Common Law Courts, Militias, and White Supremacy* (Portland, OR: Coalition for Human Dignity, 1996).

34. Lucy A. Williams, "The Right's Attack on Aid to Families with Dependent Children," *Public Eye*, vol. 10, nos. 3 and 4 (Fall/Winter 1996), p. 18.

35. Jean V. Hardisty, "The Resurgent Right: Why Now?" *Public Eye*, vol. 9, nos. 3 and 4 (Fall/Winter 1995), pp. 1–13.

36. Ibid.

37. This section is adapted from a draft of Berlet and Lyons's *Too Close for Comfort*.

38. John B. Judis, "The Republican Splintering: A Preview of the San Diego Zoo," *New Republic*, August 19, 1997, p. 34.

39. Berlet and Quigley, "Theocracy and White Supremacy," in *Eyes Right!*, pp. 15–43; Diamond, *Roads*, p. 298.

40. Diamond, *Roads*, pp. 165–172.

41. Surina Khan, "Gay Conservatives: Pulling the Movement to the Right," *Public Eye*, vol. 10, no. 1 (Spring 1996), pp. 1–10.

42. Hanna Rosin, "Walking the Plank: Henry Hyde's Abortion Problem," *New Republic*, August 19, 1997, pp. 16–20; Judis, "The Republican Splintering," p. 35.

43. Ronald Steel, "The Hard Questions," review in *New Republic*, December 30, 1996, p. 25.

44. Richard J. Herrnstein and Charles Murray, *The Bell Curve* (New York: Free Press, 1994).

45. Jason DeParle, "Daring Research or 'Social Science Pornography'?" *New York Times Magazine*, October 9, 1994, p. 48.

46. Charles Lane, "The Tainted Sources of 'The Bell Curve,'" *New York Review*, December 1, 1994, pp. 14–19; Bellant, *Old Nazis*, pp. 60–64; Bellant, *Coors Connection*, pp. 38–39, 54, 75.

47. Diamond, *Roads*, pp. 279–286.

48. Ibid., pp. 279–280.

49. Ibid., p. 284.

50. Richard Bernstein, "Magazine Dispute Reflects Rift on U.S. Right," *New York Times*, May 16, 1989.

51. See, for example, the June 1992 *Rothbard-Rockwell Report*, which defends the paleocons. For a look at the neocon view of Buchanan and the Rockford crowd, see the May 1992 issues of *First Things* published by Neuhaus ("The Year That Conservatism Turned Ugly") and *Commentary* ("Buchanan and the Conservative Crackup").

52. Sam Francis, "Stupid and Proud," in his column "Principalities and Powers," *Chronicles*, September 1993, p. 9.

53. Gregory Pavlik, review of Gottfried's *The Conservative Movement*, revised, *Conservative Review*, vol. 4, no. 5 (September/October 1993), pp. 35–37. Note that the Independent Institute and the Independence Institute are separate entities.

54. Pavlik, review of Gottfried's *The Conservative Movement*, pp. 36–37.

55. Diamond, *Roads*, p. 180.

56. Jacob Heilbrunn, "Neocon v. Theocon," *New Republic*, December 30, 1996, pp. 20–24. Rob Boston, "Divided They Fall? Hairline Cracks in the Christian Right," *Public Eye*, Vol. 11, no. 2 (Summer 1997), pp. 1–8.

57. See, for example, the newspaper *Culture Wars*, with its motto "No social progress outside the moral order."

58. Fred Clarkson, *Eternal Hostility: The Struggle Between Theocracy and Democracy*, (Monroe, ME: Common Courage Press, 1997), pp. 33, 104–106, 117–119, 153.

2

The Personal Is Political:
The Role of Cultural Projects in the
Mobilization of the Christian Right

Sara Diamond

A few short years before the dawn of a new millennium, evangelical Christianity remains the source of inspiration for the single largest and most influential social movement active in U.S. politics. The Christian Right's power is most visible at the ballot box and in the halls of Congress. It is a power rooted in organizations and in projects both inside and outside the realm of formal electoral politics.

In 1994, the Christian Coalition, along with Focus on the Family, Concerned Women for America, the American Family Association, and scores of smaller, lesser-known groups, helped deliver Congress to the Republicans for the first time in forty years. In thirty close races, the Christian Right's get-out-the vote efforts were the most obvious factor in the Republicans' victory.[1] Some ninety representatives beholden to the Christian Right quickly assembled a new Congressional Family Caucus, through which they pledged to keep the party committed to a "family values" legislative agenda.[2] The leading candidates for the 1996 Republican presidential nomination made courtship of the Christian Right central to their campaigns.

Pundits offered facile explanations for the most evident of the Christian Right's successes. Some pointed to the handful of cases in which the movement had used "stealth" tactics to slip candidates past unsuspecting voters. Others pointed to a dubious voting bloc of "angry, white men" who were credited with, or blamed for, Republican victories in 1994.

Those victories were decades in the making. The Christian Right's longevity as well as its broad appeal can be attributed to the movement's dual-track focus on conventional electoral and lobbying strategies combined with what can be called "cultural politics." Political power involves questions of who will shape and implement the public policies we all must live with. We formalize the process through elections. But it is through the informal practices of everyday life that people come to know what they think and decide how to act—or decline to act—politically. Cultural politics is about the TV and radio programs people interact with, the books they read, the churches they attend—all of which have immeasurable effects on beliefs and behavior more properly considered "political."

Long before the Christian Right came to exert power within the Republican Party, the movement mobilized through a preexisting network of evangelical subcultural institutions. These have included a multibillion-dollar broadcasting industry, a comparable independent publishing industry, plus countless "parachurch ministries" aimed at everything from counseling homosexuals to "go straight" to home schooling children to extolling the virtues of "traditional" relations between "real men" and their wives. This chapter is about how the movement deploys some of its cultural projects, not just for the sake of preaching the gospel but also in service to a political agenda.

When Pat Robertson ran for president in 1988, he told reporters he wanted to be called a businessman, not a televangelist. Yet years before Robertson became the quintessential power broker between the Christian Right and the Republican Party, he was, in fact, the first televangelist to establish a full-time Christian television network, then a university, then a law firm, then the Christian Coalition, one of the largest grassroots lobbying operations in recent history. Robertson's trajectory has typified those of lesser-known movement leaders. He began with a calling to preach the gospel, and over time, broadened the notion of "the gospel" to include a "biblical view" on virtually every political issue under the sun.

During the cold war era of the 1950s, religious broadcasters laid the groundwork for the TV and radio networks that would later become the Christian Right's greatest political assets. From the 1940s through the 1960s, evangelicals were involved primarily in interdenominational conflicts with "mainline" or liberal churches. Theological conflicts took form in a struggle over which denominations would win the lion's share of access to the federally regulated airwaves. Evangelicals astutely protected their interests by forming two related Washington, D.C.–based lobbies, the National Association of Evangelicals and the National Religious Broadcasters. During the same years, evangelicals built powerful missionary agencies. Most worked abroad in the developing countries. Evangelist Billy Graham's ministry also won multitudes of converts inside the United States. At home and abroad, the missionary groups were rigorously anticommunist. They helped legitimize, for their religious constituencies, the United States government's military buildup and foreign interventions.

Domestically, they also played an important, though little known, role in government-led Red-baiting campaigns against liberal clergy.[3]

The 1960s and 1970s saw the continued growth of evangelicals' broadcast and media resources. Among the cohort of baby boomers who entered adulthood during the Vietnam War era, large numbers joined unconventional religious movements of one sort or another.[4] Thousands of hippies joined the Jesus movement and began to make contact with some of the older leaders and ministries within the evangelical subculture. The Jesus movement expanded the numbers of evangelical churchgoers precisely at the time when secular New Right political strategists began to make common cause with up-and-coming leaders of the Christian Right. Several national news magazines labeled 1976 the "Year of the Evangelical" because, for the first time, evangelicals voted in large numbers, and most voted for Jimmy Carter, a Democrat. Carter, the Baptist Sunday school teacher, disappointed most evangelicals with his liberal policies. By 1980, the Christian Right, with logistical assistance from veteran Republican Party organizers, was in full swing behind Ronald Reagan's candidacy. Reagan, too, disappointed the Christian Right. He promised far more than he delivered on the issues of abortion and school prayer. But his crusade against "communism," particularly in Central America, enlisted the collaboration of Christian Right leaders. Throughout the 1980s, the movement's political strategists worked on two tracks. They worked collaboratively with White House foreign policy makers. They also worked as outsiders building a grassroots infrastructure that the Republican Party would not want to ignore. In the 1990s, the national policy agenda shifted to issues almost exclusively domestic, and the Christian Right's success in organizing voters began to bear fruit. By then, the broader evangelical subculture had established an unparalleled array of seemingly nonpolitical institutions, the endurance of which helps explain the success and longevity of the Christian Right as a political force.

In the rest of this chapter, I analyze the political side of several key evangelical industries and projects: the religious broadcasting industry; evangelical publishing and print media; the Promise Keepers men's rallies; and the "racial reconciliation" project to redress institutional racism within evangelical churches. All of these activities are multifaceted. They are personally meaningful to audiences and participants. At the same time, these projects help inform and galvanize activists within the Christian Right.

The Power of the Air

Among all of the Christian Right's resources, religious broadcasting has proven to be indispensable. On a day-to-day basis, evangelical broadcasters create for their audiences a media milieu in which fighting "immorality" is seen as the duty of every believer. Then, at pivotal junctures, the audiences are ready to act in large and decisive numbers. A case in point was the furor that ensued in early 1993 when the Clinton administration announced its intention to lift the ban on gays in the military. The previously unknown Antelope Valley Springs of Life church in Lancaster, California, made headlines with its promotion of *The Gay Agenda*. This twenty-minute video features scenes of flamboyant gay pride marches, interviews with antigay doctors, all to the effect that gays threaten social stability. *The Gay Agenda* first circulated during the 1992 anti–gay rights ballot initiative campaigns in Oregon and Colorado. Once the fight over gays in the military began, Pat Robertson broadcast *The Gay Agenda* for the 1 million viewers of his *700 Club* program.[5] Antigay military officers showed *The Gay Agenda* at prayer breakfasts and in Bible study groups.[6] The film was an effective piece of propaganda in the campaign, led by prominent Christian broadcasters, to flood Congress with phone calls against the lifting of the ban.[7] Under pressure from top military brass and the Christian Right, Clinton policymakers ultimately reneged on their promise to lift the ban.

A year later, religious broadcasting networks proved decisive when the Christian Right defeated a proposed amendment to a congressional education bill (H.R. 6) that would have required state certification of all home-school teachers. Michael Farris of the Home School Legal Defense Association first sent a fax alert to a network of tens of thousands of home-school families. Then Farris and other home-schooling leaders appeared on two nationally syndicated Christian radio talk shows, Dr. James Dobson's *Focus on the Family* and Marlin Maddoux's *Point of View*, calling for a congressional lobbying blitz. Home-school supporters jammed the Capitol Hill switchboard with nearly 1 million phone calls in a few days. By the time H.R. 6 came to a vote, the sponsor of the amendment, Representative George Miller (D–CA) was the only one willing to vote for it.[8]

The gays in the military issue and H.R. 6 lent themselves to the kind of grassroots lobbying campaigns in which the Christian Right's independent media outlets can prove decisive. On a more regular basis, the role of Christian broadcasting is to inculcate audiences with a coherent worldview so that when a controversial issue arises, listeners and viewers are ready to respond.

The sheer scope of the religious broadcasting industry makes it a useful political tool. As of 1995, there were 1,329 full-time Christian radio stations and 163 full-time Christian TV stations.[9] In television, access to cable networks is more important than individual station ownership. Pat Robertson's Family Channel cable network, which carries the weekday *700 Club*, was available through 10,000 cable systems to a potential audi-

Cultural Projects in Christian Right Mobilization 45

ence of 59 million. The Trinity Broadcasting Network, which hosts a weeknight talk show, often on political topics, is carried by about 3,000 cable systems to a potential audience of 27 million.[10]

On the radio dial, Christian broadcasting is the third most popular format, behind country and adult contemporary music. About one in ten U.S. radio stations identify their programming as religious, though only about 2 percent of the total radio-listening population is tuned in to these stations. Still, that gives Christian radio a core audience of 3.5 to 4 million regular listeners, mostly women.[11]

In the 1990s, Christian radio has become increasingly geared toward public affairs programming and talk shows. Focus on the Family is the leader of the pack, with a daily half-hour talk show broadcast on more than two thousand stations.[12] Marlin Maddoux of the Dallas-based USA Radio Network broadcasts his daily live call-in show for 2 million listeners. The content focuses heavily on issues such as homosexuality, sex education, and indictments of the Clinton administration.[13] Concerned Women for America president Beverly LaHaye hosts a weekday talk show aired on ninety stations. LaHaye routinely uses her show to mobilize listener-lobbyists. For example, LaHaye urged listeners to lobby their senators to approve Supreme Court Justice Clarence Thomas in 1991 and to reject Dr. Henry Foster, the Clinton nominee for surgeon general in 1995.[14]

In the 1990s, the trend in Christian television is toward huge syndicated cable networks, and the trend in radio is toward consolidation of station ownership in the hands of a few networks. Major chains, including Salem Communications, Crawford Broadcasting and Bott Broadcasting, have begun buying up stations all over the country.[15] The station formats are increasingly homogeneous, with more and more hours taken up by popular, syndicated shows and with less reliance on local producers. The typical format features a series of half-hour programs with well-known Bible teachers in the morning, followed by nationally syndicated call-in shows in the afternoon. Many stations reserve late afternoon drive time for locally hosted public affairs call-in programs.[16]

The trend toward more call-in shows reflects the popularity of secular right-wing broadcasters, particularly Rush Limbaugh, and the station managers' understanding of the political utility of talk radio. Warren Duffy, a popular Christian talk show host from Los Angeles, has explained that his listeners are beginning to see that "their Christian values are being attacked in the political arena on many levels [and] that an active faith requires involvement in the political and social causes that affect our freedom to live godly lives."[17] Along with Christian broadcasters throughout the state of California, Duffy mobilized his listeners in 1994 to lobby the governor and the legislature to eliminate the California Learning Assessment Test (CLAS). Christian Right activists opposed the reading material and evaluative type of questions found in this statewide public school achievement test.

But few would have known about the CLAS test had they not tuned in to Christian radio and TV. Media campaigns such as the one against CLAS work because they first appeal to audiences on gut-level "family values" issues. Then they give people a feasible course of action: Call or write elected officials, send a check to the Christian legal firms representing aggrieved parents.

Christian broadcasting is politically efficacious because it does much more than keep audiences abreast of the latest "attacks" on Christian values. To most outside observers, the fare on Christian radio and TV seems insipid. Much of the content consists of extrapolations of select Bible passages and testimonies by individuals who tell how the Lord intervened and rescued them from myriad problems. The formulas are repetitive, even ritualistic. Yet the formulas are popular because they help meet the audience's needs for a sense of spiritual connection with fellow believers and for hope that their own personal problems can be alleviated. By helping to meet psychological needs, the most popular Christian broadcasters cultivate the kind of loyal listeners and viewers who are then available to return the favor when it is time to take action.

The political messages and the ready-made lobbying tasks are presented within a success-oriented ideological milieu. Every individual soul makes a difference in the Kingdom of God. Therefore, no individual act of protest or pressure is too small to matter. At the same time, the strong personalities of trusted broadcasters command obedience to suggestion. If Pat Robertson or James Dobson says, "Call your senator," a high rate of compliance is guaranteed.

The Printed Word

Most of the themes and tactical campaigns presented through Christian broadcasting are reinforced in print outlets. By 1995, this echelon of the evangelical subculture included about 50 locally produced monthly newspapers, 72,500 Christian bookstores, and a $3 billion a year book publishing industry, up from $1 billion in 1980.[18]

The Christian Booksellers Association organizes an annual convention attended by about 12,000 retailers and suppliers of Bibles, videos, tapes, Christian fiction, self-help books, greeting cards, and evangelical tracts. The booming business in evangelical paraphernalia draws customers mostly from among charismatic and Baptist churchgoers. Women are almost twice as likely as men to be consistent readers of Christian books.[19] A typical Christian bookstore is like a gift shop with racks of Bibles, cards and calendars, special sections for children's literature, novels for adults,

Cultural Projects in Christian Right Mobilization 47

sections on women's and men's issues, plus a section titled "current affairs." Here one typically finds the latest books by Pat Robertson, Ralph Reed, Randall Terry and other big names on the Christian Right. There are books on how to defend "religious freedom" against the secular state; why abortion is a "holocaust"; why home schooling is preferable to public school education.

Most stores also have sections on eschatology or the study of the end-times. In these books, Bible experts debate whether scripture predicts Christ's return before, during, or after a Great Tribulation wreaks havoc on society. Evangelical readers have been treated to a series of doomsday prophets who have made false claims about Christ's imminent return.[20] Among the eschatologists, Hal Lindsey has been the biggest bestseller. His 1970 book *The Late Great Planet Earth*, which sold 15 million copies, forecasts increased "persecution" of born-again Christians and escalated violence in the Middle East as signs of Christ's likely imminent return.[21] Lindsey's 1995 best-seller *Planet Earth—2000 A.D.* identifies "berserk weather," crime, drug abuse, and AIDS as "evidence" of coming catastrophes.[22] Lindsey carefully avoids setting a precise date for Christ's anticipated return, thus ensuring that readers will not be disappointed and refuse to buy his next books.

But Lindsey and others cultivate among their readers a view that social and political problems are masterminded by Satan and are not the result of human error and certainly not resolvable through human effort. Peace treaties in the Middle East, the affairs of the United Nations—even natural disasters—are all fodder for a worldview that neglects conventional wisdom in favor of a more suspicious, even conspiracist stance toward routine news events.

Pat Robertson's best-selling book *The New World Order* was heavily criticized because of a chapter he wrote on conspiracies of "European" or "international" bankers. Such terms are well-known code for the historical charges that Jewish bankers dominate world finance. Robertson's book was also a classic reading of social trends and political events through the lens of end-times Bible interpretation. Robertson links the rise of the New Age movement and a purported United Nations plot to do away with American sovereignty to a coming "world government" foretold in the Book of Revelation.[23]

Prophecy books and all the corresponding talk about eschatology on the Christian TV and radio networks provide for adherents a sort of parallel universe, an alternate mindset that is reinforced by the themes found in popular Christian fiction. The most popular of this genre has been Frank Peretti's novel *This Present Darkness*, which had sold about 2 million copies by 1994.[24] *This Present Darkness* is a lyrically written and riveting tale. A band of Lucifer's demons, in league with a conspiratorial

New Age cult, is waging "spiritual warfare" against a small town in Middle America. God's angels intervene on behalf of the story's heroes. But the evil is so great that even some of the town's most upright churchgoers turn out to be part of the conspiracy. No one can be trusted. Evildoers are everywhere.

Evildoers are also ubiquitous in more politically explicit novels such as *The Lambda Conspiracy* by Spenser Hughes. In this potboiler, a cabal of gay New Agers pulls the strings at the White House and assassinates a U.S. senator while he is speaking at an evangelical broadcasters' convention. The protagonist is a handsome, thirty-five-year-old TV journalist who sacrifices his career to tell the truth about the homosexual plot to take over the country.[25] This is fiction, but author Spenser Hughes has been promoted as an "information" source by the Traditional Values Coalition, a leading Christian Right lobbying group in Washington, D.C.[26]

The lines between fact and fiction can get blurry. The same stores that peddle conspiracist literature also provide customers with the latest hard news from the evangelical press. Across the country, about fifty independently produced monthly newspapers offer readers local church news, plus a steady diet of nationally syndicated material from the Evangelical Press News Service (EP), which sends out a weekly packet of articles to about 280 Christian media outlets.[27] A typical evangelical newspaper, such as the *Southern California Christian Times*, features articles on local ministries and political campaigns, ads for private Christian schools and for local Christian radio stations, calendars of events, and lots of letters to the editor.[28]

By including many syndicated national news stories, the regional papers serve to unify and solidify an evangelical worldview, with political implications. In February 1995, for example, the EP reported an incident in which a dozen members of a group called Lesbian Avengers entered the Bay Area offices of Exodus International, an antigay counseling ministry. The lesbians released hundreds of live crickets and held signs urging God to send a plague on the organization. The short news item was carried in publications throughout the evangelical press network, and the message was potent. Exodus' executive director, Bob Davies, was quoted as saying that the incident was "another confirmation that many gays are not interested in tolerance and diversity." Davies warned that the incident was "a foretaste of things to come for all members of the conservative church. The lines are being drawn."[29] Indeed, the lines were drawn. Inadvertently, the Lesbian Avengers succeeded in reinforcing, in the minds of evangelical readers, the view that gay people are disrespectful toward Christians, that gay people will damage private property to get their point across. At a time when the Christian Right was seeking support for its ballot initiative campaigns against gay civil rights, this story gave legitimacy to the anti–gay rights cause.

Making Promises

More often than not, a seamless web links the content of evangelical media and the promotional work of leading movement organizations. The Promise Keepers men's movement is a prime example. Founded in 1991 by former University of Colorado football coach Bill McCartney, Promise Keepers holds the mission of drawing born-again Christian men into a more active role inside their churches and helping them restore what they call a "leadership" position in their families, so as to stem the tide of social problems caused by absentee fathers and husbands.

In 1995, the Promise Keepers men's rallies drew more than 600,000 Christian men to weekend rallies at sports stadiums in thirteen U.S. cities.[30] The phenomenal growth of Promise Keepers has been made possible through preexisting church and media networks. In 1995, Promise Keepers advertised its rallies by daily broadcasting a ninety-second promotional spot on 400 Christian radio stations.[31] In its first few years of operation, Promise Keepers relied on frequent coverage on the leading Christian TV networks and in the evangelical press. One early promoter was the popular monthly *Charisma* magazine, with a circulation over 100,000. In 1994, *Charisma*'s publisher Stephen Strang started *New Man*, the Promise Keepers' own glossy bimonthly magazine, which reached a circulation of 500,000 by 1995. *New Man* is full of easy-to-read stories about Christian athletes, happy marriages, and churches that foster interracial friendships among fellow believers. Beyond the movement's own press, in 1995 the mainstream media gave favorable coverage to the Promise Keepers rallies in major cities.[32]

At the local level, Promise Keepers brings crowds to stadiums through a network of ten thousand volunteer church coordinators called Point Men, who serve as liaisons between the national organization in Colorado and the men's groups sponsored by local pastors.[33] Some observers have been alarmed by the prospect that the Promise Keepers' self-described male "leaders" and "warriors" may have political goals more ambitious than taking charge of their own wives and children. Bill McCartney himself has been a board member of Colorado for Family Values, the group that sponsored the 1992 state ballot measure outlawing gay rights ordinances. Promise Keepers claims to be nonpartisan and apolitical, but the exhibit hall at one of its 1995 rallies included literature tables from two major Christian Right groups, Dr. James Dobson's Focus on the Family radio ministry and Gary Bauer's Family Research Council think tank.[34]

These organizations mobilize the evangelical community on a range of issues, especially opposition to abortion rights, gay rights, and much of what goes on in public schools. Representatives of both organizations appear frequently on the Christian broadcasting networks and in columns for the evangelical press. Focus on the Family, in particular, conducts "community impact seminars" all over the country to train Christians to form grassroots political committees inside their own churches.[35] No doubt such committees are active in some of the same churches where Promise Keepers volunteers organize local men's groups. The "family values" legislative agenda is mutually reinforcing, through the idea that individual men need to reclaim "leadership" within their own four walls.

Outside, the specter is one of stadiums full of men ready to do battle with women demanding equality. For the Promise Keepers, though, the time to confront feminism head-on has long since passed. Some who attend the rallies may be there for a last-gasp feeling of unadulterated male chauvinism. But the Promise Keepers' own literature is all about forging a "new man," one who is tough and protective of women, like John Wayne, but also warm, fuzzy, and a good household helper, like Alan Alda. The phenomenal success of Promise Keepers cannot be explained solely in terms of the group's effective outreach and media promotion. The rallies strike a chord in men who travel long distances and spend weekends singing, praying, even crying out loud in public. The Promise Keepers project may allow men to repent for mistreatment or neglect of their wives and families while also reminding men that they are still in charge.

Repenting for Racism

"Racial reconciliation" is a major theme of the Promise Keepers events, as it is for the Christian Right and the broader evangelical movement in the 1990s. One of the "Seven Promises of a Promise Keeper," which participants pledge to uphold, is to reach "beyond any racial and denominational barriers to demonstrate the power of biblical unity." In practice, Promise Keepers is racially integrated in its leadership, its staff, and its lineup of rally speakers. The crowds are mostly white men, but they are being taught the virtues of crossing racial lines for a shared "family values" agenda.

Precisely because there is strength in numbers, racial reconciliation has been a major goal of evangelical churches and Christian Right political projects for the past several years. The phenomenon has received scant attention in the mainstream press, though it is frequently covered in evangelical media outlets. After decades of segregation in the churches, it is the most conservative white denominations that have been publicly repenting for their racist pasts and forging new alliances with black church leaders. In fall 1994, the Pentecostal Fellowship of North America, representing twenty-one white denominations, broke with seventy years of racial segregation and formed a new body, the Pentecostal-Charismatic Churches of North America, with an executive committee of six black and six white ministers to represent 10 million pentecostals. The birth of the new interracial fellowship was marked by a ceremony at which black and white ministers washed each other's feet, as Jesus washed the feet of his disciples, and prayed for forgiveness for the sin of racism.[36] In 1995, leaders of the Southern Baptist Convention celebrated the 150th anniversary of their denomination with what many considered a long overdue apology for a history of racism.[37] The Southern Baptist Convention was originally formed out of a dispute among white Baptists over the question of whether slave owners could become missionaries. The Southern Baptists agreed with the slave owners, which is why most black Baptists formed their own denominations following emancipation.[38]

These are but two examples of a series of meetings at which white evangelical leaders have offered olive branches to their African-American and Latino counterparts. The trend in the churches is matched by increasing racial inclusiveness within the evangelical press and within the Christian Right's overtly political projects. The guest lists and hosts of Christian TV shows have become increasingly integrated. *Charisma* magazine has published a series of articles on racial reconciliation, including a June 1995 article that was favorable toward interracial marriage.[39] The rhetoric of racial reconciliation typically evades the political and economic roots of racial injustice. Instead, racism is portrayed as a sin of prejudice among individuals. Nevertheless, racial reconciliation offers great growth potential for church builders and for the Christian Right, which seeks to absolve itself of the racist stereotype while enlisting conservatives of color who oppose abortion, gay rights, and affirmative action.

Politically, the racial reconciliation project has just barely begun to pay dividends. In 1991, the Reverend Louis Sheldon of the Traditional Values Coalition organized African-American pastors to lobby for the confirmation of Supreme Court Justice Clarence Thomas. That same summer, the TVC mobilized black churches to lobby against a California state assembly bill for gay rights.[40] In fall 1993, the Christian Coalition released the results of a poll it had commissioned showing that large percentages of African Americans and Latinos opposed abortion, gay rights, welfare, and affirmative action. The validity of the poll data was dubious but the mission was clear. Christian Coalition executive director Ralph Reed pledged that his movement would no longer "concede the minority community to the political left," and he announced that the coalition would begin recruiting from within black and Latino churches.[41] Toward that end, the coalition appointed a young African-American man from Los Angeles to recruit coalition chapter leaders in urban areas and to organize them for the 1996 elections.[42]

Building a Kingdom

At one level, the racial reconciliation project looks like blatant tokenism for the sake of political expediency. However, to the extent that the movement can defy its own long-standing reputation for racism, there will be one fewer obstacle to the enactment of the movement's "family values" legislative agenda. Racial reconciliation, like other trends within the evangelical subculture, presents an opportunity for growth and genuine change in the Christian Right's base of support.

Here in this chapter, I have focused only on evangelical media, the Promise Keepers men's project, and the trend toward racial reconciliation within the churches. Many other aspects of the evangelical subculture fit the model of a cultural project through which the personal also becomes political. Home schooling is a good example because it is a private practice, a choice made by parents. Yet spokespersons for the leading Christian home-schooling associations appear frequently in evangelical media venues to encourage Christian parents to drop out of a public school system they see as evil and, instead, to train their children using school materials produced by conservative book publishers. Across the country, several dozen antigay counseling ministries, modeled after Exodus International in California, promote antigay messages under the guise of helping family members persuade their gay relatives to abandon the gay "lifestyle." Besides home schooling and antigay counseling ministries, Christian Right legal firms, antiabortion "crisis pregnancy" counseling centers, and other seemingly nonpolitical projects all reinforce ideological positions consistent with those of the Christian Right.

The most successful social movement projects are those that fulfill multiple functions. Cultural projects are ideal because they simultaneously attract people at a profoundly personal level and make them participants in some of the major controversies underway within society as a whole. A Promise Keepers rally can be a fun and cathartic weekend experience for the guys at the local church. The rally also challenges men to explore their own thoughts about male-female relations and to think about what they can personally do to bolster traditional gender roles.

White evangelical church leaders want to throw off the yoke of segregationism in order to build bigger churches. Christian Right political strategists want to make themselves indispensable to the Republican Party. To do that, they need all the voters they can get, including voters of color. Church politics and electoral politics mutually reinforce each other.

Similarly, in the realm of evangelical broadcast and print media, the religious and political themes work together. The Bible assures born-again Christians that in the end they will prevail against all evil. That is a powerful antidote to the weariness or burnout that plagues any group of longtime activists. Like church membership, evangelical media help meet people's needs for a sense of belonging and a higher purpose, beyond the mundane exigencies of daily life. Having satisfied some of their personal needs for camaraderie, evangelical activists are then available for the labor-intensive volunteer work that makes a grassroots political movement possible. On top of that, it has been through the evangelical broadcast networks and print outlets that the already converted have learned about events such as the Promise Keepers rallies and political lobbies such as the Christian Coalition.

Without access to a preexisting apparatus of media outlets and church ministries, the Christian Right would not have become the political powerhouse that it has been in the 1990s. With political skill alone, the organizational leaders of the Christian Right could not have inspired tens of thousands of believers to choose worldly politics as their most urgent mission field.

Notes

1. John C. Green, James L. Guth, Lyman A. Kellstedt, and Corwin E. Smidt, "Evangelical Realignment: The Political Power of the Christian Right," *Christian Century*, July 5–12, 1995, pp. 676–679.

2. Information on the Congressional Family Caucus provided by the office of Representative Tom A. Coburn (R–OK). See David Grann, "Congress Takes Up Social Issues, Whose Values Will Prevail?" *Washington Post*, May 7, 1995.

3. For details on the historical antecedents of the Christian Right, see chap. 4 of Sara Diamond, *Roads to Dominion: Right-Wing Movements and Political Power in the United States* (New York: Guilford Press, 1995).

4. Wade Clark Roof, *A Generation of Seekers: The Spiritual Journeys of the Baby Boom Generation* (San Francisco: HarperSan Francisco, 1993).

5. David Colker, "Anti-Gay Video Highlights Church's Agenda," *Los Angeles Times*, February 22, 1993.

6. "Challenging the Homosexual Agenda," Focus on the Family *Citizen*, April 19, 1993, p. 5.

7. Michael Weisskopf, "Energized by Pulpit or Passion, the Public Is Calling," *Washington Post*, February 1, 1993.

8. John W. Kennedy, "Mixing Politics and Piety," *Christianity Today*, August 15, 1994, p. 42; Susan Olasky, "Homeschool Hotline," *World*, March 5, 1994, pp. 18–19.

9. Sarah E. Smith, "Glory Days—Past or Future?" *Religious Broadcasting*, July/August 1995, p. 26.

10. The figures on the Family Channel and Trinity Broadcasting Network come from the 1995 National Religious Broadcasters *Directory of Religious Media*. Updated annually, the directory gives ownership and audience data on the full gamut of Christian TV and radio stations, cable networks, and individual TV, radio, and video program producers (National Religious Broadcasters, 7839 Ashton Ave., Manassas, Virginia 22110).

54   *Sara Diamond*

11. Kennedy, "Mixing Politics," p. 42.

12. Ibid., p. 43.

13. Ibid., p. 44.

14. Author's monitoring of *Beverly LaHaye Live,* the Concerned Women for America radio program.

15. Mark Ward Sr., "The Coming Shakeout in Christian Radio," *Religious Broadcasting,* September 1994, pp. 24–27.

16. Author's collection of program guides from several stations.

17. Perucci Ferraiuolo, "Riding the Rush," *Religious Broadcasting,* September 1994, p. 20.

18. "Mile-High City Draws Christian Retailers," *Colorado Christian News,* August 1995, p. 1.

19. Ibid.

20. See, e.g., Joe Maxwell, "Prophecy Books Become Big Sellers," *Christianity Today,* March 11, 1991, p. 60; Joe Maxwell, "End-Times Prediction Draws Strong Following," *Christianity Today,* June 20, 1994, pp. 46–47; Joe Maxwell, "Camping Misses End-Times Deadline," *Christianity Today,* October 24, 1994; Don Lattin, "The Man Who Prophesied the End of the World," *San Francisco Chronicle,* March 12, 1995, p. 6.

21. Hal Lindsey, *The Late Great Planet Earth* (New York: Harper Paperbacks, 1992). The cover of this edition says the book has sold 15 million copies and calls it the classic number one *New York Times* best-seller.

22. Hal Lindsey, *Planet Earth—2000 A.D.* (Palos Verdes, CA: Western Front, 1994).

23. Pat Robertson, *The New World Order* (Dallas: Word Publishing, 1991).

24. "Peretti Signs with Word," *Bookstore Journal,* August 1994, p. 28. *Bookstore Journal* is the monthly magazine of the Christian Booksellers Association. For an overview of the success of Frank Peretti and the Christian fiction genre, see "The Newest Christian Fiction Injects a Thrill into Theology," *New York Times,* October 30, 1995; "The Almighty to the Rescue," *Time,* November 13, 1995, pp. 105–107.

25. Spenser Hughes, *The Lambda Conspiracy* (Chicago: Moody Press, 1993).

26. The *Traditional Values Report,* March-April 1994, p. 8, advertised that Spenser Hughes would be a featured guest at the TVC's April 1994 Congressional Briefing for Pastors. *The Lambda Conspiracy* was sold in Christian bookstores and by the TVC.

27. These include Christian radio and TV stations, plus about 50 independent Christian newspapers published all over the country. The list of newspapers is available from the EP News Service, 1619 Portland Ave. South, Minneapolis, MN 55404.

28. Author's subscription collection to about one dozen Christian monthly newspapers.

29. EP News Service, February 10, 1995, p. 9.

30. Promise Keepers press kit, distributed at the September 29–30, 1995, Promise Keepers rally in Oakland, California.

31. Promise Keepers press kit.

32. See, for example, "Men Pack RFK on Promise of Religious Renewal," *Washington Post,* May 28, 1995; and "Men Crowd Stadiums to Fulfill Their Souls," *New York Times,* August 6, 1995.

33. Promise Keepers press kit.

Cultural Projects in Christian Right Mobilization

34. Author's observation at the September 29–30, 1995, Promise Keepers rally in Oakland, California.

35. Sara Diamond, "Focus on Some Families," *Z Magazine*, July/August 1994, pp. 29–33.

36. "The 'Memphis Miracle,'" *Ministries Today*, January/February 1995, pp. 36–38; "Pentecostals Move Toward Unity After Decades of Racial Division," *New York Times*, October 23, 1994; "Pentecostals Form Interracial Alliance," *Washington Times*, October 22, 1994; "Pentecostals Renounce Racism," *Christianity Today*, December 12, 1994, p. 58. See also the October 31, 1994, issue of the *National and International Religion Report*.

37. "Racist No More? Black Leaders Ask," *Christianity Today*, August 14, 1995, p. 53.

38. Joe Maxwell, "Black Southern Baptists," *Christianity Today*, May 15, 1995, pp. 27–31.

39. Joe Maxwell, "When Love Crosses the Line," *Charisma*, June 1995, pp. 30–34.

40. Sara Diamond, "Change in Strategy," *Humanist*, January/February 1994, p. 35.

41. "Minority Myths Exploded," *Christian American*, October 1993.

42. "New Regional Coordinator Named," *California Christian*, January 1995, p. 3. This was the newsletter of the California branch of the Christian Coalition.

3

Inventing an American Conservatism: The Neoconservative Episode

Gary Dorrien

American intellectuals have long charged or lamented that the United States lacks a genuine homegrown tradition of intellectual conservatism. In 1950, one of the key forerunners of American neoconservatism expressed this judgment with withering finality. At the outset of *The Liberal Imagination,* Lionel Trilling famously declared that liberalism was America's only serious intellectual tradition and that so-called American conservatism consisted merely of "irritable mental gestures which seek to resemble ideas."[1] A decade later, the conservative political writer Peter Viereck similarly judged that existing American conservatism consisted mostly of recycled European ideologies, nostalgia for the Old South, and a host of reactionary populisms. In its politics, he observed, American conservatism was dominated by upper-class capitalists who mistakenly called themselves conservatives and by "neo-Populist barn-burners" who idolized Joseph McCarthy. In its more intellectual versions, American conservatism rested upon such "unhistorical appeals to history" as the "traditionless worship of tradition" featured in Russell Kirk's recent writings.

Viereck urged that America deserves a more sophisticated and genuinely American conservatism than this. The American conservatism that is needed would seek to conserve American traditions and social institutions that actually exist, he contended. It would defend the American establishment that is actually there instead of mythologizing fantasized memories of Tory England or the Old South or Gilded Age capitalism. Historically it would appeal to the semiaristocratic Whig tradition of James Madison and the *Federalist.* Like Madison, it would blend the moderate conservatism of Edmund Burke with the moderate liberalism of John Locke. It would prefer Washington and Calhoun over Jeffer-

Inventing an American Conservatism   57

son and Jackson, but it would not dissociate itself from Jeffersonian democracy. It would revere the American Constitution, take a gradualist approach to politics, uphold traditional moral values, and protect the executive branch from mob pressures. In the context of current disputes, Viereck proposed that a genuinely American conservatism would oppose communism, but also oppose McCarthyism. It would support capitalism and trade unionism, upholding Locke's emphasis on property rights while accepting many New Deal reforms as a bulwark against socialism. It would restrain state power while recognizing (with Burke) that conservative ends require a strong state. A genuine American conservatism would be a new thing that defended the actually existing American establishment from its various critics.[2]

These arguments got Viereck expelled from the conservative movement of his time. In the early 1960s the very currents that he sought to define out of American conservatism consolidated instead to become a dominant force in Republican Party politics, making Barry Goldwater the party's presidential nominee. Viereck's idea of a mature conservatism that made its peace with modernity, trade unionism, and the welfare state had no place in a movement that was determined to move an already conservative Republican Party sharply to the Right. In the year that followed Lyndon Johnson's rout of Goldwater in the national election, however, the first signs of a political current that shared much of his agenda (if not his sensibility) began to appear.

For many years Irving Kristol had shared Trilling's judgment that American conservatism was too backward and immature to be taken seriously. He thought of himself as a "neoliberal" or "liberal realist." In the 1950s, he charged that liberals were failing the test of realism by failing to support America's cold war against communism.[3] In the mid-1960s, he began to complain that most liberals were also unrealistic about the limits of government-directed efforts to eradicate poverty. Without any recognition that he was becoming some kind of conservative in reaction, Kristol set himself against the Johnson administration's commitment to launch a "war on poverty." With Daniel Bell, he founded a right-leaning social policy journal, *Public Interest*, that promised to chasten liberal dreams of a big-government Great Society.

Kristol and Bell believed that liberals and other government policymakers were working with a shortage of hard information. The most celebrated social policy work at the time was Michael Harrington's *The Other America*, which relied heavily on personal anecdotes and a strong moral argument in calling for massive government efforts to eliminate poverty. Harrington appealed for national outrage "at a monstrous example of needless suffering in the most advanced society in the world."[4] *Public Interest* was decidedly more cautious, empirical, and skeptical by contrast. Bell's recent experience working with the Commission for the Study of Automation had convinced him that the social policy field was producing "a lot of sloppy thinking." Kristol judged that the problem was that the best information generated by American research universities was not getting filtered to government policymakers. This was the mission they envisioned for *Public Interest*, which proclaimed its willingness to seem "a middle-aged magazine for middle-aged readers."[5] Kristol was the most conservative figure in the magazine's founding group, but even he had no conception of their venture as a new kind of conservatism. "Conservatism in the United States at that time was represented by the Goldwater campaign against the New Deal, with which none of us had any sympathy, and by *National Review*, which we regarded as too right-wing," he later recalled. "We considered ourselves to be realistic meliorists, skeptical of government programs that ignored history and experience in favor of then-fashionable ideas spawned by the academy."[6]

Neoconservatism had deeper historical roots than this, but as a movement it began with Irving Kristol's alienation from mid-1960s academic idealism. His magazine's early issues warned against the unanticipated consequences of social engineering. Figures such as Nathan Glazer, Edward C. Banfield, Roger Starr, and Aaron Wildavsky sharply criticized Great Society housing and welfare policies; James Q. Wilson censured liberal strategies toward racism; in 1967, Daniel Patrick Moynihan gave an early warning that the war on poverty was faring as badly as America's war in Vietnam. The following year, John H. Bunzel gave an early verdict against black studies a generation before multiculturalism had a name.[7] In the name of promoting equal opportunity—a liberal ideal—*Public Interest* warned repeatedly that a bad mutation of the liberal faith was breeding dependency in the welfare class, impeding America's economic growth, and creating a vast "New Class" of parasitic public sector functionaries.

The first neoconservatives were careful to distinguish their objections to Great Society legislation from similar right-wing opposition. They explained that they were empirical social scientists, not ideologues; they worried about the unanticipated consequences of government intervention without assuming that social engineering is always wrong or misguided. By the late 1960s, however, the difference was already becoming blurred. *Public Interest* increasingly took on a movement character, blasting government redistributionist policies in principle. The rise of a war-resisting counterculture among students and younger academics drove Kristol's group to draw lines and make unexpected alliances. "Suddenly we discovered that we had been cultural conservatives all along," Kristol later recalled. "Now, we had to decide what we were for, and why. Cool criticism of the prevailing liberal-left orthodoxy was not enough at a time when liberalism itself was crumbling before the resurgent Left."[8]

This perception that a countercultural leftism was taking over the Democratic Party provoked numerous others to become neoconservatives. As editor of *Commentary* magazine, Norman Podhoretz had provided a valuable forum for New Left thinking in the early 1960s, but in the later 1960s, he had second thoughts about his contribution to a growing student rebellion. By 1970, his role in promoting New Left criticism of American culture and militarism was deeply embarrassing to him. He sought to refurbish the liberal anticommunist orthodoxy of the previous generation but found, in his reckoning, that it no longer existed. He judged that the old "Vital Center" liberals who had once held liberalism and anticommunism together were reducing the faith to meaninglessness. Liberals such as Arthur Schlesinger Jr. and John Kenneth Galbraith were accommodating feminism and Black Power and other radicalisms, while the fiasco in Vietnam and a burgeoning antiwar movement were sapping their will to fight communism anywhere. Podhoretz lurched to the right in reaction, setting *Commentary* against all of the progeny of the New Left.[9] An ideological line was established on issues that his magazine had previously debated freely. The new *Commentary* made no claim to disinterested objectivity. Its tone was defiant, aggressive, and often harsh. It specialized in personal attacks on former friends. Samuel McCracken blasted the new academic leftism, Dorothy Rabinowitz took aim at activist professors and clergy, Midge Decter and Arlene Croce dissected the ravages of feminism, and Kristol criticized the liberal "religion of democracy." A bit later, Jeane Kirkpatrick denounced the politics of "McGovernism," and Michael Novak condemned the moralistic hypocrisy of the New Class. Podhoretz later explained that his circle of writers enjoyed a crucial advantage over *National Review* conservatives in their polemics against the Left: "We knew what they really thought and felt, which did not always coincide with what they considered it expedient to say in public; and we knew how to penetrate their self-protective rhetoric." The new conservatives demystified movement-speak and denounced its penetration into the mainstream of the Democratic Party.[10]

Many of the new conservatives were former partisans of what was now called the Old Left. Some were veterans of the struggle in the 1930s to drive Communists out of the unions, when the struggle was fought with guns and clubs. Some of them claimed that they were still socialists. Many of them were Jews. Old Left social democrats such as Sidney Hook, Max Shachtman, Emanuel Muravchik, Arnold Beichman, Arch Puddington, Harry Overstreet, and Frank Trager brought a fierce anticommunism and a highly developed sense of politics as tournament into the struggle against a rising antiwar movement. Their backgrounds in the Old Left faction fights over Stalinism contributed mightily to the rhetorical style and ideological character of what came to be called neoconservatism. Like

Kristol and Podhoretz, the Old Leftists were deeply alienated from what they called the "liberal intelligentsia" or the "fashionable liberal elite."[11] This alienation later fueled their "culture war" against the New Class. It was to these figures, many of whom still regarded themselves as socialists, that the term "neoconservative" was first applied.

The term was first applied as an exercise in dissociation. Many of the Old Leftists were Harrington's former comrades in the Socialist Party. Though some of them were ambivalent about America's war in Vietnam, all of them were repulsed by the antiwar movement. The 1972 presidential election was a watershed for them, as it proved to be for all of the neoconservatives. George McGovern's Democratic candidacy represented the triumph of everything that the right-leaning social democrats detested in modern liberalism. McGovern was soft on communism, he wanted to bring America home from Vietnam, he indulged the various counterculture movements, and he catered to the self-promoting idealism of a new generational power bloc—the "New Class" children of the 1960s who were swelling the ranks of America's nonproducing managerial class. While still claiming to be socialists, many of the Old Leftists supported Richard Nixon in the 1972 election; others joined George Meany on the sidelines, holding their noses at both sides. To all of them, the McGovern candidacy represented the triumph of appeasement and New Class isolationism. For most of them, even Nixon was preferable to this betrayal of the party's cold war tradition.

Harrington and his friends at *Dissent* magazine were anxious to distinguish their form of social democracy from the rightward-moving militarism of their former comrades. They were especially eager to help younger activists see the difference between progressive and reactionary social democracy. Harrington's early attempts to explain the difference to the founders of Students for a Democratic Society had gone awry. As a youthful partisan of the Old Left he had tried to convert 1960s-generation radicals to progressive democratic socialism, but as he later recalled, "my notion of a progressive, Leftist anti-Communist made as much existential sense to them as a purple cow."[12] He spent much of the decade seeking to repair his relations with New Left activists. At the same time, he became the leader of a progressive faction of the Socialist Party that supported the antiwar movement. In 1972, Harrington's group walked out of the party after failing to gain control over it. As a way of establishing that his former comrades were no longer part of any movement to which he belonged, Harrington hung the label "neoconservative" on them. The socialists for Nixon did not constitute the right-wing of the Left, he implied, but the left-wing of the Right.

The difference was crucial, as the labeled outsiders understood. As descendants of the Old Left faction fights over Stalinism, the first neoconservatives were well acquainted with the sociological phenomenon of labeling. They bitterly disavowed their label and its insinuations. They hotly disputed Michael Harrington's right to excommunicate them from the Left. The label stuck to them, however, mainly because most of the right-leaning social democrats did go on to align themselves objectively with conservative politicians and institutions. They were joined in this transmigration by a wider circle of former liberals whom Harrington and others also called neoconservatives. After McGovern was routed in the 1972 election, a group of Democratic Party activists formed the Coalition for a Democratic Majority to purge the party of McGovern-style liberalism. The group included Podhoretz, Kirkpatrick, Moynihan, Novak, Henry Jackson, Ben Wattenberg, and numerous others with little or no background in socialist politics. They argued that a perverse new-style liberalism was servicing the ambitions of New Class baby boomers under the banner of compassion. It wanted America to be weak but government to be strong. The neoconservatives claimed at first that they were not seeking to strengthen the American Right. They were seeking only to replace the Democratic Party's liberal leaders with anticommunist moderates such as Jackson and Max Kampelman. Liberals had overreacted to Vietnam. Their "New Politics" was based on guilt. American disgust with the degradation of liberalism was shrewdly exploited by Nixon's electoral campaign, Podhoretz observed, which "exhibited something close to perfect pitch in its ear for the national mood." So-called neoconservatism was merely a self-respecting, pro-American corrective to liberal guilt-mongering.[13]

This self-understanding did not survive the factional struggles of the next campaign season, however. Neoconservatives pushed hard for Jackson in the 1976 Democratic primaries, but they gave short shrift to the moderate Southern moralist who won the party's nomination. After Jimmy Carter won the presidency, the neoconservatives failed to convince him that a massive military buildup was needed to catch up to a superior Soviet enemy. They also failed to gain a single important position in the Carter administration. Less than a year after Carter took office, the neoconservatives began to make "Carterism" a term to be invoked only as an epithet. Podhoretz charged that the same liberals who had run the Vietnam War under Kennedy and Johnson were now atoning for their sins by keeping America at home. Podhoretz noted that Carter had recently congratulated himself and his fellow Americans for overcoming their "inordinate fear of communism." For Podhoretz, this declaration epitomized the stupidity and corruption of spirit that characterized America's "culture of appeasement." Throughout the 1950s and 1960s, one of the key forerunners of neoconservatism, the former Trotskyist James Burnham, had repeatedly charged that America was surrendering to Soviet power throughout the world because American leaders secretly feared it. With virtually the same words that Burnham had used a generation earlier, Podhoretz and other neoconservatives now alleged that American leaders were cowering in fear before an emboldened Soviet enemy.[14]

This reading of the American condition and its stigmatizing rhetoric of "appeasement" and "Finlandization" had little place in the Democratic Party in the early years of the Carter administration. By the time that Carter did dramatically increase American military spending (mainly as a response to the Soviet invasion of Afghanistan), the neoconservatives were looking elsewhere for a sufficiently militant leader. Carter authorized a 5 percent increase in military spending for 1981 and the Congress authorized an additional 4 percent increase, but the neoconservatives judged that Carter lacked the will to use his enhanced firepower. In their hope that Ronald Reagan would "take the fight to the Soviets," as they often put it, the neoconservatives thus supported Reagan's presidential candidacy in 1980.

By then, most of them were reconciled to Harrington's name for them. Kristol was the first to embrace the term "neoconservative" and also the first to join the Republican Party. For him, as for many others who joined the movement in the early 1980s, "neoconservatism" was an intellectual movement originated by former leftists that promoted militant anticommunism, capitalist economics, a minimal welfare state, the rule of traditional elites, and a return to traditional cultural values. The new conservatives were highly conscious of the factors that distinguished them from their conservative allies. Neoconservatism was modernist, liberal democratic, and ideologically aggressive. It held no brief for the Old South or laissez-faire capitalism but rather pledged to defend an embattled American establishment from its numerous enemies within and without. The neoconservatives had come to the Right not by inheritance but conversion. With the passion of converts, they urged Reagan to heap new spending increases on top of Carter's escalated military budget, thus creating what David Stockman later called "the giant fiscal syllogism" that doubled American military spending in five years. They assured Reagan that traditional conservatives did not really understand the nature of communism or the power of its world-embracing ideology or the importance of ideological combat. For these reasons, they convinced him that any serious crusade against communism and the American culture of appeasement would have to be led by themselves.

These claims offended numerous old-style conservatives who resented that they were pushed aside. The undercurrent of resentment between neoconservatives and so-called "paleoconservatives" flared into a bitter faction fight during Reagan's second term. In the early years of Reagan's presidency, however, the neoconservatives achieved a stunning degree of

Inventing an American Conservatism

political success. Kampelman, Kirkpatrick, Elliott Abrams, Richard Perle, Eugene Rostow, Kenneth Adelman, and Richard Pipes were appointed to high-ranking foreign policy positions. William Bennett, Chester Finn, William Kristol, Linda Chavez, and other neoconservatives worked in various domestic policy offices. The *New Republic* warned half seriously that "Trotsky's orphans" were taking over the government. Neoconservatives provided the intellectual ballast for Reagan's military buildup and his anticommunist foreign policy, especially his maneuvers in Central America.

They were also the last true believers in the efficacy of Soviet totalitarianism. In the mid-1980s, most neoconservatives brushed aside any suggestion that the Soviet economy was disintegrating, that dissident movements in the Soviet bloc were revealing cracks in the Soviet empire, or that Gorbachev's reforms should be taken seriously. For them, the absolute domestic power of the Communist Party and the communist duty to create a communist world order precluded the possibility of genuine change anywhere in the Soviet bloc. In the early years of Reagan's presidency, Podhoretz bitterly complained that despite his militant rhetoric, his skyrocketing military expenditures, and his appointment of neoconservatives, even Reagan was capitulating to Soviet communism in the struggle for the world. Podhoretz's frustration hardened into virtual contempt in the closing years of Reagan's presidency. He ridiculed Reagan for seeking weapons agreements with the Soviets, charging that Reagan had turned into a "Carter clone." He thundered repeatedly that Reagan's insatiable greed for popularity was driving America into the arms of the Soviets and betraying the cause of anticommunism. In his reading, Gorbachev was a crafty Leninist who had figured out how to strengthen the Soviet empire and disarm the West.[15]

Though neoconservatives often quoted selectively from George Kennan's famous 1947 article on the sources of Soviet conduct, none of them put any stock in Kennan's prediction that the Soviet empire would someday collapse under the weight of its own inefficiency, tyranny, and squalor. Totalitarianism was an article of faith for them. Most of them believed that the totalitarian structure of communist rule gave the Soviet Union immense advantages over the West in its drive for world domination. In the late 1980s, however, Podhoretz's warning that the Soviets were actually winning the cold war was resisted by neoconservatives such as Irving Kristol and Jeane Kirkpatrick, who suggested that even Soviet totalitarianism was apparently not exempt from "the rules of change." Shortly after the Soviet bloc imploded in Eastern Europe, Kristol and Kirkpatrick argued that neoconservatives needed to give up their crusading struggle for the world and adopt a more restrained realpolitik in foreign policy. Neither America nor neoconservatism needed a world mission that transcended America's economic and security interests.[16]

But for most neoconservatives, this prescription was too cynical, accommodating, and provincial. With the dissolution of the Soviet enemy, they insisted that what America needs is precisely a new ideological creed that proclaims a moral and universal commitment to export capitalist democracy throughout the world. This is one of the two distinctive commitments that a dissolving neoconservative movement has contributed to a reconstituted American Right. Neoconservatives such as Podhoretz, Novak, Wattenberg, Joshua Muravchik, and Charles Krauthammer believe that the moment has arrived for a new Pax Americana, in which America should use its power to shape a new world order on American terms.[17] To these advocates of "democratic globalism," the Bush administration was a bitter disappointment. Though a handful of neoconservatives held high positions during Bush's presidency—notably Constance Horner, Paul Wolfowitz, Bernard Aronson, and William Kristol—Bush did not pretend to any interest in servicing the world-embracing ambitions of neoconservatives. He had no ideological agenda and little use for quarrelsome intellectuals of any kind. His passing references to a "New World Order" at the outset of the Gulf War gave a moment of hope to globalist neoconservatives, but he quickly fell back into realpolitik in the closing days of the war. In 1992, some neoconservatives supported Bill Clinton's presidential candidacy in the anticipation that he would pursue what he called an aggressive foreign policy "infused with democratic spirit." A few neoconservatives even hoped that Clinton would pull the Democratic Party back from its generational descent into McGovernism. Clinton pointedly avoided neoconservatives in making his key appointments, however, and he quickly put aside his campaign rhetoric about exporting democracy. Today he has virtually no support from neoconservatives.

The high-water mark for neoconservatism as a distinctive political movement has surely passed. Neoconservatives are unlikely to regain the political influence and power they attained during Reagan's presidency. The dissolution of the Soviet Union has stripped neoconservatism of its unifying enemy and ended the world-historical phase of politicization by which the movement was principally defined. It has also occasioned the ascendancy of political issues less favorable to neoconservative interests. Neoconservatives rode to power in the 1980s with a conservative administration that claimed it was "morning in America," but despite the stunning collapse of Soviet communism, the Bush administration never dared to claim that it was morning in America. American resentment over the nation's economic decline, the costs of unemployment and health care, the corruption of America's political system, the ravages of racial injustice, and the disintegration of America's cities and infrastructure created a strikingly different mood in American politics.

Inventing an American Conservatism 65

Americans no longer feared the Soviet threat but worried that Japan and Germany had won the cold war. Neoconservatives called for America to project its power aggressively throughout the world, but with episodic exceptions, most Americans are less eager to shoulder the burdens of a democratic empire. Neoconservative ideology has lost much of its coherence and energy in the process. As a generational phenomenon, neoconservatism represented the last stage of the Old Left. It was the last significant movement in American politics to be defined principally by its opposition to communism. But generational experience cannot be replicated, and the galvanizing Soviet threat no longer exists.

The irony of the neoconservative episode is that after protesting so indignantly that they were not conservatives of any kind, the neoconservatives went on to create a political movement that has now blended almost without remainder into the conservative establishment. This did not seem a likely prospect at the height of their political influence. In the mid-1980s, the neoconservatives were bitterly attacked by several factions of the traditional Right, including various Old Right elitists clustered around William F. Buckley Jr.'s *National Review* and George Panichas's *Modern Age* as well as by Thomas Fleming and other populist conservatives in the pages of Fleming's journal, *Chronicles*. The dean of American intellectual conservatism, Russell Kirk, rebuked the neoconservatives for their "ideological infatuations" ("the neoconservatives are often clever, but seldom wise") and commented wryly on their industry. "How earnestly they founded magazine upon magazine!" he noted. "How skillfully they insinuated themselves into the councils of the Nixon and Reagan Administrations!"[18]

The old conservatives were offended by the opportunism and sharp elbows of their "newcoming" allies. Kirk observed that the neoconservatives behaved like the cadre of a political machine, "eager for place and preferment and power, skillful at intrigue, ready to exclude from office any persons who might not be counted upon as faithful to the Neoconservative ideology." They were "clever creatures, glib, committed to an ideology, and devious at attaining their objects." In his view, they were also cultural and economic imperialists. They had begun as Marxists and were now reverse-Marxists. They were ideologues who acted as though they had invented conservatism. Stephen Tonsor complained that they had no business leading any part of a conservative movement. "It is splendid when the town whore gets religion and joins the church," he allowed. "Now and then she makes a good choir director, but when she begins to tell the minister what he ought to say in his Sunday sermons, matters have been carried too far."[19]

Many of the old conservatives were appalled that former liberals and socialists were seizing Old Right institutions. "We have simply been crowded out by overwhelming numbers," Clyde Wilson protested. "The offensives of radicalism have driven vast herds of liberals across the border into our territories. These refugees now speak in our name, but the language they speak is the same one they always spoke . . . Our estate has been taken over by an impostor, just as we were about to inherit."[20] Among the losses, traditional conservatives counted such previously Old Right institutions as the American Enterprise Institute (AEI), the Heritage Foundation, and the Hoover Institution. During the same period, neoconservatives developed close ties with the Scaife, Bradley, Smith Richardson, and John M. Olin Foundations. Pat Buchanan bewailed that the Right's major financial institutions were being captured "by neo-con staffers who are steering $30 million a year to front groups, magazines, scholars and policy institutions who toe their party line." Paul Fleming complained that neoconservatives were attaining "a lock on all money and the institutions created by the Right." With particular bitterness, Paul Gottfried summarized the Old Right's resentments. "The neoconservatives created an enemy on the right by vilification and exclusion," he explained. "The enemy lives increasingly for revenge and is trying to subvert the neoconservative empire. Few old rightists believe the foundations now run by neoconservatives will become theirs as soon as their enemies fall. Far more likely such resources will go to opera houses and other civic charities than to supporting old right scholars. It is burning hate, not uncomplicated greed, that fuels the old right war against the neoconservatives."[21]

The conflict between neoconservatives and various kinds of paleoconservatives, Straussians, New Right populists, and others did resemble something like a political war in the latter years of Bush's presidency. Kirk and Fleming condemned democratic globalism as the product of ideological hubris and will-to-power. Kirk speculated that neoconservatives were prone to imperialism by virtue of their utilitarian outlook. Unlike genuine conservatives, he observed, the neoconservatives had little sense of the mundane order as a realm subordinate to the transcendent order: "They are focused on the struggle for power, and are using power for their mundane purposes." Genuine conservatism finds its home in history, theology and humane letters, he contended, but the neoconservatives were social scientists and ideological activists. Their politics was therefore utilitarian, instrumental, self-promoting, and power oriented, just like the New Class liberals they derided.[22]

This kind of criticism and the barely veiled anti-Semitism of certain conservative writers moved neoconservatives to emphasize why a *new* conservatism had been needed in the first place. Podhoretz, Decter, and Richard John Neuhaus repeatedly charged that the traditional Right was still rife with racism, anti-Semitism, and xenophobia. With knowing in-

Inventing an American Conservatism 67

sight derived from recent experiences in working with paleoconservatives, Neuhaus observed that many conservative leaders were comfortable only with governments led by white males of tested genetic stock.
Like Henry Adams, they feared that America's experiment in republicanism was being trashed by America's vulgar economic system and the un-
refined immigrants it attracted. Neuhaus allowed that this was an old
story on the Right. What was new was that paleoconservatives were using the neoconservative ideology of democratic globalism as a foil for
their own attempts to reinstate a host of repressed bigotries into America's public discourse. "The list includes nativism, racism, anti-Semitism,
xenophobia, a penchant for authoritarian politics, and related diseases of
the *ressentiment* that flourishes on the marginalia of American life," he remarked. Conservative misgivings about neoconservative chauvinism
were not to be taken seriously. American conservatives were railing
against the imperialism, "democratism," and will-to-power of neoconservatives not because they were developing delicate sensibilities on
these matters, Neuhaus suggested, but rather because they clung to a
smaller and meaner image of what America should be. America's so-
called conservative intellectual leaders were still distrustful of democracy, they still believed that immigration should be restricted to people
who looked like themselves, and they still could not bring themselves to
work cooperatively with Jewish or other "ethnic" figures within the neoconservative movement. It went without saying that charges of racism
and anti-Semitism could be abused to stifle debate about legitimate issues, he conceded, but conservative leaders apparently needed to be re-
minded that the evils signified by these terms were not "merely figments
of the fevered liberal imagination."[23]

This was exactly the kind of charge that made conservatives distrust
their ostensible allies. Fleming claimed that neoconservatives were never
able to substantiate their charges of bigotry within the traditional Right.
They fell back instead, he contended, "on the last resort of the calumnia-
tor: 'code words' and 'insensitivity.'" Fleming left the implication hang-
ing: These were leftist sins. It was the Left that judged and excluded people on the basis of a sensitivity code. It was the Left that demonized its
opponents with charges of racism, anti-Semitism, misogynism, and the
like. Real conservatives did not operate on the basis of a code of political
correctness. Neoconservatives savaged the code with withering contempt when they polemicized against liberals, but they were quick to invoke it in their polemics with conservatives. Podhoretz railed against the
"nativist bigotry" and "other abominations" paraded in *Chronicles* and
declared that he was drawing a line: "I know an enemy when I see one,
and *Chronicles* has become just that so far as I personally am concerned."
Fleming replied that this kind of in-house polemic proved that neocon-

servatives did not belong to the conservative movement at all. They were more like conspiracy theorists, in his judgment: "If they know where a man stands on nuclear energy, the Trilateral Commission, the Palestinians, or the gold standard, they can locate him precisely on the grid of their paranoia."[24]

Neoconservatives thus entered the 1990s as a splintering faction of a disintegrating intellectual Right. On the level of mass politics, "conservatism" remained a potent electoral force. Among its intellectual elites, where the movement's ideological contradictions were less tolerated, American conservatism was a shambles. The unifying force of the Soviet threat was gone. The cracks in the Reagan-Bush coalition were immediately magnified as a consequence. On one extreme, Old Right isolationist nationalism made a dramatic comeback, as represented by Pat Buchanan's subsequent presidential campaigns. On the other extreme, neoconservatives crusaded for a new Pax Americana that claimed American dominion over the entire globe. "Conservatives" wanted to relinquish the empire and expand it; they wanted to make America the universal nation and restrict immigration to America; they identified America's interests with Israel's and resurrected the dual loyalty smears of the 1940s; they celebrated the triumph of corporate capitalism and condemned the commercial culture it created; they celebrated the universality of American democracy and repudiated the imperialism of democratic ideology. At the height of the faction fight between neoconservatives and various Old Right intellectuals, Stephen Tonsor remarked, "It has always struck me as odd, even perverse, that former Marxists have been permitted, yes invited, to play such a leading role in the Conservative movement of the twentieth century." He mused that if Stalin had spared Trotsky's life, Trotsky would undoubtedly be holed up at the Hoover Institution writing neoconservative tracts for *Commentary*. Neoconservatism was culturally unthinkable apart from the history of certain modern secularized Jewish intellectuals, he noted, especially those who came out of the hothouse environment of New York leftism. This was the root of the problem. Trotsky's heirs had never made good allies and they never would. They belonged too much to the modern world to ever make good conservatives.[25]

This verdict has since proved, however, to be exaggerated, if not ungenerous. Neoconservatives have made sizable contributions to the American Right that only they could have made. Many of them are no less religious than paleoconservative intellectuals; indeed, the leading religious thinkers within the intellectual Right today are Catholic neoconservatives such as Novak, Neuhaus, and George Wiegel. Some of them (especially Neuhaus) have worked hard to cultivate links with New Right fundamentalists and evangelicals. Perhaps more important, many

Inventing an American Conservatism 69

conservatives today take for granted the possibility of an American Right that has no complicity in segregationist or anti-Semitic movements of the past. This transformation of consciousness is largely a neoconservative achievement. Most of the younger activists and intellectuals who work for neoconservative institutions today think of themselves simply as conservatives. They are products of the neoconservative episode, but they have little acquaintance with the experiences that created neoconservatism. At the American Enterprise Institute these younger activists refer to Irving Kristol and Michael Novak as "the grandpas," but they do not share any of their grandpas' need to distinguish their conservatism from bad-smelling older versions. They take for granted the neoconservative belief that American conservatism should be capable of sustaining an equal-opportunity politics that does not draw upon what Neuhaus calls the "fever swamps" of the Old Right.

The first neoconservatives were raised to think of "the Americans" as aliens. America belonged to and was defined by white Anglo-Saxon Protestants. Many of the neoconservatives applied to college just as their country's doors were opening to them. Podhoretz entered Columbia University in 1946 under a 17 percent quota for Jews. Twenty years later, having prospered in the land of the Americans, he and his friends became its apologists against a younger generation of ungrateful American children. They created the possibility of a wider and more deeply American conservatism in the process. This is the second important contribution that a now-dissolving neoconservative movement has made to the American Right. Neoconservatives have brought to the American Right a vehemently conservative ideology that accepts no guilt for reactionary movements of the past. They oppose feminism, affirmative action, and multiculturalism without the baggage of a racist and nativist past. They speak to Americans' fear of a multicultural society without seeming racist. In recent years conservatives of all kinds have condemned multicultural education as an attack on American civilization and culture, but it is the neoconservatives who spearheaded the reaction against multiculturalism, just as they took the lead in condemning the feminist movement.

"Women's lib has swept over the past two decades like a tornado, leaving behind it a vast wreckage of broken and twisted lives," Podhoretz declares. In his telling, the legacy of feminism is "of children sacrificed to the 'needs' of their parents; of women driven literally crazy by bitterness and self-pity while being encouraged to see virtue and health in the indulgence of such feelings; of men emasculated by guilt and female bullying." Decter charges that the freedom demanded by feminists is the freedom demanded by spoiled children "and enjoyed by no one: the freedom from all difficulty." To indulge this illusion is to engage in child sacrifice, she warns. Feminist demands are infantile and destructive, especially self-destructive, making their purported beneficiaries miserable with self-pity. "All the demands for unneeded preference in admissions and hiring, all the absurd litigation, all the efforts at speech control and thought control, and most important, all the programs to manage and 'improve' the behavior of the men in her life, whether husband, boss, roommate or date, have left her more disaffected and more mentally self-indulgent than before," she claims.[26]

Neoconservative women such as Decter, Ruth Wisse, and Carol Iannone speak to the feelings of many women that the existence of a feminist movement demeans their personal achievements. Wisse complains that she is frequently offered endowed professorships and conference speaking engagements that she would not be offered if she were male. The deans who court her seem oblivious to the "unspeakable rudeness" of their hiring practices, she reports. The women's movement has institutionalized discrimination by gender and degraded the accomplishments of women who do not need a women's movement. "By contriving to define me as a member of a handicapped species the women's movement has deprived me of my dignity and misrepresented my aims," she explains.[27] That the women's movement has enhanced the dignity of millions of women by reducing various barriers to their achievement does not count for her as a serious objection. This truism does not address her resentment at being lumped with her inferiors. Neither does it alleviate her anxiety that like many black opponents of affirmative action, she is a beneficiary of affirmative action.

Neoconservatives trade on these potent feelings, arguing that affirmative action helps only those who do not deserve their attainments and stigmatizes those who do deserve them. Much of the considerable rhetorical power of neoconservatism has been attributable to its appeal to widespread American fears of being stigmatized or reversely discriminated against.[28] Neoconservatives understood from the outset that American conservatism must speak the language of democracy and individual opportunity. They are committed to conserving and defending most of the American establishment that actually exists. They defend what they call "the American reality," and they plainly chastise those reactionaries who, as James Nuechterlein said of Kirk, "imagine themselves superior to that reality."[29] The first neoconservatives turned to the Right at the same time and for the same reasons that millions of white ethnics and middle-class taxpayers began to vote Republican. This was the historical moment when working- and middle-class Americans could no longer expect to live better than their parents. Encouraged by Republican rhetoric to this effect, they increasingly thought of themselves not as beneficiaries of government entitlement programs but as beleaguered taxpayers. America's decline as a world economic power cost Jimmy Carter his second presidential term and propelled most neoconservatives to support not only Ronald Reagan's anticommunism but Reaganomics. To explain to Americans why their country was in economic decline, neoconservatives joined Reagan in blaming "labor elites" that strangled American productivity, a New Class of public sector functionaries that benefited from expanded government, and a welfare class that was addicted to government largesse. The image of a burgeoning welfare class that physically and economically threatened other Americans lurked behind most neoconservative rhetoric about the culture of poverty.

Irving Kristol once explained that neoconservatives had become influential by defending the prerogatives of a business class that was not adept at defending itself. "We had to tell businessmen that they needed us," he recalled. "Business understands the need for intellectuals much more than trade unionists understand it, but not enough. Basically, it wants intellectuals to go out and justify profits and explain to people why corporations make a lot of money. That's their main interest. It is very hard for business to understand how to think politically."[30] It was the neoconservatives who taught the business class how to think politically, just as they taught the American Right how to wage the cold war and the war for control of American culture. Neoconservatives alone knew how to unmask the class interests of middle-class liberalism. They alone knew how to defend a capitalist establishment that was weak at defending itself. In their highly successful rhetorical depictions, American liberals coddled the criminal class (which was disproportionately black) and the welfare class (which was also disproportionately black). They discriminated against white Americans (through affirmative action) and created comfortable public sector jobs for themselves in the process. They also kept America weak in the face of a superior Soviet enemy.

The movement's greatest strength at the high point of its influence was the militant anticommunism it inherited from the Old Left. Neoconservatives condemned the tyranny, mendacity, and brutality of communism in language that derived straight from the Old Left polemics against Stalinism. The picture of the Soviet enemy drawn by Shachtman, Hook, and Burnham was reproduced with fearsome certainty. Neoconservatives demanded a massive military buildup and a new interventionist foreign policy on the basis of this portrait. Some of them argued that the strengths of Soviet totalitarianism gave Soviet leaders immense advantages over their democratic opponents. Jean-François Revel insisted that Soviet communism was stronger than liberal democracy because liberalism permitted too much internal criticism. Podhoretz claimed that Soviet military strength and strategic geopolitical power surpassed America's. Richard Pipes warned that Soviet leaders were preparing to fight and win a nuclear war.[31] American military spending doubled between 1980 and 1985 on the basis of these claims. Neoconservatives argued later that the collapse of the Soviet Union owed much to Reagan's military buildup, which purportedly convinced Soviet leaders that they could not afford to perpetuate the arms race.

It appears likely that the pace of Soviet disintegration was, indeed, accelerated by the pressure of heightened American military spending in the 1980s. In their eagerness to attribute the dissolution of the cold war to Reagan's militarism, however, neoconservatives wrote off the enormous socioeconomic costs of the military expansion as well as its lack of necessity. Neoconservatives grossly overestimated not only the political strength and efficiency of Soviet bloc "totalitarianism" but also Soviet geopolitical force and economic strength. They thus demanded enormous military increases to outstrip a largely fantasized opponent. The United States was the world's leading creditor nation when Reagan's military buildup began, providing the largest source of capital for national economies throughout the world. By the end of Reagan's presidency, the United States was the world's largest debtor nation. America's dominant economic position in the world was squandered virtually overnight.

Moreover, the military expansion of the 1980s crowded out vital national investments in infrastructure, education, housing, soft-energy hardware, and similar needs. Federal aid to education was slashed by one-third, while workforce training and retraining were gutted. America spent more than $2 trillion on the military without raising the money to pay for it, leaving debts that devoured nearly half of every subsequent tax dollar. The Reagan military budgets sent a fantastically expensive message to a Soviet leadership that, in any case, could not have indefinitely ignored its disintegrating economic base. As early as 1983, the chief of the Soviet general staff, Marshal Nikolai Ogarkov, was telling former American officials that the cold war was over because of Soviet economic and technological backwardness. Numerous Soviet officials understood that the Soviet system was too rigid to compete with societies that put computers in the hands of every student.[32] In an increasingly internationalized world economy, the inferiority of the Soviet economic and educational systems was too obvious even for Soviet leaders to ignore. A more realistic assessment of the Soviet threat could have allowed the United States to husband its resources. Neoconservative polemics against "appeasement" made such an assessment politically impossible in the 1980s.

With the end of the cold war, neoconservatives scrambled to redefine the basis of their role in the American Right. Some called for a political and military commitment to remake the world in America's image. Others urged that the more important struggle was the war to reclaim American culture from an adversary class of well-positioned liberals and radicals. Irving Kristol counted himself in the latter group. "There is no 'after the Cold War' for me," he declared in 1993. "So far from having ended, my cold war has increased in intensity, as sector after sector of American life has been ruthlessly corrupted by the liberal ethos." In his telling, the liberal ethos promotes political collectivism and moral anarchy at the same time. "It cannot win, but it can make us all losers."[33]

Within the Right, neoconservatives were latecomers to this belief that the paramount struggle is the war for control of American culture. Though they took the lead in blasting feminism and multicultural education, they were often less aggressive on other cultural issues, or at least less inclined to ascribe a high priority to them. In 1982, New Right propagandist George Gilder could still complain that "neoconservatives, in general, are afraid to fight on ERA, abortion, sex education, pornography, school prayer, and gay liberation." Though neoconservatives generally took right-wing views on these subjects, he allowed, they could not be counted on to fight in the trenches for conservative victories. Neoconservatives were still too preoccupied with foreign policy, too devoted to their computer regressions, and too skittish about making electoral alliances with the New Right to really fight America's cultural battles. In Gilder's reading, they were still too intellectually pretentious to make good conservative allies. Gilder predicted that someday they would make better allies, however. At some future date, he conjectured, "when these trends have reached some climax sufficiently catastrophic," neoconservatives would finally enter the trenches of the cultural struggle. They would fight not merely against academic leftism but against the entire leftist assault on American culture: "They will finally grant, in essence, that Ernest van den Haag and Billy Graham were right about pornography; that Anita Bryant knows more about homosexuality than does the American Association of Psychiatrists; that Phyllis Schlafly is better at defining national priorities than is Daniel Patrick Moynihan; that the Moral Majority is a more valuable and responsible movement in our politics than is the Coalition for a Democratic Majority." Gilder confessed that the culture warriors of the New Right needed neoconservative support. Until the neoconservatives realized who their real friends were and moved all the way to the right, he warned, American conservatives had no chance of winning America's most important battles.[34]

For neoconservatives, the sufficiently catastrophic climax turned out to be the death of communism. Many of them began to appreciate Gilder's lesson only after the New Right's social agenda became, by default, their own highest priority. Decter identified the key to the change in attitude that was required of them. As she explained, hard-core cultural warfare can be fought only by those who are willing to proclaim and insistently repeat a few simplistic truisms. This was Reagan's strength. Decter re-

74   *Gary Dorrien*

called that in 1976, when Reagan challenged Gerald Ford for the Republican nomination, most neoconservatives still did not take Reagan seriously because of his lack of intellectual depth. Though they later became "his passionate supporters," it took many years for them to overcome their patronizing attitude toward him. Reagan's apparent simplemindedness reinforced their tendency to set themselves apart from other conservatives. *Neo*conservatives were too sophisticated to speak like Reagan or Schlafly. "They were still in the early stages of the process of stripping spiritual issues down to their simplicities and possibly a bit snobbish about their reluctance to push this process through to its end," she recalled.[35]

Neoconservatives gave Reagan higher marks for intelligence after he brought them to power, but it was only with the collapse of the Soviet threat that they became ordinary right-wingers. They made the purgative reduction that culture warfare requires. Having lost the galvanizing enemy that sustained their identity as a movement, they embraced the cultural resentments of people they had previously dismissed as reactionaries. They joined the culture war wholeheartedly. "Now that the other 'Cold War' is over, the real cold war has begun," Irving Kristol enthused. Podhoretz argued that the key to culture warfare was to be ready to make unexpected alliances and embrace "shocking" solutions "if we are ever to do anything about the corrupted and poisoned culture which in this country is our major problem." In November 1996, Neuhaus strayed a bit far even by this standard, charging that the "legitimacy" of the American "regime" has been thrown into question by the American government's support of abortion on demand. To some conservatives and neoconservatives, this kind of rhetoric was offensively reminiscent of the 1960s New Left diatribes against "Amerika." Neuhaus was chastised by Peter Berger, Walter Berns, and even Decter for taking the battlefield metaphors of culture warfare too literally. Some observers worried that he represented an ascending theocratic impulse in the conservative movement. Neuhaus rebuked this suggestion as a slander on his commitment to democracy, but what the controversy surely did confirm is that he, like many neoconservatives, has embraced culture warfare as a literal substitute for the cold war.[36]

Having relinquished their original support for the welfare state, the neoconservatives have no remaining basis (beyond style) for claiming any distinction for their kind of conservatism. In the 1980s, they embraced Reagan's economic policies and repeated his ritualistic calls for cuts in the capital gains tax. Irving Kristol became a leading advocate of supply-side economics, even while doubting that supply-side policy made economic sense. He had no doubt that supply side tax cuts were *politically* popular and therefore worth supporting.[37] Novak became a chief mythologist of American-style "democratic capitalism," claiming to find redemptive spiritual qualities in the practices of corporations. He explained that by virtue of their communal-religious character and their independence from the state, corporations "offer metaphors for grace, a kind of insight into God's ways in history." His later work expanded on this theme, claiming that capitalism is not only productive, virtue-producing, and spiritually true but that it also provides a universal standard "to which cultures must measure up." American democratic capitalism sets the standard by which all world cultures, political systems, and economies should be judged.[38]

This tendency to invest its political beliefs with absolute ideological or even religious significance is a distinguishing mark of a now-dissolving neoconservative movement. Figures like Moynihan and Bell dissociated themselves from the movement after it lurched all the way to free enterprise ideology and supply-side economics. Neoconservatives never quite fulfilled Viereck's hope for a new kind of conservatism. They were too polemical and much too ideological to speak in the tones that he considered intrinsic to authentic conservatism. They were too obsequious toward big business and far too militaristic to meet his tests for true conservatism. If neoconservatism never became the prudent, reflective, deeply rooted American conservatism that Viereck sought, however, it did transform the American Right in ways that made it possible for many academics and activists to think of themselves as conservatives. It brought many people into the American Right who had not expected to move there. More than a few disillusioned Swedophiles and former liberals became neoconservatives in the 1980s after being chastened by what Nathan Glazer called the limits of social policy. For them, neoconservatism was a corrective retrenchment from the overreaching commitments of the welfare state. Neoconservatives promoted entrepreneurial freedom from the state and instructed Americans on the limits of what government could do for them.

Neoconservatism is passing away as a distinctive political and intellectual movement. Recent history has washed away the factors that made two generations of neoconservatives distinctive within the American Right. The word conservative had ugly connotations to those on whom Michael Harrington first hung the label "neoconservative," but today the ideological children of Irving Kristol and Michael Novak wear the older term proudly without equivocation. Many of them write for William Kristol's *Weekly Standard,* a punchy right-wing periodical that arbitrates conservative political orthodoxy with little regard for pre-1990s in-house distinctions. Conservative activists such as William Kristol and John Podhoretz are products of the neoconservative movement. Like most of the "minicons" of their generation, they have inherited the neoconservative sense of politics as ideological tournament, but there is otherwise very little in their work that distinguishes them from the larger American Right to which they belong. More significant than any intellectual debt that they owe to neoconservatism is the fact that they have inherited from the neoconservative episode an elaborate network of corporate-funded think tanks, foundations, magazines, and lobbying agencies.

Contrary to the fears of the Old Right, these institutions have not faded away or become opera houses. Rather, they comprise a substantial segment of the infrastructure of an amply endowed American Right. Though some older neoconservatives and paleoconservatives continue to make no secret of their dislike for each other, self-interest has prevailed on both sides. Neoconservatives have made sizable contributions to the American Right, and today they have nowhere else to go. Though some of them gave Clinton a brief look during his first campaign for the presidency, virtually all of them quickly reestablished that their home is the "New Class" world of Republican Party activism and corporate-funded institutes. Clinton's triangulating opportunism does not meet any of their tests for ideological seriousness. Neoconservatives have wedded themselves, instead, to an American Right that increasingly reflects the influence of neoconservatives upon it. American conservatism has become more aggressive, more adept at political argument, and (to many) more attractive as a consequence of this influence. American conservatives today are more inclined than their predecessors to believe in the power of ideas. They believe that great things can be accomplished if they attain the right analysis of society. This conviction once belonged exclusively to liberals and progressives. For all of its internal contradictions, American conservatism today owes much of its potent political force to the living and lasting influence of the neoconservative episode.

Credits

This chapter is based on a larger book-length study by Gary Dorrien, *The Neoconservative Mind: Politics, Culture, and the War of Ideology* (Philadelphia: Temple University Press, 1993).

Notes

1. Lionel Trilling, *The Liberal Imagination: Essays on Literature and Society* (New York: Charles Scribner's Sons, 1950), ix.

2. Peter Viereck, "The Revolt Against the Elite" and "The Philosophical 'New Conservatism'—1962," in Daniel Bell, ed., *The Radical Right* (New York: Doubleday, 1963), 135–154, 155–173; quote on 158. See Russell Kirk, *The Conservative Mind: From Burke to Eliot* (Chicago: Regnery Books, 1987 [1953]).

3. See Irving Kristol, "'Civil Liberties': 1952—A Study in Confusion," *Commentary* 13, no. 3 (March 1952), 231–236; Kristol, "Liberty and the Communists," *Partisan Review* 19, no. 4 (July/August 1952), 493–496.

Inventing an American Conservatism

4. Michael Harrington, *The Other America: Poverty in the United States* (New York: Macmillan, 1962), 202.

5. Daniel Bell and Irving Kristol, "What Is the Public Interest?" *Public Interest* 1 (Fall 1965), 4; "sloppy thinking" quote in Walter Goodman, "Irving Kristol: Patron Saint of the New Right," *New York Times Magazine,* December 6, 1981, 202.

6. Irving Kristol, *Neoconservatism: The Autobiography of an Idea* (New York: Free Press, 1995), 31.

7. Nathan Glazer, "Housing Problems and Housing Policies," *Public Interest* 7 (Spring 1967), 21–51; Aaron Wildavsky, "The Political Economy of Efficiency," *Public Interest* 8 (Summer 1967), 30–48; James Q. Wilson, "The Urban Unease: Community vs. City," *Public Interest* 12 (Summer 1968), 25–39; Daniel P. Moynihan, "A Crisis of Confidence," *Public Interest* 7 (Spring 1967), 3–10; John H. Bunzel, "Black Studies at San Francisco State," *Public Interest* 13 (Fall 1968), 22–38.

8. Kristol, *Neoconservatism: The Autobiography of an Idea,* 31.

9. See Norman Podhoretz, "Reflections on Earth Day," *Commentary* 49, no. 6 (June 1970), 26; Norman Podhoretz, *Breaking Ranks: A Political Memoir* (New York: Harper and Row, 1979).

10. Samuel McCracken, "Quackery in the Classroom," *Commentary* 52, no. 4 (October 1971); Dorothy Rabinowitz, "The Activist Cleric," *Commentary* 50, no. 3 (September 1970); Midge Decter, "The Liberated Woman," *Commentary* 50, no. 4 (October 1970); Jeane Kirkpatrick, "The Revolt of the Masses," *Commentary* 55, no. 2 (February 1973); Michael Novak, "Needing Niebuhr Again," *Commentary* 54, no. 3 (September 1972); Podhoretz, *Breaking Ranks,* 307.

11. Quotes in Social Democrats, U.S.A., "For the Record: The Report of Social Democrats, U.S.A. on the Resignation of Michael Harrington and His Attempt to Split the American Socialist Movement," undated and unpublished position paper, 1–36. See Maurice Isserman, *If I Had a Hammer . . . : The Death of the Old Left and the Birth of the New Left* (New York: Basic Books, 1987), 57–75.

12. Michael Harrington, *Fragments of the Century* (New York: Saturday Review Press, 1973), 145.

13. Norman Podhoretz, "What the Voters Sensed," *Commentary* 55, no. 1 (January 1973), 6.

14. Norman Podhoretz, "The Culture of Appeasement," *Harper's* 255, no. 1529 (October 1977), 29–32. See Norman Podhoretz, *The Present Danger: Do We Have the Will to Reverse the Decline of American Power?* (New York: Simon and Schuster, 1980).

15. Norman Podhoretz, "The Neo-Conservative Anguish over Reagan's Foreign Policy," *New York Times Magazine* (May 2, 1982), 33, 96–98; Podhoretz, "How Reagan Succeeds as a Carter Clone," *New York Post,* October 7, 1986; Podhoretz, "Reagan—The Crippled Hawk," *New York Post,* June 25, 1985; Podhoretz, "The Madness of Arms Control," *New York Post,* October 1, 1985; Podhoretz, "What If Reagan Were President?" *New York Post,* April 29, 1986; Podhoretz, "Gorbachev's Salami Tactics," *New York Post,* October 20, 1987; Podhoretz, "What the Soviets Really Want," *New York Post,* November 19, 1985.

16. Irving Kristol, "The Map of the World Has Changed," *Wall Street Journal ,* January 3, 1990; Kristol, "Defining Our National Interest," *National Interest* 21 (Fall 1990), 23–24; Jeane J. Kirkpatrick, "A Normal Country in a Normal Time," *National Interest* 21 (Fall 1990), 44–45.

17. See Joshua Muravchik, *Exporting Democracy: Fulfilling America's Destiny* (Washington, DC: American Enterprise Institute, 1991); Ben J. Wattenberg, *The First Universal Nation: Leading Indicators and Ideas About the Surge of America in the 1990s* (New York: Free Press, 1991); Charles Krauthammer, "Universal Dominion: Toward a Unipolar World," *National Interest* 18 (Winter 1989), 47–49; Krauthammer, "The Unipolar Moment," *Foreign Affairs* 70, no. 1 (1991), 23–33.

18. Russell Kirk, *The Neoconservatives: An Endangered Species*, The Heritage Lectures, no. 178 (Washington, DC: Heritage Foundation, 1988), 1–10.

19. Ibid.; Stephen J. Tonsor, "Why I Too Am Not a Neoconservative," *National Review* 38, no. 11 (June 20, 1986), 55.

20. Clyde Wilson, "The Conservative Identity," *Intercollegiate Review* 21, no. 3 (Spring 1986), 66. See Jeffrey Hart, "Gang Warfare in Chicago," *National Review* 38, no. 10 (June 6, 1986), 32; Ernest Van Den Haag, "The War Between Paleos and Neos," *National Review* 41, no. 3 (February 24, 1989), 21–23.

21. Buchanan and Fleming quoted in David Frum, "The Conservative Bully Boy," *American Spectator* 24, no. 7 (July 1991), 12; Gottfried quoted in Robert Moynihan, "Thunder on the Right," *Thirty Days* (September 1989), 68. See Paul Gottfried and Thomas Fleming, *The Conservative Movement* (Boston: Twayne Publishers, 1988), 73.

22. Kirk, interview with author, October 19, 1989.

23. Richard John Neuhaus, "Democratic Conservatism," *First Things* 1 (March 1990), 65; Podhoretz, interview with author, June 12, 1990.

24. Thomas Fleming, "The Closing of the Conservative Mind," *Chronicles* 13, no. 9 (September 1989), 12; Podhoretz quoted in Moynihan, "Thunder on the Right," 69–70.

25. Tonsor, "Why I Too Am Not a Neoconservative," 55.

26. Norman Podhoretz, "The Disaster of Women's Lib," *New York Post*, August 18, 1987; Midge Decter, "The Liberated Woman," 44; Decter, "For the Family: Millions of Americans Have Been Engaging in Child Sacrifice," *Policy Review* 27 (Winter 1984), 44–45. "All the demands" quote in Decter, "Liberating Women: Who Benefits?" *Commentary* 77, no. 3 (March 1984), 36. See Decter, "Farewell to the Woman Question," *First Things* 14 (June/July 1991), 9.

27. Ruth R. Wisse, "Living with Women's Lib," *Commentary* 86, no. 2 (August 1988), 45; see Carol Ianonne, "The Feminist Confusion," in Peter Collier and David Horowitz, eds., *Second Thoughts: Former Radicals Look Back at the Sixties* (Lanham, MD: Madison Books, 1989), 150–153; Ianonne, "The Barbarism of Feminist Scholarship," *Intercollegiate Review* 23, no. 1 (Fall 1987), 35–41.

28. See Nathan Glazer, *Affirmative Discrimination: Ethnic Inequality and Public Policy* (New York: Basic Books, 1975); Edward C. Banfield, *The Unheavenly City Revisited* (Boston: Little, Brown, 1974); Dinesh D'souza, *Illiberal Education: The Politics of Race and Sex on Campus* (New York: Free Press, 1991).

29. James Nuechterlein, "The Paleo's Paleo," review of *The Conservative Constitution*, by Russell Kirk, *First Things* 15 (August/September 1991), 46.

30. Quoted in Sidney Blumenthal, *The Rise of the Counter-Establishment: From Conservative Ideology to Political Power* (New York: Harper and Row, 1988), 154.

31. Jean-François Revel, *How Democracies Perish* (New York: Harper and Row, 1985); Norman Podhoretz, "Making the World Safe for Communism," *Commen-*

Inventing an American Conservatism

tary 61, no. 4 (April 1976), 37–41; Richard Pipes "Why the Soviet Union Thinks It Could Fight and Win a Nuclear War," *Commentary* 64, no. 1 (July 1977), 24–34.

32. Ogarkov quoted in Leslie H. Gelb, "Who Won the Cold War?" *New York Times,* August 20, 1992; see Daniel Deudney and G. John Ikenberry, "Who Won the Cold War?" *Foreign Policy* 87 (Summer 1992), 123–138; Benjamin M. Friedman, *Day of Reckoning: The Consequences of American Economic Policy* (New York: Vintage Books, 1989).

33. Kristol, *Neoconservatism: The Autobiography of an Idea,* 486.

34. George Gilder, "Why I Am Not a Neo-Conservative," *National Review* 34, no. 4 (March 5, 1982), 218–220.

35. Midge Decter, "Ronald Reagan and the Culture War," *Commentary* 91, no. 3 (March 1991), 46.

36. Ibid., 486; Norman Podhoretz, "Second Thoughts," in Collier and Horowitz, eds., *Second Thoughts,* 195; editor's introduction to "The End of Democracy?" *First Things* 67 (November 1996). For responses to this symposium by Berger, Berns, Decter, and many others, see the January 1997 issue of *First Things* and subsequent issues.

37. See Kristol, *Neoconservatism: The Autobiography of an Idea,* 35–37.

38. Michael Novak, *Toward a Theology of the Corporation* (Washington, DC: American Enterprise Institute, 1981), 41–43; Novak, *The Catholic Ethic and the Spirit of Capitalism* (New York: Free Press, 1993), 226. See Novak, *The Spirit of Democratic Capitalism* (New York: American Enterprise Institute/Simon and Schuster, 1982).

4

Business Conflict and Right-Wing Movements

Matthew N. Lyons

The right-wing offensive of the last twenty years has been a gold mine for big business. The enormous cuts in taxes for corporations and the wealthy, the record-breaking federal payments to military contractors and other favored industries, the shredding of regulations on everything from toxic dumping to antitrust policy—such measures have put billions of dollars into corporate pockets. Employer bargaining power over a vulnerable workforce has been dramatically enhanced by an array of rightist-initiated campaigns, including social service cuts, attacks on unions, anti-immigrant racism, and expansion of the prison labor system. The collapse of the Soviet bloc, brought on partly by the costs of an intensified cold war, has opened vast new areas for corporate penetration and has removed a major counterweight to multinational capitalism in the Third World. Scapegoating of oppressed groups for real and imagined social problems has helped to deflect attention away from those who benefit most from human misery.

In some eyes, this broad picture indicates a simple alliance: "The Right represents big business." But in the same period, there have also been signs that neither the Right nor big business has embraced the other unanimously. The emergence of right-wing paramilitary groups that not only denounced Wall Street but were willing to take up arms against the government (the Order and the Posse Comitatus in the 1980s, various "militias" in the 1990s) pointed to a reservoir of right-wing antielitism that went beyond simple rhetoric. Pat Buchanan's presidential campaigns in 1992 and 1996 indicated that at least a few capitalists (certain South Carolina textile barons, for instance) were willing to break ranks and bankroll a populist right-winger hostile to free trade and the global economy. Meanwhile,

80

Bill Clinton's successful, well-funded presidential campaigns showed that even after the Reagan "revolution," a moderate conservative with liberal pretensions could still attract strong business support.

This chapter examines the relationship between business interests and ultraconservative movements in recent U.S. history. By "ultraconservative" I mean, roughly speaking, those forces that go beyond a conservative defense of established power relations but stop short of a fascist demand to fully eliminate liberal pluralistic institutions. Ultraconservatism includes the array of movements that emerged as a backlash against the gains of New Deal reformism and organized labor and, more recently, those of the civil rights, feminist, gay and lesbian, antiwar, and environmental movements. Many of these forces came together in the New Right that arose in the 1970s and broke apart in the 1980s and 1990s. I explore here the capitalist role in that process.

Business Conflict Analysis

As leftists and some liberals have long argued, capitalist support has been vital to the growth of right-wing movements. In making this crucial point, however, there are two common pitfalls. One is to lump all capitalists together politically, implying that class-conscious business leaders always support the Right—which they do not. The other pitfall is to focus only on the actions of individual capitalists or specific companies. Although this approach can yield a wealth of information, it often provides no explanation—beyond personality differences—as to why some capitalists but not others embrace the Right.

Fortunately, a small but growing body of literature offers us a third alternative: business conflict analysis. This approach, as I would formulate it, starts with the recognition that the capitalist class dominates politics and society as a whole under a private enterprise system. Other interests, including popular movements for social change, can and do play a role, sometimes a big one. But they face an uphill battle, and the closer they come to challenging basic capitalist interests, the steeper the field becomes. Capitalists will band together to repel any serious radical threat to its system of rule.

Serious threats to capitalism, however, have rarely been a live issue in U.S. politics, and beyond its fundamental unity, capital encompasses many competing interests. Specific policies that are good for one section of business may be useless or even harmful for another, and these disputes play a big part in shaping everyday political conflict. Historically, capitalist interests have tended to arrange themselves into factions according to industry, region, type of company, and other factors. As several writers have argued, shifting factional conflicts and alliances within the business elite have had a big role in shaping right-wing politics, and this can be seen clearly in the case of the New Right.[1]

Business conflict theory complements, but cannot replace, other tools for analyzing social movements and the structures and ideologies that frame them. The rise of the New Right embodied a right turn both "from above" and "from below," and although the elite shift influenced the grass roots, so did many other factors. Corporate-sponsored propaganda campaigns and other top-down initiatives cannot in themselves explain, for example, the massive politicization of evangelical Christians since the 1970s, the salience of abortion rights and homosexuality as right-wing targets, or the ultraconservative Right's partial shift away from explicit biological racism toward coded forms of racism and cultural nationalism.

Nonetheless, business conflict analysis does provide a key insight into right-wing antielitism. Because it is typically combined with a defense of the traditional social order, right-wing antielitism has sometimes been dismissed as sheer hypocrisy. In fact, antielite critiques have often been used by "outsider" factions of the capitalist elite as a way to mobilize popular support against the dominant "insider" faction. The outsiders cannot call into question the capitalist system itself, so they treat the insiders as a parasitic force—often a conspiratorial one—that supposedly perverts the true workings of democracy and free enterprise. For example, McCarthyism's crusade against "Communists" in federal agencies reflected (among other things) an attempt by Western and Midwestern-based business forces to depose Eastern establishment representatives from the top levels of government. Antielitism from above has often blended with a kind of right-wing antielitism from below, in which middle- and working-class whites have combined hostility toward the rich and powerful with aggressive racism, nativism, or anti-Semitism, or some combination of these sentiments.

Inventing an American Conservatism

From the 1930s until the 1970s, insider and outsider business factions were mainly defined by whether they supported or opposed the New Deal system.[2] In this section, I will sketch the outlines of that conflict as it shaped right-wing politics over these decades. Based on principles established under President Franklin Roosevelt in the 1930s, the New Deal system was consolidated and expanded from the 1940s on. Within the United States, the system involved collective bargaining between big corporations and a bureaucratized labor movement; the gradual removal (under pressure from below) of traditional forms of legal discrimination and disenfranchisement; and Keynesian policies of active government intervention in the economy, including institution of both social welfare programs

Business Conflict and Right-Wing Movements 83

and massive military spending. These measures helped provide business with a stable workforce and political base, a large consumer market, generous subsidies to defense contractors and other firms, and a governmental cushion against economic crises. Internationally, the New Deal system encompassed a global capitalist order based on U.S. military dominance; the primacy of the dollar as a world currency under the Bretton Woods system; international organizations such as the United Nations; and an overall lowering of tariff barriers through periodic General Agreement on Tariffs and Trade (GATT) negotiations, though import quotas and subsidized exports ("foreign aid") continued to target the Third World in many industries. Social reform was to be encouraged in Europe (and sometimes, in caricature form, in the Third World) both to strengthen consumer markets for U.S. exports and as bulwarks against communism; the USSR was either to be enmeshed in the global market through détente or worn down through "containment." These measures provided the framework for a vast expansion of U.S.-based capital around the world.

Thomas Ferguson has shown how a new "historical bloc" of capitalists rallied to Roosevelt's New Deal policies in 1935–1936 and went on to dominate U.S. politics for forty years. This bloc included companies in capital-intensive industries where profits depended relatively less on keeping labor costs low. This meant they could be relatively flexible about cutting a deal with the increasingly militant labor movement. In addition, many firms in this coalition were competitive or dominant internationally, thus they wanted low tariffs to boost trade and open up new markets. The bloc also included many of the big investment banks and internationally oriented commercial banks, which favored free trade and had tiny labor costs compared with other industries.[3]

This bloc, which has been dubbed "internationalist" or "multinationalist," initially included only a fraction of the business class, but it was the dynamic core of that class, and in the postwar years it grew both in members and influence. The multinationalists had outposts in various regions but were centered in the Northeast. They included an important sprinkling of Jews and Catholics but were most strongly associated with the WASP "Eastern establishment" that dominated the most prestigious universities, foundations, and newspapers, as well as the foreign service. The multinationalists saw their interests tied to Europe and emulated Britain, whose empire was their model for a globally managed economy. They controlled both the national Democratic Party and the moderate wing of the Republican Party and were represented by such bodies as the Council on Foreign Relations, the Committee for Economic Development and, later, the Trilateral Commission and the Business Roundtable.

The New Deal system was opposed by an evolving business coalition in transition from its previous role as the hub of the capitalist elite. This "nationalist" bloc was centered initially in the Midwest, later in the Sun Belt. It included many old manufacturing industries such as the textile, steel, and shoe industries, which were labor-intensive and thus especially vulnerable to labor unions, and many private or family-controlled firms steeped in laissez-faire individualism, which were hostile to social welfare policies. Also included were companies that favored protectionist policies because they could not compete internationally or were oriented toward domestic markets or regions dominated by the United States, such as Central America. Isolationist vis-à-vis Europe, nationalists favored a unilateral, predatory model of U.S. expansion southward into Latin America and westward across the Pacific into Asia—an extension of Manifest Destiny overseas. Nationalists had a presence in both major parties, but especially in the Republican Right. They were represented by the National Association of Manufacturers (NAM) and, at least in the early period, the U.S. Chamber of Commerce.

Although often happy to receive government subsidies, business nationalists were hostile to any form of "strong state" that would restrict their entrepreneurial freedom. Yet they tended to be more sympathetic to the economic nationalism of fascist Germany and Italy than to free-trading England and, like many fascists, saw the New Deal as proof of a sinister alliance between international finance capital and communistic working-class organizations. Such views easily translated into conspiracy theories centered on Wall Street, Jewish bankers, and Britain, with the English Rothschild family as a connecting link. When Midwestern business nationalists spearheaded the America First Committee in 1940–1941 in an effort to keep the United States out of World War II, the committee became a magnet for Nazis and Nazi sympathizers.

During the first two decades after World War II, the nationalist-multinationalist conflict continued to influence U.S. right-wing politics. After the 1949 Chinese Revolution, nationalists generally supported a "rollback" military strategy against communism, in contrast to the more moderate containment strategy generally favored by multinationalists. Both factions embraced the cold war crusade to purge leftists from public life—useful above all for weakening the labor movement. But nationalist-affiliated politicians such as Joseph McCarthy and Richard Nixon also turned the charge of communist conspiracy against representatives of the Eastern establishment, especially such Anglophile bastions as the State Department and the CIA. McCarthy's backers included former America First leader Robert Wood (head of Sears Roebuck) and Texas oilmen such as H. L. Hunt and Clint Murchison; multinationalist business leaders played a key role in lobbying for the Senate condemnation that ended McCarthy's Red-hunting crusade.[4]

Unable to complete their purge of Eastern elite figures from government, business nationalists provided core support for an array of ultraconservative organizations that expanded McCarthyism into even more grandiose conspiracy theories. Most notable was the John Birch Society, founded in 1958, whose early leadership included nationally oriented oil executives J. Howard Pew (Sun Oil) and Fred C. Koch (Rock Island Oil), and a number of other NAM-affiliated entrepreneurs. Squarely in the anti–New Deal tradition, the Birch Society fiercely opposed the United Nations, the income tax, and all incursions by the welfare state or "world government" and alternated between isolationism and rollback in military affairs.[5]

In 1964, Barry Goldwater's presidential candidacy offered business nationalists an opportunity to retake control of the national Republican Party. The 1964 race hinged largely on President Johnson's support for civil rights legislation and Goldwater's denunciation of federal government efforts to end segregation. But the Goldwater campaign also denounced the welfare state, the UN, and low tariffs. Phyllis Schlafly's book, *A Choice Not an Echo*, one of the key campaign tracts, argued that a sinister cabal of "kingmakers"—Eastern establishment leaders—had secretly chosen all of the Republican presidential nominees since 1936 in order to protect their own wealth and power. Faced with such a campaign, the vast majority of top corporate leaders swung behind the Democrats, making 1964 the only presidential election in this century when that has happened. Goldwater's capitalist backing was confined almost exclusively to nationalists concentrated in the Sun Belt and Midwest. A number of them later became major funders of the New Right, including Roger Milliken (textiles), Jeremiah Milbank Jr. (chemicals and other interests), and Henry Salvatori (independent oil).[6]

Although Goldwater lost to President Johnson in a landslide, his campaign helped lay the groundwork for the rise of the New Right—through its appeal to the anti–civil rights backlash, its ability to mobilize an ideologically dedicated network of activists, and its groundbreaking use of direct-mail fund-raising.

The New Right Convergence

Between Goldwater's defeat in 1964 and Ronald Reagan's presidential victory in 1980, a combination of factors moved the business community sharply to the right: first, the rising wealth and influence of "outsider" anti–New Deal business forces centered in the Sun Belt; second, the decision by many multinationalists in the 1970s that their economic goals could no longer be accomplished within the New Deal framework. These shifts—combined with the grassroots backlash against the civil rights movement, feminism, lesbian and gay liberation, and other social change movements—gave rise to the New Right.[7]

During the 1960s and early 1970s, the Sun Belt economy expanded dramatically, as Vietnam War contracts spurred industrialization and as capital fled from the Northeast in search of low-wage, nonunionized workers. Most defense contractors and other Sun Belt companies on the technological cutting edge—such as those in the aerospace, computer, telecommunications, and medical research industries—were either directly tied to Eastern multinationals or shared their general outlook. But the federally subsidized boom, ironically, also fostered a crop of laissez-faire entrepreneurs hostile to the Eastern elite and steeped in a broth of Birchite conspiracism, traditionalist Protestant morality, and cultural nationalism. Some of these capitalists were in agribusiness or labor-intensive manufacturing fields like the old nationalists of the Midwest had been. Most typically, however, they were based in real estate and mineral speculation (oil, gas, mining), and in financial and other service sectors. I will call this faction the "outsider" bloc to distinguish it from the old business nationalist bloc in which it was deeply rooted but from which it eventually began to diverge.

Probably the biggest factor within the outsider bloc was independent oil entrepreneurs, most of them small or medium-sized domestic producers. Since the days of H. L. Hunt and Clint Murchison, many oil wildcatters had been bitterly hostile to the multinational oil corporations such as Exxon, Mobil, and Shell, associated (actually or symbolically) with Rockefeller wealth. In addition, Thomas Edsall has written, independent oil

> has a highly complex and ambivalent relationship with the federal government. It has bitterly fought price controls over oil and natural gas and has angrily denounced government intervention in the marketplace. At the same time, however, independent oilmen have struggled to obtain and to keep a network of special tax breaks, all of which have given the industry a government-created market advantage over its competitors, the major oil companies. The combination of dependence upon and anger at the federal government has made independent oil the most conservative industry in the nation.[8]

After two decades of low oil prices, the steep price hikes in 1973 and 1979 led by OPEC (Organization of Petroleum Exporting Countries) sharply increased the amount of cash available to independent oil firms—and through them to ultraconservative activism. Edsall estimated in 1984 that at least one-third of all contributors to right-wing organizations and the Republican Party were independent oil producers.[9]

Sun Belt capital was instrumental in the growth of a dense network of New Right organizations in the early and mid-1970s. In one prominent example, Colorado beer magnate Joseph Coors joined with Paul Weyrich to found the Heritage Foundation in 1973 and the Committee for the Survival of a Free Congress (later renamed the Free Congress Foundation) in

1974. Evangelical Christian organizations, central to the growth of the New Right, were among those receiving major support from Sunbelt entrepreneurs such as Nelson Bunker Hunt (son of H. L. Hunt), who donated $10 million to Pat Robertson's Christian Broadcasting Network (CBN) in 1970 and major sums over the following decade to the Campus Crusade for Christ.[10]

As Sun Belt anti–New Deal forces were rising, a crisis in the New Deal system was pulling much of the U.S. multinationalist bloc to the right.[11] U.S. overseas investments and trade increased during the 1960s and 1970s, at the same time that Japan and Western Europe were gaining industrial strength. Thus, U.S. companies faced growing foreign competition both abroad and in home markets, which fueled protectionist sentiment. Although big military budgets had helped the United States enforce its economic and political primacy since World War II, arms spending became a significant drain on the U.S. economy during the Vietnam War. A massive outflow of dollars from the United States (due to trade, overseas investment, and military spending) meant that the country could no longer afford to exchange dollars for gold—and this and other factors brought an end to the dollar-based Bretton Woods monetary system. The defeat in Vietnam, followed by revolutions in Southern Africa, Nicaragua, and Iran, temporarily put U.S. imperialism on the defensive.

Domestic changes, including the expansion of government's social role in response to popular pressures in the 1960s and 1970s, also cut into the benefits that capitalists reaped from the New Deal system. The long 1960s boom pushed unemployment to unusually low levels, at the same time that growth of social programs provided workers with a somewhat greater cushion against job loss. A reduced threat of unemployment weakened capitalist leverage over employees, contributing in the late 1960s to a widespread resurgence of rank-and-file worker militancy and a sharp fall in corporate profit rates, which remained stagnant through most of the 1970s. In the early 1970s, federal government regulation of the environment, occupational health and safety, and consumer protection expanded significantly, forcing business to absorb some of the costs previously passed on to other sectors of society.

The 1974–1975 recession, partly engineered by government policymakers to raise unemployment and restore profit rates, proved to be the most severe downturn since the 1930s, pointing to deep structural problems in the U.S. economy. Several years of stagnation followed. To improve their prospects in this worsening climate, U.S. companies, including multinationals, sought to reduce labor costs through efforts ranging from plant relocation to illegal attacks on unions and tried to press for reduced government regulation and for further cuts in corporate taxes, which had already been sinking steadily throughout the 1960s.

On foreign and military issues, the political center of gravity among multinationalists also shifted rightward over the 1970s. Early in the decade, the Nixon administration had promoted détente with the USSR and had increased reliance on "regional surrogates" to police much of Africa, Asia, and Latin America. But détente, and its corollary of increased trade with the Soviet Union, benefited European companies far more than U.S. ones, and regional surrogates often failed to enforce U.S. dictates. These factors, among many others, led many multinationalists to support increased military budgets and a more directly aggressive role in the Third World, while rising competition with other capitalist powers fueled demands for a more unilateralist foreign policy.

In the mid-1970s, sharp policy debates opened within the multinationalist bloc. A dwindling liberal wing favored an international strategy based primarily on economic aid and financial leverage, co-optation of radical Third World movements, and global management in concert with Western Europe and Japan. Rightward-moving multinationalists, including a number of defense contractors among others, increasingly converged with Sun Belt ultraconservatives around a number of core goals: to crank up the cold war and military spending; to dismantle social programs, environmental legislation, and other government regulations on industry; to roll back what remained of labor union power; and to cut taxes. Both wings of this emerging business coalition channeled hundreds of millions of dollars into the array of New Right lobbies, think tanks, media organizations, legal centers, political action committees, and other organs pursuing their overall agenda. Right-wing projects outside the New Right itself also received increased funding.[12]

As noted before, the right turn from above interacted with a right turn from below, which began in the 1960s and gathered force with the economic downturn in the 1970s. Governor George Wallace of Alabama tapped the growing racist backlash among Northern working-class whites with his Democratic and American Independent presidential campaigns in 1964, 1968, and 1972. During the 1970s, the white suburban middle class took the lead. The rightist upsurge attacked school desegregation, affirmative action, abortion rights, public visibility for lesbians and gay men, and other recent social gains. The backlash involved not only defending traditional power and privileges but also scapegoating oppressed groups for genuine grievances such as unemployment, crime, declining real income, and general social fragmentation.[13]

Although these initiatives had their own dynamic, business-oriented elites also worked to promote, coordinate, and channel them for their own ends. Direct-mail specialists such as Richard Viguerie flooded the grass roots with propaganda and appeals for money, establishing direct-mail fund-raising as an important right-wing business constituency in its own right. Following George Wallace's example, the New Right denounced liberal reformism as an elitist attack on regular working people. Rather than directly attack popular New Deal programs as Goldwater had done, the New Right sought white middle- and working-class supporters by emphasizing social-issue targets such as abortion, busing, the Equal Rights Amendment (ERA), and gay rights.[14] Particularly effective as a mobilizing tool was the "tax revolt" of the late 1970s that, without mentioning race, exploited and fomented white hostility toward government programs aiding black and Latino communities. This campaign tapped widespread, deeply rooted racist sentiments, whereas the major role of business interests in bankrolling antitax propaganda (e.g., through the American Council for Capital Formation) was seldom noted.[15]

The Reagan "Revolution"

The new right-wing business coalition helped push President Jimmy Carter's administration to the right in the late 1970s and contributed to the 1980 presidential victory of Ronald Reagan. Reagan garnered support not only from rightists in both major parties but also from moderate political and business forces in the Republican Party. Under his administration, a bipartisan coalition in Congress enacted much of the New Right's economic and foreign policy program.[16] In a massive upward income transfer, the government slashed business taxes and personal income taxes for the wealthy while increasing the regressive social security tax. Although the New Deal system was not dismantled, social programs for low-income people, already declining, were reduced dramatically (while programs benefiting the middle class, notably Social Security, were better defended in Congress and received fewer cuts). The administration largely abandoned enforcement of environmental and health and safety regulations, turned over vast public resources such as timber and offshore oil to private companies at discount rates, tilted the National Labor Relations Board more heavily toward management, and broke the pivotal air traffic controllers strike of 1981. Meanwhile, Reagan's unprecedented peacetime military buildup not only subsidized military contractors and supported the revived cold war mentality and Third World intervention but also amounted to the largest application of Keynesian deficit spending in U.S. history, helping to sustain the economic boom for business in the mid-1980s.

The Reagan administration's overall attack on the New Deal system, and above all its renewal of cold war militarism, held together a broad array of capitalist supporters, yet differences persisted within the coalition. On trade policy, the administration maneuvered to satisfy its various backers, proclaiming free trade but offering protection or subsidies to specific industries. On military policy, outsider capitalists of the rollback school tended to take the cold war revival, Third World interventions, and massive arms buildup at face value, as a counterattack against "the Evil Empire" and its minions. To many multinationalists, however, these policies were a way to protect investments in the Third World and, in particular, to counteract the growing autonomy of Western Europe and Japan and ensure that the United States keep control over a unified global market.[17] Centrist-oriented multinationalists, not necessarily intent on superpower confrontation for its own sake, sometimes prevailed on the Reagan administration to soften its anti-Soviet stance. Thus, Reagan relaxed certain trade restrictions against the USSR and signed the intermediate-range nuclear forces (INF) arms control treaty, moves that many New Rightists criticized.[18]

Even within the rightist camp, which shared an ideological anti-Sovietism, there were important divisions, which would eventually lead to acrimonious splits and clashes over policy. Although ideological, cultural, and organizational differences were important factors, to a significant extent these paralleled and provided expression for capitalist factional divisions.

Within the Reagan coalition, much of the right-wing multinationalist backing went to relatively moderate voices such as the American Enterprise Institute. Founded in 1943 as the American Enterprise Association, the AEI did not become influential until the early 1970s, when it began to receive support from military contractors and other big corporations such as General Electric, Hewlett-Packard, Standard Oil of California, Texas Instruments, and Rockwell International, as well as from major banks such as Chase Manhattan and Citicorp. The Business Roundtable, a right-wing multinationalist lobbying group founded in 1972, helped channel funds to the institute. The AEI also received contributions from long-standing ultraconservative funders, such as the J. Howard Pew Freedom Trust.[19]

The AEI, in the words of Joseph G. Peschek, was "drawn more to the Republicanism of George Bush and Gerald Ford than to that of Jesse Helms or Paul Laxalt"—that is, it represented a moderate conservatism more in line with the preferences of the Eastern establishment than those of Sun Belt ultraconservatives.[20] The AEI sponsored the work of "free market" economists such as Milton Friedman and a host of neoconservatives such as Irving Kristol, Jeane Kirkpatrick, Seymour Martin Lipset, and Ben Wattenberg. The "neocons" made up an intellectual network of former cold war liberals rooted in the Democratic Party, many of them Jews or Catholics, who were alienated by the social activism of the 1960s and formed an uneasy alliance with the New Right. Through organizations such as the Committee on the Present Danger, neocons played an important role in the revival of militaristic anticommunism. However,

Business Conflict and Right-Wing Movements 91

among other differences, they tended to have a more internationalist outlook than many in the New Right, and they advocated a limited form of the New Deal system, not its complete abolition.[21]

Representing a very different sector of the business community, significantly further to the right than the AEI, was the Council for National Policy (CNP).[22] The CNP was founded in 1981 as a secretive discussion group to bring together a broad array of top right-wing evangelicals, secular activists, government officials, retired military and intelligence officers, journalists, academicians, and business leaders. Researchers such as Russ Bellant have pointed to the CNP as a key networking forum within the ultraconservative Right. Among business-affiliated CNP members in the 1980s, Sun Belt outsiders and old-line nationalists predominated. Firms represented were typically entrepreneurial (controlled by one family or individual), with about 70 percent of business members based in the South and West. The biggest bloc was in the overlapping fields of Sun Belt real estate and construction, oil and gas, and financial services. Southeastern textiles and other old (and probably labor-intensive) industries, many of them in the Midwest, were represented, as were an assortment of food, beverage, and retail industries. So, too, were many businesses directly tied to right-wing politics (e.g., religious broadcasting, direct-mail marketing).

The CNP also included a sprinkling of members linked to multinationalist firms such as CBS and Pepsico and a handful of people in international finance. However, conspicuously few CNP business members had ties with high-tech industries such as the aerospace, electronics, telecommunications technology, computer software, or pharmaceutical industries. Tobacco industry people, too, were almost completely missing from this right-wing assemblage, belying a common stereotype but consistent with tobacco's long-standing character as a multinational industry not especially tied to ultraconservative politics.[23]

On the activist side, the CNP included evangelical leaders such as Pat Robertson, Jerry Falwell, and Tim LaHaye; "secular" New Right leaders such as Edwin J. Feulner (Heritage Foundation), Paul Weyrich (Free Congress Foundation), Howard Phillips (Conservative Caucus), and Richard Viguerie; government leaders such as Senator Jesse Helms and Representatives Jack Kemp and Dick Armey; and many other well-known figures. Larry Pratt of Gun Owners of America and English First was a member; later, he would help launch the militia movement. For Christian Right leaders, the CNP was home ground. By comparison with the AEI, this gathering was more oriented toward mass organizing and toward moral traditionalism, cultural nationalism, and populist antielitism.

The CNP bore strong ties to the business nationalist-oriented Old Right. Formation of the CNP was initiated by John Birch Society leaders William

Cies and Larry McDonald, the late Democratic congressman from Georgia, who conceived the organization to counter the Eastern elite's Council on Foreign Relations. Billionaire Nelson Bunker Hunt, a JBS national council member, was a key recruiter for the fledgling CNP. Prominent on the CNP executive committee was Reed Larson, executive director of the National Right to Work Committee, which was founded by Southern business executives in 1954 as a vehicle for union busting. The CNP also included staunch protectionists such as textile magnate Roger Milliken and several leaders of the U.S. Business and Industrial Council (USBIC), probably the most protectionist of business organizations today.

Yet among the outsider business forces represented in the CNP, protectionists were offset by firms with significant links to the international market. In 1988, at least 14 percent of business-affiliated members were from companies with identifiable overseas interests (operations, sales, or imports). These included such firms as Amway and Southwire, both squarely outside the multinationalist establishment and yet both with major operations in Europe, Latin America, and Asia. Some of the bigger oil independents, including Herbert and Nelson Bunker Hunt, had long been active overseas. The W. R. Grace conglomerate had always had extensive holdings in Latin America and more recently in Europe, and Pat Robertson's media empire operated on several continents.

In some cases, such operations probably continued the expansionist side of business nationalism: overseas growth as egoistic conquest, hostile to any sort of international coordination or open competition. But to some extent at least, the movement of outsider capitalists into the world market created a stronger commonality of interests with (right-wing) multinationalists. This was a period when the State of Oklahoma, in the heart of oil wildcatter territory, signed a deal with the Morgan Grenfell investment bank (London counterpart of J. P. Morgan and Company)—despite all traditional attitudes toward English bankers. That contract was negotiated by the law firm of R. Marc Nuttle, Pat Robertson's 1988 national campaign manager and a Free Congress Foundation adviser.[24]

The Heritage Foundation and the Free Congress Foundation, core New Right organizations founded with Coors money in the early 1970s and headed by CNP members, brought together multinationalist and outsider business support significantly more than did the CNP itself. Out of 158 major FCF donors on a list for 1988–1989, at least 65 were CNP members or their direct affiliates, and they were joined by other longtime ultraconservative funders such as Los Angeles oil developer Henry Salvatori. But the list of donors also included a number of multinationalist interests such as the Amoco Foundation, Chase Manhattan, IBM, and Texaco. Richard Mellon Scaife, by far the biggest donor with over $7 million in contributions, was an heir to the vast fortune of the Mellon family (Gulf Oil, Alcoa, Mel-

Business Conflict and Right-Wing Movements 93

lon Bank, and so on)—surely a part of the Eastern establishment, though one with a long-standing involvement in right-wing politics. Contributors to the Heritage Foundation included a similar mix.[25]

As they sought broad financial support within the business community, the Heritage Foundation and FCF also cultivated links with several different right-wing political currents. The two foundations were closely connected with the Christian Right; their strong emphasis on a traditionalist approach to social policy issues and open hostility to the "liberal" establishment helped their relations with hard-line cultural nationalists. Yet the prevailing FCF and Heritage Foundation outlook was pro-Zionist and global in scope, which helped them strengthen ties with neoconservatives.

The Right Breaks Apart

For the most part, potential conflicts within the right-wing coalition were kept within bounds during the Reagan administration. But they erupted forcefully in the late 1980s and early 1990s, centering on the clash between neoconservatives and self-described paleoconservatives who upheld old-style isolationism and cultural nationalism.[26] Various factors contributed to this splintering. Many ultraconservatives distrusted Reagan's successor George Bush, an Eastern establishment figure with few ties to the New Right. On a more profound level, the collapse of the Soviet bloc beginning in 1989 removed anticommunism as a cause uniting different right-wing factions, which focused attention on divisive questions about domestic social policy and the role of the United States in a post–cold war world. The Persian Gulf crisis following Iraq's invasion of Kuwait in 1990 brought the latter issue to a head as paleoconservative opponents of U.S. intervention squared off against neoconservative and other rightist supporters of Bush's war.

Less visibly, economic trends also contributed to the right-wing breakup—aided, ironically, by Reagan administration policies. In the long term, traditional protectionism à la the textile industry was declining with more and more firms being drawn into the international market, including firms in the ultraconservative outsider bloc. Yet this spurred defensive reactions from domestic-oriented producers feeling increasingly threatened. In addition, the automobile and computer industries, among others that were once dominant internationally, faced rising foreign competition. Such industries sometimes wanted high tariffs on imports, but sometimes they wanted government research subsidies or help getting access to overseas markets, which is rather different from traditional economic isolationism.

The Reagan administration helped intensify business conflict over issues of economic nationalism during the 1980s, with monetary policies that encouraged a flood of imports and foreign investments into the United States. This expanded the business constituency that had a stake in an integrated international economy. In the process, however, it brought outrage, often misdirected, from those who faced business failures or feared that "Japan, Inc." was taking over America.[27]

The resurgence of economic nationalist sentiment was part of the context in which paleoconservatives launched their attack on neoconservatism in the late 1980s and in which paleocon Pat Buchanan opposed President George Bush in the 1992 Republican primaries. Both campaigns were efforts to resuscitate the kind of isolationist and nativist Right that had been led by Midwestern business nationalists half a century before. In paleocon eyes, Bush represented the sinister Eastern elite, whereas neocons were Jewish "dual loyalists" beholden to Tel Aviv and closet liberals who had infiltrated the Right. Buchanan's campaign platform of classic anti–New Deal isolationism condemned not only the welfare state and "the tax burden on American business" but also foreign aid and the stationing of "vast permanent U.S. armies on foreign soil." Buchanan said of Bush: "He is a globalist and we are nationalists. He believes in some *Pax Universalis*; we believe in the Old Republic. He would put America's wealth and power at the service of some vague New World Order; we will put America first."[28]

Unfortunately for Buchanan's campaign coffers, not much was left of the business constituency that had backed the Nazi-infested "America First" movement in 1940–1941. Although Roger Milliken and the USBIC endorsed Buchanan, few others from the CNP orbit joined them. Most New Right leaders stayed silent or backed George Bush, if reluctantly. Like Richard Gephardt in 1988, who campaigned for the Democratic presidential nomination as an economic nationalist, Buchanan found that a direct challenge to free-trade orthodoxy cut him off from major sources of capitalist support.[29]

Another split-off from the New Right that appealed to business nationalist traditions was the U.S. Taxpayers Party (USTP). After unsuccessfully trying to recruit Buchanan as its candidate, the USTP fielded Howard Phillips for president in 1992 and 1996. The USTP brought together several overlapping political clusters, including Phillips's Conservative Caucus, the American Independent Party (originated by George Wallace in 1968), and the most militant wing of the antiabortion movement, including Randall Terry of Operation Rescue. USTP ideology was a sort of militarized Christian libertarianism, rooted in both the John Birch and "states rights" (segregationist) traditions of uncompromising hostility to federal government authority. USTP leaders urged formation of armed militias and death to abortion providers.[30]

The USTP called for "deconstructing the post–Civil War [!] legacy of neo-Marxist welfare-state liberalism and moral decadence." Specifically,

Business Conflict and Right-Wing Movements 95

it urged abolition of the income tax, Social Security, the Federal Reserve, the civil service, the Voting Rights Act, and bilingual ballots and withdrawal from the UN, the International Monetary Fund (IMF), and the World Bank. Phillips even called for abolishing public schools because they teach "atheism," "humanism," and "sexual promiscuity." The USTP denounced the North American Free Trade Agreement (NAFTA) as a loss of sovereignty and a boon to "multinational megaliths" at the expense of small business. Although it supported a strong military, including a space defense system, the party wanted to reduce federal police forces. The USTP received contributions from a number of CNP members, including Richard Viguerie, Birch Society leader William Cies, and William Ball, of the family that controls the Ball Corporation (a former Star Wars contractor) but apparently did not attract much capitalist interest.[31]

The FCF and the Heritage Foundation, New Right coalition builders, held a sort of middle position in the feud between neocons and paleocons. Despite their cultural and ideological affinities with the paleocons, these organizations leaned overall more toward the neocon side of the dispute, refusing to abandon right-wing internationalism or pro-Zionism. For example, Robert Krieble of the FCF board of directors contributed money to Buchanan's campaign but disagreed with his isolationist politics. Krieble dismissed protectionism as "a loser" and as "short-term stuff" out of touch with the logic of capitalism:

> [It]'s a trend, a worldwide trend among . . . all businessmen to follow the market, and the market has become global. And so if you want to build a successful company . . . then in some ways the most profitable way to take advantage of that is to sell on the world market wherever you are accepted. . . . So, all businessmen who operate global companies are losing their nationality. Nations are losing their stature in the society of the new world.[32]

The collapse of the Soviet bloc, Krieble noted, enormously enlarged the potential size of the global capitalist market. His Krieble Institute, affiliated with the FCF, conducted political training seminars for rightists in Eastern Europe and the former Soviet Union. Krieble was himself the retired chairman of Loctite Corporation, a multinational chemical company, and has been a member of the CNP executive committee.

Pat Robertson's Christian Coalition also tried to steer between nationalist and multinationalist positions. Founded in 1989 after Robertson's unsuccessful bid for the Republican presidential nomination, the Christian Coalition combined the financial and propaganda resources of Robertson's media empire with solid grassroots activism to create a powerful mass organization oriented toward winning control of the Republican Party. Thus the coalition had an interest in cultivating friendly relations with at least some of the multinational capitalists who dominate the major parties, without antagonizing its own mass base, which has been largely sympathetic to paleoconservatism. Nor did the coalition want to alienate the Sun Belt outsider capitalists who have traditionally provided the core of evangelical Christianity's business support.

Echoing the paleocons, the Christian Coalition warned against a "New World Order" and the threat of U.S. sovereignty being surrendered to international institutions.[33] Robertson's 1991 bestseller *The New World Order* announced that the Council on Foreign Relations was the center of "a behind-the-scenes Establishment" with "enormous power," seeking to establish a world government and managed economy dominated by bankers. The Establishment had used Marxism as a tool for achieving this goal. In Robertson's account, Jewish bankers such as the Rothschilds and Paul Warburg, along with British imperialists such as Cecil Rhodes, featured prominently as members of the generations-old conspiracy. This rehash of Birch Society and Liberty Lobby themes was scrupulously faithful to outsider capital's traditions of Anglophobia, hatred of Wall Street, and furtive anti-Semitism.[34]

Yet Robertson and the Christian Coalition avoided identifying themselves too closely with paleoconservative positions. Despite the anti-Semitism inherent in his claim that the United States is a "Christian nation," Robertson has long used his strong pro-Zionism to build an alliance with right-wing Jews (though some groups, such as the Anti-Defamation League, eventually criticized *The New World Order*). After denouncing George Bush in 1991 as an unwitting tool of Satan, Robertson turned around and endorsed the incumbent president (and not Buchanan) in 1992.[35] The following year, Christian Coalition leaders joined the multinational establishment in supporting NAFTA and described its passage as one of the few positive steps taken by Bill Clinton's administration. This was a risky move, given their own supporters' leanings. Pat Buchanan was warmly applauded by the Christian Coalition's 1993 annual conference when he denounced NAFTA, and coalition executive director Ralph Reed publicly admitted that such criticism might lead the Christian Coalition to deemphasize its NAFTA position.[36]

But as an international businessman, Robertson had a direct stake in supporting NAFTA. Not only was his nonprofit Christian Broadcasting Network operating in dozens of countries, including Russia, China, and in the Middle East, but his for-profit International Family Entertainment (IFE) had also begun broadcasts in Europe as well as in the United States. *Newsweek* commented that Robertson "likes the [NAFTA] treaty's provision protecting intellectual property—including the television shows and movie syndicates."[37]

In addition to the much-publicized sex scandals involving televangelists Jim Bakker and Jimmy Swaggart, Robertson's 1988 presidential campaign had been hurt by a fall in oil prices and probably by the collapse of the real-estate market, which affected the Sun Belt oil and land entrepreneurs closely tied to Christian Right causes.[38] In 1989, Robertson reduced his financial dependence on Sun Belt outsider capital by creating IFE as a for-profit spin-off from CBN. In the process, Robertson formed a partnership with John Malone's Tele-Communications Inc. (TCI), the largest cable system operator in the United States and one of the most powerful companies in the cutting-edge field of information technology.[39] The full implications of this move remain to be seen, but it has significantly changed the Christian Coalition's relationship with the business community.

Confronting the Right, Confronting Elites

As I have argued, conflicts between capitalist factions have played an important role in shaping right-wing politics. For several decades, ultraconservative forces were sustained by business outsiders hostile to the prevailing New Deal system. The rise of a broad coalition spearheaded by the New Right temporarily submerged many of these conflicts, as outsider capitalists found common ground with right-wing multinationalists. But the end of the cold war helped reopen old political fissures within the business community, contributing to a fragmentation of the Right that began in the late 1980s. Such tensions were evident in the Right's disunity over the Gulf War and in the economic and social-cultural debates between ultraconservative Pat Buchanan and multinationalist-oriented candidates in the 1992 and 1996 Republican presidential primaries.

There are many topics that I could not address in this limited study, such as the role of business forces in promoting (and, in some cases, opposing) anti-immigrant racism or the contradictory relationship between capitalist interests and paramilitary rightists such as the Aryan Nations or the militia movement. Business conflict certainly does not explain everything about right-wing politics, but it offers a useful analytic tool, and there is much work to be done in this area, as capitalist factions continue to reconfigure and shift their political leanings.

As we develop strategies for confronting and reversing the right-wing attack, business conflict analysis is important for several reasons. For one thing, it helps alert us to the ways in which antielitist appeals can be used by business factions not only as empty rhetoric but to serve their own bids for power. This is particularly true of appeals that treat oppression as a conspiracy rather than an entrenched system of rule. In recent years, some left-leaning people have endorsed and promoted such conspiracism without considering its implications and in the process have lent credibility to right-wing ideology.

Business conflict analysis also points to divisions within the capitalist class that can sometimes be exploited by antioppression movements. Both the labor movement in the 1930s and the civil rights movement in the 1950s and 1960s won important gains partly because they did not face a united front of ruling-class opposition. In both cases, a large section of the power structure was intransigent, but another faction (tied to the multinationalist bloc) was prepared to make limited concessions under pressure from a sustained, militant popular movement. This is how reforms are often won. But the flip side of these examples is also important. Elites successfully contained the radicalizing potential of both the 1930s labor movement and the 1960s civil rights movement through a combination of co-optation and repression. Both movements were vulnerable to this tactic, in part, because some of their leaders were willing to place their faith in elite-controlled institutions as agents of social change.

It would be dangerous for us to base an antirightist strategy on a "moderate," "liberal," or "democratic" wing of big business. All factions of capital share a material stake in preserving a social order that is inherently oppressive and undemocratic. Genuine democracy is not achievable within a capitalist framework. Time and time again, social change movements have placed their trust in elite-controlled institutions, including the state, and time and time again this trust has been betrayed. Lasting change that benefits the oppressed can only be won by strong, autonomous social movements.

Notes

An earlier version of this article was prepared as a background report for the Blue Mountain Working Group in November 1994. Thanks to the following people and organizations for help in preparing this article: Amy Ansell, Russ Bellant, Chip Berlet, Fred Clarkson, Sandi DuBowski, John Goetz, David Lyons, Sandra Lyons, Suzanne Pharr, the Women's Project, Political Research Associates, Planned Parenthood Federation of America's Public Policy Institute, and the reference staff at Cornell University's Johnson Graduate School of Management Library. Special thanks to Jamie Buss for emergency technical assistance. Any errors of fact or interpretation herein are my responsibility.

1. For works that have helped to shape my understanding of business conflict analysis, see Franz Schurmann, *The Logic of World Power: An Inquiry into the Origins, Currents, and Contradictions of World Politics* (New York: Random House; Pantheon Books, 1974), esp. pp. 48–60; Thomas Ferguson, *Golden Rule: The Investment Theory of Party Competition and the Logic of Money-Driven Political Systems* (Chicago: University of Chicago Press, 1995); Thomas Ferguson and Joel Rogers, *Right Turn: The Decline of the Democrats and the Future of American Politics* (New York: Farrar, Straus and Giroux/Hill and Wang, 1986); Bruce Cumings, *The Ori-*

Business Conflict and Right-Wing Movements

gins of the Korean War, vol. 2, *The Roaring of the Cataract, 1947–1950* (Princeton: Princeton University Press, 1990), esp. chaps. 2 and 3; Mike Davis, *Prisoners of the American Dream: Politics and Economy in the History of the U.S. Working Class* (London: Verso, 1986); Amy Ansell, "Business Mobilization and the New Right: Currents in U.S. Foreign Policy," in *Business and the State in International Relations*, ed. Ronald W. Cox (Boulder: Westview Press, 1996); Thomas Bodenheimer and Robert Gould, *Rollback! Right-Wing Power in U.S. Foreign Policy* (Boston: South End Press, 1989); David N. Gibbs, *The Political Economy of Third World Intervention: Mines, Money, and U.S. Policy in the Congo Crisis* (Chicago: University of Chicago Press, 1991); and Ronald W. Cox, *Power and Profits: U.S. Policy in Central America* (Lexington: University of Press of Kentucky, 1994).

2. This discussion of the rise of the New Deal system and of the business factions that supported and opposed it is based on Ferguson, *Golden Rule*, chaps. 2 and 4; Ferguson and Rogers, *Right Turn*, pp. 48–50; Schurmann, *Logic*, pp. 48–60; Cumings, *Origins*, vol. 2, chaps. 2 and 3; and Davis, *Prisoners*, pp. 163–167. On U.S. trade relations with the Third World under the New Deal system, see Gabriel Kolko, *Confronting the Third World: United States Foreign Policy, 1945–1980* (New York: Pantheon Books/Random House, 1988), pp. 107, 119, 151, 292.

3. Early members of this multinationalist bloc included Standard Oil of New Jersey (now Exxon), Royal Dutch Shell, Standard Oil of California (now Chevron), General Electric, Reynolds Tobacco, American Tobacco, IBM, ITT, Mead Paper, Pan Am, and the Filene merchants, along with banks such as Brown Brothers Harriman, Chase National, Dillon Read, Goldman Sachs, Lehman Brothers, and Bank of America.

4. On the right-wing attack on the Eastern establishment during the early Cold War, see Cumings, *Origins*, pp. 106–117. On business forces supporting and opposing Joe McCarthy, see ibid., pp. 91–92; Philip H. Burch Jr., "The NAM as an Interest Group," *Politics and Society* (Fall 1973), p. 118n; Burch, *Elites in American History*, vol. 3, *The New Deal to the Carter Administration* (New York: Holmes and Meier Publishers, 1980), p. 149; Charles J. V. Murphy, "McCarthy and the Businessman," *Fortune* 44, no. 4 (April 1954), esp. p. 184; Murphy, "Texas Business and McCarthy," *Fortune* 44, no. 5 (May 1954).

5. On business interests and the John Birch Society, see Burch, "The NAM as an Interest Group," pp. 97–130, esp. pp. 120–129.

6. On business interests and the Goldwater campaign, see Ferguson and Rogers, *Right Turn*, p. 53; Burch "NAM," pp. 115 n.39, 120n, 124, 126–127; and Burch, *Elites*, vol. 3, p. 224 n. 98. On Schlafly, see Phyllis Schlafly, *A Choice Not An Echo* (Alton, IL: Pere Marquette Press, 1964).

7. The following discussion of the rise of Sunbelt outsider capital is based on Davis, *Prisoners*, pp. 167–176; and Ferguson and Rogers, *Right Turn*, pp. 91–92.

8. Thomas Byrne Edsall, *The New Politics of Inequality* (New York: W. W. Norton and Company, 1984), p. 99.

9. Ibid., p. 101.

10. See Russ Bellant, *The Coors Connection: How Coors Family Philanthropy Undermines Democratic Pluralism* (Boston: South End Press and Political Research Associates, 1991), p. 2; and Sara Diamond, *Spiritual Warfare: The Politics of the Christian Right* (Boston: South End Press, 1989), pp. 13, 53.

100   *Matthew N. Lyons*

11. This discussion of the changes that pulled many multinationalists to the right is based on M. Patricia Marchak, *The Integrated Circus: The New Right and the Restructuring of Global Markets* (Montreal and Kingston: McGill-Queen's University Press, 1991), esp. pp. 3–14; Samuel Bowles, David M. Gordon, and Thomas E. Weisskopf, *After the Wasteland: A Democratic Economics for the Year 2000* (Armonk, NY: M. E. Sharpe, 1990), pp. 63–95; Ferguson and Rogers, *Right Turn*, chap. 3; Gabriel Kolko, *Anatomy of a War: Vietnam, the United States, and the Modern Historical Experience* (New York: Pantheon Books/Random House, 1985), pp. 283–290; and Joseph G. Peschek, *Policy-Planning Organizations: Elite Agendas and America's Rightward Turn* (Philadelphia: Temple University Press, 1987), esp. pp. 46–72.

12. Important New Right organizations included the Committee for the Survival of a Free Congress (later renamed the Free Congress Foundation), the Heritage Foundation, the Conservative Caucus, the National Conservative Political Action Committee, the Eagle Forum, Accuracy in Media, the National Legal Center for the Public Interest, *Conservative Digest*, and the National Right-to-Life Committee. The movement also drew in a number of older organizations such as the American Enterprise Institute, the American Security Council, Young Americans for Freedom, and the American Conservative Union. Closely tied with the New Right were Christian Right organizations such as the Moral Majority and Christian Voice. Also allied were neoconservatives through such organs as the Committee on the Present Danger, the Coalition for a Democratic Majority, and the magazine *Commentary*.

On corporate funding for right-wing organizations and campaigns in this period, see Dan Morgan, "Conservatives: A Well-Financed Network," *Washington Post*, January 4, 1981; Institute for Southern Studies' Campaign Finance Project, "Jesse Helms: The Meaning of His Money," *Southern Exposure* 13, no. 1 (January–February 1985), pp. 17, 21; Peter H. Stone, "The Counter-Intelligentsia: The 'Free-Enterprise' Think Tanks and the Holy War on Government," *Village Voice*, October 22, 1979; and Larry D. Hatfield and Dexter Waugh, "Where Think Tanks Get Their Money," *San Francisco Examiner*, May 26, 1992.

13. On the middle-class insurgency of the 1970s, see Davis, *Prisoners*, pp. 225–228.

14. Ibid., pp. 170–171.

15. On the tax revolt, see Thomas Byrne Edsall with Mary D. Edsall, *Chain Reaction: The Impact of Race, Rights, and Taxes on American Politics* (New York: W. W. Norton and Company, 1991); and Ferguson and Rogers, *Right Turn*, pp. 102ff.

16. The following discussion of Reagan administration actions is based on Ferguson and Rogers, *Right Turn*, chap. 4. See also Sara Diamond, *Roads to Dominion: Right-Wing Movements and Political Power in the United States* (New York: Guilford Press, 1995), pp. 212–227.

17. Ferguson, *Golden Rule*, pp. 244–245.

18. Ibid., p. 250; Diamond, *Roads*, p. 225.

19. On business support to the AEI, see Peschek, *Policy-Planning*, pp. 28–29; James A. Smith, *The Idea Brokers: Think Tanks and the Rise of the New Policy Elite* (New York: Free Press/Macmillan, 1991), pp. 181–182.

20. Peschek, *Policy-Planning*, p. 30.

21. On the neoconservatives, see Diamond, *Roads*, pp. 178–202, 275.

22. Sources for this discussion of the CNP include: Russ Bellant, "Secretive Rightwing Group: The Council for National Policy," *Covert Action* 34 (Summer

1990), p. 17; Bellant, "The Council for National Policy: Stealth Leadership of the Radical Right," *Front Lines Research* 1, no. 2 (August 1994), p. 7; Council for National Policy Board of Governors membership list, 1984; CNP Membership Directory, 1988; the Lotus "One Source" databases for U.S. public and private companies; *International Directory of Company Histories*, vols. 1–9 (Chicago and Detroit: St. James Press, 1988–1994); *Who's Who in America*, various editions (Wilmette, IL: Albert Nelson Marquis, Macmillan Directory Division); and Burch, *Elites*, vol. 3.

23. Major business-affiliated CNP members included Howard Ahmanson (heir to the Ahmanson savings and loan fortune); John M. Belk (department stores); Joe, Holly, and Jeffrey Coors (brewing); Oliver Delchamps (supermarkets); Nancy S. DeMoss (insurance); Rich DeVos (co-owner of Amway); Pierre S. Du Pont IV (chemicals, oil, etc.); Jack Eckerd (drugstores); Langdon Flowers (baked goods); J. Peter Grace (W. R. Grace conglomerate); the brothers Herbert and Nelson Bunker Hunt (oil); Linda Bean Jones (L. L. Bean); Robert Krieble (Loctite chemicals); Lewis Lehrman (Morgan Stanley investment bank); Paul D. Meek (Petrofina, a Belgian oil company); Roger Milliken (textiles); Ed Prince (auto parts); James Richards (Southwire, wire and cable manufacture); and Thomas A. Roe (building materials).

24. "R. Marc Nuttle: Biographical Sketch" (c. 1993), one-page photocopy distributed by author and furnished by the Krieble Institute, Washington, D.C.

25. On Richard Mellon Scaife, see Karen Rothmyer, "Citizen Scaife," *Columbia Journalism Review* 20, no. 2 (July-August 1981), pp. 41–50. On Heritage Foundation contributors, see Peschek, *Policy-Planning*, pp. 32–34.

26. On the paleocon-neocon feud, overall fragmentation of the right-wing coalition, and factors behind them, see Diamond, *Roads*, chap. 12.

27. See Ferguson, *Golden Rule*, pp. 246–248.

28. Patrick J. Buchanan, "Why I Am Running for President," *Human Events*, December 28, 1991, p. 11. This is the text of Buchanan's December 10, 1991, speech announcing his candidacy.

29. On the Buchanan and Gephardt campaigns, see Ferguson, *Golden Rule*, pp. 334n and 260–262, respectively.

30. John Goetz, "Missionaries' Leader Calls for Armed Militias," *Front Lines Research* 1, no. 2 (August 1994); and Goetz, "Randall Terry and the U.S. Taxpayers Party," *Front Lines Research* 1, no. 2 (August 1994).

31. "Join the U.S. Taxpayers Party!" *U.S. Taxpayers Party Quarterly Review* 1, no. 2 (Summer 1993), p. 5; "United States Taxpayers Party Abridged Platform: Excerpts from the USTP National Platform"; speech by Howard Phillips to the National Committee of the U.S. Taxpayers Party, Louisville, Kentucky, December 11–12, 1992, *USTP Quarterly Review* 1, no. 1 (Spring 1993), pp. 5–6; and "NAFTA Must Be Stopped," resolution adopted by the USTP National Committee in Denver, Colorado, May 21–22, 1993, *USTP Quarterly Review* 1, no. 2 (Summer 1993), p. 1.

32. Robert H. Krieble, interview with investigative journalist, Summer 1993. The interview with Krieble was conducted by John Goetz and took place on July 3, 1993 in Ivano-Frankivsk, Ukraine.

33. See, for example, "New World Order Threat: Keyes Warns Americans Against Complacency," interview with Alan Keyes by John Wheeler, *Christian American*, January 1994, pp. 10–11.

34. Pat Robertson, *The New World Order* (Dallas: Word Publishing, 1991). Robertson's use of anti-Semitic themes and sources in *The New World Order* did not receive significant attention in the major media until several years after the book appeared. See in particular Michael Lind, "Rev. Robertson's Grand International Conspiracy Theory," *New York Review of Books*, February 2, 1995, pp. 21–25.

35. Robertson, *New World Order*, p. 37; Joe Conason, "The Religious Right's Quiet Revival," *Nation*, April 27, 1992, p. 553.

36. Martin Mawyer, "A Rift in the Ranks of the Christian Right," *Washington Post*, National Weekly Edition, October 4–10, 1993, p. 24; Gerald F. Seib, "Christian Coalition Hopes to Expand by Taking Stands on Taxes, Crime, Health Care and Nafta," *Wall Street Journal*, September 7, 1993.

37. Howard Fineman, "God and the Grassroots," *Newsweek*, November 8, 1993, p. 45.

38. Ferguson, *Golden Rule*, p. 253.

39. My thanks to John Goetz for pointing this out. On the Robertson-TCI deal and creation of IFE, see "Family Cable Channel Switches Signals from Religious to Entertainment Fare," *Wall Street Journal*, September 24, 1990; and "An Empire on Exemptions?" *Washington Post*, February 13, 1994. On the Christian Broadcasting Network, see Diamond, *Spiritual Warfare*, pp. 12–22.

PART TWO

Ideological and Policy Currents

5

Kitchen Table Backlash: The Antifeminist Women's Movement

Jean Hardisty

Attacking the vision, policies, and programs of the contemporary women's movement has been a central theme of the Right's backlash politics. Right-wing organizations and individuals have skillfully mined the public's mixed feelings about recent changes in the role of women, promoting a "traditional values" agenda intended to maximize political opposition to feminist reforms.

In fact, the Right has gone beyond tapping the backlash against the women's movement. It has made an attack on feminists (labeled "women's libbers") the central theme of its organizing of women. Feminists are attacked as a threat to the family because they "promote" abortion, divorce, lesbianism, and, of course, the sexual revolution.

This stereotyping and scapegoating of feminists (or "femi-Nazis," to use Rush Limbaugh's term) accomplishes three goals. First, it demonizes liberals (the political sector most identified with legislation for women's rights). Second, it is a vehicle for promoting the Right's vision of family values, serving as a major front in what Pat Buchanan has called the "culture war." And third, it acts as a recruiting arm for the larger agenda of the Right. Organizing conservative women to oppose feminists creates a "women's auxiliary" of the Right.

There is no question that the contemporary women's movement has been a profound agent for change in the social, political, economic, and cultural life of the United States. Women have demanded reforms to increase their legal and economic power, advocating a revolutionary transformation in their status. This advocacy has occurred within a setting of economic change that has pushed and pulled women into the workforce, altering lifestyles, power relationships, and social attitudes.

105

Such change sometimes appears to be superficial. The women's movement has not, after all, resulted in dramatic increases in the number of women holding political office. Nor has it ended sexist discrimination and harassment in many settings. The discrepancy in salaries and wages between women and men has not changed significantly. The glass ceiling still blocks most women from promotion to top positions within the corporate world. And with very few exceptions, women still have primary responsibility for housework and child rearing, despite the veneer of the more caring husband and father.

But it is a mistake to underestimate the changes the women's movement has brought about. By questioning the traditional place of women beneath men, especially in the heterosexual nuclear family setting, feminism has challenged a bedrock value of both the Christian Right and the secular Right.

In this chapter, I will look at how women are recruited to support the larger agenda of the Right through their work in the right-wing, antifeminist women's movement. The charismatic leaders of this important movement are often little known and frequently taken for granted by the Right's male leadership. These women leaders, however, do not protest. They seem content to serve as quiet, largely unheralded political helpers to the men they support.

The women's lack of public acclaim, however, should not be mistaken for lack of importance to the Right's success. The Right is militant in its intention to reverse the progressive reforms associated with liberalism in this country. Such a drastic social redirection cannot occur unless at least a sizable sector of women, especially middle-class women, supports it. It is imperative that women be brought along and equally important that those women who object be "handled." In order to roll back the gains of the 1960s, 1970s, and 1980s, the feminists of the women's movement (and their message) must be politically neutralized.

This is not easily done, since feminism has sensitized large numbers of women to the oppressive nature of sexist discrimination and patriarchal domination—both central to the Right's agenda. The Right's leadership recognizes feminist consciousness as a major threat. Neutralizing that threat is best done by women, who can don a mantle of legitimacy when speaking and organizing against feminism. Women's leadership within the Right also symbolically refutes feminism by upholding women who collaborate with the very forces identified by feminism as the source of women's oppression.

The antifeminist women's movement is also important for its concrete achievements, though these are difficult to measure accurately. Much of the evidence of the effectiveness of the movement's political work is anecdotal and of necessity relies heavily on the organizations' own self-reporting, in fund-raising pitches and public relations materials. However, one reasonable indicator is the success of campaigns in which the organizations participated publicly. Two organizations that dominate the contemporary right-wing women's movement (Phyllis Schlafly's Eagle Forum and Beverly LaHaye's Concerned Women for America) have conducted innumerable successful campaigns in support of right-wing causes. Beginning with the defeat of the Equal Rights Amendment in 1982, these include support for the military buildup of the 1980s, attacks on the Department of Education and the National Endowment for the Arts, defeat of the Clinton health care reform plan, and attacks on sex education in the schools, to name only a few.

Profile of the Movement

Phyllis Schlafly is the name most often associated with the antifeminist women's movement. Schlafly is the founder of Eagle Forum, the oldest and best-known of the mass-based right-wing women's organizations. After founding Eagle Forum in 1967, Schlafly went on to found STOP ERA in 1972. She reigned as grande dame of the antifeminist Right until 1977, the year designated by the United Nations as International Women's Year, when Beverly LaHaye, a professional right-wing Christian organizer, launched her explicitly Christian women's organization, Concerned Women for America. In the 1990s, CWA is larger and more influential than Eagle Forum, and LaHaye and Schlafly compete for dominance of the antifeminist women's movement.

STOP ERA, Eagle Forum, and CWA all flourished during the early years of the Reagan administration. As the right wing of the Republican Party—the institutional base of the New Right—consolidated its power under Reagan, social issues were at the center of the agenda. With the defeat of the Equal Rights Amendment in 1982, STOP ERA declared victory and closed. Eagle Forum and Concerned Women for America continued to grow in numbers and influence, as each organization was influential in the Right's campaign to press for legislation rolling back the social changes of the 1960s and 1970s.

Eagle Forum, Concerned Women for America, and the Reagan administration all benefited from the work of two individual right-wing theorists, Connaught (Connie) Marshner of the Free Congress Research and Education Foundation and Onalee McGraw of the Heritage Foundation, who broke much of the analytical ground for the Right's public policy on family values.[1] Drawing on the policy implications of Marshner's and McGraw's work, the administration and its congressional supporters pushed antifeminist and antigay legislative initiatives on many fronts. The most comprehensive piece of legislation proposed was the Family

Protection Act, which was repeatedly debated in Congress but was never actually passed. After playing their critically important role, both Marshner and McGraw dropped from public view. Though the Reagan administration was unable to deliver all of the changes demanded by the Right's social agenda, it gave every encouragement and succor to the Right's family values initiatives, and it did succeed in defunding abortion for poor women.

As the country entered the 1990s, journalists more often identified the Right's organizing around family values as a conservative *Christian* agenda, reflecting the Christian Right's increasing power within the larger right wing. There were two reasons for this shift in the balance of power away from the secular New Right leadership and toward conservative evangelical activists of the Christian Right. First, the Christian Right proved to be more effective at organizing at the grassroots level. It had an advantage, of course, in that its potential recruits are already organized into churches, making it easier to speak to them about family values and the threat of liberalism. Second, this sector of the Republican Party was the most aggressive in recruiting new activists to enter politics. The organizing done by Pat Robertson, through his organization the Christian Coalition, took the early work of Jerry Falwell to new heights of political power and influence. As the Right's infrastructure grew and diversified and the Christian Right gained new prominence and influence, the right-wing women's movement followed suit. CWA became larger and more well known.

Another right-wing attack came from academic women, who began to publish books and articles questioning the principal tenets of the women's movement. Eventually these women spawned an entire new wing of the antifeminist women's movement, mounting a powerful attack on women's studies and its underlying feminist principles. The handful of academic women who have made a career of attacking not just the work of feminist scholars but the practice of women's studies itself have written books and articles that inevitably have become the subject of debate within women's studies departments and courses. At the head of the pack is Camille Paglia, a self-confessed attention-grabber based at the University of the Arts in Philadelphia. Paglia is part professor and part performance artist and has turned her loud, cranky critique of feminists as prudish misfits and victims into a media career. Paglia has been joined by other critics of women's studies, most notably Christina Hoff Sommers, whose book *Who Stole Feminism?* was heavily supported and promoted by conservative foundations.[2] This support won Sommers a place at the table on countless television talk shows.

Sommers has been joined by other disaffected academic women, including Daphne Patai and Noretta Koertge, two veterans of women's studies who have jointly written an angry attack on their former affiliation titled *Professing Feminism*.[3] Elizabeth Fox-Genovese has promoted a similar critique of women's studies in *Feminism Is Not the Story of My Life*.[4] Alumni who oppose the acceptance of feminism and multiculturalism on the campuses of their alma maters have formed organizations with names such as Ivy Leaguers for Freedom and the National Alumni Forum. These organizations give voice and clout to conservative alumni who want to reverse the increase in racial and sexual diversity that has come to their (usually elite) campuses. In all cases, women's studies is a major target of this organizing.[5]

Conservative academic women are not comfortable with either the middle-class grassroots warriors of Eagle Forum or the evangelical Christian ladies of Concerned Women for America. They need their own voice and have generated a new organization to speak for them—the Women's Freedom Network (WFN). Working hand-in-hand with WFN is the Independent Women's Forum, designed to influence media coverage of the progress of women toward equality. Calling themselves "equality feminists," these women abhor all discussion of women as victims, refusing to accept that women as a class are oppressed. They believe in competing for status and success without regard to gender considerations and are viciously disdainful of women who consider gender a factor in their personal or career advancement.[6]

Ideologically, the academic sector of right-wing women is located between classical liberalism and libertarianism. Adherents to classical liberalism, as distinct from New Deal liberalism, believe first and foremost in individual freedom. Like libertarianism, classical liberalism is opposed to "big government" and supports the economic and political freedom of the individual above all else. Sometimes called "laissez-faire conservatives," these women are less extreme on social issues but vehemently opposed to feminist solutions—such as affirmative action, comparable pay, or mandatory day care—for economic and political problems.[7]

There is surprisingly little cross-fertilization within or among the sectors of the antifeminist women's movement. Each sector talks to itself, the media, and the sector of the Right to which it relates. For instance, academic women do not relate well to Newt Gingrich and the crude right-wing politics of the New Right. Their ambitions lie within academia, though they do promote their message publicly through the media.

The more political organizations of the movement, represented by Eagle Forum and CWA, reflect the ideology and agenda of specific sectors of the Right and relate to them on an ongoing basis. Eagle Forum acts as an arm of the Buchanan-Helms branch of the New Right, whose adherents are sometimes called paleoconservatives. This wing is so far right that it is barely contained within the New Right. CWA, by contrast, acts as an arm of the Christian Right.

In fifteen years of observation, I have never seen Phyllis Schlafly and Beverly LaHaye together in the same room. I have never heard or seen them refer to each other. I have never seen the Women's Freedom Network tell its members about either Eagle Forum or Concerned Women for America. In fact, in its recent publication *Neither Victim Nor Enemy*, Rita Simmons, the organizational head and prime mover of WFN, misspelled Beverly LaHaye's name.[8]

Who Are the Antifeminists?

Phyllis Schlafly's Eagle Forum and Beverly LaHaye's Concerned Women for America are the Right's answer to liberal mass-based women's organizations such as the National Organization for Women (NOW) and the National Abortion and Reproductive Rights Action League (NARAL). They are an integral part of the right-wing political movement currently in ascendance in the United States. As such, they are enjoying new levels of power and influence.

In the mid-1970s, I began to try to understand the antifeminist women who organized against the ERA. Led by Phyllis Schlafly's STOP ERA, these were often evangelical and fundamentalist Protestant Christians, as well as conservative Catholics, whose religious beliefs led them to oppose equality for women. Their work against the ERA was motivated by alarm and fear that it would create a legal mechanism for the ongoing violation of God's will. As they were told by Schlafly, the role of women as helpmates to their husbands was set by biblical law—a message often reiterated by their pastors and ministers.

It is not difficult to understand why women would oppose social change that violates their religious beliefs. For those who make political decisions using a religious yardstick, there is a long history of voting for the candidate or referendum that matches their religious convictions, be they conservative or liberal. But beyond that, I was curious to know what made these anti-ERA women become activists, especially given that their conservative religious beliefs would not naturally encourage activities outside the home, especially in the public political sphere.

In studying STOP ERA, I discovered a formula that has worked for the Right to this day. A charismatic woman, known for her savvy and wisdom and accepted and loved as a natural leader, recruits women around close-to-home issues (such as the potential for the ERA to result in same-sex bathrooms or daughters drafted into military combat), then gives them an organizing model that does not require them to leave their homes, thus allowing them to stay in a safe and familiar place (meetings around the kitchen table is a favorite). Gradually some women begin to stand out and become trusted lieutenants, and they are identified and rewarded as such by the charismatic leader. As familiarity develops and momentum builds, the agenda of the organizing effort broadens to include the wider agenda of the Right. The members are thus formed into an arm of the Right.

Questions about these women have haunted me ever since the anti-ERA campaign. Could they have been recruited by pro-ERA forces if their concerns had been addressed directly? Was it Schlafly's organizing style that proved attractive, or was it her message itself? Why was it so easy for Schlafly to paint ERA supporters as the enemy? I did not see the ERA as a threat to them but as a help to all women. Why did we see things so differently?

Phyllis Schlafly

Phyllis Schlafly is a lawyer and intellectual whose politics were heavily influenced by her late husband, Fred Schlafly. Twenty years her senior, he was a prominent member of the Old Right, obsessed with Old Right themes—paranoid anticommunism, bitter opposition to New Deal reforms, and rage over the loss of the Panama Canal.[9] The Schlaflys' politics mirrored those of the John Birch Society. Researchers have yet to settle just how closely affiliated with the notorious and discredited JBS Phyllis Schlafly was in the 1960s and 1970s.

STOP ERA was not Phyllis Schlafly's first service to the right wing of the Republican Party. She had earlier written a book during Barry Goldwater's campaign for the Republican nomination in the 1964 presidential election. Titled *A Choice Not an Echo*, it promoted Goldwater as a genuine conservative who would overthrow once and for all the politics-as-usual pattern of the Democratic-controlled Congress. The book is often identified as the factor that allowed Goldwater to capture the nomination.[10]

After Goldwater's disastrous defeat, Schlafly founded Eagle Forum and led the campaign to oppose International Women's Year in 1977, which she painted as dominated by hateful women's libbers who did not represent the majority of American women. In this battle she began to knit together the three principal themes of antifeminism: opposition to abortion, to the ERA, and to equality for women. During the 1970s, Schlafly developed—and delivered to the New Right leadership—"the political gold of misogyny."[11]

But Schlafly soon became trapped in the political realm of women's issues and, later, children's education. Despite her five books on defense and foreign policy, to this day she is seldom recognized for her expertise on defense issues. In the 1970s, Schlafly was nearly alone in defending and promoting General Daniel O. Graham in his far-out Star Wars program to defend the United States from intercontinental missiles. Graham's scheme is still being funded, despite the end of the cold war. Rumors that Schlafly wanted to be secretary of defense in the first Reagan administration were not even dignified with comment, though she undoubtedly knows more about defense than many men who have served in that job.

Nor was Schlafly ever properly rewarded by the Republicans for the service she performed in defeating the ERA. During the Reagan administrations, when she might have received such a reward, the only crumb thrown her way was a seat on the Commission on the Bicentennial of the Constitution. One explanation for this slight is that Schlafly had done her job too well. Once the Republicans gained power, Schlafly's outspokenness became a political liability. A shrewd and invaluable strategist of the Old Right and the New Right, Schlafly has been used and taken for granted by the male leadership of her movement and her party. In reviewing Phyllis Schlafly's career during the 1980s, it becomes intriguing to ask how Schlafly failed to translate her success into real power and how Beverly LaHaye succeeded in overtaking her.

The answer lies in part in the complex character of Phyllis Schlafly, but also in the somewhat old-fashioned nature of her right-wing politics. Schlafly has never been able to take two steps that are crucial to becoming truly influential in politics in the 1980s and 1990s. First, she has not aggressively pursued media exposure. Though Schlafly enjoys occasional media coverage by dint of her status as the mother of the right-wing women's movement (and most recently as a spokesperson for Pat Buchanan), she has not done what other New Right leaders have done—create her own media outlet to circumvent the mainstream media. Her once-a-week radio feature is modest by the Right's standards of media exposure. In fact, public relations and promotional material have never been her strong suit.

Schlafly's newsletter, a remarkably plain and simple four-page two-color affair titled the *Phyllis Schlafly Report,* has not changed its format in fifteen years. Although Schlafly's photo does appear in the masthead and the text (consisting entirely of a long feature article) is still written by Schlafly, these promotions of herself as the leader and visionary of the organization are modest by right-wing standards. Not that Schlafly shrinks from leadership or fame, but her particular brand of charisma stems from her career as a lawyer and intellectual. Her patrician manner and dignified self-presentation are similar to the style of the exclusive Daughters of the American Revolution. As an example of her leadership style, Eagle Forum offers a ten-day cruise on the Crystal Harmony, "probably the most beautiful ship afloat," in April 1996, complete with seminars on board by Schlafly herself. The cost of the cabins per person ranges from $2,399 to $9,930.

The Antifeminist Women's Movement 113

The second step Schlafly has not taken toward greater personal power and political leverage is to grow beyond her roots in the Old Right. True to those roots, Schlafly has always been an isolationist, a ferocious anticommunist, a strong defense advocate, unyieldingly antiabortion, and an opponent of free trade and big government. This particular mix of Old Right commitments (for which she gets strong support from her principal political sponsor, Senator Jesse Helms of North Carolina) has left her slightly askew from the ideological profile of the New Right. New Right ideological commitments tend to represent a slight revision of Old Right ideology. Anticommunism is common to both the New Right and the Old Right, but the New Right focuses much more explicitly on family values themes and on domestic economic policy. Its family values themes are built around opposition to abortion, divorce, sex education in the schools, and homosexuality; and advocacy for prayer in the schools, parental rights, and the preservation of gender roles. Although Old Right ideologues supported each of these family values, they did not place them at the center of their political agenda.

New Right domestic policy themes include reducing the budget deficit, abolishing government-imposed regulations, destroying unions, and reducing taxes. Old Right domestic themes were internal subversion by communist sympathizers, support for free-market capitalism, and opposition to New Deal reform programs. Again, there is a great deal of overlap, but a subtle difference in emphasis. The policies of the Old Right tended to benefit wealthy Brahmin Republicans. Those of the New Right tend to benefit the smaller, newer corporate entrepreneurs, sometimes known as "venture capitalists," as well as "old money" Republicans. Both ideologies threaten the interests of working-class and middle-class voters, but the New Right conceals this fact cleverly by highlighting the family values themes that enjoy widespread popularity with these same voters.

Schlafly has not been able to meld completely with the New Right. Though a brilliant political innovator, architect, and strategist, she has not been able to change her politics and her style with the times. For this reason, she has not been elevated as she might have been. However, Phyllis Schlafly's Old Right politics are not yet a thing of the past. They may not be dominant, but they are enjoying a rejuvenation in the angry, antigovernment rhetoric of Ross Perot's Reform Party and the militia movement.

Of all those currently competing for leadership of the Republican Party, Schlafly's politics are closest to those of Pat Buchanan, another Old Rightist who has been unwilling to sign onto the New Right style. Schlafly and Buchanan share a commitment to political isolationism, to right-wing anticorporate free-market populism, an ever-increasing defense budget, protectionist trade principles, and opposition to multiculturalism. Further, they are both vehemently antiabortion (Schlafly, a Roman Catholic, is the national chairman of the Republican National Coalition for Life) and is adamantly opposed to "secular humanism."

As Buchanan has become more prominent politically, Schlafly has been quick to affiliate with him. Only two days after Buchanan's victory in the 1996 New Hampshire primary, Phyllis Schlafly endorsed Buchanan at a news conference in Columbia, South Carolina.[12] Should Buchanan's brand of Old Right ideology take hold within the Republican Party, he may prove the ally that Schlafly needs to finally gain the power and recognition that she has not received from the New Right. More likely, her affiliation with Buchanan, like her close association with Senator Jesse Helms (R–NC), will continue to leave her marginalized.

Beverly LaHaye

Concerned Women for America, the "other" mass-based right-wing women's organization, is larger and more media savvy than Eagle Forum. Its budget is larger and it is arguably more influential. Its leader, Beverly LaHaye, now challenges Phyllis Schlafly's status as grande dame of the movement. Yet she is little known to feminists and even less known to the general public. CWA's budget is at least eight times that of Eagle Forum. More than three times as many members attend the CWA annual conference as attend Eagle Forum's annual conference. Eagle Forum claims a membership of 80,000 members, compared with CWA's claim of between 600,000 and 700,000. Both claims are undoubtedly inflated, but they do accurately reflect the greater wealth and mobilizing power of CWA. It is sobering to compare these membership figures with the National Organization for Women's estimated membership of 250,000.

Beverly LaHaye reached this pinnacle of women's organizing by a combination of being in the right place at the right time and knowing how to maximize her political impact through electronic media and slick public relations. LaHaye is the wife of Dr. Tim LaHaye, a cofounder of the Moral Majority and a well-known leader within the Christian Right. The LaHayes for years conducted profit-making Family Life Seminars with Christian couples, where they honed their family values themes. They have long belonged to the network of Christian Right organizations that came into its own within the Republican Party during the 1990s. In fact, it could be argued that they represent the far edge of the Christian Right. Both have been members of the board of directors of the Coalition on Revival, an organization that promotes the idea that the United States be governed by biblical law.[13]

Unlike Phyllis Schlafly, Beverly LaHaye is very much a product of the New Right. Her style is that of a preacher rather than an intellectual. She organizes her followers in prayer circles, usually made up of seven

The Antifeminist Women's Movement

women who meet "around the kitchen table." The CWA slogan is "Prayer, Praise, and Action." Each of the triad is given equal importance, so recruits are encouraged not simply to act, with specific instructions such as "call your congressman" or "speak to your librarian," but to become emotionally and spiritually engaged as well.

Beverly LaHaye claims to have decided to organize conservative Christian women when she and her husband were watching the International Women's Year Convention on television in 1977. Feeling that the events she saw did not represent her idea of womanhood, she had a revelation and declared that she must actively oppose it.

In 1963, LaHaye experienced a religious conversion. She surrendered herself completely to God and became what she calls "a spirit-filled woman." As she describes herself, before that conversion she was a "fearful, introverted person with a rather poor self-image." She has lectured on her transformation and developed her own analysis of the four types of human "temperament" and the ways that bringing the Holy Ghost into your life will strengthen each type of temperament. The LaHayes' joint organization, Family Life Seminars, offers to analyze your temperament for $29.95 for anyone willing to take a half-hour test.[14]

When LaHaye launched CWA, she was a member of the Christian Right and the wife of an established Christian Right leader. Thus, quite naturally, LaHaye set out to organize Christian women, without regard for the way that focus excludes non-Christian women. Specifically, CWA's religious style and language—that of evangelical and fundamentalist Protestants—is not altered to speak to Jews and Catholics. However, Jewish and Catholic ideologues who hold compatible political views are welcomed as speakers at CWA conferences.

Her unapologetic appeal to Christian women has made recruiting easier for LaHaye than it has been for Schlafly. The women LaHaye recruits are already part of an existing Christian-based mass movement, and the family values message is deeply part of their daily religious experience. These women merely need to be educated about the threat to those values posed by liberals, then harvested for membership in the organization. LaHaye's background as the coconvenor of Family Life Seminars gave her the training in ministry that was crucial for the task of founding a Christian Right women's organization. Not surprisingly, LaHaye's organizing style and tone is that of the church. CWA is an organization of the heart and soul rather than the intellect.

The contrast with Schlafly's style is evident in the CWA publication that parallels Eagle Forum's *Phyllis Schlafly Report*. CWA's monthly *Family Voice* looks like a magazine in booklet size. It is multicolor, printed on slick paper, and filled with organizational news and photographs. It is also a hard-hitting right-wing propaganda tool, filled with political

116   Jean Hardisty

rhetoric, misinformation, and exaggeration. Perhaps its most important organizing feature is its visual focus on Beverly LaHaye, surrounded by the leadership of the New Right and Christian Right, all bolstering her credibility as a prominent and legitimate leader. As charismatic founder and minister to the organization (LaHaye is called "President for Life"), LaHaye's presence is felt and seen throughout the magazine. Further, La-Haye has a half-hour daily radio show that is prominently promoted in the magazine. Sociologist Sara Diamond estimates that the radio show reaches an audience of 500,000.[15] All this shows an awareness and skill at public relations that are part of the explanation for CWA's success.

A Gathering of Eagles

Each year in September both CWA and Eagle Forum hold their annual conventions in Washington, D.C. In 1994, they held them on successive weekends, at the same hotel. One might imagine that the scheduling was intentional, to allow women to stay in town and attend both conventions, but there was virtually no overlap in attendance between the two, and the similar scheduling was probably unintentional.

Eagle Forum's annual attendance hovers around 250. Many of the workshops and keynote addresses focus on issue areas identified as "women's issues," such as the schools, health care reform, violence on television, or the latest misdeeds of feminists. A surprising number, how-ever, stray far afield of these issue areas, into conspiracism on a grander scale. One such theme, promoted heavily at recent Eagle Forum confer-ences, is the alleged international conspiracy behind the New World Or-der.

In the 1990s, a sector of the Right supports the idea that there is an in-ternational conspiracy to create a "New World Order." George Bush, never trusted by the Right, adopted the phrase "New World Order" to describe the U.S. international dominance expected to characterize inter-national relations after the fall of communism in Eastern Europe and the Soviet Union. Growing numbers of those within the Right now see this as code for the final arrival of "One World Government"—a long-standing right-wing concept. One World Government will prevail when the United States is finally robbed of all its sovereignty. At that time, rather than self-rule, we will have rule by the hated United Nations, which is seen as the center of the conspiracy. Aiding in this subversion are an ar-ray of coconspirators, according to the specific conspiracy theory. They range from traitorous Trilateralist elites to international Jewish bankers and other unaware coconspirators within the United States itself. This theme is a favorite of Senator Jesse Helms and is one of the extreme posi-tions that has kept him somewhat marginalized, even within the New Right. Phyllis Schlafly has written about it in the *Phyllis Schlafly Report*. It is safe to say that this theme has replaced the anticommunist theme that for many years was at the center of Old Right ideology.

In the scenario spun by right-wing conspiracy theorists before rapt 1995 Eagle Forum conventioneers, trade treaties such as the General Agreement on Tariffs and Trade were identified as furthering the cause of the One World Government conspiracy. Speakers argued that the vehicle is not only GATT itself but the "hidden provisions" within the treaty, such as the provision for a World Trade Organization (WTO). This theory was heavily featured at both the 1994 and 1995 Eagle Forum annual conventions, though not all followers of the New Right agree with it. The prominence of this theme at Eagle Forum events places Schlafly's organization well to the right of the mainstream of the Republican Party, which tends to support GATT, NAFTA, and the New World Order.

But Schlafly is careful to make the connections between the UN-sponsored New World Order and the everyday concerns of her members. In February 1995, she wrote a fund-raising letter to her members about the threat posed by the United Nations Treaty on the Rights of the Child. In this letter she states: "This UN Treaty is designed to take children away from the protection of their parents, put children under the authority of UN 'experts,' give children the legal rights of adults, and set up government lawyers to sue parents to assert the child's 'rights.'"

Interestingly, Phyllis Schlafly herself does not publicly state the extreme positions taken by the speakers featured at her convention. She does, however, introduce each speaker, bestowing in no uncertain terms her seal of approval on what is about to be said. The speakers themselves are usually men. At the 1994 Eagle Forum convention, twelve of the fifteen principal speakers were men. In some cases, they are New Right politicians who are keeping in touch with their base. In other cases, they are young men trying to break into the crowded ranks of the Right's leadership. These younger speakers are still "inexpensive" because they are not yet so well known that they charge inflated speaking fees.

Eagle Forum conventions are serious, almost somber, affairs. They usually culminate on Saturday night with a hotel banquet, featuring a special guest speaker. In 1994, Phyllis Schlafly herself was the toast of the evening. On the occasion of her 70th birthday, an impressive roster of the Right's leadership turned out to toast her, including Senator Jesse Helms, chair of the Senate Foreign Relations Committee. In the audience, her Eagles (the most tried-and-true members wearing badges of honor in the form of eagle pins) celebrated their commitment to her organization and its ideology.

Song and Praise at CWA

The annual convention of Concerned Women for America is predictably bigger, more media savvy, more stage produced, and more explicitly

Christian. The singing of Christian songs and hymns occurs throughout the convention, and on Sunday morning there is a "Concert of Praise and Prayer." Here again, most of the principal speakers are men; eleven of the fifteen speakers at CWA's 1994 convention were men. In 1995, this number (seventeen of twenty-five) was artificially inflated because every declared Republican candidate for president came to speak before the CWA audience, as well as House Speaker Newt Gingrich and Ralph Reed, the controversial executive director of Pat Robertson's Christian Coalition.

Beverly LaHaye also bestowed her imprimatur on the theory that the New World Order conspiracy threatens our daily lives. At CWA's 1995 conference, Dr. Stanley Monteith, an orthopedic surgeon who publishes a conspiracy-minded right-wing newsletter called *HIV-Watch* and runs a radio show called *Radio Liberty*, spun out a long-standing right-wing theory that traces the international conspiracy's roots to a nineteenth-century plan for a New World Order developed by British entrepreneur Sir Cecil Rhodes. In horrifying detail, Monteith described how the plan for international domination was then picked up by Andrew Carnegie, the American robber baron, and has culminated in the Council on Foreign Relations and the presidency of Bill Clinton. Throughout his talk, Monteith referred to his research in "the secret files" as the source of his information.

At the 1995 CWA Saturday night banquet, the focus was on the achievements of Beverly LaHaye, especially her recent trip to Beijing to attend the Fourth World Conference on Women. Ironically, LaHaye's attendance at the hated conference seemed to confer status on her as an involved leader at the center of important political events. A film was shown of LaHaye's trip, emphasizing her influential role at the conference, her sightseeing, and "fellowship" on the Great Wall of China. The film's tone was remarkably bland, almost travelogue-like. It was only in the spoken comments of a number of the CWA lieutenants who accompanied her on the trip that the rightist rhetoric became inflamed and the audience was encouraged to demonize the conference and its feminists and lesbians. U.S. government officials who attended were also condemned as supporters of the UN. Here, again, we see the charismatic leader herself remain free of the most extreme rhetoric, while setting the stage for the heated pronouncement of her chosen spokespersons.

While aggressively marketing her own and her husband's books, LaHaye also used the conference to promote a long-distance telephone service called Lifeline. Described as "the first long-distance carrier that is built on biblical values and centered around the Lord Jesus Christ," Lifeline donates part of the proceeds from its business to support CWA. Lifeline is promoted as an alternative to AT&T's long-distance service, which "has thrown its financial support behind numerous homosexual rights causes."

The Right-Wing, Antifeminist Worldview

There are certain obvious and visible rewards for being involved in a political movement, whatever its content. The annual conventions and regional conferences of the two mass-based right-wing women's organizations showcase those rewards. In right-wing as in progressive gatherings, the feeling of being with like-minded people working for the same goals, who see the world and its problems in the same correct way, provides a feeling of safety and acceptance. But because those in the Right—especially right-wing women—give deference and love to their leaders, it is exciting to be in the presence of the charismatic woman leader and the political notables that she can produce. This itself testifies that the movement is important and that its participants are making a difference.

But such rewards do not explain the appeal of the movement's ideology for many women who are not at these conventions. They do not explain what attracts women to oppose equality and to see themselves as subordinate to men by nature. Here the explanation lies in the conservative religious beliefs of the rank-and-file members of Eagle Forum and CWA. Their social conservatism stems from their religious conservatism. It is a conservative reading of the Bible that defines their gender role. The Bible is not just a source of advice and guidance; for many conservative religious women, it is an infallible mandate. To follow it is to follow the correct path.

The conservative Christian beliefs of Schlafly's and LaHaye's followers may be the principal reason for their hostility to women who try to achieve equality for women. Certainly it goes a long way toward explaining why they so thoroughly hate feminists, whom they see as harbingers of godless secular humanism. However, other factors also play a role.

In the late 1970s, Andrea Dworkin published an article in *Ms* magazine titled "The Promise of the Ultra-Right." In this important piece, Dworkin argued that five fundamental forms of satisfaction are provided to women by rightist ideology: form, shelter, safety, rules, and love.[16] The first, "form," refers to an understanding of the world that is based on fixed, predetermined social, sexual, and biological roles. The chaos of contemporary society they see everywhere is explained by pointing to violations of that fixed order. The other four forms of satisfaction assured by right-wing values—shelter, safety, rules, and love—follow from the first. If a woman understands her natural gender role, she will marry, then will submit to her husband as his helpmate, follow the dictates of the church, and derive her greatest meaning from serving her family and making a good home for them. In return, her husband, the head of the family, will provide both shelter and love and will protect her from violence. The rules for this exchange are clear. She must act as a proper wife and mother, being careful not to threaten the hegemony of the husband and father nor to look outside the home for satisfaction or excitement.

For conservative women with traditional values, the women's movement threatens this structure. It removes the rules and by doing so undermines the assurance of form, shelter, safety, and love. Feminists and other social reformers introduce and encourage chaos with their "unnatural" reordering of roles. Their policies are, therefore, seen as a threat to conservative women rather than as a release from oppressive gender roles.

Feminist ideology promotes the goal of self-actualization for women, a process that often leads to women breaking out of established roles and violating traditional values in the process of finding a more fulfilling life. That is, the feminist women's movement encourages women to take charge of their lives, explore their own potential, and free themselves from subordination to the whims of irresponsible or violent men. This provides something beyond the assurance of physical security. It envisions an unprecedented level of freedom and independence for women. This ideal is captured by the words "women's liberation."

But for women with conservative values and a traditional lifestyle, breaking out of traditional roles may feel less like freedom and more like foolishly high-risk behavior. They see that often liberation has its costs. A woman who steps outside her role is no longer in a position to hold her husband to his role. She may be subject to the chaos that follows from her "unnatural" behavior.

The danger of liberal reformist movements, such as the feminist women's movement, is described by rightist economist George Gilder. Gilder is a major intellectual architect of the liberalism-leads-to-chaos school of social and economic analysis. In his most influential book, *Wealth and Poverty*, Gilder fixes the blame for contemporary chaos on the breakdown of traditional gender roles. He describes young men as naturally violent and a threat to social order. Fortunately, marriage has a civilizing effect on their savage instincts. Marriage imposes order in two ways: by providing sexual gratification at any time and by forcing men to go to work to support their wives and babies. Gilder argues that traditional marriage, which is maligned and denigrated by feminists, imposes constraints on the destructive youthful energy of young men. Without traditional marriage, that destructive energy is loosed on society.[17] The result is the chaos that conservatives see in contemporary society and that stands in stark contrast to their romantic view of the 1950s.

This worldview helps to explain the heated antifeminist sentiment of the members of Eagle Forum and CWA. Their rhetoric is more characteristic of the pent-up anger and resentment of hate literature than of simple disagreement over goals and tactics. For the mass-based right-wing women's movement, opposition to feminism is a holy war, and demonization of feminists obviously touches a chord.

The Antifeminist Women's Movement

Further explanation for this vehemence lies in the right's homophobia—the fear and loathing of homosexuality. For conservatives who read the Bible literally, homosexuality is a practice condemned by God. Evidence of rabid homophobia can be found in the frequent campaigns mounted by both Eagle Forum and CWA against "the gay agenda" and "militant lesbians." When a feminist policy is under attack from either organization, it is often smeared as lesbian motivated. Any such tarring implies that the feminist position in question is antifamily, anti-Christian, and antimale.

Another source of right-wing women's animus is their interpretation of feminism as elitist. Feminism becomes a matter of what "they" are doing to "us." In this view, the source of women's oppression is not men but other women, specifically other women who are inferior morally but who have influence and power to impose their own twisted, secular priorities. "They" control popular culture and have hoodwinked the unknowing public into supporting their selfish agenda. Their ally and financial underwriter is liberalism—which is seen as the handmaiden of socialism and communism.

Whipping up the latent resentments of conservative/traditional/Christian women against feminists and their agenda serves a strategic purpose in right-wing movement building. Right-wing leaders like Schlafly and LaHaye appeal to women as women, connecting with them around the worldview described earlier, then bring them along into the broader aspects of the Right's agenda. They educate them about how feminism is a threat to the family, about the "homosexual agenda," and about the elites in Washington who want to rob "us" and "destroy this country." They draw women in with messages of support for their common worldview, follow up with political recruitment into right-wing women's work, then mobilize them in the service of building the larger movement.

Encoded Messages on Race

The Old Right placed race at the center of its political ideology and promoted policies designed to maintain white hegemony and domination. White supremacism was justified by the supposed biological inferiority of black people. But by the beginning of the 1980s, Richard Viguerie, in a book titled *The New Right: We're Ready to Lead*, stated that racism was no longer a part of the Right's agenda.[18] This, in fact, was a major motivation for the title the movement gave itself (the New Right). As overt racism was muted in the Right's rhetoric, the social issues were elevated to greater prominence. Publicly, "traditional values" and "family protection" took the place previously occupied by antiblack recruiting themes.

It is hard to find explicitly racist statements by New Right leaders. The same can be said of the right-wing women's movement. Without these statements to serve as "proof" of racism, journalists are usually unwilling to expose, or even discuss, the issue of racism within the movement. Many journalists ignore the fact that in order to understand the racism of the New Right, it is necessary to recognize that it is encoded. In order to see it, you need to look at the consequences of the movement's ideology and agenda.

Particularly revealing is the ideological justification for stereotyping and vilifying many people of color. According to the New Right, including the antifeminist women's movement, the correct measure of morality is a person's worthiness. To be worthy, you most likely are Christian (ideally, born-again), have conservative social values, support freedom, oppose communism, and take responsibility for your own actions. Anyone can meet these requirements. If you adhere to this worldview, there is no ideological reason for you to be punished or excluded because of your race.

The same pattern applies to the right-wing women's movement. Though few women of color attend the conventions or belong to Eagle Forum or CWA, those who do are welcomed. They are accepted as worthy because they oppose affirmative action, multiculturalism, and welfare. They are worthy because they believe in individualism, personal responsibility, limited government, and family values. They oppose liberalism, government programs for the needy, secular humanism, and sex education in the schools. In many cases, the policies promoted by Eagle Forum and CWA are opposed to the interests of women of color, but the label "worthy" is a powerful seal of morality and does sometimes attract women of color whose values are traditional and conservative.

Those who fail to live up to the standards of worthiness are assumed to do so because they are weak or corrupt. They are branded as greedy, lazy, or violent, and the Right blames them for social ills and advocates excluding them from society. There are many ways that a person can be classified as unworthy and be excluded. Violating one of the above requirements is one way. Those who are excluded for that reason often tend to be people of color—precisely because of the racism so prevalent in U.S. society. Accusing them of dependence, lack of conformity to strict biblical mandates, and inability to earn money, the New Right scapegoats large portions of communities of color. By scapegoating the victims, the effects of poverty and racial discrimination are camouflaged and the hegemony of white, Christian values is rescued from liberal "softness."

Another way to run afoul of the New Right is to identify with a subgroup of the dominant culture, thus setting yourself apart from the Eurocentric cultural mythology that has historically dominated our national self-image. For example, to identify primarily as African American, Latina, or Chinese American is to place yourself aside from the dominant culture. It leads, quite naturally, to the emphasis on multiculturalism so eloquently advocated by many people of color who find that to conform to the dominant culture is to deny a fundamental part of their own cultural existence. All these methods of exclusion, ostensibly racially neutral, are at the heart of the New Right's racism.

The Right adamantly maintains that racial discrimination is no longer a factor in American society and that personal failures are simply personal failures. This denial of the continuing existence of racism in U.S. society is another aspect of the New Right's racism. No speaker was more popular with CWA annual conventioneers in 1995 than Alan Keyes, an African-American radio host who passionately asserts that race is not a factor in contemporary society and who passionately defends the values of white, Christian America.

White women in the right-wing women's movement are not required to overcome their racism. In fact, they are rewarded for understanding that though racist stereotypes are not applicable across the board, they are valid when applied to those who are unworthy. Thus, the "welfare queen" or other stereotypes promoted to represent despised members of society are not seen as racist stereotypes but as accurate and honest depictions of unworthiness. Discriminating against those who fail to adhere to the values of the Christian Right is justified as upholding morality. Society's blatant racial stratification is not questioned, therefore there is no mandate for racial inclusiveness nor any concern that the organizations are nearly entirely white.

Of course, there is much debate within the Right over the exact nature of worthiness. Bitter feuds erupt every day over tenets of right-wing ideology and policy. But there is general agreement that the Anglo-European model of individualism, Christianity, and self-restraint is the blueprint for worthiness. Hardworking, churchgoing, responsible, upright, heterosexual people are eligible for worthiness. Further, Western civilization is seen as the source of the progress and advancement of the United States. Any concession to moral corruption, secularism, sexual "deviance," lack of personal responsibility, or multiculturalism is a threat to society. The basis for this "new" encoded racism is cultural white supremacism. It lies at the heart of the "culture war," and the antifeminist women's movement is enlisted for battle.

Conclusion

Metaphorically, the antifeminist women's movement is a slick, fast-talking recruiter, sent into women's social spheres to win conservative-leaning women to the larger Right. By addressing complex areas of concern and distress for conservative women who hold traditional values (school curriculum, violence on television and in rock and rap music, child-rearing practices, divorce, homosexuality) with simple, conservative solutions, it first draws them into the movement, then introduces them to the larger ideology and agenda of the Right. Its appeal is to women who are angered by and alienated from modern society's economic, social, and cultural liberalism. The movement offers an opportunity to unite with like-minded women to oppose reformed gender roles, to regain dominance and moral superiority within a smaller, more satisfying sphere, and to demonize political enemies (especially feminists), all in the cause of "defending America."

Conservative women are open to an ideology that values the superior knowledge and insight of elevated leaders and thus are willing to follow the dictates of the movement's charismatic women leaders. As the leaders introduce them to the larger agenda of the Right, they become political foot soldiers for right-wing campaigns on issues such as welfare reform, privatized health care, immigration restrictions, and antigay initiatives. Any objections they might have as women to the Right's agenda are neutralized. They become reliable supporters of an agenda that places women in a permanently inferior position "by nature."

The right-wing women's movement often appears marginal because it does not actively compete with male-led organizations for dominance within the New Right. However, the movement is strong, effective, and successful. Its political strength lies in its role as a large body of motivated activists who can be turned to whatever cause is identified by the woman charismatic leader. As such, the movement has played a crucial role in nearly every right-wing campaign of the last twenty years.

Because the organizing style of the antifeminist women's movement is lean and efficient, requiring little debate over decisions and delivering a high level of conformity to political marching orders, it is a formidable political adversary. It exists in large part to target feminists and other supporters of equal rights for women. We ignore or dismiss it at our own peril.

Credits

This chapter was previously published in *Public Eye*, vol. 10, no. 2 (Summer 1996).

Notes

1. See Constance Marshner, "The New Traditional Woman" (Washington, DC: Free Congress Research and Education Foundation, 1982). Also see Onalee McGraw, "The Family, Feminism, and the Therapeutic State" (Washington, DC: The Heritage Foundation, 1980). For an excellent discussion of Marshner's career, see Susan Faludi, *Backlash: The Undeclared War Against American Women* (New York: Crown Publishers, 1991), 241–247.

2. Laura Flanders, "The 'Stolen Feminism' Hoax," *Extra!* vol. 7, no. 5, September/October 1994:6–9.

The Antifeminist Women's Movement

3. Daphne Patai and Noretta Koertge, *Professing Feminism: Cautionary Tales from the Strange World of Women's Studies* (New York: Basic Books, 1994).

4. Elizabeth Fox-Genovese, *Feminism Is Not the Story of My Life: How Today's Feminist Elite Has Lost Touch with the Real Concerns of Women* (New York: Nan A. Talese/Doubleday, 1995).

5. Alice Dembner, "Alumni Bring View from Right to Campus," *Boston Globe,* June 24, 1995.

6. Laura Flanders, "Conservative Women Are Right for Media," *Extra!* vol. 9, no. 2, March/April, 1996:6.

7. Rebecca Klatch, *Women of the New Right* (Philadelphia: Temple University Press, 1987).

8. Rita Simmons, ed., *Neither Enemy Nor Victim: Women's Freedom Network Looks at Gender in America* (New York: Women's Freedom Network and University Press of America, 1996).

9. Carol Felsenthal, *The Biography of Phyllis Schlafly: The Sweetheart of the Silent Majority* (Chicago: Regnery Gateway, 1982).

10. Phyllis Schlafly, *A Choice Not an Echo,* rev. 3d ed. (Alton, IL: Pere Marquette Press, 1964).

11. Tanya Melich, *The Republican War Against Women: An Insider's Report from Behind the Lines* (New York: Bantam Books, 1996).

12. James Bennet, "Buchanan, Exalted, Pushes Economic Insecurity Theme," *New York Times,* February 22, 1996.

13. Fred Clarkson, "Christian Reconstructionism," in Chip Berlet, ed., *Eyes Right! Challenging the Right-Wing Backlash* (Boston: South End Press, 1995), 59–80.

14. Beverly LaHaye, *The Spirit-Controlled Woman* (Eugene, OR: Harvest House Publishers, 1995), 11–15.

15. Sara Diamond, *Facing the Wrath: Confronting the Right in Dangerous Times* (Monroe, ME: Common Courage Press, 1996), 14.

16. Reprinted in Andrea Dworkin, *Right-Wing Women* (New York: G. P. Putnam's Sons, 1983), 13–36.

17. George Gilder, *Wealth and Poverty* (New York: Basic Books, 1981).

18. Richard Viguerie, *The New Right: We're Ready to Lead* (Falls Church, VA: Viguerie Company, 1981).

6

Fulfilling Fears and Fantasies: The Role of Welfare in Right-Wing Social Thought and Strategy

Ann Withorn

I presently work three jobs to make ends meet. Or perhaps I should say four since mothering is more than a full-time job in itself. I have been on and off welfare for years because I can never make enough money and/or be there for my children in the ways they need.

I work as a crossing guard for the police. I work cleaning houses and as a visiting nurse. These are all potentially well-paying jobs but the work is not always steady and I am paid per job. . . . I have never sold myself or drugs. I have never stayed at home and watched TV and never eaten bon bons. . . .

No one should have to choose between providing for the financial or emotional survival of their family. And yet we have to. And you and the rest of government is responsible for this impossible situation.

Stop bashing mothers. Stop bashing welfare recipients. Stop all these punishing changes that will only make a bad situation worse. We have a right to survive.

—Ellen Green, testifying before the Massachusetts Legislature, 1995[1]

Although opposition to "welfare" has only rarely been a primary focus of the Right in the United States, it has often been an implicit unifying point, a place where the circles of ideological interest intersect. Almost every right-winger gets deeply satisfying rewards from being against the friendless welfare state. Racists can tell stories about ne'er-do-well blacks. Libertarians can expose the brutality of a behemoth state. Radical capitalists can show the dire costs of interfering with a free market, whereas Christian moralists can rant passionately about welfare's permissiveness regarding women's promiscuity and family "breakdown."

Historically, the role of antiwelfare argument as a linchpin among right-wing forces was not obvious. But especially over the past decade, we began to see preachers, pundits, politicians from both parties, researchers, and respondents to national polls all being quoted in ways that were even picked up in the rambling justifications of a murderer of Mass-

126

achusetts abortion clinic workers: Welfare is the epitome of all that is destroying American society—it must be stopped because it undermines the good people and rewards the bad.[2] With the successful 1996 passage of national "welfare reform," grown directly from the most conservative roots imaginable, the congruence has become screamingly visible. Today, opposition to welfare has successfully become not only a unifier for the Right but a wedge issue for infusing right-wing ideology into mainstream social policy and social thought.

This chapter reviews how "welfare" has served as a historic source of fear and fantasy for the varied right-wing views of the world and examines its role in supplying an ever more common enemy, and a shared vision, for today's successful fusion of disparate conservative forces.[3]

It is important to state that this chapter is built upon an assumption that one of the historically basic and proper divisions between Left and Right in the United States has been over the willingness to provide public resources to those in need (welfare) but that this division has been obscured because liberals and even leftists have consciously glossed over their structural intentions in order to avoid presumed public opposition. Advocates of an American welfare state knowingly sold Aid to Families with Dependent Children (AFDC) with false claims that it would be temporary, and proclaimed a "War on Poverty" that they knew could not be won in capitalist America, for example. Since the Right has historic, consistent, and logical reasons for opposing welfare, this lack of clarity and even outright liberal obfuscation has fueled right-wing fears that the welfare state *is* a leftist trick, perpetrated on the American people by socialistically oriented social workers and social planners.[4] More important, the inability of people on the Left to claim and defend welfare as a social achievement for all (regardless of its real contradictions and failures of implementation) has created an opening for right-wing ideas and proposals to enter the mainstream political arena without a base for effective opposition.[5]

Basing my arguments on my twenty-five years of activism around welfare issues, I propose here that the Right is *correct* to see welfare as a symbol of all they oppose, and I urge those of us who profess an alternative view to openly defend, redefine, and expand the broadest but most democratic vision of a welfare state.

Welfare and Historical Right-Wing Fears

Our [Massachusetts] almshouse paupers are nearly all foreigners ... Aliens and their children embrace five-sixths of all who become chargeable ... the greater proportion are lazy, ignorant, prejudiced, unreasonable, receiving charity of the state as a right rather than as a favor.

From 1857, cited in David Bennett, *The Party of Fear*[6]

Historically, the positive concept of "welfare" has presumed a general obligation of collective society to maintain all of its members at some minimal standard, and its deep and abiding opposition to this very presumption, albeit for widely differing reasons, has united the Right.[7] Any understanding of the power of the Right today must build upon an awareness of the historic force of differing fears about the nature of welfare as well as upon an understanding of how the fantasy bugaboo of welfare has been used in varied ways by separate strands of the right-wing tradition.

We might begin our story by remembering that when the leaders of the most successful right-wing movement in U.S. history sat down to write the Constitution of their Confederacy of Southern States in 1861, they quickly cribbed from the original U.S. Constitution. The only major changes created a more explicitly white supremacist society and left no doubt as to the legality of black slavery and states' rights. One of the few other substantive changes made by the reframers was the deletion of a simple clause in the Preamble: No longer was the government of a master race even to claim as one of its purposes "to promote the general welfare." And after being defeated in their national quest, racists moved on to oppose Reconstruction's minuscule social welfare efforts as fostering "dependence and unrealistic expectations" among former slaves.[8]

To move the narrative ahead, we can also observe how, over the past sixty years, whenever the Right has again threatened to eliminate "welfare," the goal was a similarly basic challenge to the goal of a liberal society. Usually the enemy was almost any form of government aid that might create guarantees and expectations of collective security—although the embodiment of all that can go wrong was most often presumed to be AFDC. This small federal program began with the Social Security Act of 1935, which since then has provided basic income maintenance to mainly single-parent families with children, while never claiming even 2 percent of total federal expenditures. Sometimes very specific criticisms emerged about what was wrong with this program as an entitlement and as a bureaucratic structure, leading to cries for "welfare reform." But in historic and even in much current conservative social commentary, "welfare" easily slips into more expansive meanings. "Long-term use of welfare," from whatever source of need-based government funds, is often listed as one characteristic of a so-called underclass. "Welfare dependency" may be defined as a problem of homeless people, many of whom are disabled and are receiving federal or state funding, or both, for basic subsistence, not AFDC. Conversely, politicians and pundits usually shrink meanings when they talk about the "welfare state," only including programs for the poorest of the poor in their definition—while denying the full array of government programs established to assist veterans, students, seniors, home buyers, and businesses after World War II.

Whatever the specific usage at any point in time, however, the very idea of a guarantee of "general welfare" has continued to be a key part of the answer whenever right-wing thinkers, across the full range of traditions, have asked what is wrong in America. Social Darwinists saw charity as "strengthening the weak, and weakening the strong." Nationalist nativists worried about our social generosity encouraging more "irresponsible aliens" to cross the border. Racists warned that welfare rewards the very laziness and propensity toward dependence that they see inherent in people of color. And always, fundamentalist Christian morality provided an overarching source of symbols, metaphors, and standards for the organization of private life that viewed any source of outside relief from intimate obligations as a profound threat to moral order.

Yet despite their mutual fears, each of the major streams of right-wing tradition also viewed the danger of welfarism in somewhat different ways. It is useful, then, to examine the varied right-wing concerns in order to understand both how they have been historically separated and how they now have, through a set of contemporary congruences that are both accidental and purposefully cultivated, joined together in a fused, self-referential fantasy.

Disparate Fears

The first set of right-wing fears about America emerge from traditional radical capitalist worries that too many fetters on rich people (or on people trying to become rich) or too much support for "nonproductive elements" would fatally weaken the society.[9] Since the economy is most productive when successful people are able to risk, invest, and hire whomever they want under any terms that suit them, poor people are either personally to blame for making bad choices or, at best, are viewed as only fulfilling a normal economic role that can be changed through their individual initiative. When they collectively claim assistance from the state—rather than just individually seeking the opportunity to find paid work, at whatever wages and terms are offered—poor people threaten the freedom of capitalists to take the most profitable course of action.

Radical capitalists have seldom presented their class interests so baldly. Instead, their positive agenda has been framed as an intense valuing of "freedom"—the economic freedom to become rich (even though in the 1880s and the 1980s we almost stepped over the edge into just admiring wealth for its own sake, with no apologies). Their negative fears have been expressed in warnings about the dire effects, not of poverty (seen as a natural economic phenomenon that even engenders personal hardiness) but of pauperism or the ability to make *any* claim on the state for economic relief. In theoretical and polemical works spanning the past century, they posit the only legitimate use of government as helping capital when business interests want help (and that, too, is risky because "robust" capitalism can be softened up by too much government help).[10] Even in times of dire depression, radical capitalists proclaimed the inevitable dangers of expanding government, no matter how compelling the populist demands. When government tries to help, so the argument goes, it still really hurts everyone—because people become less free to make and keep their money and more likely to be fooled into thinking that government will be there to bail them out when they fail. Freedom and individual creativity are stifled whenever capitalism has buffers like those erected in what Bob Dole calls our "sixty-year detour" experiment with a welfare state.

However, much of this century was a period when, as historians across a wide spectrum agree, politics were driven by assumptions that dire poverty was a greater threat to the economic order than were carefully constrained welfare programs. Thus, for years radical capitalists were pushed to the margins of social debate—as the more successful internationalist capitalists agreed to "pay the price" for social harmony. Only in the last two decades has such "fundamentalist capitalism" been rehabilitated, based in large part on a carefully orchestrated effort to link liberal capitalism to welfare statism.

Nationalism and nativism provide a second strain of fears for America.[11] This old school, the motto of which was "America is the greatest country in the world but it is being weakened by outsiders and unpatriotic Americans," historically viewed immigrants as a danger to a healthy nation and to a rewarding economy for "real Americans." It spun a vision of a united, patriotic, and militarily prepared national community threatened by a lack of national strength and by enemies that corrupted from within and without. The other side of nationalism was nativism: If anybody new came here, their "Americanism" could be questioned. Of course, if newcomers were white, acted exactly like the people who had been here before, and did not make any claims for welfare, then it was easier for them to quickly become "good Americans."

Nationalists and nativists were not as historically fearful of government or even of some forms of welfare as the radical capitalists. After all, they wanted some government and a strong military as symbol of our country's special mission. And although nativists always feared immigrants and wanted to bar services that attracted them, they also wanted a punitive government of police, courts, and even schools and social workers to do something *to* the immigrants: control them, send them back if they grew uppity, make rules for them, force them to behave like Americans. Therefore, fears of immigrants did not always translate particularly into opposition to welfare, since social programs were often a way of "controlling the dangerous classes."[12]

Welfare in Right-Wing Social Thought and Strategy 131

Third, white racists, building on arguments articulated by the proslavery movement and the Confederacy, embody deeply intertwined fears of blacks and government welfare programs. For twentieth-century white supremacists, dark people are so different culturally (and probably genetically) that, at the least, they need to stay on their own because they will corrupt and besmudge all that is strong and good in this society (they are even sometimes called "Mud People," as in the notorious *Turner Diaries*). Thus, the Civil Rights movement, like Reconstruction, is accused of undermining the natural social order, and government programs aimed at "uplifting" blacks have been seen as a new form of malevolent slavery that has merely replaced the benevolent slavery of the "old plantation." More recently, less overt racists still see government programs aimed at blacks as inevitably bound to fail because such people will be "culturally resistant" to responsibility.

The racist strand of right-wing thought builds directly on the same fears that helped defeat the abolitionists' struggle for real equality.[13] As the story goes, if only black people (and their white radical allies) had not insisted on "fatally flawed" programs like Reconstruction then, or poverty programs and affirmative action now, white people would feel safe. All our problems can be traced somehow, ultimately, to the very *presence* of black people in our midst. Repugnant as this tradition is, even to many radical conservatives, militant white supremacists (and Christian Identity movement members) like Randy Weaver find friends when they cry "freedom" from government and when they articulate fears about the reduced prospects for white men, because of the gains, and the welfare drains, of black people. Always, then, white supremacists have militantly feared the consequences of national government involvement in any "private" affair like race relations, either directly or simply by targeting resources toward mostly black urban areas.

Fourth, radical fundamentalist moralism has played an important historical role in establishing a faith-based fear of the welfare state. Usually less focused on dogma than on upholding proper "Christian" behavior (and tied to a defense of the traditional family hierarchy where god > father > mother > child), this tradition has historically been deeply Protestant, although there have been recent efforts to bridge the historic chasm between fundamentalist Protestantism and conservative Catholicism.[14] Fundamentalist groups have primarily seen the country's problems as resulting from godlessness, from a breakdown in the traditional moral order embodied in families and churches. Most recently they have seen society as profoundly threatened by the facts of divorce, "illegitimacy," teen pregnancy, homosexuality, and even more so by secular humanist values that do not judge such behavior.

But Christian fundamentalists have only been episodic members of the political Right. Historically, they have been torn by conflicting impulses: the fear of being corrupted by the secular world versus the need to stand up for God's law and order; the mandate to engage in Christian charity versus the need personally to judge sin and oppose sinners. It has always taken strong leadership to move fundamentalist Christians beyond their fears that getting involved in the state is corrupting, regardless of the sinfulness in the world. And, of course, there has always been a belief that some charity had to be provided, even to sinners, but if believers got too close to such people, without converting them, they might themselves become tainted.[15]

Finally, a fifth stream of radical elitism has historically presented profoundly conservative fears regarding America's disorderliness, reflecting a heritage more akin to European aristocratic patterns than to other domestic U.S. traditions. This perspective has influenced the world of ideas by finding society is most challenged not by the fettering of capitalism but by too much power for the ignorant and too many collectivist experiments. In this century the long-standing intellectualist and elitist tradition evolved and intersected with nationalist, anticommunist radical capitalism, arguing that socialism, and even an overly populist democracy, is bad because it is anticapitalist and disorderly and because it gives people a sense of too many rights.[16]

From the radical elitist perspective, seen for years in William Buckley's *National Review*, socialism or "collectivism" in any form is to be greatly feared because it legitimates the dangerous idea that people on the bottom can wrongly claim equality with, and resources from, those on the top. The welfare state, as the institutional embodiment of the ascendancy of the bottom, is therefore the "natural enemy of quality"; it allows people to start expecting too much and creates all sorts of programs that disrupt the natural hierarchies by redistributing wealth and rights downward.

Historical Implications

These long-standing but disparate right-wing traditions were only partially marginalized during the past century. However ineffective members of the right wing were at claiming majority national attention after the defeat of the Confederacy and the success of progressivism, their fears have always had more popular power to mobilize the citizenry than liberals wanted to admit.[17] At local levels, in churches, newspapers, and state legislatures, there have always been strong arguments, if not organized forces, to represent such radically conservative perspectives. Collections of fundamentalist sermons or congressional debates of any year yield voices just like those of today's Right. For years, the military has been a seedbed for the types of "freedom"-oriented radical nationalists who formed the militia movement—as the quest for the Oklahoma bombers briefly revealed. And the Confederate flag has remained a watered down but real symbol of cultural and racial reaction—witness Pat Buchanan's defense of it in 1996. How widespread the acceptance of such ideas has been is another question, of course. Nonetheless, it is still important to accept that capitalist, elitist, nativist, racist, and traditionally "moral" perspectives have been part of the daily culture for many ordinary white people living outside of major northern urban centers and have, indeed, presented a set of bedrock, reactionary core values upon which contemporary right-wingers currently draw.

As we can see, then, the varying streams of the right-wing tradition in America have offered the public remarkably compatible fears—fears that people at the bottom of society's economic, cultural, racial, social, and moral hierarchy would claim collective legitimacy and rights and thereby take away the opportunities for "good, hardworking, God-fearing Americans" to live well. Increasingly, twentieth-century welfare programs, provided as rights, as "entitlements" without automatic bars on ever-expanding expectations, were viewed as offering a highly dangerous opportunity for society's losers to weaken the nation, the economy, the culture, and the race. When Barry Goldwater warned against "welfarism" that stemmed from "government policies which create dependent citizens [and] inevitably rob a nation and its people of moral and physical strength," he encapsulated the common fears that began to become clearer during the last quarter century.[18]

Yet, until the 1970s, the recurring pattern was that the Right fragmented, divided, and distrusted itself because of differing goals, strategies, and tactics, with little unity gained from its shared fears. But since that time, as commentators across the political spectrum have seen, the Right began self-consciously to coalesce and, spurred by external events, to create a fusion of interests unprecedented in U.S. history. A critical part of this new fusion was the turning of long-standing mutual fears of welfare into a common fantasy regarding the possibility of reversing the gains that had been made, first by the Great Society, then by the New Deal, and finally by the whole set of efforts begun a century ago under the optimistic hopes of a "progressive movement."

Welfare and Current Right-Wing Fantasies

It is time to set the record straight. If religious conservatives took their proper proportionate place as leaders in the political and cultural life of the country, we would work to create the kind of society in which presumably all of us would like to live: safe neighborhoods, strong families, schools that work, a smaller government and lower taxes. . . . Government would be small because citizens and private institutions would voluntarily perform many of its functions. We would not need a large bloated welfare state to take care of us, for we would take care of each other. We would not need the law to threaten or cajole us, for a higher law would live in our hearts. . . . In short, we desire a good society based on the shared values of work, family, neighborhood and faith.

Ralph Reed, Christian Coalition[19]

The growing strategic and organizational unity among right-wing forces since the 1970s has been well documented.[20] My purpose is not to track the overall process by which the Right grew through Reaganism to become the powerful force we now see flexing its muscles in Congress, in presidential politics, and in the media. Instead, I want to suggest how opposition to welfare, and to welfare statism, has become an essential strategic linchpin for a new and finally successful right wing. Opposition to welfare has emerged from being an issue on the back burner, an underlying and discardable fear in the days before Reagan, emerging to become a major way in which right-wing ideas find broader legitimacy and resonance today. It now supplies one of the central fantasies that have reframed right-wing rhetoric into a popularly appealing vision for a post–cold war, postwelfare world.

Roots of Victory

Since the 1970s, several external factors have helped strategists seeking to unite the Right to use their underlying fears of welfare, pauperism, and "dependency" as a base for a new, wider vision. By exploiting these factors and bolstering them with a barrage of writing and organizing, right-wing activists have buried the historical contradictions of the varied strains of ideology under a growing, united opposition to welfare and a shared fantasy of how healthy society would be if we could just forever abolish "the failed welfare state."

First, perhaps the most pivotal change in the environment nurturing right-wing thought was the collapse of the Soviet Union and the broad-scale exposure of the problems that permeated Soviet-style systems. This colossal change has given credence to radical capitalist arguments that capitalism can be triumphant if it is untainted by socialist compromises like welfare. Without a cold war to force us to show the social benefits of American democracy, the victors need take no prisoners nor make any compromises to buffer the effects of the economic "realities" of capitalism. Despite the growing inability of global capitalism to provide the United States with the same level of economic security that it did after World War II, much less full economic justice, it faces no significant opposition as a prescription for how to organize a society or even a world.

Any remaining problems result from constraints placed on capitalism, from places where socialism has crept in and especially from people who have become dependent on its "benefits." Thus, for example, privatization—which makes sense in Russia, where every corner store was a state enterprise—is used here to gradually dismantle the U.S. welfare state and erode the social expectations it inevitably created. Now radical capitalists and those elitists who want social order can come together in a new, less crude form of anticommunism, focused primarily on replacing the dangers posed by a welfare state with Newt Gingrich's "Opportunity Society" of freewheeling entrepreneurialism.[21]

Now, too, the "cowboy" capitalists can get back at the "Yankees," who have been willing since the Progressive Era to allow government to create a social safety net, at the cost of continued assurance of social peace, favorable taxes, and tariff structures. Eastern liberal capitalists, and their political representatives, are tainted with welfare statism and are told to abandon their support for government with much the same vehemence heard from the Goldwaterites who once booed Nelson Rockefeller.[22] We can have a hegemonic anticommunism—without having to prove that anyone ever had a party membership card. Anybody who still dares to demand a responsive, dependable government or a redistributive tax system is automatically labeled a "politically correct collectivist," a "domestic socialist," who is therefore responsible for the growth of the welfare-maintained underclass. We can limit free speech—not by outlawing Communist parties but by stopping social welfare professionals from legislative advocacy if they receive any public funding, as so many do in a privatized delivery system.[23]

Second, the dramatic increase in immigration over the past fifteen years has triggered the revival of nativism, along with a fusing of radical capitalist, nationalist, and nativist sentiments in joint opposition to social programs for newcomers. Books like *The Path to National Suicide: An Essay on Immigration and Multiculturalism* and journals like the Heritage Foundation's *Policy Review* now clearly state their belief: Immigrants are still the problem. They are trouble not only because they are here but especially because they can now claim certain economic and social protections and rights unavailable to previous generations of immigrants.[24] We can still let some in, but only if they leave family behind and if they expect nothing—except the chance to work at any wage, under any conditions. Although some of the most paranoid and racist nativists find the very presence of immigrants to be a problem, for most the goal is simply getting them back into subservient positions, speaking English only and asking for nothing from a welfare state. In times of economic stagnation for the working classes, no matter how glittering the growth at the top, once again fear of immigration emerges as a bedrock reaction, with the successful attempt to curb welfare for immigrants as a cornerstone to "recovery."

Third, the Gulf War has, as was loudly proclaimed, "ended the Vietnam syndrome" and has made militaristic patriotism popular again. Few mainstream journalists now offer any criticisms of military spending, nor is war seen as an inherently problematic undertaking. The effects on our emerging fantasy are complex but seem to shore up a rekindled national consensus that social problems—in the schools and the streets—can also be cured with tough, military-style discipline, not with efforts to provide support to families and, especially, youth. Thus, we have schools run by generals and a return to uniforms and boot camps as models for youth programs.

Fourth, the changes in women's status and options since the 1960s have provided especially critical impetus for fusion of right-wing forces.[25] Despite all the failures to gain political and economic power, women over the past thirty years *have* made real challenges to the established ordering of male priorities: More women are proudly in the workforce; more are able to divorce and not be forced into remarriage; more are challenging sexual harassment, stalking, rape, and incest. These are challenges that the Right must turn back or fundamentalist morality's house of cards will come down. From the perspective of traditionalist Christianity especially, feminism is the enemy.[26]

By now radical capitalists, and even many fundamentalist Christians, have accommodated to economic pressures that require women to be more "in the world" than they have ever been in history. Conservatives seldom deny women's quests for jobs with fair wages today, although child care is usually seen as an earned benefit and any glass ceiling is viewed as resulting from women's "choices." Not even the "failure of the family" is blamed on a woman's employment, unless she takes her job too seriously. And divorce itself is tolerated, although the Religious Right waffles here, usually decrying the high rates of "no-fault" divorce and accepting the strained logic that pregnant women and girls are better off with "pressured" marriages, which are likely to end in divorce.[27]

Instead, the real danger is defined as women's ability to *choose* to live without men, not the problem of their being abandoned. The Right correctly sees that feminists celebrate women's right to raise their children without men and that they rightly find the fundamental policy base of that entitlement in AFDC. Here the Christian Right and the radical capitalists are unified: Once women can positively claim welfare, no matter how compromised, as a substitute for the "protection" of a man or an employer, then both the traditional family and the "necessities" of the workplace are threatened.

Furthermore, for thirty years women have also been opening up the secrets of the patriarchal family: the violence, the abuse, the incest. And they have done so not just to name men's sins in order to reform them but to

Welfare in Right-Wing Social Thought and Strategy 137

justify the rights of women to live without men. This work has been more radical and frightening than we feminists have often ourselves understood, but women as well as men on the Right have clearly seen the implication: that even talking about such intimate injustice cracks the whole culture of dominance of men over women.[28] Since right-wingers cannot acknowledge even to themselves that incest, battering, and rape are the systemic methods that subjugate women, they are in a pickle. But they *can* say that single families are bad, turn children into criminals, and take them away from the "love and discipline" and legitimacy that only a father can bring. They can assert that if such things happen at all it is primarily in families of the "underclass," where bad people have made bad choices while weakened by welfare. And they can blame the media and feminists for trying to "present deviance as the norm." In this context of denial, any economic right, given without punishment, that allows women to support themselves and their children outside the authority of either a husband or a boss is profoundly suspect. Women unconstrained by the discipline of marriage or workplace are inherently more likely to "blow the whistle" on all the problems at the heart of so-called family values in this country, so they must be silenced and demonized.[29]

Out of this deep material, the moralist Right has asserted leadership by creating a fearful fantasy that incorporates other streams of right-wing thought. The fantasy says that the pain Americans are feeling does *not* result from our confusion about how to handle more gender equality, especially at a time when everyone's economic expectations are being downsized—oh, no. Rather, our misery is caused by women without men who have too many rights, who do not accept their suffering gracefully. Women on welfare then represent all women who are asserting their right to live without men and to claim their rights to "child support" if not from fathers, then from the state. Unless women present themselves as total victims (and then only if they stop any claims to victimhood after a specified time limit), they find little support from a set of coalescing arguments that posit their very existence as a terrifying alternative to the male-headed family and to every citizen's "obligation" to accept any employment under any conditions.

Finally, the limited but real success of African-American social activism has also served to link varied strands of the Right, most importantly by rejuvenating the racist Right. As Jill Quadragno has pointed out, popular opposition to the Great Society was easily channeled into intertwined antiwelfare, antiminority rhetoric. Today, old racist arguments that people of color demand and receive too much have reemerged in the attacks on government as a provider and protector of economic or social rights, with welfare as a prime example of what many white people see as excessive and divisive claims by people of color. Thus, even though the evidence is less out in the open, to understand the power of today's right-wing agenda we must understand how overt racism plays into the emerging fear that "we have given it all away."[30]

Achieving Fusion

In order for these changed circumstances to coalesce into a fused, self-conscious interpretation, a unified vision was needed. Here the work of Paul Weyrich, Pat Robertson, the Heritage Foundation, and others was critical, as was the increasing influence of writers (supported by conservative foundations) who sanitized hard-right ideas for less-ideological audiences. After all, when, in 1960, the city manager of Newburgh, New York, a John Birch Society member, tried to forced welfare recipients (both General Relief and AFDC) to work off their benefits and to pick up their checks at the police station, he was stopped and was widely criticized—and few conservatives sought national attention by defending him. When Goldwater talked about "welfarism" he received cheers from right-wing audiences (and was chosen by 38 percent of the electorate) but was generally seen as too extremist.

After 1964, others, like Milton Friedman, kept writing and slowly developed a following for antistate economic theory. Conservative economists and critics began writing somewhat turgid books about the costs and bureaucracy of the welfare state that received some mainstream attention and normalized the questioning of welfare. And although George Gilder was first treated as a crank when he revealed to a more general public the evils of welfare and the need to "wean" people from the welfare state as a first step in righting the moral and behavioral wrongs of America, the election of Reagan gave credence to Gilder's ideas and served as a base from which more mainstream writers could call for "an end to welfare."

During the Reagan era, a new generation of conservative think tanks sponsored speakers, writers, and studies, which launched a reinterpretation of the whole Great Society, and of AFDC in general, as the source of a "practice and ideology" of dependency, with increasing emphasis on the danger of welfare use for families. No longer was the problem just that which had long troubled radical capitalists—a costly, ineffective governmental bureaucracy. Soon hard-right commentators joined with less-conservative writers in characterizing the poorest of the poor as an "underclass," created not by the pressures of poverty but in large part by drug abuse, crime, and illegitimacy, behaviors themselves glibly associated with "long-term welfare dependence."[31]

Therefore, when Charles Murray and Lawrence Mead hit the bookstores and airwaves in the mid-1980s with full-blown arguments that social welfare policy itself created antisocial behavior among almost all recipients, in addition to creating a permanent underclass, and that welfare programs had to be abolished or made almost totally punitive and work-oriented for the *benefit* of the poor, the basis for today's attack on welfare was complete.[32] A cohesive right-wing argument had been crafted and was presented as a "new consensus" that welfare had failed.

The new arguments pushed far into the mainstream of both political parties, so that by the early 1990s the policy discussion, if not the political rhetoric, shifted away from talking (except in select circles) about "bad people." Instead, the Right could present itself as being the political force with the *real* sympathy for those who endured the bad system that created their poverty, who only needed help to break the "habit of welfare," to attain freedom from bureaucracy, and to have a chance to participate in a rejuvenated economy and revived moral order. Mead, however, like the nativists of old, also argued for government-imposed work programs and other policies to force people to accept employment on any terms. Since welfare, especially "long-term welfare dependence of the underclass," had become a coded way to talk about people of color, "welfare reform" became an acceptable way to do something about black people without being so explicit (although both Murray and, especially, Mead were clear that blacks were the main group needing improved behavior).

Right-wing writers and politicians presented themselves as the true protectors of families (and women), by getting them off welfare and by not offering them the temptation to opt out of the work and family ethic. In Marvin Olasky's words, the way to "renew American Compassion" was by ending the welfare state.[33] Given its tradition of charity, a key step in this progression was convincing the Christian Right to join the assault on welfare. Here Newt Gingrich himself was pivotal, because years ago he made it his explicit goal to "capture the moral high ground" by showing how "no one has been more harmed by the Great Society than the poor," thereby demonstrating his, and the current Right's, "ability to take an issue, rotate it in three-dimensional space, and in the process of doing that, change the character of the debate."[34]

Thus, as the post–World War II economy's long-term retrenchment had begun, the cold war had ended, immigration had increased, and churches had revived in opposition to moral decline, it could all fit together. AFDC became the undefended symbol of all that was wrong with the economy and the people: It hurt society by creating bloated bureaucracies; it undermined the economy by artificially raising wages and giving poor people options besides the "hard labor" that had built America. It broke down families by taking fathers out of the house, by allowing mothers to run a household without fathers or jobs, and by not even caring whether parents were married. It supported a dark-skinned underclass that was already especially averse to work, and it corrupted new immigrants away from working. It destroyed the "American ethic" of personal responsibility.

With such an enemy, the vision grows clear: Society can renew itself only if it gives up its commitment to a "false compassion" and goes back to individualism and basic values of work, faith, and family, as Marvin Olasky has argued:

> The perspective from 1990 shows that the social revolution of the 1960s has not helped the poor. More women and children are abandoned and impoverished. The poor generally, and the homeless particularly are treated like zoo animals at feeding time. . . . Let's transport an able-to-work, homeless person back from the present to 1890 and ask the question, "Are you better off now than you were then?" Then he would have been asked to take some responsibility for his own life, and to help others as well, by chopping wood or cleaning up trash. Then he would have had to contact other people, whether relatives or other colleagues. Now he is free to be a "naked nomad" shuffling from meal to meal.
>
> And what of the children? Let's transport an abandoned child from the present to 1890 and compare treatment now—shuttling from foster home to foster home, or growing up without a daddy—to treatment then, when adoption into two-parent families was a priority preached about in churches and facilitated by a lack of bureaucracy.[35]

In short, welfare, the welfare state, and specifically AFDC now serve as the designated enemy for a vision of the antiwelfare society, where we have no federal floor under poverty, where social spending is so suspect that it can never again be claimed as a sign of social progress. And those who would try to defend welfare have now become the true enemies of our chance to "morally rearm" America and allow people to function as responsible citizens. They have to be shoved aside, along with other politically correct associates, if America is to reach a brighter future.

What Is Happening Now

Welfare has not been just poor policy—that's much too mild. It has been a form of social blasphemy. The truth is, for the last 30 years, our social welfare policies have trumped the accumulated wisdom of human civilization—and overturned rules set in stone ever since men and women first grew their own groceries 10,000 years ago. . . .

In some communities, government has stomped out all that was once vibrant: church, family, and neighbors—and replaced them with nothing but a small, steady, alluring and demeaning little check. The results certainly haven't been as neutral as the checks. We've shaken together a cocktail of fatherlessness and immature motherhood that turned out to be combustible. It has exploded into guns and drugs and boys who kill before they start shaving. . . .

> *Why are Republicans getting elected right and left in America today? Because we are the only ones telling the truth about the damage the Great Society has done. . . . I hope America comes up with a welfare reform law that will allow all of us to get back to the business of raising children who know there's a floor underneath them: church, family and community—the planks of civilized life—*
>
> **William Weld, Governor of Massachusetts**[36]

By 1997, the fantasy has become well framed, institutionalized in the villainous Personal Responsibility and Work Opportunity Reconciliation Act, or PRWOA (the 1996 "welfare reform" bill) and widely shared beyond the Right. And not only welfare recipients suffer. The bipartisan passage of the welfare reform bill, which could have been successfully vetoed, has ended federal entitlements to AFDC and has forced states to deny eligibility for many block-grant funds to most legal immigrants and to teen mothers living alone, among its most notable aspects. Sadly, even the defeated opposition to the bill was primarily raised based on arguments about the extent of change needed, not because there is widespread opposition to the general approach. And with the successful passage of welfare reform, the various strains of the Right have come together more powerfully than perhaps even they quite realize themselves, having created a new consensus around welfare that prepares the ground for an even more tightly constrained "vision" for all of us, not just the poor.

Now there are intellectuals who openly call for a "new nationalism" and "communitarians" who stress obligations, not rights and unity of "basic values," not a valuing of diversity; and who decry an "overemphasis" on basic conflicts in society.[37] Now it is possible everywhere to hear echoes of old elitist traditions calling for renewed order and a unified community based on presumably shared values. Families (read: women) are again to be strengthened by caring for elders and wayward daughters. We hear arguments that only white men can be unifying leaders. By definition, people of color and women are "divisive" until they prove they can rally white men to their cause.

In my view, we are approaching a point of no return in this country's betrayal of its democratic promise with the kinds of proposals that are published in every issue of the Heritage Foundation's *Policy Review*, that are put forward in documents like the Contract with America and in the broader conservative social "covenant" of the Christian Coalition, and that of course underlie the new welfare reform bill. If we can, with great fanfare, pass laws that make legal immigrants unable to receive basic social security protections, what happens to the best of the American Dream? If we can tell mothers, just because they have broken our rules about women's place, that they can be cut off from any economic support for their children after a designated time or, at best, be forced to work for

142   Ann Withorn

basic maintenance without any guarantees of child care or health care, then who is next?

We have already seen states pass rules, with federal permission, that give no benefits to a child unlucky enough to be born to a mother already on welfare. Welfare reform starts to deny disability benefits to those who might be "using" a mental or addiction problem to avoid work. And if affirmative action goes next, there will be fewer and fewer people of color in positions of any authority to make whites uncomfortable or to see what is happening. There is no buffer to the "realities" of life in America when some criminals face a "three strikes and you're out" policy, when others confront mandatory capital punishment, when no benefits are available to pregnant teens and there are family caps facing welfare mothers. The motto of New Hampshire becomes nationalized, not as "live free or die" but, instead, as "live free or we kill you."

Alternative Fantasies Without Fears

Intellectually and politically, the challenge is to define an alternative vision for combating the corrosive right-wing fears and fantasies. A chapter like this is no place to do so, especially without sounding hopelessly rhetorical. All I can do is briefly suggest a few of the basic elements of the strategy that welfare rights activists are forging in their heretofore lonely struggle to defend themselves and the rights of all to basic security.

First, welfare rights advocates know that the only way to answer the fears that poor people are "taking advantage" is to acknowledge that *most* people feel economically vulnerable. The trick is to show how the problem is structural, caused by the "choices" of rich people to protect themselves. The goal is to find ways to show how poor people *share* bad times; neither they nor the welfare system cause everyone's pain. The National Welfare Rights Union, working with the national Share the Wealth Campaign, is consciously reconnecting to traditions of left-wing populism and trying to build a campaign that shows how wealthy people both benefit from conscious decisions by politicians and are currently feathering their own nests while shifts in the world economy make the rest of us more insecure.

Second, welfare rights activists know that it is not enough just to question inordinate government wealth benefits, because that can, and does, lead some middle-class populists to simply argue that the state must be cut for everyone. Instead, the only way to turn the debate around is to expose how a fully global capitalist economy now gives most people less economic security and puts more people at greater risk of real poverty. Since that means greater job insecurity, lower wages and benefits, increased single parenthood, and constant health care "crises," then we

Welfare in Right-Wing Social Thought and Strategy 143

must organize around demands to *strengthen* the welfare state, to protect everyone with income guarantees as well as with calls for full employment at living wages. Indeed, one good effect of the criticisms of the existing welfare system as too bureaucratic is to give new power to the welfare rights movement's long-standing complaints about how the system is administered.

Third, any new programs proposed by the Left must insist on democratic and respectful processes, instead of viewing the fact of asking for assistance as an automatic sign of pathology. The goal is to break the demonization of welfare recipients and push people to admit that "there but for fortune" go their families, so that we can begin to reopen demands for "basic income" guarantees, benefit and wage subsidies, and breadwinning wages for jobs that no longer exist. Welfare rights advocates know that this will mean challenging the conventional realism of the Left that there is no "political support" for income programs, but their hope is to build on alternative democratic traditions that grow out of labor, civil rights, and feminist movements in other countries.

Fourth, the "race card" must be trumped by demanding a welfare state built upon more than calls for increased individual responsibility of black men and communities. Black leaders, especially, must not abandon welfare recipients, and white activists must work to assure that alternative proposals contain concrete strategies that neither relegate people of color to the dole nor deny access to meaningful job opportunities. This is a tough area: Because the connections between racism and antiwelfare rhetoric are very deep and because the ways in which AFDC has indeed been experienced as racist oppression, many African-American activists have traditionally had a hard time taking up the "welfare rights" banner. But if we broaden the demand to "income rights" or to the need to defend "family security" through public commitments, there is room for intellectual and strategic movement.

Finally, women on welfare know that the key will be to reclaim the "moral" arguments about what constitutes healthy families and to stop the widespread denial regarding how real people in most families really behave. We are divorced and have affairs. Most of us, not just welfare recipients, can name a relative with a drinking or drug problem. We are related to some teenager who "got in trouble" or at least could not easily find his or her way. There are more "funny uncles" and "stepfathers to stay away from" than we like to admit. If we acknowledge the *normality* of our "dysfunctions," both social and economic, then we may well be on the road to the identification across classes and identities that is our only hope for the denial built into new calls for "family values."

As depressing as the victories of the fused Right may be, I still find some hope (on some days) because now more people are forced into the

144   *Ann Withorn*

place where welfare rights activists have been for years: We *know* we have no choice but to organize the broadest movement possible. True, the Right will win more before it loses, but we can only reject the social suicide with which the Right tempts us if we understand what is happening.

This chapter began by mentioning the Confederacy, as a way of recalling just how far the American Right is willing to go and as a means of suggesting that we need to reclaim the fervor and breadth of the abolitionist movement if we are to succeed. In that effort, some of us will be called upon to preach, some to teach, some to help women and children hide. We may have to storm some barricades and plot some underground escape paths. And we will need a new vision of rights as economic and social justice that will be broad enough not only to include all diversities but to accept leadership from those who have experienced the worst this society offers. To know the fears, fantasies, and actions of today's Right is an absolute first step for any new effort to combat it. Our necessity is to create a movement as broad, visionary, and focused as the best of the one forged by our ancestors a century and a half ago.

Notes

1. This quote is from Ellen Green, a woman who is on welfare and whose statement is one of many that I have gathered in coediting, with Diane Dujon, *For Crying Out Loud: Women's Poverty in the United States* (Boston: South End Press, 1996).

2. John Salvi, the accused murderer of workers in the Brookline abortion clinics, wrote a generally incoherent statement that seemed to link welfare with his problems and the sin of abortion. *Boston Globe*, January 3, 1995.

3. Although Lucy Williams's excellent article "The Right's Attack on Aid to Families with Dependent Children" (*Public Eye*, vol. 10 [3–4], Political Research Associates, Fall/Winter 1996) was written after most of the drafts of this chapter, I have still used it as a "checkpoint" for understanding the history.

4. For the best summary of how this worked historically, see Michael Katz, *In the Shadow of the Poorhouse*, 2d ed. (New York: Basic Books, 1996). For a good example of this dramatic distrust, see "Absence of Judgment: What Social Workers Believe About the Poor Will Hamper Welfare Reform," *Policy Review* (November/December 1996), p. 50.

5. A good recent source of this argument, although it was a staple of John Birch Society conspiracy theory, is Marvin Olasky, *The Tragedy of American Compassion* (Washington, D.C.: Regnery, 1993). Theodore Lowi's earlier book *The End of Liberalism* (New York: Basic Books,1969) helped to show how this failure of liberalism worked to legitimate conservatism.

6. Cited in David Bennett, *The Party of Fear: The American Far Right from Nativism to the Militia Movement*, 2d ed. (New York: Vintage, 1995), p. 73.

7. The literature on welfare and its meanings is very large. For our purposes here, the most useful recent sources on the history are Michael Katz, *Shadow of the Poorhouse*, and *The Undeserving Poor: From the War on Poverty to the War on Welfare*

Welfare in Right-Wing Social Thought and Strategy

(New York: Pantheon, 1989). Mimi Abramowitz offers an important feminist analysis in *Regulating the Lives of Women: Social Welfare Policy from Colonial Times to the Present*, 2d ed. (Boston: South End Press, 1988). But these sources do not even touch on the extensive theoretical writing that has persistently kept growing over the past twenty years. For as good a summary as any, see Clyde W. Barrow, *Critical Theories of the State* (Madison: University of Wisconsin Press, 1993).

Recently, Italian philosopher Umberto Eco has identified "Ur Fascism" as a concept that allows us to comprehend the basic, but sometimes internally conflicting, themes that unite the modern Right across countries with different traditions and histories. His categories and approach are very useful, and I draw upon them here in trying to establish core themes. See *New York Review of Books*, October 1995.

8. W.E.B. Dubois's classic book, *Black Reconstruction*, chronicles well the absurdity of this and other white reactions to Reconstruction.

9. For me, the term "radical capitalism" is useful because it helps me think about the ideology associated with the most extreme logic of capitalism, as opposed to the very different logic that comes from capitalists who see a legitimate use of the state to help maintain a quality of life outside the market (as well as their power). As someone coming from a very strong "class struggle first" politics, it is hard for me to give capitalism any sort of credit, but I must now admit that the differences among capitalist politics are as significant as those between Stalinists and other kinds of socialists. I think the analogy of "fundamentalist capitalism" to fundamentalist religion is also useful, both of them being the more legalistic, rigid end of a spectrum that includes at the other end a more flexible, responsive set of behaviors and beliefs.

10. The sources that embody this approach are both theoretical and polemical, most notably Frederich Hayek, *The Road to Serfdom* (Chicago: University of Chicago Press, 1944); Russell Kirk, *The Conservative Mind* (Washington, DC: Regnery, 1953). For a sympathetic but useful summary see Ronald H. Nash, *Freedom, Justice, and the State* (Washington, DC: University Press of America, 1980). Also see George Nash, *The Conservative Intellectual Movement in America* (New York: Basic Books, 1976).

11. See Bennett's *The Party of Fear* for the best overview.

12. Here I am conflating a huge amount of social welfare history. Besides Katz, *The Shadow of the Poor House*, see Clarke Chambers's review of the tensions in social welfare history, "Toward a Redefinition of Welfare History," *American Historical Review* vol. 73, no. 2 (Spring 1986), pp. 18–37. See also Bruce Jansson, *The Reluctant Welfare State*, 2d ed. (Pacific Grove, CA: Brooks Cole, 1996).

13. For an eerily depressing story of the decline of abolitionist influence, see James McPherson, *The Abolitionist Legacy: From Reconstruction to the NAACP* (Princeton: Princeton University Press, 1975).

14. Interestingly, the strong stand of the Catholic hierarchy on poverty and even on welfare reform itself may have inhibited this effort.

15. See George Marsden, *Understanding Fundamentalism and Evangelicalism* (Grand Rapids, MI: Eerdmans, 1991). Ralph Reed works hard to confront these tensions in *Politically Incorrect: What Religious Conservatives Really Think* (Dallas: Word Publishing, 1994).

16. Few chroniclers of conservatism parcel out this strain very well, except for identifying its roots in Social Darwinism and tracing it through the thought of

Taft and the *National Review*. The most helpful are George Nash, *The Conservative Intellectual Movement* and Jerome Himmelstein, *To the Right: The Transformation of American Conservatism* (Berkeley: University of California Press, 1990).

17. I know this from my own growing up in the lower-middle-class white South, where fundamentalist Christianity, racism, xenophobic nationalism, and nativism were, and are, just assumed to be "what everybody thinks." Robert Wiebe's neglected book, *The Segmented Society* (New York: Pantheon, 1975), does a good job of explaining how this happens, and in a more historical way, so does the Brinkely-Yohn-Ribuffo summary of the history of conservatism in the AHR Forum, "The Problem of American Conservatism," edited by Alan Brinkely (April 1994), p. 409–452.

18. Quoted in Jonathan Martin Kolkey, *The New Right, 1960–1968, with Epilogue, 1969–1980* (Washington, DC: University Press of America, 1982), p. 52. See Lucy Williams, "The Right's Attack."

19. Reed, *Politically Incorrect*, pp. 10–11.

20. For a recent treatment, see Jean Hardisty, "The Resurgent Right: Why Now?" available through Political Research Associates, Somerville, Massachusetts, 1995.

21. The Heritage Foundation's *Policy Review* was full of especially glowing predictions about how all this would work during 1990.

22. I still find Carol Oglesby's old analysis of a *Yankee-Cowboy War* (Norman: Sheed Andrew and McNeill, 1976) between Eastern and Western, international and domestic capitalists to be useful. Oglesby's cowboys are not, however, only right wing, and not all his Yankees are liberal. As the world economy shifts, we see many Yankees attracted and divided by the notion of unfettered capitalism—just read the contradictory editorials in the *Wall Street Journal*. It is fair to say, however, that both Gingrich and elitist conservatives in the *National Review* are seldom too critical of any type of capitalism, even though they "help" some big business leaders see the error in trusting the welfare state.

23. Newt Gingrich has even claimed that newspapers that oppose ending capital gains taxes are "socialist." And although the notorious Istook amendment, which would gag almost any advocacy among anyone receiving any federal funds, has not yet passed, it has already cast a chill over many of the more mainstream advocates that I work with. I do find helpful arguments against this acceptance of triumphant capitalism, which I find endemic in my adult students at the University of Massachusetts, Boston, in the late Ralph Miliband's brilliant book, *Socialism for a Skeptical Age* (Cambridge: Polity Press, 1994).

24. Lawrence Auster argues for cutting immigration almost totally in *The Path to National Suicide* (Washington, DC: Regnery, 1993). For the view that it is not immigration that is so bad but rather the welfare states' support of aliens after they arrive, see Ron K. Unz, "Immigration or the Welfare State: Which Is the Real Enemy?" *Policy Review* (Fall 1994), pp. 88–96. For a lively and revealing debate on the issue, see comments on Unz's article in the Winter 1995 *Policy Review*.

25. Susan Faludi, *Backlash: The Undeclared War Against American Women* (New York: Crown, 1991), documented some of this, but it has also been explored in Linda Gordon's stunning introduction to *Women, the State, and Welfare* (Madison: University of Wisconsin Press, 1991).

Welfare in Right-Wing Social Thought and Strategy 147

26. See Beverly LaHaye and various issues of Phyllis Schlafly's *Report*, as well as various articles by Robert Rector for the Heritage Foundation, such as his "Welfare Reform That Is Anti-Work, Anti-Family and Anti-Poor," in *Backgrounder* (Washington, DC: Heritage Foundation, 1987).

27. See Marvin Olasky, *Tragedy*, p. 186, and Ralph Reed, *Politically Incorrect*. Also see Peter P. Arnn and Douglas Jeffrey, *Moral Ideas for America* (Claremont, CA: Claremont Institute, 1993).

28. I am especially indebted to Jean Hardisty of Political Research Associates, whose work on women of the Right helped me understand how it is that conservative women defend the existing order.

29. George Gilder is always especially telling here, but so are Charles Murray, *Losing Ground* (New York: Basic Books, 1984), and Marvin Olasky. Interestingly, a long-term study that has done extensive interviewing of women on welfare has found overwhelming evidence of the abuse and lack of nurturance that low-income women have experienced over their lives (Ellen Bassuk, "Single Mothers and Welfare," *Scientific American* October 1996, p. 60–66). Such information is often used by the Right to demonstrate the "pathology" of women on welfare, but I read it to show how dangerous so many "families," of all types, are and how they need to be fundamentally challenged as the automatic source of healthy values for *all* of us.

30. Jill Quadragno, *The Color of Welfare* (New York: Oxford University Press, 1995). For polling data on white attitudes, see Andrew Hacker, *Two Nations: Black and White, Separate, Hostile, Unequal* (New York: Simon and Schuster, 1993). Also, here Dinesh D'souza's arguments against affirmative action and the continued power of racism are critical examples of the rush away from racism as an explanation for any preventive social action. Lucy Williams does an especially fine job of tracing the powerful racism inherent in the Right's antiwelfare arguments in "The Right's Attack."

31. For an excellent review of the range of writing on the underclass, see Michael Katz, ed., *The Underclass Debate* (Princeton: Princeton University Press, 1993).

32. George Gilder, *Wealth and Poverty* (New York: Basic Books, 1981), Charles Murray, *Losing Ground: American Social Policy, 1950–1980* (New York: Basic Books, 1985), and Lawrence Mead, *Beyond Entitlement* (New York: Basic Books, 1985).

33. See Marvin Olasky's latest updating and popularizing of his earlier work *Renewing American Compassion: How Compassion for the Needy Can Turn Ordinary Citizens into Heroes* (New York: Free Press, 1996).

34. Newt Gingrich and Terry Kohler, quoted in Connie Brock, "The Politics of Perception," *New Yorker*, October 9, 1995, p. 75.

35. Olasky, *Renewing American Compassion,* pp. 222–223. Moral Rearmament (a name I have always loved) was an earlier right-wing movement, aimed at helping especially youth rebuild a commitment to national and moral values. The group has waned in recent years.

36. Statement as prepared for delivery by Governor William Weld, American Society of Newspaper Editors, October 13, 1995.

37. In the March 27, 1995, *New Republic*, John Judis and Michael Lind make a direct appeal "For a New Nationalism," deliberately harkening back to Teddy Roosevelt, pp. 19–27.

7

Why Did Armey Apologize?
Hegemony, Homophobia,
and the Religious Right

Anna Marie Smith

Why did Dick Armey apologize? Armey, the House majority leader, committed what he called a "slip of the tongue" in January 1995, in referring to Democratic Representative Barney Frank, as "Barney Fag." Armey's subsequent apology was of course highly equivocal, and he attempted to blame the media first and foremost for blowing his remarks out of proportion. But he did apologize to the extent that *New York Times* columnist Frank Rich commented, "After hearing [Armey] on the floor of the House or reading his rapid-response letter to a Times editorial accusing him of 'hate speech,' you'd expect him to don a pink triangle at any moment."[1] Rich noted that many Republicans were actively courting the homophobic vote. If opposition to abortion rights has operated as one of the unifying nodal points in Republican discourse, opposition to lesbian and gay rights is beginning to play a similar role. Antigay activism on the right is especially important at the state and local government levels and at the grass roots. Official homophobic discourse may be more muted at the national level, but it nevertheless remains quite forceful. Indeed, the Right's attack on Clinton during the gays-in-the-military debate became one of the defining moments of his first term in office. Armey nevertheless felt that it was necessary to apologize for his remark.

Rich and the spokesperson for the gay Log Cabin Republicans argue that Armey apologized because he and other Republicans have recognized that they need the gay vote and that they cannot afford to offend lesbians and gays by making such blatantly bigoted remarks. Quoting Rich Tafel, director of the Log Cabin Republicans, Rich stated, "[Armey] can't afford to alienate gay voters—and gay-friendly voters—because the

G.O.P. may need them as much as it needs the Christian Coalition in '96. Indeed, if this ugly incident accomplished anything positive, it may have been to bring the gay vote out of the closet as a political force Republicans must finally reckon with." Tafel further described the "gay vote" as a "swing vote" that is traditionally Democratic and yet fiscally conservative and disenchanted with Clinton. As such, it is supposed to be available for any number of political articulations. Rich concluded, "Since the religious right is not about to vote Democrat, it behooves a G.O.P. leader like Dick Armey to apologize to voters like Mr. Tafel rather than pander to homophobes who have 'nowhere else to go.'"[2] Rich and the Republican gays assume that political discourse is shaped first and foremost by a straightforward cost-benefit analysis: They believe that Republicans have indeed recognized lesbians and gays as a legitimate interest group. Having weighed the costs of the loss of an imaginary singular "gay vote" against the benefits of increased support from homophobes, the Republicans have supposedly decided to avoid homophobic exclusions.

Rich and the Log Cabin group, however, are wrong. Their analysis is limited by their implicit acceptance of a pluralist model of politics. They assume that political subjects are more or less fixed interest groups that merely compete for access to political resources. Politicians, by the same token, are seen as vote maximizers who attempt to appeal to different voters' blocs to earn benefits—increased numbers of votes—without incurring too many costs, that is, the withdrawal of votes. An appeal to oppressed minorities on the part of right-wing politicians, then, is supposed to be a sign that they continue to recognize the power and value of "the minority vote." Most important, Armey's apology is taken as evidence of the dispersal of power. It is assumed that even when the Republicans control both houses of Congress, the oppressed minorities who are traditionally associated with the Democratic bloc still retain enough voting power to force the Republicans to moderate their exclusionary discourse and make direct bids for their support. In other words, in the absence of a minority vote with at least some clout, the Republicans would not bother issuing apologies[3] and would not construct visions of the ideal American social order that does in fact include right-wing women, Jews, lesbians and gays and people of color.[4] This explanation is not entirely wrong: The Republicans know that they have to attract some "traditional" Democratic voters to their side in order to win elections. It does nevertheless ignore the symbolic aspect of right-wing discourse.

The Right's Evisceration of Liberal Democracy

Armey's apology should be interpreted with reference to three right-wing discourses, emanating from the Religious Right, neoconservatism, and the new racism. Briefly, the Religious Right combines right-wing antiliberalism, a theocratic rejection of secular humanism, populist moral authoritarianism, pro–free market individualism, and an exclusionary nationalism with an attack on the welfare state in the name of the restoration of the primacy of the patriarchal family. Neoconservatism emphasizes possessive individualism and anti–welfare state policies but retains the public-private distinction and tends to subordinate moral issues to economic issues; it often combines a transnationalist promotion of international capital with a racial-nationalist opposition to labor migration and nonwhite immigration in general. The new racism reproduces traditional racist exclusions but legitimates racism as the natural expression of fixed cultural differences; it overlaps and intersects with Religious Right moralism and neoconservative positions on the welfare state, immigration, education and law and order issues.[5]

These three discourses are becoming increasingly sophisticated. Their material exclusions—of lesbians and gays, the unemployed, women, people of color, and so on—have to be legitimated. These exclusions must be at least partially reconciled with the liberal democratic tradition that, for all its weaknesses and contradictions, nevertheless structures what Antonio Gramsci would call "common sense": the taken-for-granted background knowledge that supplies the hidden assumptions behind political discourse that is widely accepted as legitimate.[6] The liberal democratic tradition was to some extent redefined in Europe and the United States after decolonization and the civil rights struggle. The new racism, for example, must operate at least partially within the horizon of postcolonial cultural relativism and "multicultural race relations" in Europe,[7] and within the horizon of *Brown v. Board of Education* and the official doctrine of "color blindness" in the United States.[8]

However, the horizons or boundaries of these terms "multiculturalism" and "color blindness" are rather weak. Their meanings have been at least somewhat fixed; the blatantly racist far Right cannot redefine "multiculturalism" and "color blindness" such that they become perfectly equivalent with its fascist program. The meanings of these terms do nevertheless remain quite elastic, for they can accommodate the parasitic reinterpretations by the Religious Right, neoconservatism, and the new racism. Indeed, these three tendencies have been quite successful in constructing frameworks for right-wing identifications with such key signifiers as "freedom," "equality," "democracy," and "tolerance of difference." The Religious Right, neoconservatives, and new racists do not mount a singular attack against liberal democracy as the far Right has done; for the most part, these groups claim instead that they are the real defenders of liberal democracy. They construct their exclusions of women, people of color, the unemployed, the poor, and lesbians and gays

Hegemony, Homophobia, and the Religious Right   151

as demands for a "return" to an "egalitarian" social order and a "renewal" of "democratic rights" against the imaginary foes of leftist cultural forces dedicated to the promotion of social engineering, a redistributive state, and a reverse-racist affirmative action apparatus.

The American right redefines "freedom," "equality," and "democracy" in a possessive individualist and exclusionary manner that rules out as incoherent the radical moments of the civil rights, black power, welfare rights, feminist, and sexual liberation struggles. Ultimately, the Right's corruption of democratic values would allow it to reconcile its peculiar "democratic" discourse with the perpetuation of virtually every form of inequality. Together, the Religious Right, the neoconservatives, and the new racists have subversively borrowed the language of the civil rights struggle, eviscerated its radical meanings, and stuffed it with profoundly antiegalitarian connotations. Neoconservatives such as Governor Pete Wilson, who have never supported class-based redistribution policies such as progressive taxation, suddenly adopt the language of class equity when criticizing race- and gender-based affirmative action.[9] When Senator Dole of Kansas, the majority leader in the Senate and the front-runner for the Republican presidential nomination, speaks out against affirmative action, he actually borrows the language of antidiscrimination and social constructionist, antibiologistic antiracism, as is apparent in a Dole statement of 1995: "For too many citizens, our country is no longer the land of opportunity but a pie chart where jobs and other benefits are awarded not because of hard work or merit but because of someone's biology. . . . We have lost sight of the simple truth that you don't cure discrimination with more discrimination."[10]

The language of sexual harassment has also been appropriated and inverted by right-wing forces. In one particularly striking case, Craig Rogers, a thirty-three-year-old male student at Sacramento State University, filed a $2.5 million sexual harassment suit against Joanne Marrow, a guest lecturer in Rogers's women's studies class. Rogers claims that he was harassed when Marrow, a tenured professor of psychology who has taught at Sacramento since 1974, delivered an explicit pro-lesbian lecture on human sexuality. Rogers attended the lecture in his senior year and subsequently completed his bachelor's degree in psychology. He states that he left Marrow's lecture "wanting to vomit" and feeling as if he had been "raped." His complaint refers to the fact that Marrow joked about male genitalia, offered tips on purchasing sex toys and on masturbation, and showed slides of children's genitals. According to her lawyer, Marrow does not contest these facts but argues that Rogers's complaint amounts to "fundamentalist Christian McCarthyism" that aims to put "sexuality back in the closet." Rogers's suit rests on the argument that he was coerced by Marrow and the university to attend the lecture. He had sought but had not obtained permission to be excused from the section of the final examination that related to Marrow's presentation. He claims that he had therefore been compelled by the university to attend the class against his will. In a sophisticated attempt to occupy the subject positions of a minority wronged by hostile speech and of a woman victimized by sexual harassment, Rogers argues that Marrow's pro-lesbian lecture violated the university's ban on speech that creates an "intimidating, hostile and offensive" learning environment.[11]

Homophobic forces now tend to avoid blatant genocidal language in favor of pseudodemocratic denunciations of the "special rights" of lesbians and gay men.[12] They often position their homophobia as a populist egalitarianism by invoking the myth of the already overprivileged wealthy gay man. The Religious Right portrays gay men as a homogeneous wealthy group and cynically uses the data about the incomes of readers of gay men's up-market magazines—data that is gathered by advertising managers interested in attracting new business—to support its case. Depending on the precise definition of sexual orientation, the average income of gay men in the United States is actually between 10 and 26 percent lower than that of heterosexual men. Although there is less of a gap between the average incomes of lesbians and heterosexual women, women's income on average remains about 70 percent of men's average income.[13] The myth of gay wealth allows the Religious Right to construct its opposition to lesbian and gay "special rights" as a form of moral solidarity with those who have been laid off in the current waves of downsizing. The term "special rights" also mobilizes a racist and sexist solidarity against affirmative action. A homophobic campaign against lesbian and gay "special rights" can therefore position itself as a populist response to white male unemployment.[14]

This articulation of "special rights" is especially ironic given the fact that "special interests" referred to corporate lobbyists in the 1960s. Since the 1970s, neoconservatives have normalized a totally opposite connotation as it has repeatedly applied the term to labor, environmental, civil rights, and proconsumer groups. By the 1980s, the interests that were once affirmed as public causes were routinely delegitimated as "special interests."[15] The Religious Right's appropriation therefore parasitically draws upon the neoconservatives' redefinition of the common good. Corporate interests were once seen as "special," as external interventions coming from outside the common good that had to kept under surveillance because of their potential to bring illegitimate influences to bear on political institutions. Now corporate interests are integrated into the redefined common good and disappear into the normalized "nonspecial" sphere of "mainstream" political relations, while progressive demands are expelled as external and illegitimate.

By constructing lesbian and gay rights as an authoritarian plot, the Religious Right positions itself as a democratic movement. Indeed, the whole aim of Ralph Reed's representation of the Christian Coalition is to "mainstream" the extremism of Pat Robertson and his followers such that the movement becomes more palatable for a wider range of voters. The anti-Semitic passages of Robertson's *The New World Order* have been the subject of numerous critical reviews.[16] The Christian Coalition's initial response to these attacks was to go on the offensive against what it calls "anti-Christian bias." Then it took a more conciliatory tack. Reed denounced the Ku Klux Klan, George Wallace, and anti-Semitism and called for new coalitions between the Religious Right, African Americans, and Jews.[17] The leadership of the Anti-Defamation League of B'nai B'rith and leading neoconservative Jewish activists have entered into negotiations about joint projects with the Christian Coalition.[18]

There are, however, several limitations to conservative religious coalition building. Mormons in Idaho tactically voted against an antilesbian and antigay state initiative in November 1994 because they were concerned about the Religious Right's anti-Mormon potential.[19] In Oregon, many Catholics remember that the Ku Klux Klan specifically attacked what it called the "special rights" of the Catholic community in the 1920s. When Catholic priests and bishops expressed reservations about the antigay state initiative called Ballot Measure 9 in the 1992 election campaign, a Catholic church was vandalized and sprayed with anti-Catholic and antigay graffiti. Like the Mormons, Catholics tend to hold antigay views, but in the context of anti-Catholic sentiment in Oregon, many Catholics tactically voted against Ballot Measure 9 in 1992.[20] At the current juncture, various fractures between the Religious Right's leadership and its grassroots membership and between different conservative religious movements remain sufficiently prominent to preclude the formation of a totally unified right-wing religious bloc.

The Contradictory Character of
the Religious Right's Homophobia

The Religious Right simultaneously pursues explicit homophobic tactics and disavows its homophobia in its mainstream demands for greater support for the traditional family. Many members of the Religious Right take the absolutist position that homosexuality is, literally, the work of Satan. Their theocratic worldview is utterly antithetical to liberal democratic dialogue.[21] This perspective has informed various political initiatives. In 1995, Representative Robert Dornan introduced two openly homophobic bills: One would have banned the use of federal funds for any federal program that would "promote, condone, accept or celebrate" homosexuality, and the second would have required the military to discharge all HIV-positive service personnel immediately. Congress voted on July 19, 1995, to attach an amendment to the appropriations bill that governs the Office of Personnel Management to prevent federal funds from being used to educate employees about AIDS. The Republicans also attempted to attach an amendment to the appropriations bill for Washington, D.C., that would have prevented the use of federal funds to implement same-sex couple adoptions. Senator Jesse Helms declared that federal spending on AIDS should be reduced because AIDS is caused by "deliberate, disgusting and revolting conduct" and the HIV virus is transmitted by "people deliberately engaging in unnatural acts."[22]

The Pro-Family Contract with America of the Christian Action Network called for the reinstatement of the ban on gays in the military, the "defund[ing] of the homosexual agenda," and the abolition of the office of the surgeon general on the grounds that it promotes "condom distribution to kids" and "homosexual sex-education." Jerry Falwell asked members of Congress to sign his "Moral Contract with America." The central principle of his "contract" is that the family consists of a male husband and his female wife and not "gay, lesbian or any other strange combination." The contract offered by the Concerned Women for America also called for the reinstatement of the ban on gays in the military and rejected "phony AIDS education" and "teaching homosexuality as an acceptable alternative lifestyle." Members of the Christian Coalition were asked in a survey to name the issues that they wanted to see in their organization's "contract." Pat Robertson included a letter with the survey, in which he sharply criticized the conservative members of Congress who are afraid "to be called homophobic for saying the government should stop funding pro-homosexual 'art' projects or for opposing homosexual marriages and homosexual adoptions." One of the seven issues selected by the membership was the demand to "end federal support for homosexual marriage, 'special affirmative action rights' for homosexuals and the agenda of the homosexual lobby."[23] When Clinton barred the federal government from denying security clearances to homosexual employees on the basis of their sexual orientation, the Family Research Council strongly attacked him. Robert Maginnis, the council's spokesperson, stated that homosexuality was a legitimate barrier to security clearance "because in all healthy societies, homosexuality is recognized as a pathology with very serious implications for a person's behavior. ... Even more importantly for security concerns, this is a behavior that is associated with a lot of anti-security markers such as drug and alcohol abuse, promiscuity and violence."[24]

There are, then, many examples of the Religious Right's explicit affirmation of blatant hatred toward lesbians and gays at local, state, and national levels. It is all the more interesting to note that these affirmations are contradicted by certain absences and rhetorical maneuvers. Neither the Republicans' Contract with America nor the Christian Coalition's Contract with the American Family actually mentions lesbians and gays. The Contract with the American Family reveals its theocratic, antifeminist, and homophobic aims in its demands for allowing prayer in public places, local school funding schemes that would free local communities from Department of Education directives, the abolition of federal arts funding, the restriction of abortion rights, "parents' rights," "family-friendly" tax policies, and censorship of the Internet and cable TV. Explicit language about homosexuality, however, is entirely absent. Gabriel Rotello, a writer for the *Nation*, offers two explanations. First, given the Republicans' current strength in Congress, the Christian Coalition does not have to address lesbian and gay rights at a national level because it is highly unlikely that a national lesbian and gay rights initiative would emerge out of a congressional committee.[25] Indeed, when asked, coalition spokespersons stated that they wanted to leave antigay initiatives to organizations working at the state level.[26] Second, Rotello has stated that the Christian Coalition has omitted directly homophobic language because "it wants to locate itself in the mainstream. Having concluded that overt gay-bashing doesn't sit well with mainstream voters, it decided overtly antigay language had to go."[27] Gay rights organizations rightly charged the coalition with duplicity. Elizabeth Birch, executive director of the Human Rights Campaign Fund, the largest gay political organization, stated, "Ralph Reed is talking out of both sides of his mouth because he knows mainstream Americans reject the anti-gay agenda."[28] Richard Berke, a *New York Times* journalist, has argued that the Christian Coalition did not repudiate its basically homophobic agenda by excluding homosexuality from its contract but had only muted its homophobic demands "in an effort to make the contract palatable to a broader range of supporters."[29]

When Reed unveiled the coalition's Contract with the American Family in a Washington press conference, he was joined by a dozen members of Congress, including Speaker Gingrich; Senator Trent Lott, the Republican whip; Senator Phil Gramm of Texas, a presidential candidate; and the heads of several House committees. Although Dole did not attend, he met with coalition officials afterward. He stated that he "welcomed this set of recommendations."[30] Gingrich had differed with the Religious Right by opposing organized school prayer and supporting the availability of federally financed abortions for poor women who are the victims of rape or incest.[31] In the days leading up to the coalition's announcement of their contract, however, Gingrich signaled his support for their views. In a television interview, he stated that the social decay in American society

since the mid-1950s should be attributed to a "long pattern of counterculture belief . . . deep in the Democratic Party" that had "undervalued the
family" and "consistently favored alternative life styles." Rich noted that
Gingrich's language in this statement closely resembled that of Robertson.[32] In a fund-raising letter, Robertson claimed to speak on behalf of
"America's 40,000,000 Christian voters" and stated that "we need a second Contract with America—one that focuses on reversing the ruinous
moral decay and social breakdown caused by a 30-year war the radical
Left has waged against the traditional family and America's religious
heritage."[33] At the coalition's announcement of its contract Gingrich commented, "Here are some key values that matter overwhelmingly to most
Americans. . . . We are committed to keep our faith with the people who
helped with the Contract With America."[34]

The Populist Defense of Inequality

In actuality, the Religious Right, neoconservatives, and new racists only
pretend to champion liberal democratic rights and freedoms in order to
defend traditional class, race, gender, and sexual inequalities. Homophobia will remain a prominent right-wing formation as long as it can be intertwined with sexism and racism such that it becomes an effective political resource for the construction of a cross-class solidarity—or at least an
imaginary cross-class unity. This imaginary unity can be invoked to sup-
press anticapitalist resistance and to organize broad consent—or at least
the "astroturf" appearance of a "grassroots" consenting bloc—for the
Right's procapitalist agenda. This reference to the construction of an
imaginary cross-class unity should not be taken as an endorsement of the
view that there exists, by definition, a natural solidarity among all workers or that the objective interests of a class guarantee the primacy of class
identity over all other types of identity. This is only to recognize that
there have indeed been several attempts to organize anticapitalist resistances in contemporary American politics and that even though some of
these resistances have enjoyed popular support, they have been defeated
at every turn. The popular campaigns against the North American Free
Trade Act and in support of a single-payer Canadian-style health care
system are cases in point. It is striking, however, that these anticapitalist
campaigns have been denied access to the mass media, have been delegitimated through intensive ideological warfare from the Right, and have
been excluded from the mainstream political agenda.

The popular mobilization by the Right around a moral authoritarian
agenda is therefore highly contradictory because it is articulated to an an-
tipopular, procapitalist political agenda, an agenda that will ultimately
contribute to the massive redistribution of wealth from the poorest sec-

tors of American society to the very wealthiest. Right-wing populist mobilizations are always dangerous, for the interpellation of "the people" as a mobilized mass in opposition to the status quo could potentially slip into a genuine grassroots anticapitalist movement.[35] Populist mobilizations must therefore be combined with authoritarian organizing strategies and must be centered on reactionary causes such as racism and homophobia. The latter serve as the ideological cement that binds the right-wing populist bloc together while simultaneously displacing and foreclosing radical anticapitalist articulations. The greater the degree of popular mobilization in right-wing anti–status quo discourse, the greater the importance of ideological maneuvers to contain that mobilization.[36]

How can a political movement that openly supports policies that favor the interests of the wealthy construct itself as a populist liberal democratic defender of "the people?" Six basic strategies are key. First, the Religious Right contributes to the displacement of anxiety about economic inequality—and, to a certain extent, racial inequality as well—by constructing moral issues as the core reasons for the disintegration of American society. With each moral issue, the Religious Right constructs an imaginary cross-class bloc of "mainstream Americans" who are not only threatened by the forces of immorality but have already become "victimized" by an excessively permissive liberal establishment. Class hierarchies are thereby concealed, for the Religious Right portrays virtually every heterosexual family—wealthy or poor—as a victim of the same attack. In this sense, the poor, working-class, and middle-class families that are actually experiencing a decrease in real income and real wealth can obtain a sense of symbolic equality with wealthy families.

Second, the imaginary class-transcendent heterosexual family is portrayed as fundamentally disempowered. Power relations are thereby reversed: The oppressive system of heterosexism disappears, while the actual oppressed peoples, lesbians and gays, are symbolically transformed into the oppressors. The so-called victim, the imaginary class-transcendent heterosexual family that is "oppressed" by homosexual "special rights," can be constructed as an "underdog" subject whose rights are being attacked. The perpetuation of heterosexism and homophobia then take on the appearance of a "liberation struggle" on the part of a "minority" against an authoritarian imposition of alien values. The corporate greed that is actually tearing the fabric of real American families apart in places like Oregon is forgotten as unemployed logging industry workers rail against the "special rights" of lesbians, gays, and blacks.[37]

Third, the Religious Right and the populist Right as a whole constructs itself as the true representative of "the people" by seizing upon already existing concerns that in themselves are "floating signifiers" in that they could be defined in either right-wing or left-wing ways. The Right then offers "solutions" that resonate with popular anxieties and yet frame the popular concerns according to right-wing connotations. Various right-wing interest groups have constructed their demands in libertarian terms: the National Rifle Association (NRA) ("freedom to defend one's family"); the tobacco industry ("freedom of choice"); the corporate lobby ("freedom from oppressive regulation"); the corporate medical insurance lobby ("freedom from socialized medicine"); mining, timber, and real estate interests ("freedom from unjust 'takings'"), and opponents of civil rights laws ("freedom from quotas").[38] In response to popular anger about authoritarian government policies, the Right blames environmental activists. Where there is rising concern about the collapse of the criminal justice system, the Right offers racially framed law and order solutions. Parents' worries about increasingly underfunded schools are redirected against multicultural and pro-lesbian and gay curricula, sex education and AIDS awareness programs. Americans are steeped in an imperialist culture that promises them global supremacy. Many have become extremely disoriented and resentful as present economic conditions fail to correspond to their imperial cultural imaginary. Instead of drawing attention to the role of transnational corporations in the economy, the Right directs resentment toward impoverished immigrants.[39]

Fourth, the Religious Right holds out an alternative vision of America in which every "legitimate" citizen would have a meaningful and valuable place in society. A similar vision served as a particularly fitting conclusion to *The Bell Curve*. Richard Herrnstein and Charles Murray suggested that although many citizens cannot enjoy real power in the economic and political spheres of their lives because of their deficient genetic material, they can at least find fulfillment in the revitalized patriarchal family and in neighborhood volunteer work.[40] The promise of the return to a social order dominated by the patriarchal nuclear family is particularly attractive to heterosexual males who wish to retain authority even as their economic situation becomes more precarious.

Fifth, the Religious Right engages in a populist strategy that simultaneously mobilizes some political elements and demobilizes others. It drags the political center so far to the right that the conservative elements within the Democratic Party become more prominent and move the party as a whole to the right. This in turn contributes to the increasing alienation among the voters who traditionally support the Democrats, such as progressive lesbians and gays, workers, blacks, and feminists. Ultimately, the authoritarian populism of the Religious Right is itself contradictory since it depends simultaneously on the permanent mobilization of a small cadre of right-wing voters and the virtual disenfranchisement of the majority of the electorate. Paul Weyrich stated: "I don't want everyone to vote. Our leverage in the election quite candidly goes up as the voting populace goes down. We have no responsibility, moral or otherwise, to turn out our opposition, it's important to turn out those who are with us."[41]

Finally, the Religious Right participates in various smear campaigns to make the Democrats appear unpatriotic, extremist, and out of control. The combination and fusion of right-wing criticisms of Clinton for his failure to serve in Vietnam, his participation in the antiwar movement, his support for mild reductions in post–cold war military spending, and his pledge to drop the military's ban on lesbian and gay personnel in the military is a classic example. With his massive defeat during the gays-in-the-military debate, Clinton swiftly lost political capital in the first few months of his first term in office. This was precisely the moment in which Clinton made his first and last attempt to introduce a mildly progressive spending package that would have introduced job creation and public investment programs.

With these six strategies, the Religious Right is engaging in a hegemonic campaign to transform the political agenda. The "historic bloc" of a populist right-wing movement, however, is always complex. The Conservatives under Margaret Thatcher held power in Britain through the 1980s even though they never managed to construct a majority bloc of voters who supported their policies. Studies nevertheless found that many voters who actually preferred Labor's policies voted Conservative because the Conservatives seemed to be more unified than Labor, Thatcher appeared to be more "statesmanlike" than Michael Foot and Neil Kinnock, and Thatcher made them feel "proud to be British." Symbolic political discourse about leadership credibility, party unity, and postimperial patriotism therefore played a key role in securing the support of these crucial swing voters.[42]

We should expect a similarly complex strategic advance on the part of the American Religious Right. The Religious Right will probably fail to construct a majority bloc of supporters, but if it can effectively "mainstream" itself further within the Republican Party, convince enough Democratic voters to vote Republican on the grounds that the Democrats are morally unfit to govern, and create the conditions in which many traditional Democratic voters become alienated from the political system and give up voting altogether, then it could gain more political power. That power is already considerable: a Mitofsky International exit poll at the November 1994 elections found that just over 20 percent of voters identified themselves as Protestants who were evangelicals or born-again Christians. Seventy-five percent of those Protestants said that they voted for Republican candidates. Voting analysts estimate that this group is the largest single voting bloc among Republican voters; it represents as much as one-third of all Republican votes.[43] The Christian Coalition has made it

160   *Anna Marie Smith*

clear to Republican presidential hopefuls that it would not position its 1.5 million member organization behind a presidential ticket that included a candidate with a pro-choice position on abortion.[44] *Campaign and Elections* magazine estimates that the Christian Right will control about 20 percent of the delegates at the next Republican convention.[45]

Populism and the Contradictions of Right-Wing Identifications

While the popularity of individual right-wing leaders such as Gingrich may rise and fall, their moral authoritarian, possessive individualist, antiwelfare state, nationalist/transnationalist and racist ideologies increasingly define the terms of the mainstream political agenda. Political statements such as those found in *The Bell Curve* were considered unacceptably extremist only a few years ago; now they are taken for granted as common-sense truth. This is one of the features of hegemonic strategy: A specific discourse becomes increasingly hegemonic as it universalizes itself into a social imaginary so that it is no longer viewed as one particular position among many and its specific rules become nothing less than the horizon of political discourse as such.

In this sense, the Religious Right committed a serious error at the 1992 Republican convention in Houston. Key speeches constructed the Republicans as a party dominated by exclusionary extremists. Attempts to normalize the Religious Right's sexist and homophobic exclusions within the liberal democratic horizon were uneven and insufficient. According to Gustav Niebuhr, "a convention speech by the conservative commentator Patrick J. Buchanan, declaring that a 'religious and cultural war' was underway in the country, was widely denounced as polarizing and counterproductive to a party whose electoral fortunes depend on casting a wide net."[46] Although it is true that the Republicans will never actually "cast a wide net" in the sense of pursuing a political agenda that would actually meet the economic needs of the majority of the population, they must appear to do so in a credible manner for those voters who waver between the Republicans, the Democrats, and the Perot protest vote. In other words, the Republicans must simultaneously reaffirm their material exclusions to appease their support base and "cast a wide net" by offering cross-class inclusions at a symbolic level through their moral authoritarian campaigns.

A hegemonic discourse cannot always afford to avow its extremism in an explicit manner. If it is to become hegemonic, it must no longer be viewed as one political discourse among many; it must obtain a "centrist" and "universalist" appearance; it must locate itself within the liberal democratic tradition. Even further, it must hegemonize the democratic tradition as a whole: It must wage an ideological battle to install its interpretation of democracy as the only possible interpretation, such that leftist and centrist alternatives become increasingly marginalized. In other words, right-wing discourses must organize consent, in the sense that they need to restructure the entire political terrain so their interpretations become routinized and institutionalized.[47]

Reed's strategy—that of "mainstreaming" the Christian Coalition's rhetoric and coalition-building tactics without abandoning its basically extremist agenda—is, therefore, entirely appropriate. A more effective Religious Right would shift from a war of maneuver to a war of position.[48] It would increasingly deploy hegemonic strategies, so that the violence of its material exclusions—its contributions to the massive impoverishment of entire sectors of the population—would be concealed and its pseudoinclusions through the construction of imaginary cross-class blocs would be accepted by the imaginary "mainstream voter" as adequate substitutes for diversity. It would aim to bring a popular bloc into being that would pass as the mythical "general population" rather than as an extremist interest group.

Many right-wing discourses are becoming highly sophisticated in their management of difference at the symbolic level. Even official homophobic discourses, for example, have constructed themselves as "tolerant" of homosexuality, as long as that homosexuality obeys strict rules. The American military and the British New Right, for example, claim that they would in fact accept homosexuality as long as it conformed to what we could call the mythical "good homosexual"—the impossibly self-disciplining celibate homosexual who somehow remains homosexual while remaining utterly asexual, isolated, and silent. The British New Right banned the promotion of homosexuality by local governments in 1988 while simultaneously arguing that they accepted homosexuals as members of British society as long as they did not "flaunt" their difference and engage in "promiscuous" sexual practices.[49] The American military's ban on the "manifestation" of homosexual conduct amounts to virtually the same demand: that lesbians and gays choose between total exclusion or total assimilation and self-erasure. These official homophobic discourses thereby construct their imaginary national spaces as diverse and tolerant spaces by including the figure of assimilated otherness. Similarly, the American neoconservative intelligentsia now includes openly gay figures,[50] and American antiaffirmative action movements often champion their black supporters and spokespersons.

However, the moral authoritarianism of the American Religious Right is so profound that its hegemonic strategies reach a limit with homophobia; its pseudoinclusions extend only as far as the poor, right-wing women, blacks, and Jews. Unlike the neoconservatives, the Religious

Right does not practice even a tokenistic or imaginary inclusion of homosexuality; it is engaged in nothing less than a total war against the entire lesbian and gay community. No lesbian or gay man—not even the most fervent supporter of neoconservative politics—will be able to earn special dispensation in the Religious Right's holy war on America. For every one of the Religious Right's pseudoliberal democratic homophobic demands—that lesbian and gay rights are "special rights" and therefore would endanger genuinely "equal rights"—it indulges in an unmodified form of blatant gay bashing.

With the rise of the Religious Right, sexuality and lesbian and gay rights have become a privileged site for the establishment of Republican politicians' conservative credentials. When Gramm tied Dole in an Iowa Republican presidential straw poll in August 1995, Dole signaled his increasing respect for the Religious Right by returning a $1,000 campaign contribution from the Log Cabin Republicans. Dole's position on lesbian and gay rights has been ambiguous. When asked about the issue in a *New York Times Magazine* interview in May 1995, he stated that lesbians and gays "obviously have civil rights. No discrimination. This is America." He claimed that he had not yet decided whether the ban against lesbians and gays in the military should be reinstituted. Two weeks later, he wrote to the notoriously right-wing *Washington Times*: "I oppose the special interest gay agenda that runs from gays in the military and reaches as far as to suggest special status for sexual orientation under Federal civil rights statutes." Although Dole's campaign had actively sought contributions from the Log Cabin Republicans as recently as May 1995, his spokesperson stated that the donation was returned because "we won't accept contributions from groups that have a specific political agenda that's fundamentally at odds with Senator Dole's record and his views." To date, the Log Cabin Republicans' contribution was the only one that was returned solely for ideological reasons.[51] Dole later reversed his position and stated that his campaign staff had erred when it returned the contribution. Berke, of *The New York Times*, has speculated that Dole made this statement in anticipation of the Federal Election Commission's public release of a report on his campaign contributions. If Dole had maintained that he does not accept funds from any group with which he has policy disagreements, then he would have opened his campaign to intensive questioning about his acceptance of contributions from many other groups.[52]

The inability of the populist Right to decide—its constant shifting back and forth between a pretend-democratic inclusionary form and an explicitly antidemocratic exclusionary form—is symptomatic of its contradictory forms of identification. The Religious Right, neoconservatives, and the new racists need to invent identification frameworks that give the members of their popular blocs the means to locate themselves in a convincing manner within the liberal democratic tradition, but without

Hegemony, Homophobia, and the Religious Right   *163*

paying the price of abandoning their extremism. The right's pseudoinclusionary gestures—its construction of imaginary cross-class blocs, its actual inclusion of conservative women and African Americans as spokespersons, and its apologies to women, blacks, Jews, and lesbians and gays—should be analyzed with reference to this contradictory structure. Armey's apology, for example, may or may not have been motivated by a concern about lesbian and gay voters, but the strategic effect of the apology is to center the extremism of the Republicans. The apology is aimed, first and foremost, not at gay voters but at homophobic Republicans. It does not appeal to an already constituted interest group; it reconstructs the homophobic popular bloc.

The important point here is that the homophobic popular bloc cannot be treated as a preconstituted subject. The role of ideology is not merely to position a subject or to normalize its demands; ideology first and foremost constructs the subject. In this sense, organic ideology is performative,[53] but its performativity remains invisible. Organic ideology brings a new subject into being, but because it borrows from already normalized traditions in its construction of the subject, the new subjects do not feel new; ideological recruitment is for the most part seamless. The constitutive ideology not only provides an imaginary framework for subjects to recognize themselves as coherent and unified subjects but it gives them the means to recognize themselves as subjects who have been there all along; it allows them to position themselves as the authors of the very ideology that brought them into being.

In actual political relations, this work of constructing the subject is never complete. The Religious Right must constantly reconstruct its popular bloc such that Religious Right subjects recognize themselves as having been there all along when they are actually shifting from position to position on a highly unstable political terrain. This is especially the case as the Religious Right continues to appropriate liberal democratic discourse and to contradict itself in its ongoing maneuvers. Homophobic bigots often reverse position, for example, in one speech virtually endorsing physical assaults on lesbians and gays, in the next, claiming to "hate the sin but love the sinner," and in yet another, positioning the homophobic campaign as a patriotic defense of the Constitution and the Bill of Rights.[54] Homophobic subjects are profoundly affected by these twists and turns, learning that unmodified homophobic bigotry is perfectly acceptable but that they are supposed to construct that bigotry in some nominal fashion with reference to liberal democratic values.

Fascist Subjectivity and the Religious Right

The specificities of the Religious Right's subject can be grasped through a comparison with the fascist subject. Fascist discourse aims to mobilize a permanently energized social movement, driven by almost unbridled passion and an explicit thirst for violent revenge against the "enemies within."[55] Religious Right discourse wants to construct a subject that is also moved by bigoted passions but always recognizes the necessity of self-discipline and the primacy of the law. Extremist passions must be channeled through the official legal structure in the very moment of their incitement. If fascism wants to construct the hysterical mob, the paramilitary force that engages in open civil warfare, and, in the case of homophobia, the militant gay bashers, the Religious Right wants to construct the righteous letter writer, the concerned parent, and the committed petition gatherer, financial donor, canvasser, and voter. The ideal Religious Right subject is simultaneously mobilized and neutralized; fired up and pacified; impatient for radical change and content to leave the real action to the leaders, content to seek social reform exclusively through legislative means. As the Religious Right reconstructs its popular bloc, it operates like a special mirror for Religious Right subjects. Having incited their bigotry, it then takes that bigotry and reflects it back to them as good citizenship; it frames the subjects' extremist discourse with reference to the reassuring tradition of liberal democracy.

The lines between fascism and nonfascist authoritarianism are in fact becoming more and more blurred. Arlen Specter has stated,

> There is a continuum from Pat Buchanan's "holy war" to Pat Robertson's saying there is no separation of church and state, to Ralph Reed saying the pro-choice candidates can't be on the Republican ticket, to Randall Terry saying "let a wave of hatred wash over you," to the guy at Robertson's law school who says murdering an abortion doctor is justifiable homicide, to the guys who are pulling the triggers.[56]

To the target of such violence, the differences between the fascist and nonfascist Right may be purely academic. In the moment, one does not feel better if one is clubbed on the head at a demonstration if that club is wielded by a uniformed police officer—like the police who rioted against the peaceful demonstration for the release of Mumia Abu-Jamal in San Francisco on June 26, 1995—rather than by a brownshirt or a white-hooded member of a vigilante mob. As we have seen in the Los Angeles Police Department trials related to the Rodney King beating, the boundaries of legality with respect to officially sanctioned violence are open to a substantial degree of interpretation.

Even where Religious Right leaders reconstruct their extremist bigotry in pseudodemocratic terms, they can incite their followers to commit brutal acts of violence. In the months leading up to the vote in Oregon on the 1992 Ballot Measure 9—a state-level measure that would have overturned

Hegemony, Homophobia, and the Religious Right

local by-laws protecting lesbians and gay men from discrimination and would have required that all state agencies and schools recognize homosexuality as "abnormal, wrong, unnatural and perverse"—there were more incidents of assaults suffered by lesbians and gays in Portland than in Chicago, New York, or San Francisco. This fact is all the more remarkable given the small size of Portland's population—437,000—as compared to those of the other cities, 6,177,000, 17,931,000, and 3,484,000, respectively. During the campaign, an Oregon lesbian, Hattie Mae Cohen, and her gay male friend, Brian Mock, were murdered by arsonists who chanted homophobic slogans after they set fire to their house. One especially disturbing aspect of this violence is that the homophobic assailants concentrated specifically on attacking lesbian and gay activists and their heterosexual supporters.[57] The incendiary rhetoric of the homophobic populist Right also contributed directly to a dramatic increase in antilesbian and antigay violence in other states as well. The Gay and Lesbian Community Center of Colorado received 40 percent of its bias violence reports for the entire year of 1992 in November and December, the weeks following the passage of Colorado's antigay Amendment 2. A similar initiative, Measure 1, was defeated in Maine in the 1995 election. Hate crimes against lesbians and gays doubled during the campaign and bullet holes were found in yard signs that opposed Measure 1.[58]

A state initiative that overturns local by-laws prohibiting discrimination on the basis of sexual orientation amounts to a full-scale assault on the right of lesbians and gays to participate equally in the political process. Colorado's Amendment 2, a voter-approved amendment to the state's constitution that narrowly passed in 1992, is a case in point. After Amendment 2 was ruled unconstitutional by the Colorado Supreme Court on the grounds that it violated the Fourteenth Amendment's guarantee of equal protection of the laws, the state court's decision was appealed to the United States Supreme Court. In his arguments in defense of Amendment 2 before the Supreme Court, Timothy Tymkovich, the Colorado solicitor general, asserted that the local by-laws in question created "special rights" for lesbians and gays in the form of legal protections that are not available to the general public.[59] Only Justice Scalia and Chief Justice Rehnquist made explicit statements that were sympathetic to Tymkovich's arguments. Justice Kennedy noted that Amendment 2 was unique in that its ban against legislation protecting homosexuals against discrimination classifies homosexuals without reference to any particular issue and "fence[s] out the class for all purposes."[60] Several justices indicated that they did not believe that Amendment 2 even passed the test of "rational basis," the very lowest standard of constitutional scrutiny.[61] In 1996, the Supreme Court ultimately upheld the Colorado Supreme Court's decision and ruled that Amendment

166   *Anna Marie Smith*

2 was unconstitutional, in part because it violated the Fourteenth Amendment.[62]

Although homophobic extremism is becoming all the more common at the grassroots level, politicians who want to locate themselves within the official "mainstream" must distance themselves from that extremism. It is strategically problematic, then, for a Republican leader such as Armey to use the term "fag." The occasional use of bigoted language by a Republican politician in an official setting might be politically useful in that it might send a signal to extremist right-wing constituents that the politician has not been corrupted by the artificial "liberal" atmosphere in Washington. It is also not inconsistent for a politician to promote extremist homophobic policies, but that must always be done through pseudoliberal democratic, official-sounding phrases, preferably borrowed from the already normalized aspects of the Religious Right, neoconservative, and new racist traditions. Further, politicians must integrate homophobia into the Republican agenda so that it does not remain a floating signifier. In other words, they must avoid giving the impression that they are using homophobia to divert attention from the "real issues." Homophobia must be hegemonized rather than treated like a single issue, that is, it must be deployed as a point of condensation, a political framework for the expression of already normalized political demands. An isolated homophobic remark, for example, is vulnerable, whereas the "homosexualization" of a proposal to reduce military spending or the homosexualization of affirmative action is more "acceptable."

Armey himself has been quite active on the Joint Economic Committee and in policy areas that affect unemployment, household income, and the viability of small businesses. His political discourse is probably defined more by neoconservative discourse on economic policy than by Religious Right discourse on homosexuality. He can only remain an effective leading Republican, however, to the extent that his discourse reflects the contemporary balance of power in the ideological struggle on the American Right. Therefore, he must simultaneously acknowledge the Religious Right's homophobic demands in explicit terms, reinforce the Religious Right leadership's political credibility by constructing those demands within the horizon of "normal" official discourse, and reassure neoconservatives that he will not dwell unnecessarily on what they may regard as an inflammatory and diversionary issue.

Even if it is obvious that Armey's apology is thoroughly insincere—even if everyone knows that the Republicans deploy explicit homophobic discourse behind closed doors and openly promote policies that produce actual homophobic results—Armey's pretended antihomophobia must nevertheless be publicly written, spoken, and sent to an imaginary lesbian and gay audience. The reactions of actual lesbians and gays are irrelevant to the political effectiveness of this pretend-inclusion. What matters is the way in which Armey's discourse contributes to the mainstreaming of Republican extremism. By pretending to include one of the minorities that will bear the brunt of the Right's vicious exclusions, the Republican leadership constructs its followers as a "tolerant," "pluralist," and "democratic" subject. Republican homophobic subjects are thereby positioned in a way that allows pursuit of their contradictory desire: They are allowed—even encouraged—to enjoy homophobic bigotry as a perfectly legitimate political interest, but they are simultaneously reassured that they remain perfectly "normal" liberal democratic subjects.

Notwithstanding the "landslide" Republican triumph in the 1994 congressional elections, the populist Right is not wholly free to pursue its agenda in an unmoderated fashion. It must continue to observe an intricate set of rules. An unmoderated bigoted discourse might alienate those right-wing voters who have come to expect a homophobia that imitates liberal democracy, cause a breach in the always fragile articulation between the Religious Right and the neoconservatives who are moderate on social issues, or incite expressions of uncontrollable homophobic passions that would ultimately contradict the Republicans' strategy. We could refer in this sense to the "relative autonomy" of official discourse: Official homophobia is not the direct reflection of particular homophobic interests, for it moderates those interests, and yet it does so not to negate homophobia but to construct the conditions for its perpetuation and institutionalization over the long term.[63]

If we note that right-wing politicians must continue to observe in some nominal way the rules of the liberal democratic tradition, then it might be tempting to conclude that that tradition is in some meaningful sense still operating as a defining framework for political discourse. The problem, however, is that the Right is not merely borrowing liberal democratic terminology in a superficial public relations exercise to mask its basically antidemocratic agenda. It is indeed pursuing an antipluralist and antidemocratic agenda, but it is legitimating that agenda by redefining the very meaning of the democratic tradition. It is attempting to present its fundamentally contradictory version of democratic values as if it had exhausted the possibilities of all legitimate discourse.

In psychoanalytic terms, the effectiveness of the fictitious apologies to minorities that are deployed by the populist Right has nothing to do with the response of the actual minority communities in question. The real aim of these apologies is to construct a new system of imaginary and symbolic identifications. The populist Right must not only construct an attractive ideal image of its followers; it must not only portray its supporters as "the good American people," in order for its supporters to become likable to themselves (imaginary identification). It must also construct a point of view from which its supporters will want to be seen, so that the supporters will be able to conceive of themselves as likable insofar as they are observed from that place (symbolic identification).[64] The enduring "organic" or normalized character of the liberal democratic tradition is such that it offers a highly effective framework for symbolic identification. If people can imagine that they are carrying out their political actions under the approving gaze of the liberal democratic tradition, as it were, then they will have little difficulty in defending the legitimacy of their actions. It is almost as if the populist Right must reconstruct the political terrain such that its right-wing supporters could imagine Locke, Jefferson, Madison, John Stuart Mill, and even Martin Luther King Jr. actually smiling down upon them as they attack affirmative action or the mythical promotion of homosexuality in the schools. In this manner, the extremism of their views is concealed. Indeed, the populist Right often goes to great lengths to invoke such figures in explicit terms or to integrate references to Enlightenment ideals, the Constitution, and the civil rights struggle into its discourse. The meaning of liberal democracy, however, is vulnerable to the corrosive effects of right-wing interpretations. Lacanian theorists overstate the case when they argue that political values are perfectly "empty signifiers" and that the effectiveness of an ideological fantasy depends solely on its coherent form.[65] It is nevertheless true that the radical moments of a tradition such as liberal democracy can in fact be almost totally suppressed insofar as reactionary movements like the populist Right gain political ground and pass off their eviscerated versions of that tradition as the real thing.

The radical democratic critic cannot assume, then, that the Right can be defeated merely by demonstrating that it has concealed its exclusions behind the superficial mask of liberal democratic tolerance; instead, it must be demonstrated that the very meaning of democracy itself is the stake in ideological struggle. In this moment of ideological crisis, the fragile consensus on the basic definition of key terms such as "democracy" that was achieved in the formation of the welfare state and in the introduction of civil rights reforms has disintegrated. The radical democratic critic cannot afford to assume that liberal democratic values are so well entrenched that the Right's efforts to redefine them will ultimately collapse in a heap of contradictions; the limits of political discourse are always historical rather than essential. In any event, hegemonic discourses can gain a tremendous degree of normalization and institutionalization while remaining profoundly self-contradictory. The radical democratic critic, then, must not stop short at merely identifying the contradictory and undecidable character of right-wing discourse; the shifting limits of political legitimacy as they are constructed through ideological contestation must be mapped out. When the Right engages in pseudotolerant gestures, it is not only disguis-

Hegemony, Homophobia, and the Religious Right 169

ing or recoding its basically intolerant discourse, it is also transforming the entire political terrain and threatening to obliterate the few remaining progressive moments of the liberal democratic tradition.

Notes

This paper was originally part of a talk that I gave at the New School Graduate Faculty on April 19, 1995. Although I gave the talk in the afternoon, I was at that time unaware that the federal building in Oklahoma City had been bombed in the morning. I would like to thank David Plotke, Aristide Zolberg, and Zillah Eisenstein for their comments on various aspects of the paper. My thanks also to Heather MacDonald for directing her important documentary film *Ballot Measure 9*, to Janine Jackson and Laura Flanders of *Counterspin*, a weekly radio program produced by Fairness and Accuracy in Reporting (FAIR), and to Chip Berlet for his excellent paper on the Religious Right.

1. F. Rich, "Closet Clout," *New York Times*, 2 February 1995.

2. Ibid.

3. Apologies to minorities from the right have been quite common in the first half of 1995. There were apologies by Senator Alfonse D'Amato for his racist imitation of Judge Ito; by Governor Christine Todd Whitman for her remarks about black men fathering children out of wedlock; by Edward Rollins, former political consultant for Whitman and Bob Dole, for his description of two Jewish congressmen as "Hymie boys"; and by Representative Randy Cunningham for his comments about "homos in the military." We have also seen a rebuke and a retreat: Governor George Pataki criticized Joseph Bruno, state senator and majority leader of New York, for the latter's remarks about blacks and Latinos on welfare, and Newt Gingrich backed away from his call for the reinstitution of the total ban on lesbians and gays in the military.

4. In this sense, the analysis by Rich and the gay Log Cabin Republicans bears a striking resemblance to Dahl's pluralist theory of power (Roald Dahl, "The Concept of Power," *Behavioral Science* 2 (1957), 201–205), in which the power of actor A ("the gay voters' bloc") is equivalent to A's ability to make actor B (Armey) do something (apologize for a homophobic remark) that B would not do if A were absent. The following analysis is therefore intended narrowly as a critique of the analysis by Rich and the Log Cabin Republicans, and more generally as an alternative approach to theorizing power, subjectivity, and discourse.

5. C. Berlet, "The Rise of the Religious Right," paper delivered at the Brecht Forum, New York, 28 September 1994; Z. Eisenstein, *Feminism and Sexual Equality: Crisis in Liberal America* (New York: Monthly Review Press, 1984); and A. M. Smith, *New Right Discourse on Race and Sexuality: Britain, 1968–1990* (Cambridge: Cambridge University Press, 1994). The differences between these three tendencies are of course quite complicated, for there are both tensions and articulations among them. The shifts in these discourses since the 1970s are such that these categories may have to be redefined. The breadth of these discourses is also enormous; for the purposes of this paper, I will focus exclusively on specific moments of their representation of sexuality and race.

6. A. Gramsci, *Selections from the Prison Notebooks*, Q. Hoare and G. Nowell Smith, trans. and eds. (London: Lawrence and Wishart, 1971).

7. E. Balibar, "Is There a Neo-Racism?" in E. Balibar and I. Wallerstein, *Race, Nation, Class: Ambiguous Identities* (London: Verso, 1991), 17–28.

8. For a critique of "color blindness," see P. Williams, *The Alchemy of Race and Rights* (Cambridge: Harvard University Press, 1991), 98–132. For a neoconservative interpretation of the civil rights tradition, see C. Thomas, "Civil Rights as a Principle Versus Civil Rights as an Interest," in D. Boaz, ed., *Assessing the Reagan Years* (Washington, DC: Cato Institute, 1988), 391–402.

9. Wilson was a strong critic of the University of California's affirmative action policy. After dismantling the policy on July 20, 1995, the Board of Regents ordered that consideration should be given to individual applicants for admission "who, despite having suffered disadvantage economically or in terms of their social environment (such as an abusive or otherwise dysfunctional home, or a neighborhood of unwholesome or antisocial influences), have nonetheless demonstrated sufficient character and determination in overcoming obstacles to warrant confidence that the applicant can pursue a course of study to successful completion, provided that any student admitted under this section must be academically eligible for admission" (William Honan, "College Admission Policy Change Heightens Debate on Impact," *New York Times*, 22 July 1995). Framed in these terms, the new policy replaces categories that reflect historical macrosocial relations with a whole set of clinical criteria that atomize each applicant and place that person under an unprecedented degree of psychological surveillance.

10. S. Holmes, "G.O.P. Lawmakers Offer a Ban on Federal Affirmative Action," *New York Times*, 28 July 1995.

11. S. Morgan and C. Gamber, "Campus News," *Lesbian and Gay Studies Newsletter of the Modern Language Association* 22, 2 (Summer 1995), 19–20.

12. Berlet, "Rise of the Religious Right."

13. A. Gluckman and B. Reed, "The Gay Marketing Moment: Leaving Diversity in the Dust," *Dollars and Sense* (November/December 1994), 19.

14. For striking examples of unemployed white heterosexual males' expressing their economic anxieties in terms of an opposition against "special rights" for lesbians and gays, see *Ballot Measure 9* (documentary film, H. MacDonald, dir., 1995. 35mm., distributors: Zeitgeist Films, New York).

15. M. Pertschuk, "How to Out-Talk the Right," *Nation*, 26 June 1995, 921–924.

16. M. Lind, review of Pat Robertson, *The New World Order*, *New York Review of Books*, 2 February 1995; F. Rich, "The Jew World Order," *New York Times*, 9 March 1995; A. Lewis, "The Crackpot Factor," *New York Times*, 14 April 1995.

17. P. Gailey, "Mainstreaming Godliness," *New York Times Book Review*, 5 March 1995; G. Niebuhr, "Olive Branch to Jews from Conservative Christians," *New York Times*, 4 April 1995.

18. D. Levitas, "Sleeping with the Enemy: A.D.L. and the Christian Right," *Nation*, 19 June 1995.

19. S. Pursley, "With the Lesbian Avengers in Idaho: Gay Politics in the Heartland," *Nation*, 23 January 1995, 90–94.

20. See *Ballot Measure 9*, documentary film.

21. Berlet, "Rise of the Religious Right."

Hegemony, Homophobia, and the Religious Right 171

22. K. Seeyle, "Helms Puts the Brakes to a Bill Financing AIDS Treatment," *New York Times*, 5 July 1995.

23. G. Rotello, "Contract on Gays," *Nation*, 19 June 1995, 873.

24. T. Purdum, "Clinton Ends Ban on Security Clearance for Gay Workers," *New York Times*, 5 August 1995.

25. G. Rotello, "Contract on Gays," 873.

26. R. Berke, "Christian Coalition Unveils 'Suggestions,'" *New York Times*, 18 May 1995.

27. Rotello, "Contract on Gays," 873.

28. Berke, "Christian Coalition Unveils 'Suggestions.'"

29. Ibid.

30. Ibid.

31. D. Johnston, "Gingrich Diverges with the Right on Abortions and School Prayer," *New York Times*, 10 April 1995.

32. F. Rich, "Gingrich Family Values," *New York Times*, 14 May 1995.

33. Ibid.

34. Berke, "Christian Coalition Unveils 'Suggestions.'"

35. E. Laclau, "Fascism and Ideology," in *Politics and Ideology in Marxist Theory* (London: Verso, 1977), 81–142.

36. Ibid., 135.

37. *Ballot Measure 9*, documentary film.

38. M. Pertschuk, "How to Out-Talk the Right," 921.

39. Berlet, "Rise of the Religious Right."

40. R. Herrnstein and C. Murray, *The Bell Curve: Intelligence and Class Structure in American Life* (New York: Free Press, 1994), 509–552.

41. Eisenstein, *Feminism and Sexual Equality*, 44.

42. Smith, *New Right Discourse*.

43. G. Niebuhr, "The Religious Right Readies Agenda for Second 100 Days," *New York Times*, 16 May 1995.

44. Berke, "Christian Coalition Unveils 'Suggestions.'"

45. F. Rich, "Breach of Faith," *New York Times*, 28 May 1995.

46. Niebuhr, "Religious Right."

47. Gramsci, *Selections from the Prison Notebooks*.

48. Ibid., 236–239.

49. Smith, *New Right Discourse*.

50. J. Atlas, "The Counter Counterculture," *New York Times Magazine*, 12 February 1995.

51. R. Berke, "Dole, in a New Bow to the Right, Returns Gay Group's Money," *New York Times*, 27 August 1995.

52. R. Berke, "Dole Says His Staff Erred in Refunding a Gay Group's Gift," *New York Times*, 10 October 1995.

53. On the concept of performativity, see J. Derrida, *Limited Inc.* (Evanston: Northwestern University Press, 1988) and J. Butler, *Gender Trouble: Feminism and the Subversion of Identity* (London: Routledge, 1990).

54. *Ballot Measure 9*, documentary film.

55. S. Payne, "The Concept of Fascism," in S. Larsen et al., *Who Were the Fascists?* (Oslo: Universitetsforlaget, 1980), 14–25; and R. Paxton, "Comparative Fascisms," Cornell University, 31 March 1995.

56. F. Rich, "David and Goliath," *New York Times,* 7 May 1995.

57. *Ballot Measure 9,* documentary film.

58. "Task Force Asks Attorney General Reno to Take Action on Oregon Killings," press release, National Gay and Lesbian Task Force, 13 December 1995 (at web page address http://www.ngltf.org), p. 32.

59. *Romer v. Evans,* U.S. Sup.Ct. 94-1039, arguments heard on 10 October 1995.

60. L. Greenhouse, "U.S. Justices Hear, and Also Debate, a Gay Rights Case," *New York Times,* 11 October 1995.

61. Ibid.

62. *Romer v. Evans,* U.S. Sup.Ct. 94-1039.

63. Here I am referring to that strand of Marxist theory that holds that the state is relatively autonomous from the class struggle. As a relatively autonomous institution rather than an instrument of the ruling class, the state is able to mediate between the conflicting interests of various fractions of the capitalist class and to neutralize the demands of the workers. Ultimately, however, the state does so to secure the reproduction of capitalist relations over the long term. See K. Marx, "The Eighteenth Brumaire of Louis Bonaparte," in R. Tucker, ed., *The Marx-Engels Reader* (New York: W. W. Norton and Co., 1978), 594–617; N. Poulantzas, "The Problem of the Capitalist State," *New Left Review,* 58 (1969), 67–78; *Political Power and Social Classes* (London: New Left Books, 1976); *State, Power, Socialism* (London: New Left Books, 1976).

64. S. Zizek, *The Sublime Object of Ideology* (London: Verso, 1989), 105–106; R. Salecl, *The Spoils of Freedom* (New York: Routledge, 1994), 33, 65.

65. Zizek, *The Sublime Object of Ideology.*

8

The Color of America's Culture Wars

Amy E. Ansell

W.E.B. DuBois once wrote that the deepest fissure on the American political landscape is the color line. From the perspective of only a few short years before the end of the millennium and nearly one hundred years after DuBois unveiled "the souls of black folks," such a statement remains all too relevant. Although there has been a relative silence around race in the post–civil rights era in the United States,[1] events in the past several years have revealed that there is a simmering cauldron of resentments and anxieties beneath the public silence, serving as a reservoir to be exploited by personalities and organizations on the right wing of the political spectrum. The Rodney King beating by the Los Angeles Police Department and the subsequent Los Angeles "race riots" in spring 1992, together with the more recent public obsession over the racial meanings surrounding the O. J. Simpson trial and the contrived innocence and inclusive pageantry broadcast during the 1996 presidential election convention season (both Republican and Democratic), are only the most salient examples of the degree to which racial symbols remain compelling in the American political imagination in the post–civil rights era.

In the run-up to and in the wake of the conservative Republican victory in the 1994 midterm elections, the reservoir of white backlash sentiments began to express itself politically in the form of anti-immigrant politics (Proposition 187) and the politics of reverse racism (the California Civil Rights Initiative). And in the academy, recent controversial publications such as *The Bell Curve* by Richard Herrnstein and Charles Murray, *The End of Racism* by Dinesh D'Souza, and *Alien Nation: Commonsense About America's Immigration Disaster* by Peter Brimelow testify to the degree to which political manipulation of the explosive depth of the color line remains intellectually pertinent.

Although many regard the renewed salience of race in U.S. politics and society as a result of the near spontaneous combustion of white backlash sentiments or as a reasonable response to objective problems concerning mutually antagonistic "race relations" in multicultural democracies such as the United States, this chapter argues that the racial dimension of America's right turn is fundamentally a social phenomenon in need of explanation.

From the sociological point of view, it is not surprising that race has exploded onto the national political landscape at this particular historical juncture. There has been an unmistakable drift of political opinion to the right in U.S. society since the late 1970s, as new players on the right wing of the political landscape—defined here as the New Right[2]—have succeeded in constituting a new climate of opinion that is deeply hostile to the type of liberal egalitarianism that marked the postwar era. Race has become a key symbol in the formation of a new authoritarian democratic consensus, organized around the New Right defense of individual liberty, market freedom, traditional values, and white racial nationalism. Furthermore, changes in the international context, and in particular the end of the cold war, have produced an identity crisis of sorts at home that is bringing to the fore questions related to the meaning of American pluralism and national identity, domestic questions at the heart of what many have characterized as the culture wars.

This chapter aims to examine the degree to which these conservative-led culture wars have a color, that is, to analyze the degree to which the categories of assumptions about national identity mobilized in the culture wars carry implications for how people differentiated by race and ethnicity are either included within or excluded from the framework of the national community. I will argue that the conservative-led culture wars are part of an ongoing contest in American society to define the "we" to whom specific moral obligations apply and the "they" to whom nothing is owed.[3] The culture wars imply a politics of indirect exclusion as they serve to define categories of people as outside the broader universe of obligations, thus challenging many liberal assumptions that have dominated American society and politics for the past half century. In order to reconcile America's democratic ideals with the politics of indirect exclusion, conservatives have contested previously dominant cultural codes and liberal assumptions related to the pursuit of racial equality.

In the process, the conservative-led culture wars have brought in their wake a new breed of racism, one characterized largely by an absence of mean-spirited affect or antiblack sentiment.[4] The new racism operates on the basis of ideas such as individual rights and color blindness, denying that it is a theory about race at all, its principles all the while serving to justify the retreat from racial justice in thought and policy. The new

The Color of America's Culture Wars

racism actively disavows racist intent and is cleansed of extremist intolerance, thus reinforcing the New Right's attempt to distance itself from racist organizations such as the John Birch Society and the Ku Klux Klan. It is a form of racism that utilizes themes related to culture and nation as a replacement for the now discredited biological referents of the old racism. It is concerned less with notions of racial superiority in the narrow sense than with the alleged threat blacks pose—either because of their mere presence or because of their demand for "special privileges"—to the economic, sociopolitical, and cultural vitality of the dominant (white) society. It is, in short, a new form of racism that operates without prejudice, and even without the category race. It is a new form of exclusionary politics that operates indirectly and in stealth via the rhetorical inclusion of people of color and the sanitized nature of its racist appeal.

The new racism is couched within, not against, America's civil religion, taking on the vocabulary of equal opportunity, color blindness, race neutrality, and, above all, individualism and individual rights.[5] It has operated by circumventing the vocabulary of the civil rights movement itself. As is evident from the California Civil Rights Initiative that won voter approval during the 1996 presidential election, it is the New Right that currently champions the idea that people should be judged on the "content of their character" and not the color of their skin. Words and phrases such as "color blindness" and "opportunity" have been similarly highjacked and repackaged so as to service a different agenda, this time in favor of a politics that is, albeit indirectly, exclusionary rather than inclusionary in spirit. Accordingly, analysis of the new racism need not be driven by a search for the irrational or the bizarre. Rather, it is important to trace the way in which the new racism is becoming a hegemonic discourse as a function of the New Right's successful attempt to center its discourse on race and normalize it in relation to other more mainstream political discourses and cultural codes.

For the most part, mainstream social science has failed to track the emergence of the new racism precisely because of its symbolic recoding and, most important, because of its apparently benign race-neutral form. For similar reasons, the new racism has penetrated popular ways of thinking on the part of social groups that are caught up in the confusion and chaos of the period and are looking for answers yet are unresponsive to those who employ blatant tactics of scapegoating or explicitly express intolerant or exclusionary sentiments.

Although they do not directly focus on race per se, four current controversies at the center of national political debate today—immigration, affirmative action, welfare, traditional values—mobilize a set of meanings about the difficulties inherent in a democracy constituted by peoples of different racial, ethnic, and cultural backgrounds. The fact that the conservative reaction to such policy areas is so out of proportion to the actual threat demands analysis of the process by which society has come to perceive diversity as an index of the disintegration of the social order, as a sign that the "American way of life" is being threatened. Race in America has become the ideological conductor of the politics of indirect exclusion. An understanding of the new racism of the New Right is crucial if progressives are to effectively intervene in and combat recent political debates that assume a nonracialist form but nevertheless serve to establish and maintain relations of racial inequality. I will briefly examine these four controversial policy areas, using them to shed light on the ways in which the new racism has penetrated and dislodged many of the assumptions that previously guided the policymaking process in the postwar United States, with telling effects for the politics of indirect exclusion.

Immigration

The United States is commonly lauded as a "land of immigrants," a "melting pot" of diverse ethnic and racial groups, or at least a "salad bowl" combining the best tastes each respective cultural group has to offer. As compared to the exclusive nature of European conceptions of national identity and the xenophobic movements that have historically been linked to them, national identity in the United States has been in principle more inclusive in character. Explicit reference to nationalism and xenophobia has historically been limited in its expression to the extreme fringes of the American political spectrum.

The liberal temperament of American national identity helps explain why, throughout the 1970s and 1980s, political exploitation of the issue of immigration was more characteristic of the Far Right (individuals and groups such as the Liberty Lobby, David Duke, the Federation for American Immigration Reform, English First, and the English Only Campaign) yet was virtually absent in the politics of the New Right. By contrast with the New Right in Europe during this same period, much of the American New Right, especially the intellectual wing (i.e., the neoconservatives), expressed support for liberal immigration policies. Indeed, the "American way of life" has long been conceived as being about regard for universal values such as equality, individual rights, and achievement. Such universal values, by the New Right's own admission, prove to be assimilable by immigrants.

By the time of the run-up to the 1994 midterm elections, it was clear that this liberal temperament was open to challenge, provoking a new willingness on the part of certain factions of the New Right to take a second look at the issue of immigration. To explain this change in temperament, one would be ill-advised to simply look for clues in objective measures of the number of immigrants and asylum seekers, for even the most bloated estimates fail to explain the degree to which the issue captured the symbolic imagination of the media and the voting public. Beginning in 1993, there emerged a series of media stories reinforcing the idea that immigrants—both legal and illegal—constitute a threat to the "American way of life." Implying that the ethos of America as a melting pot may be reaching the point of a boiling cauldron, the mainstream media were blitzed in the run-up to the 1994 vote on the anti-immigration measure Proposition 187 with images of the Statue of Liberty in distress. For example, a July 1993 *Newsweek* article illustrated what it called the "immigration backlash'" with a cover depicting the Statue of Liberty up to her nose in a rising tide of boat people. *Chronicles* magazine ran a headline story titled "Bosnia USA," accompanied by a picture of a throng of pointy-eared, fiendish creatures scrambling up a crying Mother Liberty.

The success of Proposition 187 in winning voter approval on the 1994 California ballot first sent the signal that immigrants would be among those to be moved outside of the culturally constructed universe of obligations. Proposition 187 was geared to deny undocumented immigrants education, social services, and nonemergency health care. Under the proposition's terms, educators, social workers, health professionals, and law enforcement agents would be required to report suspected illegal immigrants and their families to the appropriate governmental authorities. California Governor Pete Wilson made Proposition 187 a cornerstone of his successful reelection campaign, with many attributing his reelection to his backlash-pandering positions on immigration and affirmative action.

Also in 1994, as a spin-off of the Republicans' "Contract with America," congressional legislation was drafted that would have barred most legal immigrants from sixty federal programs, prohibiting them from receiving free childhood immunizations, housing assistance, Medicaid, subsidized school lunches, and many other federal benefits. The contract itself included proposals to significantly increase efforts to limit illegal entry into the country and to make illegal migrants ineligible for almost all federal, state, and local welfare benefits, with the exception of emergency medical services and nutrition programs. The contract also allowed for the deportation of legal immigrants who receive more than twelve months of public assistance during their first five years' residency in the United States.

Rather than offer a counterstory, President Bill Clinton responded to the conservatives' story about an invasion of undeserving immigrants in a manner that reaffirmed the discursive links being forged by the New Right—in this case, between welfare dependence and (Hispanic) immigration—by issuing a directive that called for a crackdown on employers of illegal aliens and more money (an extra $1 billion in fiscal year 1996) to thwart illegal entry into the United States. The welfare bill that he signed in August 1996 follows through on most of the stipulations outlined here and also places a ban on most forms of public assistance and social services for legal immigrants who have not yet become citizens.

Although it is certainly legitimate in a liberal democratic society to entertain open debate about the merits and proper levels of immigration, the national conversation in these cases revolved around the illiberal premise that misguided welfare policies were serving as a magnet attracting a flood of unassimilable illegal immigrants from Mexico and elsewhere in Latin America and the Caribbean. Despite contradictory evidence in the social science literature regarding the economic and social impact of immigration, supporters of Proposition 187 and drafters of the congressional legislation portrayed immigrants as "welfare schemers" and "embezzlers of public funds" and as responsible for stealing jobs and worsening social problems such as crime, thus feeding into a long cycle of scapegoating immigrants during periods of economic strain.

Such legislative activity around the immigration issue led to vigorous debates within New Right circles. Neoliberals writing for the *Wall Street Journal* favored open borders and warned of the potential for such activity to lead to a mandate for bigotry and racial discrimination. Neoconservatives supported a policy of assimilation for legal entrants in the pages of *Commentary* and were concerned that any type of anti-immigrant plank would be a loser for the GOP in the long run. Paleoconservatives such as Peter Brimelow advocated a fortress America, to protect against any further dilution of the nation's white racial stock. It is the latter group that deserves particular attention as it is spearheading the effort among conservatives to reconstruct the color white as a dominant nonracist cultural identity.

In previous years, conservatives attempted to erode liberal racial policies such as multiculturalism in the name of constitutional principles of fairness. In the wake of the 1994 Republican landslide, however, the paleoconservative strand of the New Right coalition began arguing for a more formative, bold defense of the dominant (white) culture against challenge, thus demonstrating a new willingness to introduce the question of the racial and ethnic composition of the United States into the public debate. A number of paleoconservative intellectuals—most notably John O'Sullivan (editor of the *National Review* and an emigrant from Britain) and Peter Brimelow (senior editor of *Forbes* and also an emigrant from Britain)— have begun to lay the foundation for a new ideological war that transcends conservative policy proposals to combat illegal immigration and instead challenges the heart of the national creed of America as a nation of immigrants. Sounding suspiciously similar to right-wing populists in Europe, such paleoconservatives warn that in the context of Census Bureau

The Color of America's Culture Wars 179

projections that the majority of the U.S. population will become "nonwhite" by the year 2050, current high levels of black and Hispanic immigration will drastically alter the U.S. national identity and in fact lead down the road to national suicide. Peter Brimelow begins his book *Alien Nation* with the words, "There is a sense in which current immigration policy is Adolf Hitler's posthumous revenge on America." In warning against this "alien nation," Brimelow and other paleoconservatives advocate a new willingness to embrace a national identity defined in explicitly racial and ethnic terms. Translated into the political sphere, right-wing personalities such as Patrick Buchanan, who are keen on exploiting the issue of immigration as part of an aggressive bid for power, are serving as a bridge between a Far Right that has long exploited the racial referents of the immigration debate and the wider New Right movement concerned more about economic and citizenship issues.

Demonstrating the continuing tension between those New Rightists concerned with liberal free market policies and limited government and those who advocate cultural conservatism and a racial-nationalist agenda, deep internal divisions within the New Right coalition over the issue of immigration signal a likely strategy of evasion in the near future. This means that the enemies of the "American way of life" will likely continue to be "illegals" who break the law and the impersonal liberal social policies such as welfare that destroy the fabric of society, whereas the racially coded symbol of the black or Hispanic immigrant will remain subtextual, there for those who wish to discover it.

Affirmative Action

The policy of affirmative action has been one of the most contentious, long-standing, and arguably most effectual institutional legacies of the civil rights movement in the United States. In large part due to this legacy but also for fear of being branded racists, New Rightists did not fundamentally challenge the policy throughout most of the Reagan/ Bush era. This is not to imply that the New Right was not unified in its opposition to affirmative action: It was. Beginning in the early 1970s, neoconservative intellectuals developed a principled critique of the policy. Affirmative action for people of color beyond the guarantee of individual equality of opportunity, according to New Rightists: (1) discriminates against the (white) majority and so constitutes "reverse racism"; (2) creates a special class of people protected by the law and thus makes people of color more equal than others; (3) harms the very groups that it sets out to help; (4) causes and perpetuates, rather than resolves or rectifies, racial conflict and polarization; and (5) fuels the tyranny of the "new class" of liberal government bureaucrats.[6]

Despite a quite solid consensus against affirmative action, conservative opposition was, for the most part, not expressed politically throughout the 1980s. It was not until the 1994 so-called Republican revolution that affirmative action entered center stage on the U.S. political scene; all of a sudden, resentment of state-order "preferences" became politically smart. Then Senate majority leader Bob Dole (Kansas Republican), a one-time supporter of affirmative action, began to criticize the policy as ineffectual and unfair. In early 1996, two other important presidential hopefuls besides Dole—Senator Phil Gramm of Texas and Governor Pete Wilson of California—promised to abolish racial "preferences" if elected. President Clinton eventually came round to give his tepid support to affirmative action, as captured by the bumper-sticker phrase "Mend it, don't end it," but only after commissioning a five-month Labor Department internal review process to study its effects, thereby sending a signal of less than total commitment.

The transmutation of affirmative action from a subterranean-movement concern to a winning campaign strategy dovetailed with the emergence of a new consensus on affirmative action that replaced conservative solicitude for individual rights (versus group rights) and equality of opportunity (versus outcome) with vigilance for whites (and especially white males) as victims of black special interests. Such symbolic construction of victimhood on the part of whites and the blatant hypocrisy it evokes was captured in a *New York Times* editorial cartoon published in June 1995 following a series of Supreme Court decisions limiting affirmative action. The cartoon showed a white man bounding down the steps of the Supreme Court shouting "Free at last. Free at last. Thank God almighty, free at last."[7] Despite such rhetorical reversals of victim and perpetrator, reliable economic indicators continue to demonstrate that although whites have suffered losses in terms of security, income, and jobs because of broad long-term structural trends, they have not lost power and advantage.[8]

Reinforcing this shift in consensus toward white victimhood was reform of affirmative action spearheaded by a number of different players: state lawmakers bolstered by anti–affirmative action local campaigns; a new Republican congressional majority taking aim at the Democrats' civil rights record and proposing color-blind legislative initiatives; and the courts, where cases were being decided that challenged race-based affirmative action in student admissions, federal contract assignments, and employment.

It was the California Civil Rights Initiative (CCRI), or Proposition 209, as it appeared on the 1996 November ballot in California, that first broke the mold. Referred to as "the son of 187," Proposition 209, which also won voter approval and has since been upheld by the courts, will effectively amend the California constitution to prohibit programs that work to open up opportunities for people of color and women in public employment, education, and contracting. The CCRI was a triumph for New Rightists, allowing them to claim moral authority on the subject of civil rights.[9] For example, Rush Limbaugh taints the Democrats as bigots for opposing the CCRI: "This is such a great thing because it points out the truth here about who's racist and who's not, who's bigoted and who's not. And guess who it is that's sweating this out, guess who it is that's biting their nails? . . . It's Democrats. . . . What are we going to call them? Bigots. They will be bigots. The people who oppose ending discrimination."[10]

The New Republicans in Congress have sought to jump on the bandwagon, thereby maximizing electoral benefit from such local and state legislative and bureaucratic activity and from the popular sentiments they purportedly reflect. Although earlier congressional initiatives had taken aim at affirmative action, it was not until the 1995 legislative session that it appeared that the Republican Party was willing to tackle the issue of affirmative action head-on. For an answer to the question "Why now?" one would be ill-advised to look for any significant change in public opinion. Rather, the reasons can be found in two simple facts: First, Republican victories in 1994 meant that critics of affirmative action now controlled key congressional committees, and second, the 1996 presidential campaign season was around the corner. Newt Gingrich in particular used his newfound power as Speaker of the House to lampoon liberalism on the issue: "The founders guaranteed the pursuit of happiness, not happiness quotients, happiness set-asides, the Federal Department of Happiness."[11] Conservative Republicans introduced the Equal Opportunity Act, informally referred to as the Dole-Canady bill and essentially a federal version of Proposition 209. Although the act never came up for a vote in either chamber, ostensibly because of the summer break but also because of conservative Republican prevarication on the issue,[12] if passed, it would have barred the federal government from giving any preference by race or gender or obliging others to do so.[13]

Just when it appeared that affirmative active was last year's issue, an important Supreme Court ruling in March 1996 in *Cheryl Hopwood v. the State of Texas* brought it back to political life. The Court's decision on the Hopwood case (referred to by many as Bakke II), involving a two-track admissions system at the University of Texas Law School, essentially proscribed the use of race-based preference devices in institutions of higher learning unless they can be shown to serve a compelling government interest and are narrowly tailored to satisfy that interest.[14] The Hopwood case was in fact only the culmination of a series of decisions taken by an increasingly conservative Supreme Court, decisions that have chipped away at the legal foundation and narrowed the scope of affirmative action.

It was in this historical context, marked by multiple cultural and institutional sites of backlash, that New Rightists took seriously the prospect of organizing around the issue of affirmative action in the run-up to the 1996 presidential election. In the words of Grover Norquist (confidant of Gingrich, founder of Americans for Tax Reform, and leader of the Leave Us Alone Coalition), opposition to racial preferences is the perfect issue: "It unites the Republican team, divides the Democrats, and it's worth winning."[15] According to Norquist, whereas conservatives have been on the defensive since the 1950s because of their lack of support for a color-blind society and as a result "wet their pants whenever they think about Selma and feel bad,"[16] it is now the Left that is on the defensive. Norquist sees the issue of color-blind public policy as the Achilles heel of the Democratic Party and summons conservative leaders willing to recover and uphold the original, color-blind principles of the civil rights movement. Norquist's call to arms expresses a widespread sentiment in contemporary conservative circles that when it comes to the civil rights establishment, there is only one hand clapping.

Whereas the New Right has over the years built counterestablishments to fight, for example, the feminist and gay rights lobbies, virtually nothing has existed on the civil rights front. Two important exceptions have been the Institute for Justice, founded by Chip Mellor and Clint Bolick, and the National Center for Neighborhood Enterprise, directed by Robert Woodson. In 1995, there emerged for the first time a conservative think tank primarily concerned with issues related to race and public policy—the Center for Equal Opportunity, directed by Linda Chavez (former director of the U.S. Commission on Civil Rights and author of *Out of the Barrios*). Around the same time, a group calling itself Project 21 emerged to give black conservatives a national voice and to counter what the organization regards as increasingly out of touch black leaders. The Center for New Black Leadership is the newest organization to have emerged and is similarly oriented toward advocating alternatives, such as school vouchers and enterprise zones, to those traditionally favored by the so-called civil rights establishment. Such counter–civil rights establishment organizations have been augmented by a range of black conservative publications that have joined the more established *Lincoln Review* and *Issues and Views*. Most notable among these new publications is *National Minority Politics*, a monthly publication that features black and Hispanic conservative columnists. Its success has led its founders, Willie and Gwen Richardson, to establish an associated broad-based conservative organization called Minority Mainstream, the self-stated objective of which is to give the mostly white conservative wing of the GOP majority a black and Hispanic presence.

Despite this burst of energy, opposition to affirmative action, the much celebrated battering ram against the Democrats, began to inflict ugly splits within the Republican Party itself, at a time when, in the run-up to the 1996 presidential election, party unity was essential. Although conservatives were united in their opposition to liberal preferentialism, they were confused and divided on what was to replace it (i.e., the proper nature and limits of colorblindness). Strategic divisions also emerged: Those in Congress who conceived of using antiaffirmative action as an effective tool against the Democrats or who were ideologically tied to the New Right advocated a "full steam ahead" approach, whereas those who were concerned about the potentially destructive impact of the issue on the Republican's own team or who worried about prospects for outreach to communities of color encouraged a "go slow" approach. This tension led to a series of disagreements and prevarications on Capitol Hill. With the latter group emerging as victorious as the election season rounded the corner, the project of keeping up inclusive appearances once again took precedence over the Republican case against affirmative action.

Welfare and Traditional Values

New Right support for conservative welfare reform, like its narratives about affirmative action and immigration, reinforces a narrative regarding the meaning of American pluralism and identity in the post–cold war era. Conservatives believe in a society in which individuals rise and fall in the social hierarchy on the basis of individual merit. Indeed, the acceptance of inequality as a social inevitability, even a social good, is a definitive hallmark of the conservative movement. It is from this wider perspective that conservatives oppose government entitlement programs. Since inequality is merely an inevitable consequence of differences in individuals' natural or inherited abilities, conservatives argue, it is impossible to eradicate it below its natural level and wrong for government to attempt to do so. Policies born to redress race and class inequality are said to produce "dependency," itself an affront to the deep and abiding Protestant belief that individuals make their own lives and are responsible for their own success or failure. Thus, by relocating the source of inequality from the social structure to individual ability and by celebrating the laudable goals of colorblindness and equal opportunity, conservatives render problematic those cultural references to notions of collective identity, group rights, and social justice that had in the past supported New Deal and Great Society welfare rights and provisions.

Throughout the 1970s and 1980s, conservatives sought to stigmatize the Great Society legacy as an overly indulgent form of social engineering. Neoconservative intellectuals such as George Gilder, Charles Murray, and Irving Kristol castigated welfare programs for destroying traditional gender roles and replacing free market mechanisms with less efficacious government handouts.[17] Besides drawing on the then current mantra that "government is part of the problem, not the solution," right-wing welfare reformers made use of the significant racial subtext beneath the Reagan challenge to "welfare state liberalism." The administration attempted to appeal, without saying so directly, to voters who felt that Democratic welfare programs are tilted toward "special interests" and toward blacks and Hispanics in particular. In fact, there is a great deal of evidence to venture further and suggest that conservative policymakers deliberately fed such a misperception. Cutbacks in social spending were justified consistently with racialized stereotypes about welfare, drugs, and crime. For example, Reagan repeatedly spoke of "welfare cheats" picking up their checks in Cadillacs and "welfare queens" having more and more babies in order to get increased benefits.[18] Such welfare abusers were almost always depicted as black—this despite the fact that roughly two-thirds of welfare recipients were, and continue to be, white.

Racial subtext or not, it became clear that by the late 1980s a new consensus on welfare was emerging within Congress and within the political culture more generally. The 1988 Family Support Act (requiring benefit recipients to participate in workfare-related education, training, and placement programs, among other things) punctuated the end of a long process whereby a new "dependency" paradigm was replacing the poverty paradigm that had reigned from the New Deal and Great Society eras and beyond, with an attendant shift in focus by policymakers from structural sources of inequality to the behavioral habits of the poor. This new paradigm was captured by Senator Daniel Patrick Moynihan (Democrat of New York and author of the controversial *Moynihan Report*) when he said, "Just as unemployment was the defining issue of industrialism, dependency is becoming the defining issue of post-industrial society."[19] The dependency paradigm reflects and evokes a revival of nineteenth-century fears of the low morality and antisocial behavior of the poor, or those who are referred to today as the "underclass," as well as distinctions between the so-called deserving and undeserving poor. The policy upshot of this paradigm shift has been a change in focus from a war on poverty to a war on the poor.

The response by Bush administration officials in the immediate aftermath of the 1992 Los Angeles disturbances illustrates the degree to which this line of reasoning remains compelling in the post-Reagan era. White House spokesman Marlin Fitzwater said that the social welfare programs of the 1960s and 1970s were responsible for the "riots" and, specifically, for their effect of making poor people feel they had no responsibility for their own "deviant behavior."[20] Vice President Dan Quayle added fuel to the conservative fire by launching an attack on *Murphy Brown*, a popular television show, for legitimating single motherhood as "just another

The Color of America's Culture Wars   185

lifestyle" and for thus contributing in its own way to the outbreak of violence in Los Angeles.

Publication of *The Bell Curve* represents a new face, if a controversial one, of the New Right assault on liberal egalitarianism in the 1990s. The arguments presented in the book signal a shift from a focus on the "dysfunctional" behaviors of the poor that riveted the attention of most underclass warriors in the 1980s (including Murray), to low IQ as the explanatory variable for many important negative social and economic indicators in the black and Hispanic community. Whereas the so-called dependency culture previously served as the ideological articulator of the conservative assault on the welfare state and its associated democratic values, now it is the alleged genetically constituted intelligence deficit of the black and Hispanic underclass that is justifying more aggressive policies of benign neglect. Evoking what he calls a "wise ethnocentrism," Murray cheerily imagines "a world in which the glorious hodgepodge of inequalities of ethnic groups . . . can be not only accepted but celebrated."[21] Dubbed an "intellectual snake charmer," Murray plays into widespread public anxieties over crime, illegitimacy, and racial friction, all the while vehemently denying that he is a racist. The effect of Herrnstein and Murray's foray into the terrain of racial determinism has been to make conservative arguments about the government's role vis-à-vis the pursuit of race and class equality, regarded as extremist less than a decade ago, appear mainstream.

It was not until after the 1994 midterm elections, however, that truly radical conservative welfare reform became politically possible. It is interesting to note that although Democrats had led efforts related to welfare reform during most of the postwar period up to the present, it is now the New Republicans, with New Democrat collusion, calling the shots and redefining the nature of the social contract between the government and the poor. One of the ten planks in the New Republicans' Contract with America was welfare reform, thus turning to Republican advantage Clinton's 1992 pledge to "end welfare as we know it." Nine of the ten planks outlined in what critics became fond of referring to as the "Contract on America" were successfully turned into bills during the first ninety-three days of the 104th Congress, including the welfare plank (only term limits went down to defeat). Newt Gingrich justified the new welfare legislation with a rhetoric of compassion for poor people that has become the most recent sidekick of the new racism: "By creating a culture of poverty, we have destroyed the very people we are claiming to help. Caring for people is not synonymous with care-taking for people," Gingrich opined.[22] Armed with this new tough-love approach, New Republicans have transmuted the Reagan-era argument that poor people are abusing welfare programs to one that avows that the programs are abusing poor people.[23] When a journalist highlighted this rhetorical twist, Gingrich reportedly smiled and said, "You cracked the code."[24]

Regardless of whether Republicans argue that the poor are abusing welfare programs such as AFDC or the reverse, the fact is that such welfare reform is occurring at a time when benefit levels have reached their lowest point in over twenty years.[25] Despite this contradiction between the symbolic dimensions of welfare policy reform and the material dimensions of poverty, the basic architecture of the 1994 Personal Responsibility Act (PRA) became law in the form of the 1996 Personal Responsibility and Work Opportunity Act. True, the addition of the "WO" to the acronym softens the blow rhetorically and adds a touch of structure to a debate that otherwise has focused, on both sides of the congressional aisle, on the culture of the poor. Yet notwithstanding this seemingly compassionate wink, the act effectively abolishes the whole system of welfare policies and their associated assumptions about responsibility, work, race, and human nature in place for the past half century.[26] In announcing the bill, President Clinton said, "Today we are taking a historic chance to make welfare what it was meant to be: a second chance, not a way of life." By signing the bill, Mr. Clinton has ensconced himself fully within the dependency paradigm of the New Right's making.

Some berate Mr. Clinton for selling out the poor, but it is important to recognize that the Democrats lost the debate on welfare long ago. They lost the debate neither because of the wishy-washy character of party leaders nor because of opportunistic or misplaced electoral ambitions but rather because the New Right won the debate on values. In other words, the Democrats lost the debate on welfare because they lost the broader debate on what the debate was about; by acquiescing to the New Right's construction of the "problem" of poverty as one of values and culture, the Democrats ceded control of the assumptions and symbols that drive the struggle for legitimacy in the policymaking arena and thus surrendered their ability to defend the poor. In this sense, the Clinton administration is complicitous with the New Right in constructing welfare recipients as scapegoats for a whole myriad of negative social and negative indicators: family breakdown, economic downturn, joblessness, crime and violence, a sense of pervasive normlessness, and so on. Such a simplistic explanation for today's troubles—suggesting that if only the poor could be rehabilitated through government coercion or benign neglect, then the nation's past glory can be reclaimed—represents a cynical and profoundly unsociological narrative that is more concerned with the construction of meanings and assumptions about U.S. society and how it works than with concrete policy effects. Having won the debate on values, the New Right has been able to strengthen its hold, and it has been difficult to dissuade those who agree with the New Right that the way to eradicate poverty is to spend less on the poor.[27]

The Center Moves Right

As this discussion demonstrates, race has been an important interpretative vehicle for orchestrating the New Right challenge to the postwar consensus, around which contemporary debates about civil rights, social justice, citizenship, and the meaning of equality have been expressed and amplified. Race has served as an ideological conductor for populist anxiety that the national way of life is coming apart at the seams and has also helped bolster the credibility and power of those who promise to put it back together again.

The appeal of racial issues today is related to the current identity crisis of contemporary U.S. society. With communism gone as the external enemy, there has been a search for a new internal enemy against which to rally. As any student of the sociology of deviance can attest, social identities are commonly defined in relation to an unacceptable other who is excluded from one's moral community. This is the "them" versus "us" theory of political discourse popularized by poststructuralism, suggesting that the definition of one's community revolves around the symbolic construction of insiders and outsiders. According to this theory, it should come as no surprise that the end of the cold war has produced a crisis in self-conception for the West and a search for a new enemy around which to articulate the values for which the "we" stands firm.

As has been demonstrated earlier, racialized others are among those standing in for the once-commanding communist threat. Blacks have been presented as scapegoats in a long effective political tactic to explain away social problems by identifying a certain group of individuals as personifying their cause. Pseudosolutions to the economic problems facing the contemporary United States have been offered via the construction of racialized others presumed to be lacking a healthy work ethic and acting as a drain on scarce fiscal resources. Simplistic analyses of a variety of difficult political challenges have been proffered that portray blacks and relevant governmental agencies as illegitimate "special interests" demanding that blacks and other people of color be treated more equally than others, thereby distorting the system of representative democracy. A myriad of social and cultural controversies has been racialized as conservatives revamp "culture of poverty" theories that explain rising negative social indicators in the black community as a result of a deficit of functional values. As is usually the case, such racial symbolism reveals more about the society that has invoked it than about any objective social problems to which the symbol ostensibly refers. In this way, blacks have come to symbolize the chaos and confusion associated with the disintegration of consensus politics in the post–cold war era.

In its attempt to reconstruct an alternative ideological bloc around a set of conservative assumptions and expectations, the New Right has succeeded in winning a major ideological reversal: discrediting the currents of thought and argument of the opposition and transforming the underpinning ideologies of consensus politics to conservative advantage. The symbol of race has been employed symbolically to stigmatize alternatives ("political correctness") and to construct political enemies (Hispanic immigrants and "welfare queens"), thus furthering the disintegration of the postwar liberal consensus and its positive vision of the role of government in pursuing racial equality policies. Race has also been used, in a more subtle way, to help forge a new political imagination and right-wing consensus that links recipes for national revival to racialized and often exclusionary images of the national community and its purported stock of cultural values. In this way, the New Right has aimed to radically change the balance of political forces by altering the symbolic terrain on which the struggle is conducted, shifting that terrain dramatically to the right.

Conservative Republicans attached to the New Right have used race as one means by which to construct moral authority for themselves and to undermine that of the opposition. Racial symbols such as Willie Horton and "welfare queens" have been deployed to demonize the so-called permissiveness of the Democratic Party on racial issues. Casting their opposition to so-called race liberalism as a defense of national values, such symbolic mobilization of racial issues in electoral politics is important because of its potential to appeal to a large number of people who feel that they are losing out: people who are looking for an easy explanation of the causes or, worse still, for somebody to blame. In conflating race with so-called liberal permissiveness, conservatives have found a way to deflect attention from complex structural changes and at the same time offer a response that justifies the reorganization and defense of white privilege.

It is precisely because the new racism is characterized by public disavowals of racist prejudice and avoidance of overt discriminatory practices that outcomes-oriented public policies such as affirmative action are so necessary in the post–civil rights era.[28] If the national community is serious about the pursuit of racial equality and justice, then it is more essential than ever to address practices that are fair in form but discriminatory in operation. If public ire, government policy, and judicial action are targeted exclusively on combating more traditional forms of racism and discriminatory exclusion, then the silence that speaks so loud in the face of the new forms of racism and indirect exclusion will facilitate a deterioration into an increasingly undemocratic public arena more interested in protecting the nonracist self-image of the dominant society than in building a truly equal, open and nonracist society.

Conclusion

Thus, there is a color to America's culture wars. By rearticulating previously dominant cultural codes, the culture wars are redrawing the socially constructed boundary between deserving and undeserving citizens, with potentially serious consequences for the politics of indirect racial exclusion. Those who are concerned with an inclusive definition of American pluralism must focus not only on the overt forms of discriminatory practice but also on those indirect forms of exclusion established and maintained by relatively more mainstream cultural codes and institutional practices. If there is to be an effective counterresponse, then consideration must be given to symbolic reversals in the more general arena of social thought as well as to those reversals at the level of policy formation that concern much of mainstream social science.

Notes

1. Jeffrey Prager, "American Political Culture and the Shifting Meaning of Race," *Ethnic and Racial Studies* 10 (January 1987), pp. 63–81.

2. The New Right, from the mid-1970s to today, has acted as the leading entrepreneur of contemporary and often racialized moral panics around a whole variety of issues: from obscene art and the spread of HIV/AIDS to inner-city crime and "political correctness" and against so-called welfare scroungers and black youth. Significant differences have existed among different strands of the New Right vis-à-vis the politics of race since the movement's emergence. For example, the secular-political arm of the New Right has been engaged in a project of employing code words around crime and welfare to speak to the racial anxieties of its voting constituency, while the neoconservative arm of the movement has been engaged in a more intellectually based project of deliberating the meaning of constitutional principles of inclusion in the post–civil rights era United States. Despite these differences of style and orientation, however, the New Right has operated in practical political terms as a hegemonic coalition. In fact, one of the central characteristics defining the New Right coalition as distinct from the Old Right (or self-described paleoconservatives), as well as from the contemporary Far Right, relates to a softer, more subtle and superficially tolerant posture vis-à-vis the controversial racial issues of the day.

3. William A. Gamson, "Hiroshima, the Holocaust, and the Politics of Exclusion," *American Sociological Review* 60, no. 1 (February 1995), pp. 1–20.

4. Important scholarship on the subject of the "new racism" includes Martin Barker, *The New Racism: Conservatives and the Ideology of the Tribe* (London: Junction Books, 1982); Pierre-André Taguieff, "The New Cultural Racism in France," *Telos* 83 (Spring 1990), pp. 109–122; Etienne Balibar, "Is There a Neo-Racism?" in Etienne Balibar and Immanuel Wallerstein, *Race, Nation, Class: Ambiguous Identities* (London: Verso, 1991); Nancy Murray, "Anti-Racists and Other Demons: the Press and Ideology in Thatcher's Britain," *Race and Class* 3 (Winter 1986), pp.

1–19; and Amy E. Ansell, *New Right, New Racism: Race and Reaction in the United States and Britain* (New York: New York University Press/Macmillan, 1997).

5. Stanley Fish, "How the Right Highjacked the Magic Words," *New York Times,* op-ed, 13 August 1995.

6. For more detail, see Ansell, *New Right, New Racism.*

7. Cartoon quoted in Leslie Carr, "Color Blindness and the New Racism," Washington, DC, paper delivered at the 1995 American Sociological Association Annual Convention, p. 5.

8. For a survey of studies that indicate continued and pervasive asymmetrical relations of inequality between whites and people of color in the areas of housing, employment, income, wealth, and education, see Amy E. Ansell, *New Right, New Racism.* In addition, studies are presented that show that such indicators are the consequence of the continued existence of systematic racial discrimination and not just a result of the operation of a color-blind market economy or disparate human capital. *New Right, New Racism* also reviews studies that demonstrate the erroneous foundation of evidence supporting the New Right's charge that white men are being victimized by "reverse racism."

9. True to the tenets of the new racism, the way in which the initiative was worded confused even strong supporters of affirmative action into believing that it advances civil rights, prompting a legal battle over whether the words "affirmative action" must be included in the title to make clear what the initiative is actually about.

10. Rush Limbaugh, *The Rush Limbaugh Show,* 14 September, 1994.

11. Newt Gingrich, quoted in letters to the editor, *Washington Post,* 2 August, 1995.

12. Steven Holmes, "Preferences Are Splitting Republicans," *New York Times,* 29 July 1995.

13. The EOA went so far as to actually block federal efforts to provide remedies for proven racial and gender discrimination as well as to severely restrict civil rights enforcement through the courts. It would have virtually eliminated the Executive Order 11246 "goals and timetables" program, used as a measure to cure discrimination since the Nixon administration, which bars discrimination by government contractors.

14. To strive for the goal of racial diversity in an entering class, said the court, "is no more rational on its own terms than would be choices based upon the physical size or blood type of applicants." Quoted in Carl Cohen, "Race, Lies, and 'Hopwood,'" *Commentary* (June 1996), p. 44. Referring to the decision as "a stunning blow to affirmative action," the *Chronicle of Higher Education* concluded that Hopwood would have a huge impact on the laws governing race-based programs in higher education and, at least in the short term, inevitably result in decreased minority enrollment.

15. Personal interview of Grover Norquist by the author, Washington, DC, August 21, 1995.

16. Ibid.

17. For a discussion of these neoconservative authors and others, see a survey of their work in Michael Katz, *The Undeserving Poor: From the War on Poverty to the War on Welfare* (New York: Pantheon, 1989).

The Color of America's Culture Wars 191

18. Ronald Reagan, "The Queen of Welfare," *Conservative Digest* (March 1977), p. 19.

19. Daniel Patrick Moynihan, quoted in Sanford F. Schram, *Words of Welfare: The Poverty of Social Science and the Social Science of Poverty* (Minneapolis: University of Minnesota Press, 1995), p. 132.

20. Marlin Fitzwater, quoted in David Rosenbaum, "White House Speaking in Code on Riot's Cause," *New York Times*, 6 May 1992.

21. Charles Murray, quoted in Tom Morganthau, "IQ: Is It Destiny?" *Newsweek*, 24 October 1994, pp. 53–62.

22. Jason DeParle, "Rant/Listen, Exploit/Learn, Scare/Help, Manipulate/Lead," *New York Times*, 28 January 1996, p. 56.

23. Ibid.

24. Ibid., p. 57.

25. According to a report published by the Center on Social Welfare Policy and Law, the current level of benefits leaves families well below the poverty line in all fifty states and the District of Columbia; in forty-two states, AFDC benefits plus food stamps come to less than 75 percent of the poverty line. Current benefits are worth a mere 63 percent of their 1975 levels (roughly $366/month for a family of three). Since 1988 alone, there has been a loss of purchasing power of 10 percent or more in forty-five states. And as the report shows, at the same time that benefit levels have reached a historic low, the need for AFDC has increased to the highest point ever. See Center on Social Welfare Policy and Law, *Living at the Bottom* (New York: Center on Social Welfare Policy and Law, 1994).

26. James Atlas, "Clinton Signs Bill to Cut Welfare and Change with State Role," *New York Times*, 23 August 1996.

27. Schram, *Words of Welfare*, p. 100.

28. John F. Dovidio, "Affirmative Action and Contemporary Racial Bias: Need and Resistance," paper presented at the Annual Meeting of the American Psychological Association, Toronto, Canada, August 1996.

9

The Military-Industrial Complex and U.S. Foreign Policy: Institutionalizing the New Right Agenda in the Post–Cold War Period

Ronald W. Cox

Of all the programs the new Republican Congress targeted for cuts in 1995 and 1996, the military budget was the glaring exception to the budget-axe rule. Although the Newt Republicans threatened the elimination of welfare programs as entitlements, the same body of representatives and senators proclaimed the necessity of maintaining defense spending at rates above the cold war average. The rationale for the 1996 defense budget of $265 billion was hardly new, however, or linked exclusively to Republican congressional hawks. Instead, the ideological arguments were forged over the past twenty years by executive branch officials within the White House; the Departments of State and Defense; military contractors; and foreign investors concerned about threats to U.S. interests in the less-developed world.

This long-term commitment to high rates of military spending is an economic and institutional expression of the interests of the ruling elite within the United States. What is often labeled the "New Right" is a diverse array of organizations, think tanks, and policy currents that tend to gain increased legitimacy during times of perceived threats to U.S. national interests in general and business interests in particular. It is no coincidence that the New Right emerged on the scene during the late 1970s and early 1980s. This is the period when U.S. business groups were increasingly concerned about emerging threats to their foreign investment opportunities in the less-developed world (especially the Middle East and Central America) and when business firms dependent on high rates of military spending lobbied aggressively for dramatic increases in the military budget.

192

The Military-Industrial Complex and U.S. Foreign Policy

Although business groups differed in their attitudes toward the Reagan administration's massive military buildup, by 1980 many prominent foreign investors were lobbying for increases in the U.S. capacity to respond to perceived threats to foreign investments. In Central America, direct foreign investors relied on the Association of American Chambers of Commerce to lobby for increased U.S. military assistance to regimes friendly to the United States.[1] In the Middle East, prominent U.S.-based oil firms, engaged in marketing and refining Persian Gulf oil, supported an increased military readiness to intervene militarily in wars that might disrupt the flow of oil from the region.

At the same time, the Committee on the Present Danger, established in 1972, brought together retired military officials, former politicians, and U.S. firms dependent on military spending to lobby for increases in the U.S. military budget during the mid- to late 1970s. High-level policy connections allowed the organization to secure meetings with White House officials, including numerous meetings with President Carter, and State Department and National Security Agency officials including Cyrus Vance and Zbigniew Brzezinski, respectively.[2] Although not formally connected to the committee, a number of New Right organizations contributed to the broad ideological arguments in favor of increased military spending, including Paul Weyrich's Committee for the Survival of a Free Congress, which organized regular luncheon meetings on foreign policy issues with congressmen and their aides to brief them on defense and foreign policy issues; the Heritage Foundation, a New Right think tank with offices on Capitol Hill, which provided the Reagan administration with a blueprint program for raising defense spending by $35 billion; the Madison Group, composed of conservative congressmen who met regularly to coordinate lobbying strategies; the National Conservative Political Action Committee (now defunct); the Conservative Caucus; and a range of groups associated with the Religious Right.[3]

The common argument is that the influence of these groups had decreased considerably by the late 1980s and early 1990s, coinciding with the end of the cold war. However, this argument misses the larger point that the New Right never had power on its own but was highly dependent on political officials and business elites, whose commitment to increases in military spending provided legitimacy for New Right arguments during the 1980s. Similarly, despite the decline of the cold war, congressional conservatives have joined the executive branch in a bipartisan effort—extending from the Bush administration to the current Clinton presidency—to create a warfighting doctrine that preserves many of the weapons systems ostensibly created to fight the Soviets and championed by New Right organizations. Thus, many of the New Right proposals for increasing the military budget have been effectively institutionalized during the post–cold war era.

The continuity in high rates of military spending from the time of the revived cold war, or "second cold war," in the late 1970s through the post–cold war period is evidence of the institutionalization of a political program advanced by the New Right but legitimized by a wide range of institutional actors in Congress and the executive branch. As I will document in this chapter, the new war-fighting doctrine that allows for the retention of the most costly and technologically advanced weapons systems has enjoyed much bipartisan support, including widespread agreement among Democrats, Republicans, and important business constituents. The development of a new war-fighting doctrine has been used to justify maintaining military spending at above cold war levels. In this sense, the current rates of military spending should be understood as a reflection of broad national priorities rather than as an exclusive project of the New Right. The origins of a U.S. commitment to massive increases in military spending date from the beginning of the second cold war and have been extended during the post–cold war period by executive branch leadership (reflecting similar priorities under both Bush and Clinton), the congressional ascendancy of the Newt Republicans in 1994, and business interests dependent on military contracts or with a stake in foreign investments.

During the second cold war of the late 1970s and 1980s and the post–cold war administrations of Presidents George Bush and Bill Clinton, international investors joined with military contractors to advocate the development of increasingly sophisticated high-tech weapons systems that could be used to defend U.S. business interests against instability caused by designated rogue states, especially in key geostrategic regions such as the Persian Gulf, where U.S. oil firms have become more active in distributing and refining oil produced by U.S. allies such as Kuwait and Saudi Arabia.[4] In addition, domestic military contractors have been lobbying aggressively for increased rates of military spending ever since the formation of the Committee on the Present Danger in 1972.

Both international investors and domestic military contractors have contributed to the Committee on the Present Danger, which became an influential advisory body to the presidential administrations of Jimmy Carter and Ronald Reagan.[5] The committee served as a kind of transmission belt for conservative and New Right influences on U.S. foreign policy, establishing close ties to both Democratic and Republican presidents during the beginning of the second cold war. Under the last two years of the Carter administration, the committee scored several political victories, including a defeat of the Strategic Arms Limitation Treaty (SALT) II, rapid introduction of new weapons systems such as the hardened silo construction for Minuteman III missiles, the Trident nuclear submarine program, and the development of strategic schemes for development and

The Military-Industrial Complex and U.S. Foreign Policy

deployment of the MX missile system.[6] Under the Reagan administration, personnel of the Committee on the Present Danger staffed many of the most influential policymaking positions in the State and Defense Departments, while helping to usher in a military budget that approached $1.5 trillion over five years.

The scope and significance of the budget increase was impressive, leading many observers to label the later Carter years and the Reagan period the "second cold war," marked by the largest peacetime increase in military spending in U.S. history. The overwhelming majority of the spending increases were to provide for the creation of new, sophisticated nuclear and conventional weapons systems, especially an expanded and modernized strategic force of B-1 bombers and MX missiles, an augmented theater nuclear force in Europe, a navy with fifteen battle groups, and a rapid deployment force. In the research and development phase, the military buildup was justified by military competition with the Soviet Union, especially the "window of opportunity" that was thought to be available to Soviet leaders contemplating a first strike (which helped provide justification for the MX missile).

Competition with the Soviet Union was most intense in the less-developed world, with the Reagan administration increasing the defense budget to enable the United States to secure rapid deployment of sophisticated new military hardware and troops to guard, secure, and defend designated strategic and economic interests throughout the world. The definition of U.S. interests was never solely informed by the Soviet threat but rather by the relative importance of key weapons systems to the profitability of weapons contractors and the long-term institutional interests of the Pentagon. In addition, the choice of weapons systems was also determined by their usefulness in defending regions of importance to influential foreign investors, especially those in the oil-rich and financially lucrative Middle East.

As long as the Soviet Union remained intact, promilitary interests could justify high military appropriations with relative ease, given the bipartisan consensus that characterized discussions of U.S. vital interests. However, these interests faced significant obstacles to maintaining high rates of spending with the collapse of the Soviet Union and the emergence of the post–cold war period, as the Defense Department now had to grapple with the problem of creating a new ideological rationale to justify its enormous budget.

It is in this context that the timing of the Gulf War was ideal for promilitary business and state interest blocs looking for a workable strategic plan to justify high levels of military appropriations. The Defense Department, military contractors, and foreign investors converged around the Gulf War to promote a new strategic doctrine for the United States in the post–cold war period. This doctrine had the advantage of producing the strategic rationale for a range of weapons systems that might otherwise have to be dismantled in the wake of the cold war. In addition, the Gulf War itself provided a kind of testing ground on which the Pentagon could lobby for the effectiveness of its new computer-guided delivery systems and arsenals.

But the war also provided a chance for unity among those liberal internationalist firms within the business community that had previously advocated reductions in military spending and among companies dependent on military contracts for profitability.[7] Both groups of firms had a stake in the Gulf War, which made it an ideal showcase for a reinvigorated commitment by the U.S. State Department to support a military doctrine that would simultaneously protect the profits of foreign investors while providing for long-term justification of cold war levels of military spending. Thus, current debates regarding the levels of appropriate military expenditure have been shaped by the range of ideological and economic interests that championed the Gulf War.

The following sections trace the interaction among executive branch officials, corporate elites, and congressional Republicans in developing a new strategic doctrine that has legitimized the maintenance of cold war military weapons in the post–cold war period. The bipartisan support at the highest state levels for maintaining a military budget above cold war levels and for an interventionist, aggressive U.S. military doctrine has given ideological, political, and economic legitimacy to the newly elected Newt congressional Republicans, whose close ties with military contractors and ideological predilections have resulted in congressional appropriations for military spending at levels above Pentagon requests.

State Interests and Military Doctrine

In order to understand the importance of the Gulf War in providing the strategic rationale for increases in the military budget, it is necessary to examine the major bureaucratic and economic interests that have contributed to the perpetuation of cold war ideology in the post–cold war period. Although the Republican leadership in the House and Senate is committed to escalating the military budget, the ideological context for such increases has been shaped by the interaction of various actors: the executive branch, especially the State and Defense Departments; the four branches of the military service; corporate investors whose assets are concentrated in strategically sensitive regions of the world; and military contractors whose profit margins are heavily dependent on military budget increases and international weapons sales. These four actors have played a key role in shaping a military doctrine whose agenda is the ba-

The Military-Industrial Complex and U.S. Foreign Policy 197

sis for congressional action regarding the military budget, and they have essentially established the framework for shifting the political debate on weapons spending to the right.

What some observers have labeled the "right turn" in U.S. foreign policy has in fact been the product of a complex array of interactions among establishment institutions, politicians, and corporate elites within the highest decisionmaking bodies of the United States, and that has systematically legitimized escalating rates of military spending from the high-water mark of the Reagan cold war years to the post–cold war period. As part of this history, the New Right is often associated with the ideological extremes of the Republican Party, from currents of the Reagan administration to the Newt Republicans' ascendancy in 1994. But the right turn in U.S. foreign policy was much broader than the ascendancy of Far Right ideologues. In fact, all the most influential sectors of the U.S. foreign policy establishment shifted to the right starting with the second cold war and have continued to argue for high rates of military spending long after the cold war has ended.

With the collapse of the Soviet bloc, there was considerable institutional pressure on the State and Defense Departments, as well as the armed services, to develop a new military doctrine to replace the outmoded war-planning documents that had guided U.S. defense strategy during the cold war. While the Soviet Union was still intact, military hard-liners within the Reagan and Bush administration justified maintaining and modernizing the most sophisticated nuclear weapons system by pointing to the need to counter the ambitions of military hawks in the Soviet Union, still portrayed as the primary military threat to U.S. strategic interests in the world. Even after the collapse of the Warsaw Pact in 1990, Secretary of Defense Richard Cheney insisted that "while cooperative aspects of the U.S. relationship with the Soviet Union are growing, the United States must be prepared to remain in long-term competition with the Soviet Union."[8]

The only major nuclear weapons treaties negotiated by the United States and the Soviet Union during the waning days of the cold war, the Intermediate-Range Nuclear Forces Treaty (INF) and the Strategic Arms Reduction Treaty (START), covered a narrow range of obsolete weapons systems for elimination, while allowing for modernization and escalation of more sophisticated weapons systems. The INF treaty of 1987 covered a very narrow range of weapons—nuclear missiles launched from the ground and with a range of between 300 and 3,000 miles—and therefore did not attempt to limit some 96 percent of the superpowers' nuclear weapons. Furthermore, each superpower was free to replace some of the ground missiles with air- and sea-launched cruise missiles. The new missiles were given the same targets previously covered by the ground-launched missiles and, in the case of new cruise missiles, were upgraded to fly at three times the speed of sound, as opposed to the speed of an airliner.

The START talks ratified in 1991 went further in eliminating other categories of weapons systems, but again the primary targets for arms reduction were obsolete weapons systems. The reduction of nuclear warheads from 21,000 to 18,500 looks less impressive when considering that START allowed an increase in nuclear warheads on the most accurate delivery systems such as air-launched cruise missiles and short-range missiles. In addition, strategic bombers were counted as one warhead, when in fact they typically carry eight or ten. The U.S. Navy's nuclear capable aircraft was exempt from the reductions. In the final analysis, START did little more than remove large numbers of obsolete systems, while leaving in place around 17,000 modern strategic weapons.

Nevertheless, the START treaty, along with a unilateral U.S. decision to retire many tactical nuclear weapons, did significantly reduce some areas of the nuclear arsenal by the time President Clinton assumed office. For example, intercontinental ballistic missiles were reduced from 1,000 to 550, and submarine-launched ballistic missiles dropped from 608 to 440. The collapse of the Soviet Union gave ammunition to those critics of defense policy, especially liberal and moderate congressional Democrats, who supported going much further in nuclear weapons reductions. Even former Secretary of Defense Robert McNamara suggested that the United States could cut its nuclear stockpile in half and ban all future production of nuclear weapons material.[9]

Although most representatives and senators were not willing to go as far as McNamara proposed, many were willing to consider a series of smaller reductions in Pentagon appropriations. House Budget Committee Chairman Leon E. Panetta noted in early 1990 that a major military spending cut was on the way. Senate Budget Committee Chairman Jim Sasser drew up a long list of military programs for possible cancellation or reduction, including the B-2 stealth bomber, the mobile MX missile, the C-17 cargo plane, and the Reagan administration's much-vaunted Strategic Defense Initiative (popularly known as "Star Wars"). Other members of Congress, including such prominent Republicans as Senator John W. Warner of Virginia, also began compiling lists of possible military cuts.

In response, the Defense Department and the Joint Chiefs of Staff, under both the Bush and Clinton administrations, drafted a series of policy recommendations for a new military doctrine that would justify a continuity in military spending levels from the cold war to the post–cold war period. The proposals have taken as their starting point the military assessments of capabilities and requirements for fighting two Gulf-type wars at one time, identifying scenarios and rogue enemy states that would require the United States to maintain its current war-fighting capabilities. Current debates over military spending begin with these assessments, with some congressional Democrats supporting a military budget that allows for the U.S. to fight one and one-half wars at one time, and the newly elected Republican majority, bolstered by the Contract with America, supports a war-fighting posture that allows conducting two wars at once.

The election of the Newt Republicans signals a congressional commitment to a two-war military budget and has promised to increase military appropriations to allow for the implementation of that scenario. However, well before the congressional Republicans took office, the Joint Chiefs of Staff under the direction of General Colin Powell began the first systematic attempt to reorient the post–cold war military doctrine of the United States toward the two-war fighting strategy. Powell, working closely with the Defense Department, aimed to shift the U.S. military strategy away from the containment of the Soviet Union and toward the threat posed by "rogue states" whose ideologies, leaders, and weapons capabilities would justify current levels of nuclear weapons expenditure and capability.

Powell and his staff drew on recommendations made in a January 1988 report by the U.S. Commission on Integrated Long-Term Strategy, a group consisting of thirteen senior policymakers handpicked by the Reagan administration to develop a long-term strategic military doctrine for the United States. Powell and the Joint Chiefs of Staff used and expanded upon the report in developing the strategic and political rationale for maintaining the existing cold war military apparatus in the post–cold war period. The final product was a proposed "base force" designed to counter threats to U.S. national security from Third World states possessing chemical, nuclear, and large-scale conventional forces.

The Powell plan proved to be an ideal solution for the military-industrial complex, aiming to preserve existing nuclear and conventional weapons capabilities against post–cold war budget cuts. As Powell and his staff recognized, the post–cold war environment would not automatically allow for a retention of cold war weapons capabilities. Although right-wing Republicans in both the Bush administration and Congress still identified post-Soviet Russia as a significant threat to U.S. national security, congressional Democratic leaders such as Senator Sam Nunn, chair of the Senate Armed Services Committee, argued that any new proposals for military appropriations would have to take into account the collapse of the Soviet Union and the new strategic environment of the post–cold war period. In other words, Russia did not constitute the same threat as the former Soviet Union, nor would it justify the same military budget.

The Powell plan, then, had to fulfill two primary goals: (1) the proposal had to move away from the cold war assumption of containing the Soviet Union as the foremost rationale for existing nuclear and conventional capabilities, and (2) the plan also had to justify strategically and politically the usefulness of U.S. weapons systems and personnel by devising potential war-fighting strategies illustrating the precise ways in which the U.S. military would be deployed and utilized in the future. The result was a two-war fighting proposal that helped legitimize maintaining most of the U.S. nuclear and conventional arsenal against the threat of several states identified as security threats.

Not one of the potential "rogue" states would justify the Pentagon's enormous cold war stockpiles. Instead, the scenario adopted by Powell and his staff focused on the separate dangers posed by several "rogue" states whose adventurous experiments with chemical or nuclear weapons capabilities, as well as their political tendencies, would justify U.S. military readiness and war preparation. The scenario envisioned by Powell involved the U.S. fighting two wars simultaneously against two of the so-called "rogue" states: Iraq, Iran, North Korea, Libya, Pakistan, and Syria. Such a scenario, far from recommending dramatic reductions in U.S. force capability, called for only small cuts in U.S. nuclear and conventional weapons. The proposed budget would remain in line with the average levels of spending (adjusted in real dollars) during the cold war. Table 9.1 is a summary of the Powell recommendations.

Politically, the proposed base force protected many of the new, high-tech weapons systems developed during the second cold war period under the Reagan administration and championed by many right-wing organizations.[10] The plan also allowed for the retention of the heavy armored divisions and the bomber wings previously intended for all-out war with the Warsaw Pact. Most important, the base force provided the United States military with the capability of rapidly moving 1.5 to 1.75 million troops to fight two wars simultaneously. If there were any political obstacles to the approval of the base force, the advent of the Gulf War and the recent election of the Republican Congress helped to eliminate them.

The Political Implications of the Gulf War

The centrality of the Gulf War is crucial for understanding the coalescence of U.S. economic and political interests supporting the two-war fighting strategy. First, Colin Powell and the Joint Chiefs of Staff identified Iraq as a rogue threat to U.S. interests in the Middle East, which increased the likelihood that the Pentagon would take action against Iraq after the invasion of Kuwait. Second, a broad range of corporate interests supported the Gulf War, giving further legitimacy to the two-war fight-

The Military-Industrial Complex and U.S. Foreign Policy 201

TABLE 9.1 The Proposed Base Force

	Actual 1990 Force	*Proposed Force*
Army forces		
Active divisions	16	12
Reserve divisions	10	6
Navy forces		
Combat ships	530	450
Carrier battle groups	15	12
Active naval air wings	13	11
Reserve air wings	2	2
Marine Corps		
Active divisions	3	3
Reserve divisions	1	1
Air Force		
Active fighter wings	22	15
Reserve fighter wings	12	11

SOURCE: Michael Klare, *Rogue States and Nuclear Outlaws* (New York: Hill and Wang, 1995).

ing doctrine advanced by Powell and his congressional supporters. Third, the Gulf War permitted the various branches of the U.S. military to showcase their high-tech weapons systems in a post–cold war confrontation with a designated rogue state, further legitimizing maintaining a military budget at cold war levels.

The Iraqi invasion of Kuwait threatened the vested interests of three important sectors of the U.S. business establishment. First, Gulf War states, led by Kuwait and Saudi Arabia, have invested close to $1 trillion in United States financial markets, linking them with the largest U.S.-based investment banks in the world. The importance of the Gulf states to the U.S. international banking interests is crucial, given the fact that there are only three capital-generating sources in the global system: Germany, Japan, and a few oil producers in the Gulf. U.S.-based financial institutions and banks with links to Saudi Arabia and Kuwait saw the preservation of these two oil monarchies as important for global profitability, and they supported the Gulf War as a result.[11]

Second, U.S. oil firms also championed the Gulf War, largely because of their role in refining oil that is produced in the Middle East. After the wave of nationalization of U.S. and European oil firms in the early 1970s, U.S. firms began to move aggressively into refining, marketing, and distribution of oil, linking these firms with Gulf states such as Saudi Arabia and Kuwait in vertical production arrangements. Saudi Arabia and Kuwait own the production facilities; U.S. firms control the refining and distribution, providing the Gulf states with much-needed outlets for the sale of oil products that are more remunerative than exports of crude oil. U.S. firms with close ties to Saudi Arabia and Kuwait include Mobil, Chevron, Exxon, Texaco, and Amoco, all of which refine and distribute oil produced in the Gulf states. In the 1980s and through the early 1990s, the Middle Eastern oil trade has become crucial for the handful of U.S.-based oil companies that control the distribution of the vast majority of the region's oil.

The international oil trade also has significant effects on global financial markets. Leading U.S. international banks depended on huge deposits of dollars available from the Middle Eastern oil trade to finance investment and lending ventures in the 1970s and to help cover debts during the crisis of the 1980s, when less-developed countries threatened to default on interest payments to international private banks. In addition, oil companies increasingly depended on revenues from distribution of Middle Eastern oil to cover outstanding debts to investment banks. During the late 1970s and early 1980s, the booming oil business spurred huge amounts of borrowing by international oil firms to finance risky exploration and drilling. When production began to decline, the dependence of major U.S. firms on other sources of revenue such as distribution and refining increased in order to cover debts. Finally, the price of Middle Eastern oil has now become a central factor in determining worldwide prices for oil.[12]

Thus, the Gulf War provided a crucial arena where the interests of the U.S. State and Defense Departments coincided with the particular economic interests of leading U.S. oil companies and commercial banks. The membership of the Committee on the Present Danger initially brought these economic interests under the same lobbying tent, which formed a crucial network for the influence of the New Right on U.S. military policy during the late Carter and early Reagan years. Using the committee as a springboard for economic and political access, U.S. financial institutions and oil companies continued to use their institutional connections to lobby for a military capable of intervening to protect key investments in trouble spots such as the Middle East.

Such an analysis helps explain the emphasis on types of expenditures in military procurement whose explicit purpose is to project force or carry out operations in the less-developed world, with a particular emphasis on military weapons systems targeted for use in Middle Eastern conflicts such as the Gulf War. For example, the role played by armor, electronics, and naval weapons in the Gulf War, especially carrier-based aircraft and ship-based Tomahawk cruise missiles, illustrates the importance placed on weapons developed during the second cold war for use in conflicts with designated rogue states.[13] The investment bloc of U.S. industries lobbying for such weapons systems were members of the Committee on the Present Danger, which included both prominent U.S.-based oil companies and commercial banks with considerable economic interests in the Middle East.

A third important component of private-sector support for the Gulf War is the military-industrial complex, an institutional matrix of firms and state bureaucrats with a material and ideological stake in increasing military appropriations. Whereas U.S. investment bankers and international oil firms have strong ties to both Democratic and Republican candidates, firms tied to the military-industrial complex and dependent primarily on domestic military production have given disproportionately to the Republican Party, especially during the 1992 and 1994 congressional elections. These firms formed an important part of the lobbying network committed to increasing the military budget and saw the Gulf War as an opportunity to showcase key weapons systems and secure congressional support for a two-war fighting military doctrine.

In summary, the Gulf War was crucial in bringing together sectors of international capital, the U.S. State and Defense Departments, and Congress to back the two-war fighting doctrine designed and proposed by Colin Powell and the Joint Chiefs of Staff. The election of the congressional Republican majority in the 1994 midterm elections further solidified the existing coalition committed to expanding the military budget by further institutionalizing the influence and lobbying clout of the domestic sector of the military-industrial complex. As we will see in the next section, however, there remains a consensus among Democrats and Republicans regarding maintaining a high defense budget, largely due to the fact that the business and political coalitions supporting a high military budget are so diverse and powerful.

Military Spending, the Clinton Administration, and the Newt Republicans

Sitting at the crossroads of domestic and international politics and at the helm of the leading world military power, U.S. presidential administrations have the interests, ability, and influence to significantly affect the global political agenda. Like its predecessors, the Clinton administration has adopted a foreign policy approach whose broadest outlines can be labeled liberal internationalist, in keeping with over a half century of U.S. commitment to global institutions and foreign economic policies forged in the environment of the cold war. Unlike most of his predecessors, however, Clinton has to deal with the new realities of the post–cold war period while seeking to maintain U.S. military hegemony to advance long-term U.S. foreign economic goals.

The outlines of liberal internationalism involve maintaining high rates of military spending for both global and domestic purposes. Globally, the

Clinton administration wishes to maintain U.S. military commitments in regions deemed crucial to U.S. foreign political and economic interests. The maintenance of high troop levels in South Korea and Japan, the pressure being exerted by the administration on Saudi Arabia to secure long-term military bases in the Middle East, and the leadership role exerted within NATO to pressure European allies for military intervention in the Bosnian crisis all illustrate the extent to which U.S. military capability is being utilized in the post–cold war environment.

In keeping with the continuity from one administration to another, the prosecution of the Gulf War by the Bush administration is indicative of the military and economic trade-offs sought by post–cold war U.S. presidents. The Bush administration tied the U.S.-led intervention in the Gulf War to other economic objectives vis-à-vis Western Europe, Japan, and the Middle East. First, the administration worked to ensure that the U.S. military operated as a kind of "mercenary for hire," whose costs and deployment were picked up by Japan, West Germany, and Saudi Arabia, in particular. Regarding Saudi Arabia, the United States hoped to cash in its military commitment in the Gulf War for a permanent military base in that country. Second, the United States worked to ensure that Japan would recognize that the U.S. effort and commitment in the Gulf War necessitated Japanese cooperation in two areas: Political and economic negotiation sought by the United States to reduce Japanese trade barriers should continue, and the Japanese should continue to play a pivotal role in financing the burgeoning U.S. debt. This strategy was continued, but in a more aggressive fashion, by the Clinton administration. And finally, the military commitment borne by the United States in the Gulf War helped to ensure a U.S. role in negotiating the terms of the transition to a European Union, which U.S. policymakers supported as a conduit for increased U.S. trade and investment in the region.

Under Clinton, this liberal internationalism has also involved the first serious effort to globalize the arms industry to increase profit-making opportunities for the military-industrial complex and to use sales of conventional military weapons to achieve U.S. objectives in the post–cold war period. Moreover, the Clinton administration has prepared policy guidelines that would factor the financial health of U.S. weapons makers and the shape of the domestic economy into decisions on foreign arms sales. The policy has been endorsed by the Rand Corporation, an elite think tank with close ties to the military-industrial complex, and the Aerospace Industries Association.[14]

U.S. defense firms have come to dominate the worldwide arms market, now accounting for 55 to 80 percent of international arms transfers. In fiscal 1993, U.S. firms signed agreements for a record $33.2 billion in arms exports, although the figure dropped to $12.9 billion in 1994, prompting the Clinton administration to actively promote conventional weapons sales. In the three years preceding the end of the cold war, the United States agreed to sales of $28.2 billion. In the three years after the cold war, sales shot up to $70.2 billion. The Lockheed F-16 jet fighter, the McDonnell Douglas F-15 fighter and the General Dynamics M-1A1 tank will all be kept alive by export sales. Economic considerations appear to have motivated the decision to sell Taiwan the F-16 fighter and Saudi Arabia the F-15.[15]

However, it would be a mistake to view the recent political efforts to promote exports of conventional military weapons as strictly designed to benefit individual arms dealers. Arms sales are part of a broader effort between the United States and its political allies in the less-developed world to respond rapidly to crisis situations. The use of arms sales helps bolster the conventional war-fighting ability of strategic U.S. allies and prepares those allies for integration into the two-war fighting strategy that the Joint Chiefs of Staff developed. In this sense, the arming of strategic and political allies is nothing new but rather has been used extensively during the cold war period for spreading the costs of maintaining U.S. political and economic interests around the globe.

The difference between the post–cold war and cold war periods, however, is the relative emphasis on economic benefits to military contractors in determining the authorization of weapons sales to less-developed countries. Although strategic decisions still play a role, a major objective of the Clinton administration is to integrate the defense industry into the global commercial economy while dropping complex military specifications, streamlining defense procurement rules, and investing in research that can be applied to both military and commercial products. The beneficiaries of this approach, of course, are the traditional constituents of the military-industrial complex: defense firms, the Pentagon, and international investors who depend on advanced weapons systems to secure valuable protection for foreign investments.

The ties between military contractors and the Clinton administration have been institutionalized by both the political commitment to a two-war fighting strategy and the objective of integrating the defense industry into the global commercial economy. In addition, the election of the Newt Republicans in the 1994 congressional races has further reinforced a commitment to increased military appropriations. As just one example, the Contract with America advocates a return to a full-blown space-based missile defense system that would generate billions of new dollars for contracts for Lockheed Corporation. The aerospace company funneled $5,000 to Gingrich during the final weeks of the 1994 campaign, after kicking in $10,000 to underwrite his controversial satellite lecture series *Renewing American Civilization* in 1993.[16]

The Republican Congress has aggressively pushed for financing of the air force's F-22 fighter, a next-generation stealth aircraft that is slated to cost over $160 million per plane and will be built by Lockheed. In addition, there is wide bipartisan support of the plan to upgrade and export Lockheed's F-16 fighter planes, a move that would benefit Lockheed twice: first through contracts to upgrade the plane and then through sales to Morocco, Tunisia, and the Philippines, whose expenditures would be used by the air force to fund contracts for new planes. The Clinton administration encouraged the sale when it authorized the arms export loan guarantee fund, which offers further subsidies to arms exporters such as Lockheed.[17]

Following the Lockheed example, House Republicans have been the most aggressive in lobbying for new weapons system, even those that the Pentagon does not want. For example, Congress lavished $44.4 billion on twenty B-2 bombers and then voted twice not to build more of them. But House Republicans added $493 million to the budget for a down payment on two more B-2s with an eye toward building twenty additional bombers at an estimated cost of $24 billion, even though the air force does not want any more B-2s. The plane's primary purpose—to penetrate radar defenses and attack Soviet targets—has vanished. And the B-2 has no mission that other strategic bombers cannot fill. The bomber has radar that cannot distinguish a rain cloud from a mountainside, has not passed most of its basic tests, and is not as stealthy as claimed, according to a report by Congress' General Accounting Office.[18]

In addition, Congress authorized $538 million in the 1996 budget to build six more Trident II submarine missiles at $90 million each, though the Strategic Arms Reduction treaties require a two-thirds reduction of the U.S. strategic nuclear arsenal. The already deployed Trident I and Trident II are judged by many Pentagon experts as more than adequate for deterrence. The U.S. currently has more than fifteen missile-carrying submarines, each loaded with more destructive power than all of the weapons exploded in both World Wars I and II.

House and Senate Republicans, joined by a number of Democrats, have led the way in supporting bills that would authorize $821 million (House) and $672 million (Senate) for the Strategic Missile Defense System, or Star Wars. So far, about $36 billion has been spent on Star Wars, without one working system to show for it. Congressional support for additional funding was much greater than the Pentagon's request for $371 million. House Republicans were calling for a network of ground-based missiles located at several sites that would be guided by space-based sensors to defend against accidental and unauthorized missile launches from Russia and the less-developed world.

However, building more than one site would violate the 1972 Antiballistic Missile Treaty (ABM) with Russia and could force Russia to stop dismantling thousands of nuclear weapons under the first Strategic Arms Reduction Treaty, now in effect. In addition, START II would be jeopardized because key provisions of the treaty cannot be fulfilled unless the United States agrees to full compliance with the Antiballistic Missile Treaty.

Conclusion

Despite the propensity of House Republicans to demand the highest levels of military spending, there is clearly broad bipartisan support for keeping military expenditures around the $265 billion mark. This is due in large part to the powerful corporate, political, and bureaucratic-institutional interests that support the two-war fighting strategy recommended by the Joint Chiefs of Staff during the Bush administration. Despite some misgivings on the part of Democrats, the Clinton administration and the Republican Congress are prepared to hammer out a military budget that will involve a commitment to the two-war fighting strategy. Although some congressional democrats have advocated a one and one-half war strategy, the justification for a range of weapons systems backed by the congressional Republicans and endorsed by Clinton remains the two-war fighting doctrine.

Foreign investors dependent on a quick U.S. response to guarantee stability and protect profits are an important part of the coalition advocating continued high rates of military spending. The multinational business community also favors commercializing and globalizing the defense industry for several reasons. First, there is widespread recognition that defense spending generates profits for other sectors of the commercial economy, even for firms that do not depend on military contracts for the bulk of their commercial transactions. Second, multinationals with interests in Europe and Asia, along with those hoping to make inroads into the Japanese market, are convinced of the potential to link U.S. military strength to protection of European, Japanese, and U.S. investments in the less-developed world. Business internationalists close to the Clinton administration, which I label "aggressive internationalists," support the U.S. leadership role in NATO and the UN for precisely these reasons.

However, another group of internationalists in the Republican Party, which I label "cautious internationalists," supports a more modified version of U.S. commitments that would eschew involvement in trouble spots such as Bosnia and Haiti. Nationalist Republicans would go further to greatly limit (or eliminate) U.S. commitments to the UN and NATO. The ensuing ideological battle played itself out in the Republican presidential primaries, with Pat Buchanan using populist economic messages to advance a right-wing nationalism opposed to GATT, NAFTA, and the

UN. Other Republican internationalists are disturbed by this rhetoric, though they had one eye on public opinion polls in opposing U.S. troop deployments in Bosnia and Haiti, where they broke with the Clinton administration's expansive definition of U.S. international commitments.

The divisions between nationalists and internationalists, with the exception of Pat Buchanan, are not extreme, however. Both groups are now advocating a military budget well ahead of the cold war average. The economic base for the nationalists—domestic industry and domestic military contractors—is becoming increasingly blurred as defense firms internationalize their arms sales, linking them with liberal internationalists who have investments in crucial geostrategic regions such as the Middle East. These linkages are best appreciated by noting the involvement of various types of firms, investment bankers, oil firms, and military contractors on the advisory board of the Committee on the Present Danger, the single most influential organization committed to escalating the military budget during the second cold war.

To the extent that there are differences between U.S. foreign policy currents, they are often attributable to the conflicting views of aggressive internationalists and cautious internationalists. Aggressive internationalists, particularly the executive branch and President Clinton, have advocated a broad interventionist and leadership role for the United States in using military troops in areas that others perceive as without significant U.S. national interest, such as Bosnia and Haiti.[19] Cautious internationalists, however, especially the Republican Congress, have been critical of such interventions, raising numerous questions regarding the lack of a "national interest" in Bosnia and Haiti.

To a large extent, these divisions are simply political posturing by both parties, though they also reflect the historic differences between an executive branch located at the crossroads of international politics and a Congress more concerned with the particular interests of its localized constituency.[20] The Republicans, with one eye on public opinion polls, have found it useful to hammer away at the theme that the Clinton administration has an ill thought out and overly expansive foreign policy. By contrast, Clinton has often responded to the broader pressures and perceptions of the international environment in making decisions regarding the scope, capacity, and appropriateness of U.S. intervention.

Given the economic context in which these debates are occurring, however—a rising gap between the lavish pay increases doled out to those CEOs at the top of the income pyramid and the middle and working classes—advocates of economic nationalism may well be able to gain a voice among those working-class constituents who feel most betrayed by the New World Order. Thus, Pat Buchanan's nationalism (or some other variant) will likely continue to surface in political debates. However,

The Military-Industrial Complex and U.S. Foreign Policy

there is little sign that the nationalists will emerge victorious. International business coalitions have too much stake in perpetuating a global political and economic agenda and are far too powerful to allow Pat Buchanan's shock troops to spoil the party.

What both nationalists, aggressive internationalists, and cautious nationalists have in common, however, is a commitment to a post–cold war military budget that is easily above the cold war average in real dollars. This is something political scientists who embraced the realist view of military spending as tied to a perception of national interest cannot easily explain—unless, of course, one takes the view that what is best for military contractors is best for America. This sounds sort of like the 1950s all over again, except that ordinary working-class people are not experiencing gains in their standard of living and are already beginning to object to a system that leaves them with second-rate jobs, while those who define the "national interest" increase their salaries at will.

Notes

1. See my *Power and Profits: U.S. Policy in Central America* (Lexington: University of Kentucky Press, 1994).

2. For the best account, see Jerry Sanders, *Peddlers of Crisis: The Committee on the Present Danger and the Politics of Containment* (Boston: South End Press, 1983).

3. Amy Ansell, "Business Mobilization and the New Right," in Ronald W. Cox, ed., *Business and the State in International Relations* (Boulder: Westview Press, 1996), pp. 65–66.

4. For details of U.S. business interests in the Middle East, see Paul Aarts, "Democracy, Oil and the Gulf War," *Third World Quarterly* 13, no. 3 (1992), 525–553.

5. For an extensive account, see Sanders, *Peddlers of Crisis*. Also see Holly Sklar, ed., *Trilateralism: The Trilateral Commission and Elite Planning for World Management* (New York: Monthly Review Press, 1981). For more recent analysis of the military industrial complex and the connections to the New Right, see Amy Ansell, "Business Mobilization and the New Right," and, in the same volume, David Gibbs, "The Military-Industrial Complex, Sectoral Conflict, and the Study of U.S. Foreign Policy," in Ronald W. Cox, *Business and the State in International Relations* (Boulder: Westview Press, 1996).

6. Tom McCormick, *America's Half-Century: United States Foreign Policy in the Cold War* (Baltimore: Johns Hopkins University Press, 1989), p. 214.

7. For an examination of the shift of international business elites from doves to hawks, see Thomas Ferguson and Joel Rogers, *Right Turn: The Decline of the Democrats and the Future of American Politics* (New York: Hill and Wang, 1986). Most recently, see Thomas Ferguson, *Golden Rule: The Investment Theory of Party Competition and the Logic of Money-Driven Political Systems* (Chicago: University of Chicago Press, 1995).

8. Michael Klare, *Rogue States and Nuclear Outlaws* (New York: Hill and Wang), p. 10.

9. Ibid., p. 9.

10. For details of right-wing organizations and their support for increased defense spending during the Reagan years, see Sara Diamond, *Roads to Dominion: Right-Wing Movements and Political Power in the United States* (New York: Guilford Press, 1995), pp. 214–227.

11. For a detailed analysis of these connections, see Paul Aarts, "Democracy, Oil and the Gulf War."

12. John L. Boies, *Buying for Armageddon: Business, Society, and Military Spending Since the Cuban Missile Crisis* (New Jersey: Rutgers University Press, 1994), p. 132.

13. Ibid., p. 127.

14. Ralph Vartabedian and John Broder, "U.S. Weighs New Arm Sales Policy," *Los Angeles Times*, November 15, 1994.

15. Ibid.

16. William D. Hartung, "The Speaker from Lockheed," *Nation*, January 30, 1996, pp. 124–126.

17. Ibid.

18. Karen M. Paget, "Military Immunity; Pentagon Budget Escapes the Knife— But Should It?" *Baltimore Sun*, September 24, 1995.

19. For a discussion of the relationship between U.S. business interests and the U.S. military occupation of Haiti, see my forthcoming "Private Interests and U.S. Policy in Haiti and the Caribbean Basin," in David Skidmore, ed., *Contested Social Orders and International Politics* (Nashville, TN: Vanderbilt University Press), pp. 187–207.

20. For examples of how these divisions play themselves out in U.S. foreign economic policy, see my "Corporate Coalitions and Industrial Restructuring: Explaining Business Support for Regional Trade Agreements," *Competition and Change: The Journal of Global Business and Political Economy* 1, no. 1 (October 1995), pp. 13–30. See also Ronald W. Cox and Daniel Skidmore-Hess, "The Politics of the 1993 NAFTA Vote," *Current Politics and Economics of the United States* 1, no. 2/3 (1995), pp. 131–144.

10

The New Right's Economics:
A Diagnosis and Counterattack

Richard D. Wolff

Very little about the New Right's economic strategy is new. It restates the enduring catechism of one traditional wing of the Right, which holds that all economic progress depends ultimately on the freedom of private enterprises to seek maximum profitability. Constrict that freedom and social decline follows.[1] The greater that freedom—from state or union or community interference—the greater will be prosperity and individual happiness. This rightist recipe for well-being dates back at least two hundred years. This traditional wing of the Right—referred to here as the Liberal Right—has secured the loyalty of the contemporary New Right, at least so far.[2]

The "New" attached to Right these days successfully appeals to an (old) cultural fetish with newness. "New" also underscores a comparison to the decades after the 1929 stock market crash. The Right now aims to negate state economic interventionism since the 1930s, labeling it "old" and "failed." Hence, the adjective "new" works well.

The Great Depression also teaches important lessons about the economic thinking of another faction of the Right—referred to here as the state capitalist Right—with a view that has been important in the twentieth century. The economic collapse of the 1930s not only traumatized the societies it ravaged. It also demonstrated the awful risks and dangers inherent in the private capitalism championed by the Liberal Right. Uncontrolled, unregulated—that is, "free"—private enterprise came to define "the economic problem." The "obvious solution"—increasingly practiced by groping governments and most influentially theorized by Keynes—was a strategy of government supervision, regulation, and interventionist management of the private enterprise economy. On one side, corporatist and fascist arrangements that largely merged the state and

211

concentrated capitalist enterprises composed the state capitalist Right. This sector of the Right—dedicated to the destruction of communism and all movements seen to be for it—played crucial roles in the histories of Germany, Italy, Spain, and other countries.

On the Left, welfare states and Keynesian economics rose triumphantly from the ashes of the Great Depression and the Liberal Right's disgraced recipe for success. Marxists joined Keynesians in denouncing private capitalism, but in the main they departed from the Keynesians in finding state management and regulation of private capitalism a much too inadequate form of state intervention. Taking their cue from what had happened in the USSR, most Marxists favored outright state ownership and management of enterprises. In effect, this amounted to a left state capitalism in which state officials replaced private individuals as owner-managers of industrial enterprises and in which communism was the official goal.[3] In the decades after 1929, state-managed (Keynesian) private capitalisms and Left and Right state capitalisms displaced "free" private capitalisms to varying degrees in many, many countries.

In the United States, Franklin Roosevelt rode the triumphal wave, while a humiliated Liberal Right retreated. Rich financial backing remained available to it—for countless "freedom" foundations aimed at shaping academic and popular discourse, for politicians willing to repeat the Liberal Right truths, and so on. Classics of Liberal Right economic theory continued to be produced and widely read.[4] Yet its economics could not emerge from the margins for several decades.

Republican President Nixon had to declare his conversion to Keynesian economics. Milton Friedman and his liberal rightist cohorts and students at the University of Chicago could not prevail in shaping academic and popular discourse with their version of "neoclassical economics" (Friedman 1962). Their elegant formal reasonings—fully clothed in the latest scientist language—claimed to prove absolutely that private individuals buying and selling within a perfect market (one without individuals, groups, or a state able to manipulate exchanges) yielded the best of all possible economic results for everyone. They called that result an "optimum" equilibrium that fully utilized all resources including labor power (in other words, a full employment equilibrium). Their neoclassical economics insisted that both theory and history had proved absolutely that any state economic intervention (other than merely protecting such perfect markets) could produce only suboptimal results (i.e., unemployment) and was therefore utterly unwarranted. Neoclassical economics in their hands rediscovered and mathematically repackaged the traditional Liberal Right catechism.

But Keynes and his followers enjoyed ideological hegemony while Friedman and friends languished on the margins. Keynesians offered

The New Right's Economics 213

endless examples of how actual markets did not work as Friedman's models of perfect markets implied. "Real world" market imperfections converted the achievement of Friedman's optimum into an academic exercise in the worst sense of the term. The dominant discourse in the United States and across the world dismissed the policy implications of Friedman's neoclassical economics—dismantling state interventions in the economy—as dangerously impractical and misguided. Since the Keynesians believed that only state economic interventions could avoid or offset the very real depression potential of private capitalism, they argued that the "fanatical" Friedmanites actually jeopardized capitalism with their unrealistic theories and inappropriate policies. Often, "strict" neoclassical economists were treated as the dinosaurs of the profession, unwilling to jettison obviously outmoded economic theories and the policies derived from them. Marxists joined with Keynesians in attacking neoclassical theories for failing to understand or foresee the depressive potential of private capitalism and for impotence or worse when depression arrived. Neoclassical economic theory was described then in precisely the terms many neoclassical theorists use now to try to marginalize Keynesianism and Marxism. In a classic role reversal, neoclassical theorists today denounce Keynesianism and Marxism for failing to understand, foresee, forestall, or solve the crises that have engulfed state-interventionist economies over the last two decades.

What primarily enabled Right economics to revive in the United States were the mounting economic problems besetting state-interventionist capitalisms. Just as the difficulties of the private form of capitalism had ushered in the Great Depression and the collapse of the Liberal Right, in the 1980s and 1990s, the difficulties of both the state-managed forms of private capitalism and of Soviet-style state capitalisms created a new opportunity for the Liberal Right to return. Although the opportunity was new, the Liberal Right that returned was not. The message was the same: Since private capitalism was the absolutely best economic system, current economic problems were all caused by state economic intervention and would be solved by dismantling it.

Oscillations Between Private and State Capitalisms

The fall and rise of the Liberal Right as a set of economic theories and policy prescriptions closely matched the fall and rise of the private form of capitalism. Although the tendency of capitalist economies to experience regular, recurring instabilities (periodic business cycles, booms and busts, crises, and so on) is well known and documented (Flamant and Singer-Kerel 1970; Beaud 1983), there exists another much less recognized and much less frequent level of capitalism's periodicity. Throughout its history, capitalism displays oscillations between private and state-interventionist (or, in summary terms, "state") forms. Both forms display the cyclical tendencies characteristic of capitalism, although how the tendencies are realized (with what unique timing, political consequences, and so forth) varies from one form to the other. The relationship between business cycles within each form and shifts from one form to another is complex.

Capitalist business cycles, especially when their decline phases are extreme (when employment, production, and income fall dramatically) have almost always generated theories and policies with the limited aim of overcoming, muting, or shortening the cycles. However, on those occasions when other, noneconomic social problems (political, religious, ethnic, cultural, and so on) reached crisis points that coincided with one of capitalism's cyclical downturns, a full-blown social crisis could arise. That usually plunged society into agonized tumult and searching for "the solution" to whatever came to be defined as "the problem." In such situations, debate crosses the usual limits—determining proper countercyclical policies—and raises the issue of a social shift from one form of capitalism to another. In the social crises of the 1930s, private capitalism emerged as *the* problem and state capitalism as *the* solution. In the 1980s and 1990s, another social crisis overwhelmed both state-managed and state capitalisms. It yielded a reverse outcome: State economic intervention emerged as *the* problem and comprehensive privatization as *the* solution.

State-capitalist systems experienced repeated business cycles from the 1940s to the present. However, the post–World War II recovery, the cold war, technical changes, and huge economic stimulations by interventionist states combined to produce a long trend of economic growth, notwithstanding the periodic recessions and inflations. So long as that growth continued and trickled down to rising real incomes for the masses of welfare state citizens, state forms of capitalism remained secure. Temporary downturns were endured and blamed on external forces or special circumstances; they provided no opportunity for liberal rightist movements to mount an effective assault on state capitalism as the culprit.

Sometimes, however, cyclical downturns coincided with other, noneconomic problems to plunge state-interventionist capitalisms into severe social crises. This was the general experience, although timing and particulars varied from country to country. The 1970s were difficult for most countries, including the United States. Rapid inflation and deep recession signaled that interacting business cycles and other social problems were provoking social crises spreading beyond the state's control. However, rooted in the post-1929 definitions of economic problems and their necessary solutions, most administrations, including both Republicans and Democrats in the United States, responded by adjusting (not

The New Right's Economics

challenging or abandoning) state interventionist policies. They expanded many state programs (especially the military), altered tax rates, and identified convenient scapegoats (Arab oil monopolists, domestic welfare cheats, criminals, and so forth). State interventionist capitalisms in the United States and elsewhere were deeply strained, but they survived.

However, the time came when state-interventionist capitalisms' cyclical downturns and noneconomic problems congealed into social crises. Just as historians can now recognize the signals of economic and social crisis maturing in the United States across the 1920s, we can chart a parallel picture for the 1980s and early 1990s. The difference is only that the first was private capitalism's distress, whereas the second was a state capitalism's trouble.

Recent business cycles coalesced with other social problems (changing global position of the United States, industrial restructuring, struggles over multiculturalism and alternative life styles, and so on) to yield a deepening mass dissatisfaction with social conditions. Unlike 1929, when a great cataclysm erupted to mark a key moment of change, the last fifteen years display a sort of social festering worsened by economic cycles. Pressures mounted for something to break the United States out of its widely perceived "trend of decline." At roughly the same time, parallel pressures mounted against state-interventionist economies and economics in Western Europe, the Third World, as well as in Soviet-style socialist societies (Kolko 1988; Evans, Rueschmeyer, and Skocpol 1985; Nove 1983, 68–117).

Now reenter the Liberal Right, for this was its new opportunity. Having fallen from power because of the intolerability of the private form of capitalism, the Liberal Right's revenge would be to use the intolerability of state capitalism to wreck "the Left." In the United States, the Right defined the Left as a continuum of all it hated. At one end were the Keynesians who wanted the state to supervise and coordinate private capitalism; they were thus the least offensive ideologically but most intensely hated, because Keynesians had dominated state economic policy since the 1930s. In the middle were the socialists, who were defined as wanting massive, intrusive state controls and supervision of private capitalist enterprises. "Socialist" became an epithet used for the secret desires that Liberal Right critics forever found hidden just below the surface of duplicitous or duped Keynesians. At the far end of the Right's list of enemies were the communists, reviled as proponents of the ultimate in state economic interventionism, the actual state takeover of private enterprise (as exemplified in the USSR). Communism was suspected by Liberal Right critics to be the eventual destination of all those who distrusted private capitalism. The Keynesians and socialists failed to recognize this as their final destination only because of ignorance of Liberal Right truths about economics or because of evil ulterior motives.

The 1980s proved a remarkable decade for the Liberal Right. Everywhere, deepening social crises provided the context in which increasingly powerful social forces declared state economic interventionist capitalism to be no longer tolerable. In the United States, Reagan, Bush, and the Republicans assaulted Keynesian dominance at all governmental levels. They effectively mobilized mass dissatisfaction with social conditions by defining the problem as "the state"—meaning its interventionist regulation of the economy and society. They offered as the solution a repackaged set of old liberal rightist nostrums: Dismantle state intervention, privatize, liberate free enterprises to compete freely in markets, and so forth. In Western Europe and across the Third World, socialists of all sorts confronted much the same attack. Where they had presided over state capitalisms now perceived to be in trouble, state intervention was blamed for it. The solution offered was likewise a return to free market privatized capitalism.

The liberal rightist sense of the historical moment received its starkest and most dramatic confirmation in the demise of the USSR and its Eastern European allies. There state capitalism had gone the furthest. State officials had replaced the owners and the boards of directors in industrial enterprises. The collapse of that system provided a great surge of persuasive strength for Liberal Right economic theories and policies around the world.

In the USSR of 1917, revolution had proclaimed the advent of socialism as an intermediate stage toward the goal of communism. An egalitarian collective ownership and management of all productive enterprises *by the productive workers within them*—communism—was to replace both private and state forms of capitalism. However, the actual history of the USSR made the achievement of such a communism an increasingly distant goal. Instead of the workers taking charge of production, state officials did so. Other than these changes from private to state owners/directors, the operation of the industrial enterprises—in terms of who decided what to do with outputs—remained remarkably like what it was in most capitalist economies. Indeed, as Lenin had often said, the USSR had had to stop at the stage of state capitalism to prepare the economic and social bases for a future renewal of the march toward a communist future.

However, what Lenin recognized as a form of state capitalism presented a deep ideological problem for subsequent Soviet leaderships. "Maintaining state capitalism" was utterly inadequate as a justification for the enormous sacrifices needed to recover from World War I, the revolution, and the civil war and to survive in a hostile world. The Soviet solution was to rename its extreme form of state capitalism as "socialism en route to communism." In a stunning irony, this Soviet definition mirrored that of the Liberal Right. As noted above, the Liberal Right also de-

The New Right's Economics

fined communism as the most extreme form of state intervention in the economy, accomplished by state takeover of formerly private enterprise.

The Soviet form of state capitalism encountered its social crisis in the 1970s and 1980s. Economic downturns had previously been managed or deferred by the huge state interventions and mass mobilizations for recovery from and resistance against military invasions and threats. However, by the mid-1970s, détente with the West had disabled the rationales for the mobilizations; superpower status had vastly increased demands on a relatively poor economy; and long-postponed demands for consumer goods and civil liberties had erupted in militant dissatisfaction with the existing state and social conditions. In this situation, the state could not cope with an economic downturn, while the mass dissatisfaction bubbled over into direct hostility to the state. The conditions had ripened for a political rising; the only questions were what kind of rising and with what objectives.

Because communism had been rendered as at best a distant future possibility or at worst the name of the hated state apparatus, the political rising could not discuss, explore, or take a communist direction. It could not define state *and* private capitalisms as "the problem," much as it could not define "the solution" as a social transition, for the first time, to a genuine workers' collective production and appropriation of their own surplus labor (communism).

Instead, and almost automatically, it took the other, traditional option in a social crisis of capitalism: an oscillation from one form to the other, here a transition back from state to private capitalism. Soviet state capitalism—described and understood as socialism or communism—was defined as "the problem," whereas free private capitalism emerged as the only and obvious "solution." These developments in the USSR and across Eastern Europe meshed perfectly with the Liberal Right's self-image as the new globally hegemonic force. The Liberal Right's old recipe for economic well-being and individual freedom—private capitalism— seemed totally confirmed, as *the* antidote alike to Keynesianism, to communism, and to socialism and social democracy.

Prospects for the Right's Economic Agenda

The Liberal Right's economic agenda—dismantling state interventions— will prevail so long as it avoids provoking an opposition capable of stopping it. Some radical economists in the late 1980s saw possibilities of labor mounting such an opposition as its living standards fell (Green and Sutcliffe 1987, 339–249; Magdoff 1989; Tabb 1989). The relevant statistics were then and still remain a clear pointer toward such a *possibility*. Consider first the exemplary history of average gross weekly earnings of U.S. production workers adjusted for price changes:[5]

1950	$318.56
1955	$365.13
1960	$393.81
1965	$437.86
1970	$419.26
1975	$420.46
1980	$412.78
1985	$401.66
1990	$382.19
1993	$373.64

These numbers show how *real* labor incomes rose steadily and rapidly to the decade 1965–1975 and then began the accelerating descent that illustrates quite literally the rise and fall of state-managed capitalism in the United States.

Elaborating this picture, note that between 1975 and 1993, the top 5 percent of U.S. households raised their share of aggregate personal income from 16.6 to 20.0 percent; over the same period, the bottom 80 percent of U.S. households experienced a fall in their share of aggregate personal income from 56.4 to 51.8 percent (May 1995, 57). In the decade from 1970 to 1979, the average number of persons in the United States living below the official poverty level was 24.8 million, or 11.8 percent of the U.S. population. In the period 1980–1993, these numbers rose to 33.8 million, or 14 percent of the U.S. population (May 1995, 11).

In the words of one of the most recent and comprehensive studies of the distribution of wealth in the United States (Wolff 1995, 7): "After the stock market crash of 1929, there ensued a gradual if somewhat erratic reduction in wealth inequality, which seems to have lasted until the late 1970s. Since then, inequality of wealth holdings, like that of income has risen sharply. ... The rise in wealth inequality from 1983 to 1989 ... is particularly striking."[6]

The social shifts revealed by such statistics surely had much to do with the Republicans' triumphs in the 1994 congressional elections. Gingrichism has so far effectively tapped enough workers' resentments and angers to shift enough of their votes to empower the Liberal Right economic agenda. Deeply disappointed by the post-1975 performance of state-interventionist capitalism, significant numbers of U.S. workers have accepted the Liberal Right's diagnoses of what happened in the United States and in the USSR. They see state intervention and state capitalism as different degrees of the same problem; the only hope left seems to be a program of return to more private capitalism.

There has not been and is not yet a serious workers' opposition movement to seek a noncapitalist solution instead. Nor have the Keynesians

The New Right's Economics

been able to alarm workers sufficiently about their losses under Reagan and Bush and the prospects of much more under Dole and Gingrich to rebuild any significant enthusiasm among them for reviving a state-managed form of capitalism. The evidence for workers in the former USSR or Germany or Brazil, for example, suggests similar reluctance to pursue either noncapitalist solutions or a return to the types of state capitalism or state interventionism that had existed there earlier.[7]

Nor do the prospects for a renewed workers' movement in opposition to the Liberal Right economic agenda seem very hopeful. In that fact lies a historic irony. Union struggles, radical political movements, and established socialist and communist parties were often crucial components in campaigns for proworker social changes (social security, unemployment insurance, subsidized medical, educational, and housing benefits, and so on), especially in the decades after 1929. Their leaderships looked to the state as the guarantor of the changes they had won. In effect, workers' movements encouraged, supported, and became willingly, even enthusiastically, identified with state interventionist capitalisms.[8] In the United States, unionists and radicals virtually merged in large numbers with the Democratic Party regimes; in Western Europe, unions and radicals worked similarly with and within labor and socialist parties in and out of power.

Although such collaborations facilitated the goal of securing state support for the social gains won by long, hard worker struggles, they also cemented an identification of labor, radical, and state interventionism that presented the Liberal Right with an ideal target. In the United States, for example, the Liberal Right could and did argue that the interventionist state had been "captured" by the "special interests" of labor unions and radicals of all sorts. This line harnessed mass dissatisfaction with declining social conditions not only to an interventionist state but to the special interests—unions and radicals—purportedly controlling it from behind the scenes. When Reagan fired the entire membership of the Air Traffic Controllers union early in his presidency, it was explained and understood as an integral part of his assault on the welfare state and its collusion with evil union interests.

The effectiveness of the Liberal Right's attack lay in its disorienting and demoralizing the union and radical movements. This forced them further into a defensive stance just as the deepening cyclical problems of state interventionist capitalism in the United States were provoking mass layoffs, "restructurings," capital flights, and technical changes detrimental to the traditional sources of union and radical strength. In sum, the Liberal Right's attack on unions and radicals demobilized the very social forces that might otherwise have been expected to resist and at least try to organize a mass opposition to the assault on state interventionism.

Of course, it is possible that the increasingly privatized capitalisms in the United States and elsewhere will encounter yet again the business cycles that have never ceased to plague all capitalisms. However, as argued above, such cycles by themselves will not undermine whatever form of capitalism they disturb. The cycles to come will be managed and rationalized as they always have been in the private capitalisms of the past. Indeed, Liberal Right economics has honed a well-developed discourse for that purpose. It represents business cycles as the temporarily painful but necessary and ultimately salutary weeding out of inefficient producers. Business cycles are merely difficult moments in a Darwinian struggle that ensures victory to the best and fittest enterprises, those that can and will deliver the best possible economic results in the future. Such a discourse comforts, distracts, and dissuades those who might otherwise respond to the ravages of business cycles (destroyed businesses, lost jobs, deferred educations, disturbed families, state fiscal emergencies, and so on) by advocating state intervention to prevent them.[9]

Were the cyclical downturns of restored private capitalisms to coalesce with noneconomic crises there, transitions back to state interventions of all sorts and degrees could unfold. Moreover, the many contradictions besetting the restoration of private capitalism suggest multiple possibilities for transition-provoking social crises. For example, if privatizations were to entail consistently less state intervention in maintaining borders, more "freedom" for labor mobility might provoke complex struggles over multiculturalism intertwined with wage reductions and competition among workers. This has explosive possibilities of all sorts. If privatization were to coincide with a decline of the U.S. global political position, with military adventures, or with ecological emergencies, Democrats might dramatize the association, blame privatization, and thereby perhaps swing the population back toward state interventions of one sort or another. If competition among major trading blocs (the United States, Japan, Europe, the Third World) were to produce serious frictions and so accelerate the decline of wages and living standards across the globe, the rapidity of adjustment might provoke all sorts of opposition that a slower pace has so far precluded.

Even if the contemporary restoration of private capitalisms around the world did encounter fully social crisis points and even if they provoked transitions to state interventionism, those transitions might take directions better described as rightist than leftist. The results of private capitalism's social crises in Germany and Italy after World War I were transitions from private to state capitalisms, but the latter capitalisms were fascist and corporative. State interventionism has hardly been a uniquely leftist phenomenon.

The Right has its splits, too. In terms of economics, the liberal kind of Right comprises devotees of private market capitalism, individualism,

The New Right's Economics 221

and so on. The state capitalist Right prefers a strong state leading or even absorbing private enterprises into an "organic" nationalism. If its restoration of private capitalism were to hit a social crisis that provoked a New Left movement toward a Keynesian interventionism or a socialist state capitalism, the Liberal Right would face at least two options. On the one hand, it could try to block, defeat, and destroy that New Left movement for the sake of preserving a private capitalism. On the other hand, it could try to co-opt that movement, accepting a transition to a state capitalism but striving to make it fascist as opposed to Keynesian or socialist. The Liberal Right could, then, form an alliance with the state-capitalist Right. Which option would be selected depends on the relative strengths of the different kinds of Right today, the strength of the Left state-interventionist movements, the preferences of private capitalists, and indeed the entire social context in each nation where such a choice of options might present itself. In any case, there is surely no warrant for presuming that "it can't happen here."[10]

Countering the New Right

The foregoing analysis implies two alternative paths of response to the New Right. One entails a campaign to thwart the restoration of private capitalism and preserve or even strengthen one or another of the twentieth century's forms of state interventionism. The other makes a break with capitalisms regardless of their private or state forms. Explicitly or implicitly, all opponents of the New Right decide which of these paths to stress.[11]

Slowly and haltingly across the globe, supporters of state- managed capitalisms are regrouping and building or rebuilding coalitions. Everywhere, they strain to deny or minimize the New Right's devastating association of their statist commitments with the social declines or disasters of the period after 1975. At the same time, they try to associate every new economic and social problem, from business cycles to cultural tensions to political scandals, with the New Right's hegemony. Republicans and Democrats in the United States, laborites and conservatives in the United Kingdom, Chirac and the Socialists in France, Yeltsin and the critics of his privatization plans in the former USSR, and their counterparts in many other countries are now locked in such battles. In this war of position, the New Right has been gaining over recent years, but its victory is still far from decisive. The outcome remains uncertain. Everywhere, the combatants look over their shoulders at fascist Right alternatives lurking or strutting in the background.

The leaders of the groupings that favor a return to state-managed capitalism have thus chosen the first path of response to the New Right. In effect, they are all counting on the periodicity of capitalism. Sooner or later, they presume, the current reign of private capitalism will become problematic and give way to a restoration of state-managed capitalism as the solution. Their strategic deliberations thus focus on (1) how to make the restoration of state-interventionist capitalism happen sooner rather than later and (2) how far to take state intervention this time around. Meanwhile, they wait, snipe at the New Right at every opportunity, and regroup their adherents.

To conclude this discussion of the economic aspects of the New Right's current ascendancy and to stimulate new discussions, I would like to offer a sketch of the alternative counterstrategy. My basic premise is this: The twentieth century's oscillations between private and state capitalisms have had consequences that make further oscillations increasingly undesirable to increasing numbers of people. A base for an alternative social program—one not committed to either pole of such oscillations—is thereby being born. To facilitate this birth, theoretical midwifery might help.

The transition from private capitalism in Russia to state capitalism in the USSR was deeply traumatic. It left a legacy of resentments and hostilities toward the inequities of private capitalism that sustained popular support for an austere state capitalism for decades. That legacy is the major obstacle to Russia's current drive to restore private capitalism. At the same time, the injustices and sufferings of Soviet state capitalism have left their profound legacies as well. These represent the major obstacle to any return to state capitalism in the near and perhaps also the distant future. In short, the dilemma of the former Soviet Union is entrapment between alternative forms of capitalism increasingly seen as almost equally unattractive.

Less dramatically, similar situations are taking shape in other countries. In many Third World nations, the "development" achieved under state-managed capitalisms proved so inadequate to needs and expectations and so unfairly distributed that a reopening toward global private capital and privatization could gain ascendancy. Yet, that ascendancy is fast reproducing a similarly poor record of "development." However, to return to state-managed development makes much less sense to increasing numbers of people whose memories permit few illusions about its prospects. Something new and different is wanted.

In Western Europe, proud social democracies held sustained power so long as they presided over a state-managed (Keynesian) capitalism that relied on postwar recovery and cold war tensions to overcome business cycles and noneconomic crises of all sorts. Now, completed recovery, the collapse of the cold war, and renewed, intense competition from Japanese and U.S. capitalisms have combined to overdetermine multidimensional social crises that create shifts in their liberal and state-capitalist right

The New Right's Economics

wings as well. Illustrations abound: the dramatic shift from Mitterand to Chirac in France, from socialist governments in Italy to ruling alliances including fascists, from the seeming invincibility of Swedish socialism to its rapid contraction, and from a solid antifascist consensus across German society to the active revival of fascist sentiment and organizations there. The parallels to Gingrichism are unmistakable, notwithstanding the differences reflecting each country's unique history and current circumstances.

Suppose a clear and persuasive case were made for a new way to overcome not only the restoration of private capitalism but also the dead end of repeated oscillations between private and state capitalisms. Suppose the birth of a new definition of communism (and a rewording such as "communitarianism") removed it from both the utopian clouds of a far and dimly grasped future and from its debilitating association with extreme forms of state capitalism.[12] Suppose communism described an economy in which productive enterprises were so collectively operated by the workers within them that they appropriated their own surpluses (revenues in excess of what they paid themselves in wages).

Such an arrangement would entail positions of participation, responsibility, and power that workers never enjoyed in either private or state capitalisms. It could elevate collectivity and community in relation to individuality in ways unknown within private or state capitalisms. It would position worker collectives in society as the third force between the individual and the state, replacing the private or state capitalists who occupied that position within all capitalisms; this would correspondingly transform politics and culture as well as economics. Such a communism would indeed be something new and different to consider in terms of coping with today's social problems and the current hegemony of the New Right's visions and policies. It could offer a new option and choice to the growing base of those interested neither in private nor state capitalisms.

Worker apathy and alienation could reasonably be expected to decline sharply in such a communism, with attractive consequences for productivity as well as all other interpersonal relationships. Democracy would expand to cover not only individuals' relationships with the state (politics) but also their relationships to enterprises (economics). Education and other cultural activities would undergo basic transformations under the pressure to cultivate in *all* individuals the sophistication, recreation, and breadth of knowledge needed to participate fully in *all* aspects of economic activity. Visions of such a communism would be a pleasure to construct, disseminate, and debate.

Of course, one problem would be to disentangle such a communism from the few, more or less similar past experiments along such lines. We would have to show, for example, why Yugoslavia, despite early efforts in this direction, actually displayed a kind of state capitalism. Likewise, the Kibbutzim of Israel and the Mondragon enterprises of Spain differ in key ways from what is envisioned here. However, these experiments all provide elements of the communism I want to project; no dismissive attitude toward them is warranted or intended. Rather, they represent rich resources for this project as well as evidence of the attractiveness such a communism has had for people even under conditions that rendered their actualization extremely difficult and hazardous.

In conclusion, whatever might be the "best" way to counter the New Right in the United States and elsewhere, it is surely wise to mount several different campaigns. Time and struggle will show which campaigns succeed and what alliances among them might succeed still more. The post-1929 experiences with Keynesian state-managed private capitalisms and with leftist state capitalisms have bequeathed more than enough devotees of those paths to ensure that their ideas and projects have entered the lists against the New Right. What is needed now are people willing to offer and organize around a noncapitalist path to counter the New Right. The notion of communitarianism or communism sketched earlier, if actively projected, may find a sufficient base of openness and interest to become socially influential. The history and prospects of the New Right as well as the history of oscillations between private and state forms of capitalism may finally have produced the sufficient—as well as the necessary—conditions for a successful campaign for a noncapitalist alternative.

Notes

1. The Right's demonization of the Soviet economic system also represents its fascination with what was so utterly opposite to its own teaching. In remarkable ways—discussed in the text later on—the histories of the Right and the USSR were intricately intertwined.

2. The term "liberal" is used here in its classic sense—still common in Europe—of a laissez-faire attitude hostile to almost all state intervention in the private economy. It is thus different from (and nearly opposite to) the usage common in the United States over recent years: "liberal" as an attitude of support for state intervention to promote general welfare.

3. The argument that the Soviet economy is best described as state capitalism is straightforward. The point is that converting private industrial property into state property and substituting state officials for private citizens on corporate boards of directors are not sufficient conditions to establish the radical alteration in economic structure that has inspired socialists and communists for the last century. The collective of workers does not necessarily come to manage and control the disposition of its own surplus simply because the state owns and operates industrial enterprises. Indeed, if workers in state-owned and -operated enterprises still produce and deliver their surpluses to others (state officials) in ways differ-

The New Right's Economics

ing only slightly from the same processes within private capitalism, it makes more sense to speak of a state capitalism than a socialism or communism (Resnick and Wolff 1993, 1994a, 1994b).

4. Perhaps the greatest of these was *The Road to Serfdom*, written in 1943 by Friedrich A. Hayek (1962). It celebrated the great virtues of capitalism as located in its individualism and free markets. It likewise denounced the inevitable descent into totalitarianism that sprang from state economic intervention aimed at meeting peoples' "needs." Despite its millions of readers and admirers, Hayek's direct assault on Keynesianism failed to dislodge it from its hegemonic position in both academic and popular economic discourse.

5. The data are taken from the study *1993 Poverty and Income Trends* prepared by Richard May (1995) for the Center on Budget and Policy Priorities in Washington. Based on the Current Population Reports of the U.S. Bureau of the Census, the data cover all nonsupervisory employees on private nonagricultural payrolls. The weekly earnings in the chart are calculated in 1993 CPI-X dollars.

6. In his foreword to this study, the president of the Twentieth Century Fund, Richard C. Leone, refers to Wolff's findings on wealth inequality as "shaking traditional American optimism" and being "a root cause of the anger that is shaking the democratic system" (Wolff 1995, v–vi). He stresses as well the findings that wealth inequality now far exceeds that of European countries, "those class ridden societies." Edward Wolff is not related in any way to Richard Wolff.

7. This analysis serves to clarify the role of workers and their movements. In the 1940s, 1950s, and 1960s, rising wages and incomes helped to secure worker loyalties to welfare state capitalisms. Union struggles, radical political movements, and established Socialist and communist parties were often crucial components in campaigns for proworker social conditions—and for the state as their guarantor. In the 1970s, 1980s, and 1990s, it is falling wages and incomes that are helping to secure worker loyalties to private capitalisms instead. In a historic irony, the Right used workers' dissatisfactions with declining state capitalisms and with their leftist defenders to weaken worker opposition to a return to private capitalism.

8. This process was aided immeasurably by the dominant tendency among socialists and communists that defined their social goals in terms of *state* ownership of productive assets and *state* operation of industrial enterprises rather than in Marx's terms of how the production, appropriation, and distribution of surplus labor was organized (Resnick and Wolff 1994b).

9. The basic Right economic mantra of "efficiency" resurfaces here. Cyclical downturns become engines of efficiency; they are the wolves that prey upon genetically inferior, weaker sheep and thereby improve the herd. The "benefits" of such weeding out are celebrated and counted, whereas the "costs" in peoples' lives and the damaged productivities of affected family members for years to come are ignored. Predictably, the resulting calculations confirm the net efficiency—the excess of benefits over costs—of cycles. This is a kind of naturalization of cycles to minimize the threat they might otherwise present to whichever form of capitalism is then in place.

10. It may be worth pointing out that fascisms need not always display the particular demonic features associated with Hitler and Mussolini. More or less

226   *Richard D. Wolff*

"friendly fascisms" may emerge from situations like those described in the text (Gross 1980). Perhaps David Duke, Pat Buchanan, and H. Ross Perot might function as conscious or unconscious midwives in the process (Langman 1994).

11. It is possible, of course, to try to combine both paths into a strategy that would support state interventionism against private capitalism ("reformism") while also campaigning to move beyond capitalism ("revolution") as the ultimate goal. Indeed, Marxist movements in the twentieth century often articulated such programs—in terms of formal strategies if not actualized tactics.

12. This is not the place to debate whether such a communism would require a new, different name to play the role suggested here. On the one hand, it should be called communism because of that word's long history, before and after Marx's critical contributions to it, in the utopian longings, social experiments, and critical social theory of masses of people. On the other hand, its negative associations and connotations may make a new term necessary.

References

Beaud, Michel. 1983. *A History of Capitalism, 1500–1980*. Trans. T. Dickerman and A. Lefebvre. New York: Monthly Review Press.

Evans, Peter B., Dietrich Rueschmeyer, and Theda Skocpol. 1985. *Bringing the State Back In*. Cambridge: Cambridge University Press.

Flamant, Maurice, and Jeanne Singer-Kerel. 1970. *Modern Economic Crises and Recessions*. New York: Harper and Row.

Friedman, Milton. 1962. *Capitalism and Freedom*. Chicago: University of Chicago Press.

Green, Francis, and Bob Sutcliffe. 1987. *The Profit System: The Economics of Capitalism*. Harmondsworth: Penguin Books.

Gross, Bertram. 1980. *Friendly Fascism*. New York: M. Evans.

Hayek, Friedrich A. 1962. *The Road to Serfdom*. London: Routledge and Kegan Paul.

Kolko, Joyce. 1988. *Restructuring the World Economy*. New York: Pantheon.

Langman, Lauren. 1994. "From Capitalist Tragedy to Postmodern Farce: The Eighteenth Broomstick of H. Ross Perot." *Rethinking Marxism* 7, 4 (Winter), 115–137.

Magdoff, Harry. 1989. "A New Stage of Capitalism Ahead?" In *Instability and Change in the World Economy*, ed. Arthur MacEwan and William K. Tabb, 349–362. New York: Monthly Review Press.

May, Richard. 1995. *1993 Poverty and Income Trends*. Washington, DC: Center on Budget and Policy Priorities.

Nove, Alec. 1983. *The Economics of Feasible Socialism*. London: Unwin Hyman.

Resnick, Stephen, and Richard Wolff. 1993. "State Capitalism in the USSR: A High Stakes Debate." *Rethinking Marxism* 6, 2 (Summer), 46–68.

_____. 1994a. "Capitalisms, Socialisms, Communisms." In *Current Perspectives in Social Theory*, vol. 14, ed. Ben Agger, 135–150. Greenwich and London: JAI Press.

_____. 1994b. "Between State and Private Capitalism: What Was Soviet 'Socialism'?" *Rethinking Marxism* 7, 1 (Winter), 9–30.

The New Right's Economics

Tabb, William K. 1989. "Capital Mobility, the Restructuring of Production, and Politics of Labor." In *Instability and Change in the World Economy,* ed. Arthur MacEwan and William K. Tabb, 259–280. New York: Monthly Review Press.

Wolff, Edward N. 1995. *Top Heavy: A Study of the Increasing Inequality of Wealth in America.* New York: Twentieth Century Fund Press.

11

Mastering the New Political Arithmetic: Volatile Voters, Declining Living Standards, and Non-College-Educated Whites

Ruy A. Teixeira and Joel Rogers

American voters have become notably volatile in the 1990s. First, in 1992, they shattered the Republican presidential coalition, with George Bush registering the third-largest decline in support for an incumbent president in history. Then in 1994, they took fifty-two seats away from the Democrats and gave Republicans control of Congress for the first time in forty-two years. Finally, in 1996 they easily reelected a Democratic president who had been massively unpopular only a short time before. Thus, in the space of only three elections, the bastions of both parties—presidential for the Republicans and congressional for the Democrats—have crumbled.

Some interpret this volatility as suggestive of big ideological swings in the electorate; others say changing values are behind these electoral shifts; still others point to the increased role of religion in politics. In this chapter, we argue that these explanations are only partial and that the chief cause of voter volatility lies in declining living standards and the persistent failure of either political party to successfully address this problem.[1]

Perot Voters and the 1992 Election

Although the drop-off in Republican support in 1992 was of historic proportions, Democrats were not the direct beneficiary. Clinton received only

43 percent of the popular vote, actually down slightly from the 45 percent Dukakis received in 1988. The "party" that gained was Ross Perot—who claimed 19 percent of the vote, the most for a third party or independent candidate since 1912. Voters thus not only rejected the incumbent president in historic numbers but also embraced a maverick candidate outside of the two-party system at almost unprecedented levels.

Those who made these choices most directly—Perot voters themselves—provide a privileged point of entry for understanding current electoral dynamics. Who were these people who deserted the Republicans but failed to attach themselves to the Democrats? What were their demographics, material circumstance, attitudes, and beliefs?

Reflecting the basic structure of the U.S. electorate,[2] Perot voters were overwhelmingly (76 percent) non-college educated[3]—as were the supporters of Bush and Clinton (both over 70 percent). More significantly, Perot's supporters were drawn heavily from the ranks of non-college-educated whites (NCEWs). Sixty-seven percent of Perot's overall support came from this NCEW group, compared to 63 percent of Bush's support and just 48 percent of Clinton's. A second characteristic of Perot voters was their rapidly deteriorating economic position. Analysis of Current Population Survey (CPS) wage data merged with the 1992 VRS exit poll reveals that although both Clinton and Perot voters came from groups that experienced wage losses in the 1980s and early 1990s, Perot voters' losses were uniformly larger.[4] A third characteristic of Perot voters was their gloomy outlook on the economy and its likely future path. In the 1992 exit poll, 70 percent of Perot voters said they thought the economy was in long-term decline rather than experiencing a temporary downturn. And in terms of prospects for the future generation, Perot voters were easily the gloomiest: Fifty percent said they thought life for the next generation would be worse, compared to 40 percent for Clinton voters and 28 percent for Bush voters. A fourth characteristic of Perot voters was their economic nationalism. The 1992 exit poll showed that Perot voters, by a 55 percent to 40 percent margin, believed that trade lost more jobs than it gained, a view they shared with Clinton voters. Later polling, especially around the time of the NAFTA vote, confirmed this economic nationalism; indeed, it suggested that it had strengthened, since Perot voters/supporters were easily the most adamantly opposed to the free trade agreement.[5]

The final key characteristic of the Perot voters was the one most widely cited in the press and in political discussion: their relative conservatism on both values issues and the role of government. But a close reading of the data suggests that Perot voters were hardly conservative ideologues on either the sanctity of traditional values or the wonders of the market. Instead, their "conservatism" was largely driven by a sense that middle-class values were no longer being rewarded and that operationally the government was not doing its job and was therefore a waste of tax money (as opposed to not having a job to do, as free market ideologues would contend). Thus, although Perot voters tended to agree with Bush voters on the desirability of a government that provides less in services but costs less in taxes (72 percent and 79 percent support, respectively) and were most likely to cite the budget deficit as a voting issue, their views on the utility of government activism tended to be midway between those of Bush and Clinton voters.[6] Asked if government neglect of domestic problems (as opposed to a values breakdown) could be held responsible for social problems in the country, for example, 50 percent of Perot voters blamed government neglect compared to 25 percent of Bush voters and 70 percent of Clinton voters. Similarly, 50 percent of Perot voters agreed that government should do more to solve national problems, a view held by 36 percent of Bush voters and 73 percent of Clinton voters.

And in the traditional "culture wars," Perot voters looked very much like Clinton supporters.[7] For example, Perot voters' support for abortion rights was comparable to that of Clinton voters. In addition, a majority of both Perot and Clinton voters endorsed a "hands off" posture for government in promoting values. But on issues of middle-class values—particularly in the sense that those who cleave to those values and work hard are not being rewarded properly—Perot voters and Bush voters were of the same mind. For example, in the 1993 Greenberg/DLC poll, 76 percent of Perot voters and 75 percent of Bush voters (compared to 59 percent of Clinton voters) agreed that "it's the middle class, not the poor, who really get a raw deal today." By 69 percent and 70 percent, respectively, Perot and Bush voters also endorsed the view that "too many of the poor are trying to get something for nothing" (compared to 53 percent of Clinton voters).

Taken together, these demographic, economic, and attitudinal data help explain the worldview and behavior of Perot voters. They were, again, primarily non-college-educated whites who objectively were experiencing, and recognized themselves to be experiencing, a sustained erosion of their living standards. This erosion had come despite their hard work and substantial tax contributions—leading to the view that the first was unrewarded ("middle-class values in decline") and that current government policies were not particularly beneficial to them. If this is a "conservative" view at all, it was driven less by ideological commitment than by a need to make sense of their life experience as NCEWs in America over the last fifteen to twenty years. Their electoral behavior followed. Fed up with Bush and the Republicans because their administration had only seemed to accelerate the decline in living standards but unable to embrace the Democrats because that party was implicated in promoting both values and government that did not seem to benefit

Mastering the New Political Arithmetic 231

them, they struck out on their own and embraced what seemed a radical alternative.

The 1994 Election

What led from the Democrats' 1992 election victory to their catastrophe in 1994? We believe that basic economic trends, and the failure to even appear to want to confront them through a coherent legislative or policy agenda, were the key.

Despite some healthy economic indicators, voters in the 1994 election had much to be concerned about. Between 1992 and 1994, the median wage fell 3.3 percent, even as the economic expansion continued. Consistent with post-1979 economic trends, this wage decline was not equally distributed, with wages for the non-college educated declining in line with the median wage trends while wages for the college educated actually increased. Comparing wage and income levels in 1994 with 1989— the peak of the last business cycle—makes the numbers clearer. Over the period, the wage losers were high-school dropouts (down 5 percent; men down 9 percent); high-school graduates (down 2 percent; men down 4 percent); and those with some college (down 6 percent; men down 7 percent). The qualified winners were four-year college graduates (up 2 percent; women up 6 percent) and those with advanced degrees (up 4 percent; women up 9 percent).[8] With losers vastly outnumbering winners, however, median household income was still 6.6 percent below its 1989 prerecessionary peak. Thus, despite the economic recovery touted by the Clinton administration, the situation of the average voter had failed to improve. Coming on top of the particularly severe income and wage losses of the 1990–1991 recession, not to mention the overall deterioration in living standards since 1979, this was a bitter pill for the average voter to swallow.

Clinton campaigned in 1992 on an economic populist program of "Putting People First." The administration promised a deliberate reversal of misfortune for average Americans, led by an ambitious program of domestic investment. But this investment program was abandoned under Wall Street pressure—prompting James Carville to announce his hope to come back in the next life as "the bond market"—and there was little economic populism in 1992–1994. And with little positive news offered economically, the divisive cultural issues that Clinton had deliberately pushed off the agenda in his campaign entered as an exploitable distraction. The cultural issues—for example, the brouhaha over the appointments process and "gays in the military"—arose almost immediately. They did damage to Clinton's reputation as a cultural conservative, an injury probably not helped by later administration activity around gun control and abortion rights, despite the relative popularity of these as individual issues.

More centrally, however, beginning with the titanic struggle around the 1993 budget, the image of Clinton as an economic populist became blurred to near extinction. He backed off from a tax cut and instead passed gas and general tax increases. And even though the latter applied only to the upper 2 percent of households, the lack of an explicit connection to any populist, job-oriented initiatives facilitated the tax hike's portrayal as another "middle-class" soak. Instead, virtually the entire administration justification for the budget, and its associated taxes and spending cuts, was to cut the deficit—a policy priority that essentially made such initiatives impossible. Rhetorically, the ceaselessly probusiness justification for cutting the deficit—that it would calm the bond markets, keeping interest rates low and thereby promoting business investment and expansion—suggested a "trickle-down" economic approach at odds with the "Putting People First" rhetoric of Clinton's campaign.

The waters were further muddied by the struggle over NAFTA. The North American Free Trade Agreement was never popular with the public, particularly the non-college educated, who remained opposed to it until the end.[9] The only way the treaty passed was through an astounding mobilization of elite opinion and "vote buying" in the House. More to the point, Clinton's full-bore pressing of the issue damaged his populist credentials. Although NAFTA itself never became a voting issue, Clinton's behavior sent a clear negative signal to the voting public about administration interest in protecting people's jobs and wages. And, although the administration has sought to remedy this damage through its familiar "in the long run" story (since trade is good for business, and business is the source of wages and income, things will work out all right in the end), the public does not believe that story. In October 1995, almost two years after the passage of NAFTA, poll respondents told Times-Mirror pollsters by a 55–36 percent margin that more free trade treaties would be likely to hurt, not help, the job situation.[10]

Finally, it would be hard to overemphasize the deleterious, antipopulist effect of the administration's failed health care reform effort. A series of tactical blunders culminated in an extremely complicated plan that the public did not understand or see clear benefits from. This confusion allowed the Republican opposition and its allies in the health insurance industry to successfully portray the reform plan as yet another big government program that would do little for the middle class.[11]

Given this combination of declining wages and incomes in the midst of economic growth, perceived social liberalism, and elitist economics, the Democrats were extraordinarily vulnerable to a Republican counterattack based on populist antigovernment themes. The Republicans argued,

Mastering the New Political Arithmetic

in essence, that the Democrats were more interested in promoting big government than in solving the public's problems and pointed as "evidence" to the fact that little good had come from the first years of Clinton's term. The non-college-educated public, still suffering declining standards, was open to this argument. If government could not do any better than it had, why not at least reduce its size and quit wasting tax money? And if Republicans could not be looked to for any real solution to large-scale economic and social problems, could they not at least be counted on to reduce taxes and the size of government?

Data from the 1994 election confirm this essentially negative populist rejection of the Democrats. Non-college-educated voters, specifically NCEW voters, deserted the Democrats in droves. Compared with 1992, support for Democratic House candidates declined 10 percentage points among high-school dropouts, 11 points among high-school graduates, and 12 points among those with some college. It held steady among those with college degrees. The shift away from the Democrats in 1994 was most pronounced among non-college-educated whites; black support for Democrats actually went up slightly. Among white men with a high-school education, Democratic support declined 20 percentage points (to 37 percent), and among white men with some college, Democratic support declined 15 points (to 31 percent). But non-college-educated white women also deserted in droves: Among both white women with a high-school diploma and those with some college, Democratic support dropped 10 percentage points. Thus, to ascribe the falloff in Democratic support to "angry white men" misses a good part of the picture.

Thus, desertion of the NCEWs was the story behind the Democratic debacle in 1994—a pattern of desertion that is consistent with the differential effects of economic trends in the 1980s and 1990s. For some, however, this close correlation between declining living standards and Democratic desertion may seem paradoxical. Why would those comparatively disadvantaged by the economy desert the Democrats, who had historically taken the part of the common man and woman, for the Republicans, traditionally the party of the relatively well-off and privileged? To desert the Democrats for Perot is one thing; to leave for Republicans might seem something entirely different.

Who takes the political blame for adverse changes in the economy and in society, however, depends not only on timing—on who was in power when the changes occurred—but on the story the average person believes about the causes and nature of the changes. This is particularly true for long-term changes of the sort that concern us here. Whereas changes in the business cycle (booms and recessions) generally simply benefit (or hurt) the incumbent party, such secular shifts as declining living standards may affect either the incumbent or the challenger party, de-

234   *Teixeira and Rogers*

pending on where the finger of blame is pointed.[12] Thus, the incumbent Democrats, the "party of the common man," got hurt by declining living standards in 1994 because the story much of the public believed about this long-term change cast the Democrats as the villain.

Indeed, at least as far back as the late 1970s, the dominant story among the general public has been that long-term decline in living standards is caused—directly or indirectly—by useless government spending (especially on the poor and minorities), inefficient and obtrusive public administration, high taxes, selfish behavior by interest groups, and excessive social tolerance and valuelessness. This viewpoint is richly illustrated by a recent Washington Post/Kaiser Family Foundation/Harvard University survey. The study (1996) shows that the public blames both government action and inaction for the decline in living standards, especially including widening inequality and the lack of good jobs.[13]

Since the Democrats are the party of government, as well as the party of poor people, liberal interest groups, and social tolerance, it is therefore the Democrats who tend to be blamed for declining living standards. And accepting this blame means that the Democrats start most elections with two strikes against them. This disadvantage does not mean they cannot win under the right circumstances; although this version is generally dominant, the antigovernment story does not always take this form. Thus, it was possible for Bush to be defeated in 1992 because his administration had become identified with declining living standards and for Dole to be defeated in 1996 because he was identified with Republican attacks on popular programs. But under normal circumstances, with the antigovernment story dominating, the Democrats are severely handicapped, no matter what the rate of economic growth; hence, they were trounced in 1994 despite being at a relatively favorable point in the business cycle. Whatever the proincumbent effect of decent aggregate economic growth was—again, it did not show up as wage and income increases for much of the population—it was swamped by the anti-Democratic effect of long-term decline in living standards, a situation blamed on the government.

From the 1994 Election to Mid-1996

From the 1994 election to the middle of 1996, yet another stunning reversal took place. The Republican revolution swept into Washington with Bill Clinton's approval ratings in the low forties and Clinton losing out to Dole in trial presidential heats by five percentage points or more.[14] By the middle of 1996, Clinton claimed approval ratings in the low to mid-fifties and was decisively beating Dole in trial heats by fifteen to twenty points. Furthermore, Democrats were beating Republicans in generic

Mastering the New Political Arithmetic

congressional trial heats, while job approval of the Republican-dominated Congress had declined up to 20 points since spring 1995. Finally, the public reported disagreeing more than agreeing with what the Republicans were doing in Congress (the percentage disagreeing was up 21 points since early 1995) and judged the Republican Congress as more a failure than a success (the percentage saying failure up 14 points from early 1995).[15]

To understand this shift, we again look to basic wage and income trends and the key legislative and policy battles that are refracted through them. The economy continued to grow in the 1994 to mid-1996 period. Indeed, from the perspective of 1996, the economy was in the sixth year of a recovery that officially began in March 1991. Reflecting this growth, the economy had now easily met the administration's goal of 8 million new jobs in the 1992–1996 period. In addition, inflation had been low and the unemployment rate had also been relatively low, in the 5.3–6 percent range.

Unfortunately, the continued expansion of the economy in this period (quite weak by historical standards) did not do much for the living standard of the average American. For example, wages continued to decline, with the wage of the median worker declining 1.2 percent in the 1994–1995 period. This left the wage of the median worker 4.6 percent behind its level in 1989, the last business cycle peak (the median male worker was down 6.3 percent; the median female worker was down 1.7 percent). Moreover, this post-1989 wage decline/stagnation has not been equally distributed. The non-college educated have fared worse (losing 5 percent in real wages in the 1989–1995 period) than those with college degrees (up 2 percent) or more advanced degrees (up 3 percent). By sex, non-college men lost 7 percent in wages, male college graduates held steady, and men with advanced degrees gained 4 percent; non-college women lost 2 percent; female college graduates and those with advanced degrees each gained 6 percent.[16]

To be sure, household incomes did rise in this period, despite the continuing wage decline. This is because families—particularly non-college-educated families—could take advantage of an expanding economy by increasing work hours and having more household members work. But even the resulting gains—2 percent in 1994–1995 among the non-college educated—were not nearly enough to bring these families back to where they were in 1989. Indeed, at the end of 1995, median household income among the non-college educated was still 6 percent below its 1989 level.

Thus, despite the continued expansion of the economy after the 1994 election, living standards for the typical voter did not improve much and remained substantially below 1989 levels. Declining living standards combined with continued and widely publicized downsizing at many prominent companies was more than enough to make most voters nervous about their economic future.

In retrospect, however, it seems clear that Newt Gingrich and the congressional Republicans overestimated their mandate. But it was not obvious at the time. Many observers seemed to believe as profoundly as the victorious Republicans that U.S. voters had taken a distinctly ideological turn against government and would support wholesale deregulation and dismantling of government programs. Yet, with respect to the 1994 election, this view was fundamentally mistaken.[17] Rather than taking an ideological turn against government, voters turned on the Democrats because, operationally, government did not seem to be working: Living standards continued to decline and other social problems worsened, even as government expenditures continued apace. Given this assessment, it was time, reasoned the voters, to get rid of the Democrats and their style of government and try something different.

But "different" in their view did not mean getting rid of, or even significantly trimming, government programs they liked. Once it became apparent that such cuts would be included in the Republican drive to balance the budget, voters began to lose their enthusiasm for budget balancing in particular and for the Republican revolution in general. This loss of enthusiasm then set the stage for the Democratic comeback in late 1995.

It is important to stress that this comeback was driven by confrontation with Republican budget-balancing plans rather than by conciliation with the overall goal of a balanced budget. Examination of poll data convincingly shows that Clinton's embrace of the balanced-budget goal in June 1995 did little to increase support for Clinton and the Democrats.[18] It was only later in the year, in the period shortly before the government shutdown on November 14, that the poll numbers started turning in favor of Clinton and the Democrats and against the congressional Republicans and their proposals.[19] And this, of course, was the time that the White House finally joined congressional Democrats in a united front against the Republicans' plan. Evidently, confrontation was the key to the Democrats' rise in popularity—not any shift in thinking on the desirability of a balanced budget or the proclamation of the "end of the era of big government."

In light of the economic trends just reviewed and the earlier analysis of the 1994 election, it is easy to see how this confrontation strategy worked. Voters essentially "fired" the Democrats in 1994 because they had failed to make significant progress in solving the voters' economic and other problems. But the Republicans, instead of solving these problems, were now threatening to make things even worse. On top of continued deterioration in living standards, they were proposing to remove environmental safeguards; defund education programs, including school lunches; and, most important of all, cut Medicare, a critical part of most voters'

Mastering the New Political Arithmetic

economic security (current or future). To add insult to injury, they were proposing to reward the rich with new tax cuts.

This was simply unacceptable to most voters. Indeed, what the Republicans succeeded in doing was to point the finger of blame for declining living standards at themselves and their wealthy allies rather than at the Democrats and government, where it had previously been. And as long as this judgment continues and voters tend to see Republicans as the greater threat to their living standards, the Democrats will continue to have the upper hand.

The results of the 1996 election support this analysis of the swing back toward the Democrats. Exit poll results identified the economy/jobs (21 percent), Medicare and Social Security (15 percent), and education (12 percent) as the key issues that moved voters into the Clinton column (three-fifths to three-fourths of voters who said these issues were their most important concerns voted for Clinton). This compares very favorably to voters motivated by New Democrat–style issues, where, among Clinton voters, crime/drugs garnered just 40 percent (7 percent of the electorate) and the budget deficit gathered only 27 percent (12 percent of the electorate).

A postelection survey conducted by Stanley Greenberg for the Campaign for America's Future (CAF) found similar motivations among Clinton voters. Almost three-fifths (59 percent) of Clinton voters in this survey cited his support of domestic programs (education, Medicare, and the environment), compared to less than one-third (31 percent) who cited his support of New Democrat–style positions (welfare reform, anticrime measures, balanced budget, moderation).

Combined with evidence presented earlier on the timing of Clinton's popularity surge in 1995, these data suggest that Clinton may have moved to the "center" (the conventional interpretation) and that doing so helped win him the election but that the center had more to do with not-so-new Democrat issues (protecting Medicare, Medicaid, education, and the environment, referred to as "M2E2") than New Democrat issues.[20] Now, this does not mean that some New Democrat issues may not have helped Clinton add on to his lead at the margin, but it did not create the basic advantage that Clinton rode to his reelection. Instead, his stalwart defense of "M2E2" should be credited. By doing so, he was able to tap public commitment to the basics of the welfare state and connect to public sentiment that the Republicans were extreme and only likely to make things worse, if allowed to have their way. Combined with substantial improvements in public perceptions of the economy in the months immediately prior to the election (attributable to continuing increases in household income), this political stance gave him an insuperable advantage in the election campaign.

The class-divided nature of Clinton's increase in support in 1996 provides further support for the critical role of the non-college educated. Analysis of exit poll data reveals that Clinton's increased support came overwhelmingly from non-college-educated voters, particularly those with just a high-school diploma (up 8 points) and those with some college (up 7 points). In contrast, college-educated voters increased their support of Clinton by just 3 points.[21]

These figures suggest that increased support from non-college-educated voters accounted for about three-quarters of Clinton's overall increase in support.[22] Indeed, this could easily be an underestimate, given the apparent (and traditional) exit poll overstatement of college graduate representation in the electorate.[23] For example, if the representation of four-year college graduates was really 43 percent of the voting electorate, as implied by the exit polls, this would imply essentially 100 percent turnout of college graduates in the 1996 election—hardly a plausible scenario. Based on census data and historic patterns of exit poll overrepresentation, a better estimate for the college graduate proportion of voters is about 30 percent. This would, in turn, imply an even heavier contribution to Clinton's victory from non-college-educated voters.

By giving the Democrats another chance in 1996, however, those voters were not saying they now believe that Democrats have the solution to declining living standards or that they have lost their suspicion of government. On the contrary, these voters are unconvinced the Democrats can make things much better, and they remain wary of the government and government activism. This, of course, could provide the basis for a Republican comeback in future elections.

The potential for volatility and a swing away from the Democrats is thus very much present; indeed, in the longer run, another large swing away from the Democrats seems almost inevitable. The combination of continued economic anxiety and strong antigovernment sentiment will provide fertile ground for an aggressive Republican attempt to reindict the government and Democrats for persistently declining living standards. And assuming that the current lack of progress on living-standards issues continues, non-college-educated voters—especially non-college-educated whites—are likely to be listening.

Mastering the New Political Arithmetic

The evidence presented in this chapter suggests that capturing the loyalty of electorally volatile white non-college-educated Americans suffering long-term and uninterrupted declining living standards is the central challenge of U.S. politics today. Whichever party meets this challenge, thereby mastering the new political arithmetic, should dominate politics

Mastering the New Political Arithmetic 239

for many years to come. And yet the Democrats, who seem well situated to represent these voters' interests, have had tremendous difficulty capturing their loyalty for more than brief periods. Why can the Democrats not do the new math?

There are several reasons for the Democrats' difficulties. First, as long as the antigovernment story about declining living standards remains generally dominant, the political terrain favors the Republicans. The Democrats can occasionally shift blame in the Republicans' direction, but the underlying view of politics held by most Americans, and the policies that follow from this antigovernment viewpoint, intrinsically favor the Republicans.

The second reason is that the current Democratic approach to countering that story and shifting the political terrain is weak. Consider the following elements of that strategy. Perhaps the best-known element is the New Democrat approach, popularized by the Democratic Leadership Council (DLC). This approach focuses obsessively on the idea that Democrats need to improve their negative image—to convince voters that the Democrats are not the party of wasteful government spending, inefficient public administration, high taxes, selfish liberal interest groups, opposition to family values, and so on. Although such an image improvement is obviously desirable, it cannot, by definition, shift the political terrain in the Democrats' favor since it leaves untouched—indeed, implicitly accepts—the dominant, antigovernment story about the decline in living standards.

This is why the New Democrat approach is ultimately limited to helping Democrats, at the margin, in already favorable situations. For example, the Democrats in 1992 faced an incumbent president who was taking the blame for a bad economy and deteriorating living standards. Given this situation, Clinton's New Democrat stance probably helped voters move away from Bush, since it "inoculated" Clinton, in the words of Chairman Al From of the DLC, from charges of being soft on crime, against family values, in favor of wasteful spending, and so on. But it did not create, or even decisively shape, that favorable situation.

Similarly, in 1995–1996, it was the Republicans' errors in attacking Medicare and other popular programs, and a confrontational stance by the Democrats toward those attacks, that shifted voter support away from the Republicans. A New Democrat stance may be helping Clinton and the Democrats add to that lead at the margin. But it did not create that lead and will not forestall a decline if and when the Republicans reunite economic anxiety and antigovernment sentiment.

Another element of current Democratic strategy is to blame declining living standards on a neutral process of globalization and technological change about which little can or should be done. This process, the Democrats say, is ushering in a new global economy based on information technology, in which government's role is primarily to help workers acquire new skills and adapt to change. At some unspecified point in the future, living standards will actually start to rise again, but until then, workers can only hope to adapt with a minimum of pain.

This argument takes the heat off government as a cause of declining living standards, but it also makes government seem almost irrelevant to any possible solution. Moreover, the nature of the argument promotes hopelessness: Someday, living standards will improve, but when is someday? This is hardly the kind of argument that provides a vigorous counterweight to Republican assertions about the culpability of government. In addition, the public does not buy the idea that a neutral technological process is responsible for all the negative economic trends people see around them. For example, a recent poll found that by more than two to one (59 percent to 28 percent), the public thought that when companies downsize or eliminate jobs, they do it mainly "to boost short-term profits, stock prices, and executives' salaries" rather than "doing what they need to compete and survive in the global economy."[24]

Nor does the public believe that acquiring more skills through education and training will do much to change the current economic environment. For example, by 55 percent to 37 percent, respondents said they believe that "working hard often isn't enough anymore, because companies aren't loyal to their employees" rather than believing that "if you get a good education and work hard today, you can really do well and get ahead." And they do not see government investment in education and training as a particularly effective way to boost incomes and improve their economic situation (ranking seventh out of eight choices offered, behind health insurance portability, encouraging company profit sharing, raising the minimum wage, lower interest rates, and two other policy options).[25]

Still another element of current Democratic strategy is addressing voters' concerns about declining values with proposals such as the V-chip and school uniforms rather than engaging those concerns as an integral part of the living-standards issue. But for non-college-educated voters, as Greenberg's (1996) research convincingly shows, values and the struggle to maintain a decent standard of living are not artificially separated in the manner implied by this approach. For these voters, economics is a values issue, since it is their values of loyalty and fairness that are being contravened by current economic trends, and it is their values of responsibility and hard work that enable them to get by in this difficult economic environment. Thus, no amount of talk about teen curfews or more educational programming on TV can substitute for identification with, and facilitation of, the values-based economic struggles of these voters.

The third reason that the Democrats have not been able to shift the political terrain in their favor is that they have ceded so much ground to the Republicans that there is very little they can do—or even talk about doing—to raise living standards. Indeed, they have imprisoned themselves, along with the Republicans and most of the economics profession, in an "iron triangle" of economic policy principles that effectively exclude any active attempt to improve the lot of the average American.[26] The first vertex of the triangle is support for the high-unemployment, high–interest rate, slow-growth macroeconomic policy favored by Chairman Alan Greenspan of the Federal Reserve Board, Wall Street bond traders, and other economic elites. The second vertex is commitment to a fiscal policy centered on reducing the deficit, up to and including balancing the budget. The third vertex is commitment to expanding free trade, including more free-trade treaties, unimpeded by labor standards and other "peripheral" issues.

Staying within this triangle, however, rules out any serious attempt to improve living standards. Reduce unemployment far enough that labor markets tighten and wages rise? No, that would produce an explosion of inflation, the inflation fighters say. Lower interest rates and push for faster growth? No, the economy cannot grow more than 2.5 percent per year without tightening labor markets, again leading to disastrous inflation. Spend more money on infrastructure and research and development to boost demand and the long-run productivity of the economy? No, this cannot be done without increasing the deficit, which must be avoided at all costs. How about more money for education and training, which current Democratic strategy says is necessary for workers to adapt to the "new economy"? No, same problem: It is still too expensive to do while trying to reduce the deficit. Try to reduce trade deficits to improve the jobs and wages of American workers? No, too much pressure on our trading partners interferes with free trade. And so on.

But without tangible progress on improving the living standard of the average American, it will be hard to convince non-college-educated voters that Democrats and activist government are worth their loyalty. Of course, current Democratic thinking asserts that over the long run, staying within this iron triangle will produce growth in living standards.

Voters, however, may not be willing to wait, especially since they are far less committed than Democratic policymakers to the iron triangle's economic principles. To begin with, there is no evidence that voters understand, much less endorse, the concept that low unemployment leads to accelerating inflation. But they know, and do not approve of, the resulting economic environment in which "no matter how good a job you do for your company, there's always someone else waiting to take your job for less pay." Nor do voters believe the balanced budget will pay off for them personally. By 55 percent to 40 percent, they believe a balanced budget would either hurt or have no effect on their family financial situation.[27] And it will probably be hard to convince them otherwise when the government's own analysts predict a growth rate dividend of an underwhelming one-tenth of a percentage point from a balanced budget.[28] Finally, most Americans have been and remain skeptical about the benefits of free trade.[29] For example, two recent NBC/Wall Street Journal polls found that the public believes by more than a two to one margin that free trade treaties, on balance, cost the United States jobs.[30] This simply underscores a long-standing viewpoint within the U.S. public.

These factors help explain why the Democrats have not been able to retain the loyalty of non-college-educated white voters for any length of time. The antigovernment story is still dominant, the Democratic counterstory, centered around New Democrat image management and platitudes about the new economy, is weak, and the party has imprisoned itself within an iron triangle of economic principles that preclude any efforts to raise living standards. The result is what we see: occasional Democratic successes in a climate of intense electoral volatility.

Conclusion

For Democrats to have a chance at long-run success, they must build a political alternative that breaks out of the iron triangle, raises living standards, and consolidates support among non-college-educated, particularly white, voters. Recent developments suggest a promising direction for the Democrats. To begin with, the evolution of public opinion around the budget battles of 1995–1996 suggests the softness of public commitment to balancing the budget as a policy goal. Although the public supported (and still supports) balancing the budget in the abstract, it consistently chooses preserving Medicare, Social Security, and other programs it deems worthy over balancing the budget. The problem, then, is not to change the entire structure of public opinion about government spending, taxes, deficits, and balanced budgets but rather to find other government programs and causes the public deems equally worthy.

What might motivate the public to find such programs and causes worthy? The answer lies in the emergence of a strand of public thinking about declining living standards that is challenging the dominance of the antigovernment interpretation. This new strand of thinking focuses on the ways in which corporations and other dominant interests are taking advantage of economic change to enrich themselves and break down the norms that previously enabled ordinary workers to prosper.

This "new economy populism" is now so powerful that it sometimes outweighs antigovernment sentiments in polling results. For example, a

Mastering the New Political Arithmetic

recent survey asked people how responsible different factors were for the nation's current economic problems.[31] Whereas "government taking too much in taxes from working people" ranked second as a "very responsible" factor (44 percent), the only factor selected as "very responsible" by a majority of respondents was "corporations have become too greedy" (53 percent). Similarly, when asked to select the biggest problem with government economic policies today, 48 percent chose "government is too concerned with what big corporations and the wealthy special interests want, and does not do enough to help average working families," compared to 35 percent who chose "government spends too much, taxes too much, and interferes too much in things better left to individuals and business."[32] Such relatively strong support for new economy populism is an important change from the public opinion climate of the early 1990s.

Here, then, is a way to motivate public support for government programs. The public is well aware that the country is going through a vast economic transformation, but it believes this transformation is destroying old rules to the advantage of those with economic power. Instead of arguing with the public (i.e., "things really are getting better," "all you need is a little bit more education," "some pain is inevitable but will usher in a bright tomorrow"), politicians might be well advised to agree with the public's belief that "the old rules are being destroyed and you really are being taken advantage of by those with the most economic power."

This view provides a compelling rationale for breaking out of the iron triangle and asserting the centrality of government action to raise living standards. If government does not help set new rules and prevent those with the most economic power from taking advantage, who will?[33] If government does not spend money on helping workers and communities become more productive and gain from the new economy, who will? Put in this way, the public can potentially be won over to the idea that government actions and programs specifically designed to raise living standards, even if they involve regulation and cost money, are necessary for a better future.[34] Conversely, if the public is not convinced of this necessity, a jaundiced view of government action and programs will continue to prevail. This in turn will make action to raise living standards impossible, ensuring that Democratic victories are episodic and unstable.

But if this new economy populism provides a potentially effective rationale for government action and programs, it runs the risk of seeming detached from the basic values that animate so many voters and anchor their lives. As argued earlier, for most voters, economics is a values issue and must be dealt with in those terms. Such a new synthesis of economics and values, of economic program and moral statement, is not difficult, in principle, to envision. After all, the economy and its ordering reflect political decisions—an old notion that the current administration tends to dismiss—and lurking behind politics are not only material interests but competing moral visions of social order. That morality can and should be pluralist and should accommodate a wide range of more specific views, but it does need to have a universalist core. That core is readily available in the belief systems of average Americans, who value contribution, responsibility, and loyalty, as well as democracy and fairness—and who find those values violated at least as much by irresponsible corporate interests (against whom no one stands as their advocate) as by the sins of the welfare state, real and imagined. A broadly populist economic program that declares itself as rooted in those values, and willing to do battle for them against all assailants, is the key to returning large numbers of NCEWs to the Democratic Party.

Of course, the approach just sketched here does not tell us precisely what policies to advocate in these areas and precisely how to advocate them. But this is less important than clarity on the basic project: framing living standards as a values issue so that every policy dispute can be seen through that prism. Does a given policy choice raise living standards and defend the values of the center against elites or not? If that question becomes routine in the American political conversation, it could give the Democrats a built-in values advantage over the Republicans in every election.

And it would have other beneficial effects as well, chief among them that it would provide a popular rationale for active government and allow the pursuit of policies that would materially improve the lives of the non-college-educated women and men at the heart of the electorate. This, in turn, would further build support for active government and allow the implementation of additional policies to raise living standards. Thus, a sort of "virtuous circle" would be created that could consolidate a stable electoral majority for the Democrats.

This contrasts with the current situation, where a vicious circle obtains: Concessions to the Republicans undermine support for active government, which prevents pursuit of policies to materially improve voters' lives, which further undermines support for active government, leading to more concessions—and so on. The Democrats are progressively left with less and less room in which to maneuver, while a volatile electorate waits impatiently in the wings to throw them out once again. No new majority is possible under such circumstances.

Instead, the political terrain must be shifted toward a broad national program to raise American living standards, as described herein. Lacking such a program, current Democratic strategy seems adrift—designed to push away the very non-college-educated voters on whom a new majority depends. Unless Democrats believe that Newt Gingrich and Bob Dole,

Mastering the New Political Arithmetic   245

or their equivalents, will always be there to bring them back, the case for forging a new approach and making living standards a values issue seems compelling.

Notes

1. This chapter is based on our more extensive analysis found in Ruy A. Teixeira and Joel Rogers, *Volatile Voters: Declining Living Standards and Non-College-Educated Whites* (Washington, DC: Economic Policy Institute, 1996).

2. For more discussion of the U.S. electorate and how heavily it is dominated by non-college-educated voters, see Ruy Teixeira, *The Politics of the High Wage Path: The Challenge Facing Democrats* (Washington, DC: Economic Policy Institute, 1994).

3. Those with a four-year college degree.

4. For some comparative data on Perot and Clinton voters' wage losses over various time periods, see Teixeira, *Politics of the High Wage Path*, table 3.

5. For more data and discussion on Perot voters and economic nationalism, see Ruy Teixeira and Guy Molyneux, *Economic Nationalism and the Future of American Politics* (Washington, DC: Economic Policy Institute, 1993).

6. 1992 VRS exit poll results.

7. This part of the discussion draws on Stanley Greenberg's useful study of Perot voters: "The Perot Voters and American Politics: Here to Stay?" in *The Road to Realignment: The Democrats and the Perot Voters* (Washington, DC: Democratic Leadership Council, 1993).

8. All wage data in this section are based on Lawrence Mishel, Jared Bernstein, and John Schmitt, *The State of Working America 1996–97* (Armonk, NY: M. E. Sharpe and Economic Policy Institute, 1997).

9. According to a Gallup-CNN poll on the eve of the final House vote, non-college-educated Americans opposed it by a 43–34 percent margin.

10. Poll conducted October 25–30, 1995. This almost exactly reverses the results of a March 1994 Times-Mirror poll in which, in an initial burst of post-NAFTA optimism, 52 percent of respondents felt more free trade treaties would help the job situation, compared to 32 percent who thought such treaties would hurt. Note also that the NBC/Wall Street Journal poll found, in both January and March of this year, that about three-fifths of the public thought free trade agreements with other countries cost the United States more jobs than they created.

11. For a detailed recounting of this episode, see Theda Skocpol, *Boomerang: Clinton's Health Security Effort and the Turn Against Government in U.S. Politics* (New York: W. W. Norton and Company, 1996).

12. This analysis helps explain the recent failures of election forecasting models driven by business cycle indicators of overall economic growth. For example, because the economy was already recovering before the 1992 election, many of the leading presidential forecasting models predicted a Bush victory (for example, Yale economist Ray Fair's model). And in 1994, because of the continued business cycle expansion under Clinton, a leading House forecasting model predicted very modest Democratic losses—just five seats (Michael Lewis-Beck and J. M. Wrighton, "A Republican Congress? Forecasts for 1994," *Public Opinions* [Fall

1994]). These models are obviously leaving out some important factors, chiefly, we would argue, the political effects of declining living standards.

13. For more on how people blame the government for favoring the wealthy and failing to act to protect the economic interests of the average citizen, see Hart/Mellman/AFL-CIO poll (April 19–22, 1996). See also the Business Week/Harris polls, reported in the March 13, 1995, and March 11, 1996, issues of the magazine.

14. Various NBC News/Wall Street Journal and CNN/USA Today/Gallup polls, November 1994 through February 1995.

15. May 1996 NBC News/Wall Street Journal poll; May 9–12, 1996, CNN/USA Today/Gallup polls.

16. All wage data based on Mishel, Bernstein, and Schmitt, *State of Working America*.

17. Even given our attention to the "story" that people believe, our interpretation of the 1994 election may strike many as insufficiently ideological. Some would argue that the relationship we observe between living standards and Democratic decline is spurious, that the real driving force behind the pro-Republican surge was increased ideological conservatism among voters. At first blush, the argument has some plausibility, as the proportion of self-identified conservatives in the 1994 electorate did rise over 1992 levels—from 30 percent to 37 percent—as did the rate at which they voted Republican, from 72 percent to 81 percent. For the most detailed explication of this viewpoint, see Fred Steeper, *This Swing Is Different: Analysis of the 1994 Election Exit Polls* (Southfield, MI: Market Strategies, 1995). However, closer examination of these data make the ideology claim less impressive. Our analyses show that the shift in the share of conservatives in the electorate did make a contribution to the decline in the Democratic vote in 1994, explaining about 18 percent of it. But it also shows that the anti-Democrat shift among economic pessimists made a much larger contribution and that an anti-Democrat shift among conservatives—that is, their increased rate of Republican voting—made no contribution at all. For a more detailed discussion of this debate as well as a critique of views that focus on values and turnout, see Teixeira and Rogers, *Volatile Voters*. For a detailed discussion of these points concerning the 1980 and 1984 elections, see Thomas Ferguson and Joel Rogers, eds., *The Hidden Election: Politics and Economics in the 1980 Presidential Campaign* (New York: Pantheon, 1982); and Thomas Ferguson and Joel Rogers, *Right Turn: The Decline of the Democrats and the Future of American Politics* (New York: Hill and Wang, 1986).

18. For data and a lucid discussion of the evolution of the Democrats' battle with the Republicans, see Thomas B. Edsall, "Confrontation Is the Key to Clinton's Popularity," *Washington Post*, December 24, 1995.

19. See, for example, the data in the November 6–8, 1995, CNN/USA Today/Gallup poll.

20. Interestingly, another clear demonstration of the relative importance of M2E2 comes from a distinctly underpublicized result from a Democratic Leadership Council (DLC) postelection poll. That poll, conducted by Mark Penn, asked voters several questions on what "this election was about." The clear winner was "preserving Medicare, Medicaid, education and the environment" over such

Mastering the New Political Arithmetic

New Democrat favorites as "expanding opportunity, responsibility and working together as a community" and "ending old-style liberalism and bringing the Democratic Party into the mainstream."

21. For more analysis of the demographics of Clinton's increased support, particularly in terms of the key role of non-college-educated women, see Ruy Teixeira, "Finding the Real Center," *Dissent* (Spring 1997), pp. 51–59.

22. An estimate that finds general support in results from the Greenberg/CAF survey. That survey found that 78 percent of new Clinton voters (those who voted for him in 1996 but not in 1992) were non-college educated.

23. See Teixeira and Rogers, *Volatile Voters,* for a discussion of exit poll education bias in 1992 and 1994.

24. Hart/Mellman/AFL-CIO, April 19–22, 1996.

25. NBC/Wall Street Journal, May 10–14, 1996.

26. We thank Rick McGahey for conversations on this subject.

27. Pew Research Center poll, January 11–14, 1996.

28. Congressional Budget Office forecast reported in Bruce Bartlett, "Yes, We Can Afford a Federal Tax Cut," *Wall Street Journal,* June 11, 1996).

29. See Teixeira and Molyneux, *Economic Nationalism,* for a review of pertinent polling data.

30. NBC/Wall Street Journal, March 1–5 and May 10–14, 1996.

31. Hart/Mellman/AFL-CIO, April 19–22, 1996.

32. Ibid.

33. In this sense, new economy populism is consistent with the sort of new economy progressivism advocated by Dionne (E. J. Dionne, *They Only Look Dead* [New York: Simon and Schuster, 1996]). Illustrating this hunger for new rules and limits on economic power, by a 2 to 1 margin (62 percent to 31 percent), the public says "government needs to be more involved in holding corporations to a higher standard of responsibility" rather than saying that "if government tries to interfere with free enterprise by telling corporations what they can and can't do, it will only make things worse" (Hart/Mellman/AFL-CIO, April 19–22, 1996).

34. It is important to emphasize the term "won over." Just as it took the Republicans much strenuous effort to successfully mobilize antigovernment populism, so the Democrats will have to work hard to mobilize new economy populism. This will be particularly true when they are faced with opposition from the business community and from conservatives within Congress. As Clinton's record demonstrates, refusal to mobilize public opinion gives these well-entrenched forces more than enough room to block new initiatives. For a lucid recounting of several choice points in the Clinton presidency where a mobilization strategy was rejected, forcing him to give up on key components of his campaign program, see John Judis, "Bill Clinton's Second Coming," *GQ* (August 1996).

Notes on Editor
and Contributors

Amy E. Ansell is assistant professor of sociology and director of international programs at Bard College. She is the author of *New Right, New Racism: Race and Reaction in the United States and Britain* (NYU/Macmillan, 1997) and "Business Mobilization and the New Right: Currents in U.S. Foreign Policy" in *Business and the State in International Relations,* edited by Ronald W. Cox (Westview, 1996). Her current research is on white racial discourse and the symbolic dimensions of political conflict and change in post-Apartheid South Africa.

Chip Berlet has spent over twenty years researching and organizing against political repression and bigotry and advocating for democracy and diversity. He works as the senior analyst at Political Research Associates in Somerville, Massachusetts, and is editor, most recently, of *Eyes Right! Challenging the Right-Wing Backlash* (South End Press, 1995). He is currently finishing a book, with Matthew Lyons (also a contributor to this volume), titled *Too Close for Comfort: Right-Wing Populism, Scapegoating, and Fascist Potentials in U.S. Political Traditions* (South End Press, forthcoming).

Ronald W. Cox is associate professor of political science at Florida International University. He is the author of *Power and Profits: U.S. Policy in Central America* (University of Kentucky Press, 1995) and editor of *Business and the State in International Relations* (Westview, 1996).

Sara Diamond holds a doctorate in sociology from the University of California at Berkeley and has taught journalism and sociology at several California universities. She is the author of *Spiritual Warfare: The Politics of the Christian Right* (South End Press, 1989); *Roads to Dominion: Right-Wing Movements and Political Power in the United States* (Guilford, 1995); and *Facing the Wrath: Confronting the Right in Dangerous Times* (Common Courage Press, 1996). Her next book, on the cultural politics of the Christian Right, will be published by Guilford Press in 1998.

Gary Dorrien is a religious studies professor at Kalamazoo College and author, most recently, of *The Word as True Myth: Interpreting Modern Theology* (Westminster, 1997). Parts of this chapter are adapted from his books, *The Neoconservative Mind: Politics, Culture, and the War of Ideology* (Temple, 1993) and *Soul in Society: The Making and Renewal of Social Christianity* (Fortress, 1995).

Murray Edelman is professor emeritus at the University of Wisconsin at Madison. He is the author of numerous books, including *From Art to Politics: How Artistic Creations Shape Political Conceptions* (University of Chicago Press, 1995); *The Symbolic Uses of Politics* (University of Illinois Press, 1964); *Political Language:*

249

Words That Succeed and Policies That Fail (University of Chicago Press, 1977); *Politics as Symbolic Action: Mass Arousal and Quiescence* (Markham, 1971); and *Constructing the Political Spectacle* (University of Chicago Press, 1988).

Jean Hardisty, a political scientist with a Ph.D. from Northwestern University, taught and researched conservative political thought for eight years, then left academia and opened Political Research Associates (PRA), a research center based in Somerville, Massachusetts, that analyzes right-wing authoritarian and antidemocratic trends and publishes public education material on the right. In addition to serving as executive director of PRA for sixteen years, Jean has been an activist for social justice issues, especially women's rights and civil rights, for over two decades. She is currently writing a book titled *Treacherous Politics: The Resurgence of the Right* (Beacon, forthcoming).

Matthew N. Lyons is research associate for the Hansberry-Nemiroff Archival, Educational, and Cultural Fund. He is a historian, activist, and writer whose work has focused on systems of oppression and social movements. He is the author of *The Grassroots Network: Radical Nonviolence in the Federal Republic of Germany, 1972–1985* (Cornell University Center for International Studies, 1989) and coauthor with Chip Berlet (also a contributor in this volume) of *Too Close for Comfort: Right-Wing Populism, Scapegoating, and Fascist Potentials in U.S. Political Traditions* (South End Press, forthcoming).

Joel Rogers is professor of sociology, politics, and law at the University of Wisconsin at Madison, where he also directs the Center on Wisconsin Strategy. National chair of the New Party, Rogers is author or coauthor of numerous books and articles on American politics, political theory, and comparative political economy. Among recent works are *Works Councils: Consultation, Representation, and Participation in Industrial Relations* (University of Chicago Press, 1995) and *Associations and Democracy* (Verso, 1995).

Anna Marie Smith is assistant professor of political theory in the Department of Government at Cornell University. She is author of *New Right Discourse on Race and Sexuality* (Cambridge University Press, 1994). She is currently finishing a second book titled *Laclau and Mouffe and the Radical Democratic Imaginary* (Routledge, forthcoming).

Ruy A. Teixeira is director of the Politics and Public Opinion Program at the Economic Policy Institute (EPI). He is the author of numerous books and articles on American politics and labor markets, including *Why Americans Don't Vote* (Greenwood, 1987); *The Disappearing American Voter* (Brookings Institution, 1992); and *The Politics of the High Wage Path* (Economic Policy Institute, 1994). Before going to EPI, Teixeira was a visiting fellow at the Brookings Institution and director of political studies at the Progressive Foundation.

Ann Withorn is professor of social policy at the University of Massachusetts, Boston. She is a longtime welfare rights activist and has written on poverty, women, and welfare state ideology. She recently completed, with Diane Dujon, a revised version of her earlier anthology *For Crying Out Loud: Women's Poverty in the United States* (South End Press, 1996).

Richard D. Wolff is professor of economics at the University of Massachusetts at Amherst. He is author of *Knowledge and Class: A Marxian Critique of Political Economy* (University of Chicago Press, 1987) and coauthor, with Stephen Resnick,

Notes on Editor and Contributors

of *Economics: Marxian Versus Neoclassical* (Johns Hopkins University Press, 1987) and, with Harriet Fraad and Stephen Resnick, *Bringing It All Back Home: Class, Gender, and Power in the Modern Household* (Pluto Press, 1994). He is also a political activist in New Haven, Connecticut, and an economic adviser to many local trade unions and was a candidate for mayor of New Haven in 1985 on the Green Party ticket.

Index

ABM. *See* Antiballistic Missile Treaty
Abortion issues, 25, 26, 29, 32, 35, 43, 51, 52, 74, 82, 88, 89, 94, 108, 111, 113, 155, 160, 164, 230
Adoptions, 154
AEI. *See* American Enterprise Institute
Aerospace Industries Association, 204
AFDC. *See* Aid to Families with Dependent Children
Affirmative action, 17, 33, 36, 51, 69, 70, 71, 88, 109, 142, 151, 152, 161, 170(n9), 175, 177, 179–183, 188
African Americans. *See* Blacks
AIDS, 154, 158
Aid to Families with Dependent Children (AFDC), 127, 128, 136, 138, 139, 140, 141, 143, 191(n25)
Aircraft, 198, 205, 206
Air Traffic Controllers, 219
Alien Nation (Brimelow), 173, 179
America First Committee, 84, 94
American Cause, 34
American Enterprise Institute (AEI), 66, 69, 90
American Family Association, 41
Amway company, 92
Ansell, Amy E., 190(n8)
Antelope Valley Springs of Life Church, 44
Antiballistic Missile Treaty (ABM), 206, 207
Anti-Defamation League, 153
Anti-Semitism, 18, 20–21, 22, 28, 34, 66, 67, 69, 82, 96, 101(n34), 153
Armey, Dick, 10, 91, 148–149, 163, 166–167
Arms reductions, 26, 90
Arms sales, 204–205, 206, 208
Asians, 20
Association of American Chambers of Commerce, 193

Authoritarianism, 18, 21, 31, 37, 157, 161, 174
  fascist vs. nonfascist, 164

Bakker, Jim, 26
Ball, William, 95
Banfield, Edward C., 58
Bauer, Gary, 49
Beichman, Arnold, 59
Bell, Daniel, 57, 58, 75
Bellant, Russ, 91
Bell Curve, The (Herrnstein and Murray), 33, 158, 160, 173, 185
Bennett, Bill, 31, 63
Berger, Peter, 74
Berke, Richard, 155, 162
Berns, Walter, 74
Betz, Hans-Georg, 30
Bible, 119, 121
Bigotry, 67, 164, 167, 178, 181
Billings, Robert, 25
Birch, Elizabeth, 155
Blacks, 20, 33, 36, 51, 71, 137, 143, 153, 173, 175, 180, 184, 185, 187, 233
  black conservatives, 182
  Black Power, 59
Bolick, Clint, 182
Bosnia, 207, 208
Bott Broadcasting, 45
Branch Davidians, 30
Brimelow, Peter, 173, 178, 179
Brookings Institution, 24
Bruno, Joseph, 169(n3)
B–2 bombers, 206
Buchanan, Pat, 28, 29, 30, 31, 34, 35, 66, 68, 80, 94, 95, 96, 97, 105, 112, 113–114, 133, 160, 164, 179, 207, 208
Buckley, William F., Jr., 22, 24
Budget issues, 232, 236, 237, 241–242

253

Bunzel, John H., 58
Burke, Edmund, 56, 57
Burnham, James, 61
Bush, George, 26, 64, 66, 93, 94, 96, 116, 184, 194, 204, 209, 228, 229
Business, 9, 71, 80–98, 192–193, 194, 201, 232
  business conflict analysis, 81–82, 97–98
  business cycles, 213, 214, 215, 220, 222, 225(n9), 233, 245(n12)
  insider/outsider factions, 82, 85, 86, 96, 97
  multinationalists/nationalists, 83–84, 85, 87, 88, 90, 92, 94, 95, 96, 97, 99(n3), 207. *See also* Republican Party, nationalists/internationalists in
  See also Corporations
Business Roundtable, 83, 90
Busing, 89

California, University of, 170(n9)
California Civil Rights Initiative (CCRI), 1, 175, 180–181
California Learning Assessment Test (CLAS), 45–46
Campaign and Elections magazine, 160
Campus Crusade for Christ, 87
Capitalism, 74–75, 80, 81, 83, 97, 98, 142, 146(nn 22, 23), 172(n63), 220
  anticapitalist campaigns, 156, 157
  fundamentalist vs. liberal, 130, 145(n9)
  radical capitalists, 129–130, 134, 136, 145(n9)
  state capitalism, 212, 213–217, 218, 219, 221–222, 223, 224, 225(n7)
  See also Business
Carnegie, Andrew, 118
Carter, Jimmy, 43, 61, 62, 70, 89, 193, 194
Carville, James, 231
Catholics, 21, 29, 35, 68, 83, 90, 110, 114, 115, 131, 153
CBN. *See* Christian Broadcasting Network
CCRI. *See* California Civil Rights Initiative
Censorship, 155
Center for Equal Opportunity, 182

Center for New Black Leadership, 182
Center for Religion and Society, 33
Center on Social Welfare Policy and Law, 191(n25)
Central America, 193
Charisma magazine, 49, 51
Chavez, Linda, 63, 182
Cheney, Richard, 197
Cheryl Hopwood v. the State of Texas, 181, 190(n14)
Children, 69, 117, 136, 140, 141, 142
Choice Not an Echo, A (Shlafly), 85, 111
Christian Action Network, 154
Christian Anti-Communist Crusade, 23
Christian Booksellers Association, 46
Christian Broadcasting Network (CBN), 87, 96
Christian Coalition, 5, 28, 35, 41, 42, 51, 95–96, 97, 108, 141, 153, 154, 159–160, 161
  Contract with the American Family, 155–156
Christian Identity, 19, 131
Christian Right, 8–9, 19, 23, 24–26, 27–28, 29, 31, 32, 34, 35, 91, 93, 100(n12), 108, 109, 114, 115, 136, 139, 148–169, 193
  and cultural projects, 41–53
  See also Christian Coalition
Chronicles, 34, 65, 67, 177
Cies, William, 91–92, 95
Civil rights movement, 23, 85, 98, 131, 151, 175
  counter-civil rights establishment organizations, 182
CLAS. *See* California Learning Assessment Test
Clash of Civilizations and the Remaking of World Order, The (Huntington), 32
Class hierarchies, 157
Clinton, Bill, 1, 45, 64, 76, 81, 118, 148, 154, 159, 177–178, 180, 186, 194, 203, 204, 205, 206, 207, 208, 228–229, 231, 232, 234, 237, 238
CNP. *See* Council for National Policy
Coalition for a Democratic Majority, 61, 73
Coalition on Revival, 114

Index

255

Coalitions, 9, 12, 22, 31, 35, 83, 89, 95, 97, 153, 179, 189(n2), 203, 209, 221. *See also* Christian Coalition; Christian Right
Cohen, Hattie May, 165
Cold war, 2, 5, 23, 26, 27, 42, 57, 63, 72, 73, 84, 88, 134, 187, 203, 205, 222
  and cultural warfare, 74
  perpetuation of ideology concerning, 196
  second cold war, 194, 195, 197, 200
Collective bargaining, 82
Collectivism, 21, 28, 73, 132, 135, 223
Colorado, 165–166
Colorado for Family Values, 49
Color blindness, 150, 174, 175, 180, 182, 183
Commentary, 33, 59, 178
Commission for the Study of Automation, 58
Committee for the Survival of a Free Congress, 193
Committee on the Present Danger, 90, 193, 194–195, 202–203, 208
Common good, 152
Common law courts, 30
Communism, 19, 21, 22, 27, 28, 42, 43, 59, 60, 61, 62, 63, 65, 71, 73, 82, 84, 113, 116, 121, 135, 212, 215, 216, 217
  anti-communist organizations, 23
  new form of, 223–224, 226(n12)
Communitarianism, 223, 224
Computers, 24, 72, 73, 93
Concerned Women for America (CWA), 28, 41, 107, 108, 109, 114–116, 117–118, 119, 120, 121, 122, 123, 154
  compared with Eagle Forum, 114
Condoms, 154
Confederacy of Southern States, 128, 133, 144
Congressional Family Caucus, 41
Conspiracy theories, 27, 28, 31, 35, 37, 68, 84, 85, 96, 97, 116–117, 118
Constitution, 57, 128. *See also* Fourteenth Amendment
Contract with America, 141, 155, 177, 185, 199, 205
Contras, 29
Coors, Joseph, 86

Corporations, 240, 243, 244, 247(n34)
Council for National Policy (CNP), 91–93, 101(n23)
Council on Foreign Relations, 83, 96, 118
Counterculture, 25, 58–59, 60
Crawford Broadcasting, 45
Crime, 33, 88, 138, 165, 178, 237
Cultural issues, 41–53, 122–123, 223, 231
  cultural hegemony, 34
  cultural politics, 8–9, 42
  cultural relativism, 150
  culture of poverty, 185–186, 187
  culture wars, 6, 32, 33, 60, 73, 74, 105, 123, 160, 173–189, 230
  monoculturalism, 32, 33
  See also Multiculturalism
Cunningham, Randy, 169(n3)
CWA. *See* Concerned Women for America

Dahl, R., 169(n4)
D'Amato, Alfonse, 169(n3)
Davies, Bob, 48
Death penalty, 25
Decter, Midge, 59, 66, 69, 70, 73–74
Defense Department, 195, 198, 199, 202
Democracy, 98, 150, 151, 161, 167, 168, 223
Democratic globalism, 64, 66, 67
Democratic Party, 59, 61, 158, 159, 181, 182, 219, 234, 237, 239–242, 244
  desertions from, 233
  New Democrats, 239, 242
Desegregation, 88
Détente, 88, 217
Development, 222
Dewey, John, 22
Diamond, Sara, 19, 21, 25, 116
Dilling, Elizabeth, 21
Direct mail, 24, 85, 88
Directory of Religious Media (National Religious Broadcasters), 53(n10)
Discrimination, 70, 71, 82, 122, 151, 165, 178, 179, 181, 188
Dissent magazine, 60
Diversity, 176. *See also* Pluralism
Divorce, 136
Dobson, James, 27, 35, 44, 49
Dole, Bob, 32, 130, 151, 155, 162, 180, 234

Dollars, 87
Dominionism, 24–25, 34
Dornan, Robert, 153–154
Douglass, Frederick, 35
DuBois, W.E.B., 173
Duffy, Warren, 45
Dworkin, Andrea, 119

Eagle Forum, 107, 109, 110, 111–114,
  116–117, 119, 120, 121, 122
  compared with Concerned Women for
  America, 114
Eastern establishment, 83, 84, 85, 86, 90,
  93, 135
Eco, Umberto, 145(n7)
Economic issues, 11, 22, 25, 64, 70–71, 82,
  87, 93, 138, 139, 142, 158, 205,
  211–224, 231, 237, 243
  debt, 72
  economic growth, 214, 232, 234, 235,
    241, 245(n12)
  economic nationalism, 229
  global economy, 201, 240
  Keynesian economics, 211, 212–213,
    215, 218–219, 221, 222, 224,
    225(n4)
  neoclassical economics, 22, 212–213
  supply-side economics, 74
  and values, 240, 243, 244, 245
  See also Foreign investments;
    Government's role, economic
    intervention; Incomes; Populism,
    new economy populism
Edsall, Thomas, 86
Education, 22, 28, 69, 73, 190(n14), 223,
  236, 237, 240, 241, 246(n20)
  federal aid to, 72
  home schooling, 44, 52
  multicultural, 69, 73, 158
  non-college-educated whites
    (NCEWs), 12, 229, 230, 233, 238,
    242, 244
  and wages, 229, 231, 235
  See also Education, Department of;
    School prayer; Sex education
Education, Department of, 26, 107, 111,
  155
Elections 228–234, 245(n12), 246(n17),
  247(n22)

Elites, 27, 30, 34, 71, 88, 98, 132, 192, 241,
  244
  antielitism, 80, 82, 97, 121
  See also Eastern establishment
Entitlements, 128, 136, 141, 183, 192
Environment, 236, 237, 246(n20)
EOA. See Equal Opportunity Act
EP. See Evangelical Press News Service
Equality, 6, 7, 11, 17, 19, 50, 58, 132, 150,
  151, 156–160, 185, 188, 218, 234
  equal opportunity, 175, 179, 180,
    183
  for women, 110, 111, 119
Equal Opportunity Act (EOA), 181,
  190(n13)
Equal Rights Amendment (ERA), 89, 107,
  110, 111
ERA. See Equal Rights Amendment
Eschatology, 47
Eugenics movement, 20, 21, 33
Europe, 21, 30, 56, 83, 84, 87, 88, 90, 150,
  176, 178, 215, 216, 219, 220, 222
  Eastern Europe, 217
  European Union, 204
Evangelical Press News Service (EP),
  48
Evolution, 21
Exclusion, 7, 8, 11, 66, 122, 123, 149, 150,
  160, 161, 174, 175, 176, 187, 189
Exodus International, 48, 52
Extremism, 2, 10, 13, 160, 163, 164, 166,
  168. See also Right, Far Right

Falwell, Jerry, 24, 25, 91, 108, 154
Family Channel cable network,
  44–45
Family Life Seminars, 114, 115
Family Protection Act, 107–108
Family Research Council, 49, 154
Family Support Act (1988), 184
Family values, 3, 41, 46, 50, 52, 105, 108,
  113, 114, 115, 137, 143
Family Voice, 115–116
Farris, Michael, 44
Fascism, 22, 31, 37, 84, 145(n7), 163–169,
  211, 221, 225(n10)
FCF. See Free Congress Foundation
Fears, 133. See also Welfare, historical
  fears concerning

Index

Feminism, 36, 50, 59, 69–70
  antifeminism, 10, 29, 73, 85, 105–124, 136–137
  as elitist, 121
Ferguson, Thomas, 83
Financial markets, 201, 202
Fitzwater, Marlin, 184
Fleming, Thomas, 34, 65, 66, 67–68
Focus on the Family, 35, 41, 44, 45, 49, 50
Folk devils, 7
Ford, Henry, 20
Foreign investments, 193, 194, 195, 196, 201, 202, 205, 207
Foreign policy, 11, 22, 24, 26, 32, 42, 43, 63, 64, 71, 73, 88, 89, 192–209
  liberal internationalist, 203–204, 208
  right turn in, 197
Foster, Henry, 45
Fourteenth Amendment, 165, 166
Fox-Genovese, Elizabeth, 109
France, 221, 223
Francis, Sam, 34
Frank, Barney, 10, 148
Free Congress Foundation (FCF), 26, 29, 86, 92, 93, 95
Free Congress Research and Education Foundation, 107
Freedom, 150, 151, 174, 211
Freedom Foundation, 23
Free market, 3, 11, 28, 174, 179, 216
Free trade, 83, 94, 242, 242, 245(n10)
Friedman, Milton, 22, 90, 138, 212–213
Fundamentalism, 27, 34, 37, 115, 129, 131–132, 136
Fusionism, 22–23, 24, 25, 138–140

Galbraith, John Kenneth, 59
GATT. *See* General Agreement on Tariffs and Trade
Gay Agenda, The (video), 44
Gay and Lesbian Community Center of Colorado, 165
Gays/lesbians, 25, 45, 48, 52, 73, 82, 85, 88, 124, 151
  gays in the military, 44, 148, 154, 159, 161, 162, 169(n3), 231
  gay vote, 149

gay wealth, 152
  See also Homophobia; Rights, special/gay rights
Gender, 3, 6, 22, 31, 52, 70, 109, 119, 120, 181
General Agreement on Tariffs and Trade (GATT), 83, 117
Gephardt, Richard, 94
Germany, 65, 84, 201, 204, 212, 219, 223
Gilder, George, 73, 120, 138, 183
Gingrich, Newt, 5, 109, 118, 135, 139, 146(n23), 155–156, 169(n3), 181, 185–186, 218, 223, 236
  lecture series of, 205
Glazer, Nathan, 58
Goldwater, Barry, 23, 29, 57, 85, 111, 133, 138
Gorbachev, Mikhail, 63
Gottfried, Paul, 34, 66
Government's role, 7, 11, 32, 57, 58, 82, 86, 87, 130, 185, 188, 229–230, 233, 236, 240, 243, 244, 247(n34)
  and antigovernment sentiment, 238, 239, 242, 247(n35)
  economic intervention, 211, 212, 213, 214, 215, 218, 219, 220
  government spending, 12, 234, 243. *See also* Military spending/buildup
Graham, Billy, 23, 42
Graham, Daniel O., 111–112
Gramm, Phil, 155, 162, 180
Gramsci, Antonio, 34, 150
Great Britain, 83, 84, 159, 221
  New Right in, 161
Great Depression, 211, 213
Great Society, 1, 58, 133, 137, 138, 139, 141, 183
Green, Ellen, 126
Greenberg, Stanley, 237, 240
Greenspan, Alan, 241
Gulf War, 28, 93, 97, 136, 195–196, 200–203, 204

Haiti, 207, 208
Hardisty, Jean, 31
Harrington, Michael, 57, 60, 61, 75
Hate crimes, 165
Hayek, Friedrich A., 22, 225(n4)
Health care, 64, 107, 124, 156, 232

Hegemonic strategy/discourse, 159, 160, 168, 175, 189(n2)
Helms, Jesse, 91, 113, 116, 117, 154
Heritage Foundation, 19, 29, 66, 86, 92, 93, 95, 107, 135, 138, 193
Herrnstein, Richard J., 33, 158
Himmelstein, Jerome L., 22–23
Hispanics, 182, 184, 185
Homelessness, 128, 140
Home School Legal Defense Association, 44
Homophobia, 10, 18, 37, 121, 148, 149, 152, 153–156, 157, 161–162, 163, 165, 166, 167. *See also* Gays/lesbians
Hook, Sidney, 59, 71
How Should We Then Live? (Schaeffer), 24
Hughes, Spenser, 48
Human Rights Campaign Fund, 155
Hunt, H. L., 84, 87
Hunt, Nelson Bunker, 87, 92
Huntington, Samuel, 32

Iannone, Carol, 70
Identity. *See* National identity
Ideology, 3, 29, 56, 65, 69, 75, 113, 122, 124, 157, 168, 187–188, 196
role of, 5–6, 7–8, 163, 246(n17)
IFE. *See* International Family Entertainment
Immigration, 7, 17, 20, 21, 30, 33, 36, 67, 68, 124, 130, 135, 141, 150, 158, 173, 175, 176–179, 188
Incomes, 143, 152, 157, 208, 209, 217–218, 225(n7), 229, 231, 232, 234, 235, 237, 240
Independent Institute, 34
Independent Women's Forum, 109
Individualism, 3, 22, 84, 109, 123, 140, 150, 175, 223
INF. *See* Intermediate-Range Nuclear Forces Treaty
Inflation, 214, 241
Institute for Justice, 182
Institute for the Study of Man, 33
Intellectuals, 68, 71, 141, 161, 178, 179
Intercollegiate Review, 33
Interest groups, 149, 158, 234
Intermediate-Range Nuclear Forces Treaty (INF), 197–198

International Family Entertainment (IFE), 96, 97
Internet, 155
Isolationism, 28, 34, 60, 68, 84, 93, 94
Israel, 68, 94, 224
Istook amendment, 146(n23)
Italy, 84, 212, 223
Ivy Leaguers for Freedom, 109

Jackson, Henry, 61
Japan, 65, 87, 88, 90, 94, 201, 204, 220, 222
Jesus movement, 43
Jews, 29, 49, 68, 69, 83, 84, 90, 94, 96, 115, 153, 161. *See also* Anti-Semitism
John Birch Society, 23, 24, 27, 28, 85, 96, 111, 138
Johnson administration, 57
Judis, John, 31

Kampelman, Max, 61, 63
Kemp, Jack, 91
Kennan, George, 63
Keyes, Alan, 123
Keynesian economics. *See under* Economic issues
Kirk, Russell, 23, 56, 65, 66, 70
Kirkpatrick, Jeane, 59, 61, 63, 90
Koch, Fred C., 85
Koertge, Noretta, 108
Kopff, E. Christian, 34
Krieble, Robert, 95
Kristol, Irving, 9, 57, 58, 59, 62, 63, 69, 71, 74, 75, 90, 183
Kristol, William, 63, 64, 75
Ku Klux Klan, 20, 153
Kuwait, 194, 201–202. *See also* Gulf War

Labor movement/unions, 82, 83, 84, 88, 98, 219, 225(n7)
LaHaye, Beverly, 27, 28, 45, 107, 110, 112, 114–116, 118
LaHaye, Timothy, 24, 27, 91, 114
Lambda Conspiracy, The (Hughes), 48
LaRouche network, 19
Larson, Reed, 92
Late Great Planet Earth, The (Lindsey), 47
Latin America, 84
Latinos, 33, 51

Index

Left, 37, 58–59, 67, 127, 142, 143, 212, 215
  New/Old Left, 5, 59–60, 71, 221
Lenin, V. I., 216
Leone, Richard C., 225(n6)
Lesbian Avengers, 48
Liberal democratic tradition, 1–2, 3, 7, 13,
  149–153, 160, 163, 164, 167, 168, 169.
  See also Liberalism
Liberal Imagination, The (Trilling), 56
Liberalism, 21, 22, 24, 28, 56, 59, 60, 61,
  66, 71, 105, 106, 120, 121, 127, 157,
  184, 188, 224(n2), 232
  classical vs. New Deal, 109
  liberal churches, 42, 43
  neoliberals, 57, 178
  See also Left; Liberal democratic
  tradition
Libertarianism, 22, 28, 31, 33, 94, 109,158
Liberty Lobby, 19, 23, 27, 28, 96
Lifeline long-distance service, 118
Limbaugh, Rush, 45, 105, 181
Lindsey, Hal, 47
Living standards, 12, 37, 217, 220, 228,
  230, 231, 233–234, 235, 236, 237, 238,
  239–240, 241, 243, 244, 245
Locke, John, 56
Lockheed Corporation, 205, 206
Loctite Corporation, 95
Los Angeles rebellions, 184
Lott, Trent, 155
Ludwig von Mises Institute, 34

McAteer, Ed, 25
McCarthy, Joseph, 56, 57, 82, 84, 85
McCartney, Bill, 49
McCracken, Samuel, 59
McDonald, Larry, 92
McGovern, George, 60, 61, 64
McGraw, Onalee, 107–108
McNamara, Robert, 198
Maddoux, Marlin, 44, 45
Madison, James, 56
Madison Center, 29
Madison Group 193
Maginnis, Robert, 154
Maine, 165
Mainstream. *See under* Right
Marriage, 51, 119, 120
  homosexual, 154

Marsden, George, 27
Marshner, Connaught (Connie), 107–108
Marxism, 213, 225(n8)
Mead, Lawrence, 138, 139
Media, 36, 43, 53, 109, 112, 114, 156, 177.
  See also Radio broadcasting;
  Publications; Television
Medicare, 236, 237, 239, 242, 246(n20)
Mellor, Chip, 182
Mexicans, 20, 36
Middle class, 12, 35, 70, 71, 88, 89, 106,
  113, 157, 229, 230, 232
Middle East, 194, 195, 201, 202, 204, 208.
  See also Gulf War
Military doctrine. *See* Two-war doctrine
Military-industrial complex, 192–209
Military spending/buildup, 62, 63,
  71–72, 80, 83, 87, 88, 89, 107, 113,
  136, 192, 194, 195, 196, 197, 198, 199,
  200, 201(table), 203, 207, 209
Militia movement, 19, 30, 80, 94, 113, 133
Miller, George, 44
Milliken, Roger, 85, 92, 94
Minicons, 5, 9
Minorities, 149, 167, 169(n3), 182,
  190(n14), 234. *See also* Blacks;
  Hispanics
Minority Mainstream, 182
Missiles, 194, 195, 198, 202, 205, 206
Mock, Brian, 165
Monteith, Stanley, 118
Moral Majority, 25, 73, 114
Moral Rearmament, 147(n35)
Morgan Grenfell investment bank, 92
Mormons, 153
Morrow, Joanne, 151–152
Moynihan, Daniel Patrick, 58, 61, 73, 75,
  184
Multiculturalism, 69, 73, 113, 122, 123,
  150, 158, 178
Multinationalists. *See* Business,
  multinationalists/nationalists
Muravchik, Emanuel, 59
Muravchik, Joshua, 64
Murchison, Clint, 84
Murders, 165
Murphy Brown, 184–185
Murray, Charles, 33, 138, 139, 158, 183,
  185

NAFTA. *See* North American Free Trade
  Agreement
NAM. *See* National Association of
  Manufacturers
NARAL. *See* National Abortion and
  Reproductive Rights Action League
National Abortion and Reproductive
  Rights Action League (NARAL),
  110
National Alumni Forum, 109
National Association of Evangelicals, 42
National Association of Manufacturers
  (NAM), 23, 84, 85
National Christian Action Council, 25
National Endowment for the Arts, 107
National identity, 174, 176, 179, 183, 187
National interest, 208, 209
Nationalism, 3, 26, 30, 34, 68, 82, 93, 129,
  130, 141, 174, 176, 207, 208–209, 221,
  229
National Minority Politics, 182
National Organization for Women
  (NOW), 110, 114
National Religious Broadcasters, 42,
  53(n10)
National Review, 22, 24, 33, 58, 65, 132, 178
National Rifle Association (NRA), 158
National Welfare Rights Union, 142
Nativism, 20, 34, 67, 82, 94, 129, 130, 135
NATO. *See* North Atlantic Treaty
  Organization
NCEWs. *See* Education, non-college-
  educated whites
Negroes, 20. *See also* Blacks
Neither Victim Nor Enemy (Simmons), 110
Neoconservatism, 8, 9, 19, 28, 29, 32, 33,
  56–76, 90–91, 93, 94, 100(n12),
  149–150, 151, 152, 153, 161, 166, 176,
  178, 179, 189(n2)
  as label, 60–61, 75
Neo-Nazis, 30
Neuhaus, Richard John, 33–34, 66–67, 68,
  74
New Age movement, 47
New Class, 58, 59, 60, 61, 66, 71, 179
New Deal, 17, 21, 22, 28, 57, 81, 82–85, 87,
  91, 109, 113, 133
New Man magazine, 49
New Republic, 63

New Right. *See under* Right
New Right, New Racism (Ansell), 190(n8)
New Right, The: We're Ready to Lead
  (Viguerie), 121
Newsweek, 177
New World Order, 27, 28, 64, 94, 116, 117,
  118, 208
New World Order, The (Robertson), 47, 96,
  101(n34), 153
New York Times, 33–34
Niebuhr, Gustav, 160
Nixon, Richard, 24, 60, 84, 88, 212
Norquist, Grover, 182
North American Free Trade Agreement
  (NAFTA), 95, 96, 117, 156, 207,
  232
North Atlantic Treaty Organization
  (NATO), 204, 207, 229
Novak, Michael, 59, 61, 64, 68, 69,
  74–75
NOW. *See* National Organization for
  Women
NRA. *See* National Rifle Association
Nuclear weapons. *See* Weapons systems,
  nuclear
Nuechterlein, James, 70
Nunn, Sam, 199
Nuttle, R. Marc, 92

Office of Economic Opportunity, 24
Ogarkov, Nikolai, 72
Oglesby, C., 146(n22)
Oil companies, 85, 86, 92, 194, 201–202,
  203
Oklahoma, State of, 92
Oklahoma City bombing, 30
Olasky, Marvin, 139, 140
One World Government, 116, 117. *See also*
  New World Order
OPEC. *See* Organization of Petroleum
  Exporting Countries
Operation Rescue, 26, 94
Opinion polls. *See* Poll/surveys
Oregon, 153, 157, 164–165
Organization of Petroleum Exporting
  Countries (OPEC), 86
O'sullivan, John, 178
Other America, The (Harrington), 57
Overstreet, Harry, 59

Index 261

Paglia, Camille, 108
Paleoconservatives, 67, 93, 94, 96, 109,
  178–179. *See also* Right, Old Right
Palmer raids, 21
Panetta, Leon E., 198
Patai, Daphne, 108
Pataki, George, 169(n3)
Patriarchy, 26, 32, 37, 106, 136, 150
Patriot movement, 30
Penn, Mark, 246(n20)
Pentecostal-Charismatic Churches of
  North America, 51
Pentecostal Fellowship of North
  America, 50–51
Peretti, Frank, 47
Permissiveness, 21, 188
Perot, Ross, 31, 34, 113, 228–231
Personal Responsibility and Work
  Opportunity Reconciliation Act
  (1996), 141, 186
Peschek, Joseph G., 90
Pew, Howard, 85
Phillips, Howard, 24, 25, 26, 35, 91, 94, 95
Phillips, Kevin, 29–30
Phyllis Schlafly Report, 112, 116
Pioneer Fund, 33
Pipes, Richard, 63, 71
Planet Earth–2000 (Lindsey), 47
Pluralism, 2, 29, 149, 169(n4), 183, 189,
  244
Podhoretz, John, 75
Podhoretz, Norman, 59, 61, 62, 63, 64, 66,
  67, 69, 71, 74
Point of View, 44
Policy issues, 6, 7, 32, 33, 44, 58, 75, 81,
  113, 139, 176, 182, 184, 235, 241, 243,
  244. *See also* Foreign policy
Policy Review, 29, 135, 141
Political correctness, 188
Polls/surveys, 51, 229, 230, 232, 234, 236,
  237, 238, 240, 242–243, 245(nn 9, 10),
  246(n20), 247(n22)
Populism, 6, 25, 27, 29, 30, 31, 37, 56,
  113, 142, 152, 156–163, 178, 207,
  231, 232
  new economy populism, 242–243, 244,
  247(nn 34, 35)
Pornography, 73
Poststructuralism, 187

Poverty, 71, 122, 129, 130, 185–186, 234
  poverty line, 191(n25), 218
  See also Homelessness; Underclass;
  War on poverty
Powell, Colin, 199–200
Power relations, 6, 17, 157, 169(n4)
Pratt, Larry, 91
Prayer. *See* School prayer
Preferences, 180, 181. *See also* Affirmative
  action
Privatization, 135, 214, 216, 220, 222
Profits, 87, 195, 196, 201, 204, 207, 211,
  240
Prohibition, 21
Project 21, 182
Promise Keepers, 49–50, 52
Proposition 187, 177, 178
Proposition 209. *See* California Civil
  Rights Initiative
Protectionism, 93, 95, 113, 183
Protestantism, 23, 24, 27, 35, 37, 69, 110,
  115, 131, 159
Publications, 46–48, 49, 51, 53, 76, 112,
  115–116
Public Interest, 57–58
Public opinion, 242, 247(n35). *See also*
  Polls/surveys
Puddington, Arch, 59

Quadragno, Jill, 137
Quayle, Dan, 26, 184–185

Rabinowitz, Dorothy, 59
Racial issues, 3, 6, 10–11, 26, 31, 33, 64,
  121–123, 173–189, 189(n2), 190(n14)
  racial determinism, 185
  racial reconciliation, 50–51, 52
  racism, 11, 18, 19, 21, 23, 28, 51, 58, 67,
  69, 82, 88, 89, 121, 122, 123, 131,
  137–138, 143, 150, 151, 156, 157,
  173–174, 176, 179, 188
  white supremacy, 20, 23, 121, 123,
  131
  See also Discrimination; Education,
  non-college-educated whites
*Radical Right-Wing Populism in Western
  Europe* (Betz), 30
Radio broadcasting, 42, 43–46, 49, 116
Rand Corporation, 204

262   *Index*

Reagan, Ronald, 1, 4, 9, 26, 43, 62–63, 72, 74, 107, 112, 138, 184, 194, 195, 199, 200, 219
 and business conflict, 93–94
 Reagan revolution, 89–93
Recessions, 87, 214, 231, 233
Reconstructionism, 25
Reconstruction period, 128
Reed, Ralph, 28, 29, 51, 96, 118, 133–134, 153, 155, 161, 164
Regulations, 80, 87, 88, 89, 236, 243
Religious Right, 148–169, 193. *See also* Christian Right
Republican Party, 23–24, 57, 85, 108, 181, 203, 232–233
 Log Cabin Republicans, 148–149, 162
 nationalists/internationalists in, 207–208, 208–209
 Newt Republicans, 5, 192, 196, 199, 205
 1992 convention, 29, 160
 Protestant vote for, 159
 Republican revolution, 1, 2, 180, 234, 236
 splits in, 183, 207
Responsibility, 3, 123, 140, 240
Revel, Jean-François, 71
Rhodes, Sir Cecil, 96, 118
Rich, Frank, 148–149, 156
Richardson, Willie and Gwen, 182
Right
 conventional view of, 17
 divisions within, 31–35, 62–63, 65–68, 90, 93–97, 179, 183, 220–221
 electoral right, 28–29, 31–35
 Far Right, 19, 23, 34, 81, 176, 179. *See also* Extremism; Ultraconservatives
 foundations for, 34, 66, 76
 Liberal Right, 211, 212, 213, 215–217, 218, 219, 220–221
 and mainstream, 1–2, 3, 7, 8, 10, 12, 13, 18, 127, 152, 153, 155, 157, 160, 161, 166, 167, 175, 185
 New Right, 4–5, 6–8, 11, 19, 25, 28, 31, 43, 81, 82, 85–89, 90, 97, 100(n12), 107, 109, 112, 113, 114, 121–122, 123, 174, 175, 176, 179, 183, 186, 189(n2), 192, 193, 197, 211–224

Old Right, 20–23, 25, 26, 31, 33, 34, 62, 65–66, 68, 111, 112, 113. *See also* Paleoconservatives
 organizational currents in, 8
 sectors of, 18, 19, 35
 sources of contemporary right, 20
 state capitalist right, 211, 212, 221
 themes concerning, 3, 17, 18–19, 67, 113, 122, 150, 189(n2)
 See also Christian Right
Rights, 3, 132, 137, 151, 155, 174, 180
 special/gay rights, 10, 29, 32, 48, 51, 89, 148, 152, 153, 154, 157, 162, 165
 See also Welfare, welfare rights advocacy
Roads to Dominion (Diamond), 19
Road to Serfdom, The (Hayek), 225(n4)
Robertson, Pat, 26, 28, 42, 44, 47, 87, 91, 92, 95, 96–97, 101(n34), 108, 138, 153, 154, 156, 164
Rockford Institute, 33–34
Rogers, Craig, 151–152
Rogue states, 198, 199, 200, 201
Rollins, Edward, 169(n3)
Roosevelt, Franklin D., 21, 212
Roosevelt's Red Record (Dilling), 21
Rotello, Gabriel, 155
Ruby Ridge, Idaho, 30
Russia, 199, 206–207, 222. *See also* Soviet Union

Salem Communications, 45
SALT. *See* Strategic Arms Limitation Treaty II
Salvatori, Henry, 85, 92
Salvi, John, 144(n2)
Sasser, Jim, 198
Saudi Arabia, 194, 201–202, 204
Scapegoating, 27, 28, 30–31, 35, 36, 37, 80, 88, 105, 122, 175, 178, 186, 187, 215
Schaeffer, Francis A., 24
Schlafly, Fred, 111
Schlafly, Phyllis, 73, 85, 107, 110, 111–114, 116, 117
Schlesinger, Arthur, Jr., 59
School prayer, 26, 43, 155
Scopes trial, 21, 23
Secular humanism, 27–28, 114, 119, 131
700 Club, 44

Index 263

Sex education, 29, 32, 45, 107, 154, 158
Sexism, 18, 156
Sexual harassment, 151–152
Sexuality, 6, 32, 151
Shachtman, Max, 59, 71
Share the Wealth Campaign, 142
Sheldon, Louis, 51
Simmons, Rita, 110
Slavery, 128, 131
Smear campaigns, 159
Social crises, 214, 215, 217, 220, 221, 222
Social Darwinism, 129
Socialism, 21, 57, 60, 121, 132, 215, 216, 221, 223
Socialist Party, 60
Social science, 175, 178
Social Security, 89, 128, 237, 242
Sommers, Christina Hoff, 108
Southern Baptist Convention, 51
Southern California Christian Times, 48
Southwire company, 92
Soviet Union, 61–62, 63, 64, 65, 72, 134, 195, 197, 212, 216, 217, 219, 221, 222, 224(nn 1, 3). *See also* Cold war; Russia
Spain, 212, 224
Special interests, 152, 180, 184, 187, 219
Specter, Arlen, 164
Starr, Roger, 58
START. *See* Strategic Arms Reduction Treaty
Star Wars, 111–112, 198, 206
States' rights, 128
Steel, Ronald, 33
Stockdale, James B., 34
STOP ERA, 107, 110
Stormer, John, 27
Strang, Stephen, 49
Strategic Arms Limitation Treaty (SALT) II, 194, 207
Strategic Arms Reduction Treaty (START), 197, 198, 206
Submarines, 194, 206
Subsidies, 93
Sun Belt, 85–87, 88, 91, 96, 97
Sununu, John H., 26
Supreme Court, 165–166, 180, 181
Swaggart, Jimmy, 26

Sweden, 223
Symbolism, 6, 7, 149, 157, 159, 167, 168, 173, 180, 187, 188

Tafel, Rich, 148–149
Tariffs, 83, 85, 93
Taxes, 17, 29, 70, 74, 80, 86, 87, 88, 89, 155, 230, 232, 233, 237, 243
TCI. *See* Tele-Communications Inc.
Tele-Communications Inc. (TCI), 97
Television, 24, 42, 49, 51
televangelism, 26, 42, 43–46
See also Media
Terminology, 4, 18, 60–61
Terry, Randall, 94, 164
Texas, University of (Law School), 181
Textiles, 85, 93
Thatcher, Margaret, 159
Think tanks, 17, 24, 33, 36, 76, 138, 204
Third World, 80, 83, 88, 199, 215, 216, 220, 222
This Present Darkness (Peretti), 47–48
Thomas, Clarence, 45, 51
Tobacco industry, 91, 158
Tonsor, Stephen, 65, 68
Trade, 83, 94, 204, 220, 232. *See also* Free trade; North American Free Trade Agreement; Tariffs
Traditionalists, 23, 25, 29, 33, 56, 119–120, 123, 175
Traditional Values Coalition, 28, 48, 51
Trager, Frank, 59
Trilling, Lionel, 56
Trinity Broadcasting Network, 45
Trotsky, Leon, 68
Two-war doctrine, 198–199, 200–201, 203, 205, 207
Tymkovich, Timothy, 165

Ultraconservatives, 81, 93, 97. *See also* Right, Far Right
Underclass, 137, 138, 139, 184, 185
Unemployment, 36, 64, 87, 152, 212, 235, 241
United Nations, 47, 85, 116, 207
Treaty on the Rights of the Child, 117
USA Radio Network, 45
USBIC. *See* U.S. Business and Industrial Council

U

U.S. Business and Industrial Council (USBIC), 92, 94
U.S. Commission on Long-Term Strategy, 199
U.S. Taxpayers Party (USTP), 35, 94–95
USTP. *See* U.S. Taxpayers Party

V

Values, 3, 12, 33, 46, 57, 119–120, 123, 133, 141, 168, 175, 176, 186, 187, 229–230. *See also* Family values; *under* Economic issues
Viereck, Peter, 56–57, 75
Vietnam War, 61, 85, 87
  antiwar movement, 59, 60
  Vietnam syndrome, 136
Viguerie, Richard, 24, 25, 26, 88, 91, 95, 121
Violence, 25, 31, 120, 164, 165

W

Waco, Texas, 30
Wages, 229, 231, 232, 234, 235, 240. *See also* Incomes
Wallace, George, 88
Wall Street Journal, 178
Warner, John W., 198
War on poverty, 57, 58, 127, 184
Washington Times, 162
Wattenberg, Ben, 61, 64, 90
Wealth and Poverty (Gilder), 120
Weapons systems, 193, 194–195, 196, 201, 202, 205, 206
  nuclear, 197–198, 200, 207
Weaver, Randy, 131
Weld, William, 140–141
Welfare, 1, 7, 10, 17, 30–31, 33, 51, 71, 82, 124, 126–144, 175, 183–186
  benefits, 186, 191(n25)
  historical fears concerning, 127–133
  reform of, 127. 128, 139, 141, 142, 178, 183, 184, 185, 186
  welfare dependency, 58, 128, 133, 138, 139, 177, 183, 186
  welfare rights advocacy, 142–144

See also Aid to Families with Dependent Children
Welfare state, 75, 85, 127, 128, 130, 132, 134, 135, 139, 140, 184, 212, 219, 237
Weyrich, Paul, 25, 32, 86, 91, 138, 158–159, 193
Whitehead, John W., 24
Whitman, Christine Todd, 169(n3)
Who Stole Feminism? (Sommers), 108
Wiegel, George, 68
Wildavsky, Aaron, 58
Williams, Lucy A., 30–31
Wilson, Clyde, 66
Wilson, Pete, 151, 170(n9), 177, 180
Wisse, Ruth, 70
Wolff, Edward, 218, 225(n6)
Women, 25, 29, 32, 45, 161, 233, 235
  academic, 108–109
  Fourth World Conference on Women, 118
  International Women's Year (1977), 111, 115
  neoconservative, 70
  recruiting, 110–111, 115, 121, 123–124
  teen mothers, 141
  on welfare, 143, 147(n29)
  without men, 136, 137
  women's studies, 108–109
  See also Feminism; Gender; *under* Equality
Women for America, 45
Women's Freedom Network, 109, 110
Wood, Robert, 84
Woodson, Robert, 182
Workers, 223, 224(n3), 225(n7), 235
World Trade Organization, 117
Worthiness, 122, 123
W.R Grace conglomerate, 92

X

Xenophobia, 30, 31, 33, 176

Y

Yugoslavia, 223–224

CPSIA information can be obtained at www.ICGtesting.com
Printed in the USA
BVOW08s1958080216

436007BV00001B/18/P